Eponyms in Psychology

EPONYMS IN PSYCHOLOGY

A Dictionary and Biographical Sourcebook

LEONARD ZUSNE

GREENWOOD PRESS

New York • Westport, Connecticut • London

Library of Congress Cataloging-in-Publication Data

Zusne, Leonard, 1924–
  Eponyms in psychology

  Includes index.
  1. Psychology—Dictionaries.   2. Eponyms—
Dictionaries.   I. Title.
BF31.Z87   1987   150′.3′ 21   87-255
ISBN 0-313-25750-7 (lib. bdg. : alk. paper)

British Library Cataloguing in Publication Data is available.

Library of Congress Catalog Card Number: 87-255
ISBN: 0-313-25750-7

First published in 1987
Greenwood Press, Inc.
88 Post Road West, Westport, Connecticut 06881

Printed in the United States of America

The paper used in this book complies with the
Permanent Paper Standard issued by the National
Information Standards Organization (Z39.48-1984).

10   9   8   7   6   5   4   3   2   1

Contents

Preface

This dictionary was prepared to provide information about individuals whose names have become part of terms in common use among psychologists, psychological eponyms. The eponyms in this book comprise not only psychological eponyms but also selected eponyms from related fields that psychologists are likely to use as they practice psychology as an academic discipline, a research field, or a profession: statistics, neuroscience, education, psychiatry, psychoanalysis, linguistics, and artificial intelligence. The dictionary provides three types of information. First, it gives the definitions of 852 eponymous terms, both current and historical. About 60 percent of these terms cannot be found in psychological dictionaries. Second, it provides references to where the eponymous phenomenon, syndrome, apparatus, or theory was first described and, if applicable, the name of the individual who coined the term. Third, it presents a short biography of each eponym, the name giver, with a list of sources of additional biographical information. The dictionary should be of use to students and teachers of psychology and to anyone else curious about the individual behind a phrase that has made him or her immortal.

An eponym is both the person after whom something is named and that which is named after the person. The eponym as a name giver need not be a person, however; place names also serve as eponyms. If it is a person's name, it need not be his or her real name; a pseudonym can become an eponym, as in Student's *t*. Nor need the name appear in its original form. Although there is no one named Therblig, it is an eponymous term because the Gilbreths chose to use their name to coin it, albeit by reversing it. The case of the therblig is a rare exception. Almost all eponyms that are names of phenomena, diseases, syndromes, methods, theories, and so on are coined not by the persons who first described the concept but by someone else, often many years later.

When the name of a place becomes part of a term, this almost invariably happens because the formulator of the term decided to use it from the outset. A large class of objects in psychology that often have a place name as part of their complete designation are the psychological tests. Generally the tests are named after the universities or hospitals where they were first constructed, and also the constructors often incorporated their own names into the test name. Of the 1,409 entries in the *Ninth Mental Measurements Yearbook,* about 19 percent have a person's name in them. As many or more begin with a place name. Are all these tests eponyms? "The Binet," "the Wechsler," and "the Rorschach" undoubtedly are, as are quite a number of other psychological instruments that have become sufficiently well known. When does a name-carrying test become eponymous? No definite rule may be given here. I made the decision whether to include a test on the basis of the impressions that my colleagues and I had gained from the pertinent literature concerning the frequency and manner of their use. Similarly, there is the question of when a person's name that precedes the name of a theory is an intrinsic part of the term and when it serves merely to identify the individual who was the author of the theory. The transitional stage in the development of an eponym represents an area of uncertainty and is a major reason why different compilers are certain to arrive at lists of eponyms that will differ in number and identity of the entries.

It will be noted that the biographical information for a number of eponyms is incomplete. In fact, no biographical information of any sort could be found for twenty-one of the 681 eponyms who are actual persons from recent times (rather than literary and mythological figures and figures from the ancient world). For a strictly biographical dictionary the selection of persons to be included is guided by their characteristics, such as their fame and contributions. This also means that biographical material on these persons will be found in commonly available sources. The writing of a biographical dictionary of eponyms must begin with the eponymous terms themselves. Only after the corpus of the terms has been established does the search for biographical materials begin. The inclusion of a name as part of a term, however, in no way depends on how well the person is known at the time, nor does it mean that this person will become well known in the future because of the eponym. While many of the eponyms included in this dictionary are names of famous persons, a very large number include the names of people who were modest practitioners of their trades and who lived and died in anonymity in spite of their eponyms. Such people are not included in professional and membership directories, biographical listings, or *New York Times* obituaries, even their passing being noted perhaps by only their hometown newspaper. Even their immediate families may be unable to supply such items as their birth and death dates.

The eponyms in this dictionary are arranged in alphabetic order, as are all other entries, such as cross-references to terms and names. Thus, not all terms that have a person's name in them will necessarily appear together. The listing depends on the position of the name within the term and on whether the person's name is or is not in the genetive form. There is no rule that determines whether a person's name will or will not have an *'s* after it in an eponym. It depends on usage, and usage may depend on no more than whether one form sounds better than the other.

The entries are structured as follows. If an eponym contains the name of only one person, that person's biography immediately follows the definition of the eponym. Eponyms containing more than one name are followed by the biographies of the owners of the names in the order in which they appear in the eponym. The exception is when a person's name in the second or third position is also the first or only name in a different entry. His or her biography then appears under that entry, and the reader is referred to it. There are a few persons whose names appear both in the first place in an eponym and in some other position in a different eponym that begins with a word other than a name. The biography of such a person is given in one place only, right after the eponym that has that person's name in the first position. The other eponym is provided with a definition and an indication that the biography must be sought under a different entry. An asterisk after a name indicates that a separate entry for that name is alphabetically listed in the book.

The following guidelines were observed concerning biographical references. An effort was made to locate English-language biographical information for all eponyms. References to sources in other languages are given only when English references are not available or they are meager. If more than one biographical reference is available, these are given, but no effort was made to make an exhaustive listing. For persons with rich biographical material, only the most important and the most accessible sources are listed. Except for book titles that are biographies or autobiographies, most other biographical sources are abbreviated. A key to these abbreviations precedes the body of the dictionary. In some cases no published biographies were found, and the word *unavailable* appears under the "Biographies" heading, even when some biographical data are supplied. These data were obtained as isolated items from various published sources, unpublished documents, and personal communications.

Periodical and Book Title Abbreviations

Abh. Kön. bayr. Akad. Wiss.	*Abhandlungen der Königlichen bayrischen Akademie der Wissenschaften*
Abh. Kön. böhm. Ges. Wiss.	*Abhandlungen der Königlichen böhmischen Gesellschaft der Wissenschaften*
Abh. Sächs. Ges. Wiss., math.-phys. Cl.	*Abhandlungen der Sächsischen Gesellschaft der Wissenschaften, mathematisch-physische Classe*
Acta otolaryng.	*Acta otolaryngologica*
Acta path. microb. scand.	*Acta pathologica microbiologica scandinavica*
Acta physiol. scand.	*Acta physiologica scandinavica*
Acta psychiat. neurol. scand.	*Acta psychiatrica et neurologica scandinavica*
Acta psychol.	*Acta psychologica*
ADB	*Allgemeine deutsche Biographie.* 56 vols. Leipzig: Duncker & Humboldt, 1875–1912. (Partially reprinted 1967).
Albany Med. Ann.	*Albany Medical Annals*
Albrecht v. Graefes Arch. Ophthal.	*Albrecht von Graefes Archiv der Ophthalmologie*
AL J. Med. Sci.	*Alabama Journal of Medical Science*
Alleg. Z. Psychiat.	*Allgemeine Zeitschrift für Psychiatrie*
Allibone	S. Austen Allibone. *A Critical Dictionary of English Literature and British and American Authors.* 3 vols. plus 2 suppl. Philadelphia: Lippincott, 1881–1891.
AMA J.	*American Medical Association Journal*
AM&WS	*American Men and Women of Science.* New York: Jacques Cattell Press/R. R. Bowker Co. (P, Physical and Biological Sciences; S, Social and Behavioral Sciences).

Amer. Imago	American Imago
Amer. J. Dis. Ch.	American Journal of Diseases of Children
Amer. J. Insanity	American Journal of Insanity
Amer. J. Ment. Defic.	American Journal of Mental Deficiency
Amer. J. Ophthal.	American Journal of Ophthalmology
Amer. J. Orthopsychiat.	American Journal of Orthopsychiatry
Amer. J. Phys.	American Journal of Physics
Amer. J. Physiol.	American Journal of Physiology
Amer. J. Psychiat.	American Journal of Psychiatry
Amer. J. Psychol.	American Journal of Psychology
Amer. J. Sci.	American Journal of Science
Amer. J. Syph.	American Journal of Syphilis
Amer. Orthopsychiat. Ass., Res. Monog.	American Orthopsychiatric Association, Research Monographs
Amer. Perfumer Essent. Oil Rev.	American Perfumer and Essential Oil Review
Amer. Psychologist	American Psychologist
Amer. Scientist	American Scientist
Amer. Sociol. Rev.	American Sociological Review
Amer. Statistician	American Statistician
AMS	American Men of Science. New York, Lancaster, Pa.: Science Press, R. R. Bowker Co., Jacques Cattell Press. (P, Physical and Biological Sciences; S, Social and Behavioral Sciences).
Ann. chim. phys.	Annales de chimie et de physique
Ann. Eugen.	Annals of Eugenics
Ann. Math. Stat.	Annals of Mathematical Statistics
Ann. Med. Hist.	Annals of Medical History
Ann. méd.-psychol.	Annales médico-psychologiques
Ann. Phys. Chem.	Annalen der Physik und Chemie
Ann. Phys., Leipzig	Annalen der Physik, Leipzig
APA Dir.	American Psychological Association. Directory of the American Psychological Association. Washington, D.C.: American Psychological Association.
Arb. Gesamtgeb. Psychiat. Neuropath. R. Krafft-Ebing	Arbeiten aus dem Gesamtgebiet der Psychiatrie und Neuropathologie von R. Krafft-Ebing
Arch. Anat. Physiol.	Archiv für Anatomie und Physiologie
Arch. Augenheilk.	Archiv für Augenheilkunde
Arch. d'ophthal.	Archives d'ophthalmologie
Arch. ges. Physiol.	Archiv für die gesamte Physiologie
Arch. ges. Psychol.	Archiv für die gesamte Psychologie
Arch. ital. biol.	Archivio italiano di biologia
Arch. ital. psicol.	Archivio italiano di psicologia
Arch. mikrosk. Anat.	Archiv für mikroskopische Anatomie
Arch. neurol.	Archives de neurologie
Arch. Neurol. Psychiat.	Archives of Neurology and Psychiatry
Arch. Ohrenheilk.	Archiv für Ohren-, Nasen- und Kehlkopfheilkunde
Arch. Ophthalm.	Archives of Ophthalmology

Arch. Otolaryng.	Archives of Otolaryngology
Arch. Physiol.	Archiv für Physiologie
Arch. psicol. neurol. psichiat.	Archivio di psicologia, neurologia e psichiatria
Arch. Psychiat.	Archives of Psychiatry
Arch. Psychiat. Nervenkr.	Archiv für Psychiatrie und Nervenkrankheiten
Asimov	I. Asimov. Asimov's Biographical Encyclopedia of Science and Technology. Garden City, N.Y.: Doubleday, 1972.
Atti Accad. naz. Lincei	Atti dell'Accademia nazionale dei Lincei
Behav. Monog.	Behavior Monographs
Behav. Res. Meth. Instr.	Behavior Research Methods and Instrumentation
Beitr. Psychol.	Beiträge zur Psychologie
Beitr. Psychol. Philos.	Beiträge zur Psychologie und Philosophie
Bell Syst. Tech. J.	Bell System Technical Journal
Berliner klin. Wschr.	Berliner klinische Wochenschrift
Ber. naturf. Ges. Freiburg i.B.	Berichte der naturforschenden Gesellschaft Freiburg in Breisgau
Ber. ü. Verh. kön. sächs. Ges. Wiss. Leipzig, math.-phys. Cl.	Berichte über die Verhandlungen der königlichen sächsischen Gesellschaften der Wissenschaften zu Leipzig, mathematisch-physische Classe
Ber. wetterau. Ges. ges. Naturk.	Berichte der wetterauischen Gesellschaft für die gesamte Naturkunde zu Hanau
Biog. Dir. APA	American Psychiatric Association. Biographic Directory. Washington, D.C.: American Psychiatric Association.
Biog. Mem. Fellows Roy. Soc.	Biographical Memoirs of the Fellows of Royal Society of London
Biog. Mem. NAS	Biographical Memoirs: National Academy of Sciences. New York: Columbia University Press, 1877—.
Biometr. Bull.	Biometrics Bulletin
Blue B.	The Blue Book. London: St. James Press, 1976.
Bonin	W. F. Bonin. Die grossen Psychologen. Düsseldorf: ECON Taschenbuch Verlag, 1983.
Boston Med. Surg. J.	Boston Medical and Surgical Journal
Brit. J. Educ. Psychol.	British Journal of Educational Psychology
Brit. J. Med. Hypn.	British Journal of Medical Hypnosis
Brit. J. Med. Psychol.	British Journal of Medical Psychology
Brit. J. Ophthal.	British Journal of Ophthalmology
Brit. J. Psychol.	British Journal of Psychology
Brit. J. Stat. Psychol.	British Journal of Statistical Psychology
Brit. Med. J.	British Medical Journal
Brockhaus	Brockhaus Enzyklopedie (20 vols.). Wiesbaden: F. A. Brockhaus, 1966–1976.
Bull. Acad. roy. belge	Bulletin de l'Académie royale belge
Bull. Acad. roy. sci. lett., Bruxelles	Bulletins de l'Académie royale des sciences, des lettres et des beaux-arts de Belgique, Bruxelles
Bull. Acad. sci. belge	Bulletins de l'Académie des sciences belge

Bull. Brit. Psychol. Soc.	*Bulletin of the British Psychological Society*
Bull. Hist. Med.	*Bulletin of the History of Medicine*
Bull. Inst. Hist. Med.	*Bulletin of the Institute of History of Medicine*
Bull. Isaac Ray Med. Libr.	*Bulletin of the Isaac Ray Medical Library*
Bull. Johns Hopkins Hosp.	*Bulletin of the Johns Hopkins Hospital*
Bull. méd.	*Bulletin de médecine*
Bull. Menninger Clin.	*Bulletin of the Menninger Clinic*
Bull. NY Acad. Med.	*Bulletin of the New York Academy of Medicine*
Bull. Soc. anat.	*Bulletin de la Société anatomique*
Bull. Soc. anthrop.	*Bulletin de la Société anthropologique*
Bull. Soc. Med. Hist.	*Bulletin of the Society of Medical History*
Canad. Biog.	*The Macmillan Dictionary of Canadian Biography,* 1963
Canad. Med. Ass. J.	*Canadian Medical Association Journal*
Canad. Who	*Canadian Who's Who.* Toronto: Trans-Canadian Press.
CE	M. J. McDonald (ed.). *New Catholic Encyclopedia.* 15 vols. New York: McGraw-Hill, 1967.
Charité Ann.	*Charité Annalen,* Berlin
Chem. Ind.	*Chemistry and Industry*
Chic. Trib.	*Chicago Tribune*
Child Dev.	*Child Development*
Clark Univ. Libr. Publ.	*Clark University Library Publications*
Clin. Endocrin.	*Clinical Endocrinology*
Clin Soc. London, Trans.	*Clinical Society of London, Transactions*
Cogn. Psychol.	*Cognitive Psychology*
Collier's	*Collier's Encyclopedia.* 24 vols. New York: Macmillan Educational Co., 1986.
ConAu	*Contemporary Authors.* Detroit: Gale Research Co.
C. r. hebd. séances Acad. sci.	*Comptes rendus hebdomadaires des séances de l'Académie des sciences*
C. r. hebd. séances mém. Soc. biol.	*Comptes rendus hebdomadaires des séances et mémoires de la Societé de biologie*
C. r. Soc. biol., Mém.	*Comptes rendus de la Societé de biologie, Mémoires*
CurBio	*Current Biography.* New York: H. W. Wilson Co.
DAB	*Dictionary of American Biography.* 22 vols. plus 7 suppl. New York: Charles Scribner's Sons, 1928–1958.
DBF	*Dictionnaire de biographie française.* 13 vols. to date. Paris: Libraire Letouzey et Ané, 1933—.
DcNAA	W. S. Stewart. *A Dictionary of North American Authors Deceased before 1950.* Toronto: Ryerson Press, 1951.
DE	R. Hendrickson. *The Dictionary of Eponyms.* New York: Stein & Day, 1985.
Deutsch. med. Wschr.	*Deutsche medizinische Wochenschrift*
Dir. Med. Spec.	*Directory of Medical Specialties.* Chicago: Marquis Who's Who.

DNB	L. Stephen & S. Lee (eds.). *Dictionary of National Biography.* 63 vols. plus index, 7 suppl., 4 twentieth-century vols. London: Smith, Elder & Co., Oxford University Press, 1885–1950.
DSB	C. C. Gillespie (ed.). *Dictionary of Scientific Biography.* 15 vols. plus index. New York: Scribner's, 1970–1980.
Dublin Hosp. Rep. Comm. Med. Surg.	*Dublin Hospital Reports and Communications in Medicine and Surgery*
EA	*Encyclopedia Americana.* 30 vols. Danbury, Conn.: Grolier, 1985.
EB	*Encyclopaedia Britannica.* 24 vols. Chicago: Encyclopaedia Britannica, 1967.
Edinb. Med. J.	*Edinburgh Medical Journal*
EI	*Enciclopedia italiana.* 35 vols. plus 3 suppl. and index. Rome: Instituto della Enciclopedia Italiana, 1949.
EJ	C. Roth (ed.). *Encyclopedia Judaica.* 16 vols. New York: Macmillan, 1972.
EncAmerBio	J. A. Garraty (ed.). *Encyclopedia of American Biography.* New York: Harper & Row, 1974.
Encycl. Soc. Sci.	*Encyclopedia of Social Sciences*
EP	P. Edwards (ed.). *The Encyclopedia of Philosophy.* 8 vols. New York: Macmillan, 1967.
Ergeb. inn. Med. Kinderheilk.	*Ergebnisse der inneren Medizin und Kinderheilkunde*
EUI	*Enciclopedia universal ilustrada europeo-americana.* 70 vols. plus 10 appendixes. Madrid: Espasa-Calpe, 1907–1930.
Excep. Child.	*Exceptional Children*
Exp. Brain Res.	*Experimental Brain Research*
Fischer, *Biog. Lex.*	I. Fischer (ed.). *Biographisches Lexikon der hervorragenden Ärzte der letzten fünfzig Jahre (1880–1930).* 2 vols. Berlin: Urban & Schwarzenberg, 1962.
Gaz. hebd. méd. chir.	*Gazette hebdomadaire de médecine et de chirurgie*
Gaz. hebd. sci. méd. Bordeaux	*Gazette hebdomadaire des sciences médicales de Bordeaux*
Gaz. méd. Paris	*Gazette médicale de Paris*
Gesch. Psychol.	*Geschichte der Psychologie*
Harvard Educ. Rev.	*Harvard Educational Review*
Haymaker	W. Haymaker. *The Founders of Neurology.* 2d ed. Springfield, Ill.: Thomas, 1970.
Hirsch, *Biog. Lex.*	A. Hirsch et al. (eds.). *Biographisches Lexikon der hervorragenden Ärzte aller Zeiten und Völker.* 3d ed. 5 vols. plus 1 suppl. Munich: Urban & Schwarzenberg, 1962.
Hist. Psychol.	*History of Psychology*

HPA	C. Murchison (ed.). *A History of Psychology in Autobiography.* vols. 1–3. Worcester, Mass.: Clark University Press, 1930, 1932, 1936.
	E. G. Boring et al. (eds.). *A History of Psychology in Autobiography.* Vol. 4. Worcester, Mass.: Clark University Press, 1952.
	E. G. Boring & G. Lindzey (eds.). *A History of Psychology in Autobiography.* Vol. 5. New York: Appleton-Century-Crofts, 1967.
	G. Lindzey (ed.). *A History of Psychology in Autobiography.* Vols. 6, 7. Englewood Cliffs, N.J.: Prentice-Hall, 1974; San Francisco: W. H. Freeman & Co., 1980.
IDP	International Union of Psychological Science. *International Directory of Psychologist.* Assen: Van Gorcum & Co., 1966.
IESS	D. L. Sills (ed.). *International Encyclopedia of the Social Sciences.* 18 vols. New York: Macmillan, 1968–1979.
InternWho	*The International Who's Who.* London: Europa Publications.
Intern. Z. ärztl. Psychoanal.	*Internationale Zeitschrift für ärztliche Psychoanalyse*
Intern. J. Psycho-Anal.	*International Journal of Psycho-Analysis*
Intern. Z. Psychoanal.	*Internationale Zeitschrift für Psychoanalyse*
J. Abn. Soc. Psychol.	*Journal of Abnormal and Social Psychology*
J. Acoust. Soc. Amer.	*Journal of the Acoustical Society of America*
J. Amer. Acad. Child Psychiat.	*Journal of the American Academy of Child Psychiatry*
J. Amer. Med. Ass.	*Journal of the American Medical Association*
J. Amer. Psychoanal. Ass.	*Journal of the American Psychoanalytic Association*
J. Amer. Stat. Ass.	*Journal of the American Statistical Association*
J. Anat. Physiol.	*Journal of Anatomy and Physiology*
J. Anim. Behav.	*Journal of Animal Behavior*
J. Anthrop. Inst.	*Journal of the Anthropological Institute*
J. Appl. Psychol.	*Journal of Applied Psychology*
J. Avi. Med.	*Journal of Aviation Medicine*
Jber. phys. Ver. Frankf.	*Jahresbericht des physikalischen Vereins Frankfurt-a.-Main*
Jber. schles. Ges. vaterl. Kult.	*Jahresbericht schlesischer Gesellschaft für vaterländische Kultur*
Jb. Kinderheilk.	*Jahrbuch der Kinderheilkunde*
Jb. Psychiat. Neurol.	*Jahrbücher für Psychiatrie und Neurologie*
J. Chem. Ed.	*Journal of Chemical Education*
J. Chem. Soc.	*Journal of the Chemical Society*
J. Comp. Neurol.	*Journal of Comparative Neurology*
J. Comp. Physiol. Psychol.	*Journal of Comparative and Physiological Psychology*
J. Consult. Clin. Psychol.	*Journal of Consulting and Clinical Psychology*
J. Consult. Psychol.	*Journal of Consulting Psychology*

J. Ed. Psychol.	*Journal of Educational Psychology*
Jewish	I. Landman (ed.). *The Universal Jewish Encyclopedia.* 10 vols. New York: Universal Jewish Encyclopedia, 1939–1943.
J. Exc. Children	*Journal of Exceptional Children*
J. Exp. Psychol.	*Journal of Experimental Psychology*
J. Genet. Psychol.	*Journal of Genetic Psychology*
J. Hist. Behav. Sci.	*Journal of History of the Behavioral Sciences*
J. Hist. Med.	*Journal of History of Medicine*
J. IEE	*Journal of the Institute of Electrical Engineering*
J. Indiv. Psychol.	*Journal of Individual Psychology*
J. Inst. Actuaries	*Journal of the Institute of Actuaries*
J. Ment. Sci.	*Journal of Mental Science*
J. Nerv. Ment. Dis.	*Journal of Nervous and Mental Disease*
J. Neurol. Psychopath.	*Journal of Neurology and Psychopathology*
J. Neurol. Sci.	*Journal of Neurological Science*
J. Neurophysiol.	*Journal of Neurophysiology*
J. Opt. Soc. Amer.	*Journal of the Optical Society of America*
J. Otto Rank Ass.	*Journal of the Otto Rank Association*
J. Pediat.	*Journal of Pediatrics*
J. Pers.	*Journal of Personality*
J. Pers. Assmt.	*Journal of Personality Assessment*
J. Personnel Res.	*Journal of Personnel Research*
J. Pers. Soc. Psychol.	*Journal of Personality and Social Psychology*
J. Phil.	*Journal of Philosophy*
J. physiol. exp. pathol.	*Journal de physiologie expérimentale et pathologique*
J. physiol. l' homme anim.	*Journal de la physiologie de l' homme et des animaux*
J. physiol. path. gén.	*Journal de physiologie et de pathologie générale*
J. Project. Techn.	*Journal of Projective Techniques*
J. Psycho-asthen. Monog. Suppl.	*Journal of Psycho-asthenia Monograph Supplement*
J. Spec. Educ.	*Journal of Special Education*
Klin. Mittbl. Augenheilk.	*Klinisches Mitteilungsblatt der Augenheilkunde*
Kolle	K. Kolle (ed.). *Grosse Nervenärzte.* 3 vols. Stuttgart: Georg Thieme Verlag, 1963–1970.
Korrespbl. schw. Ärzte	*Korrespondenzblatt schweizer Ärzte*
Landw. Jb.	*Landwirtschaftliche Jahrbücher*
L'Année psychol.	*L'Année psychologique*
Larousse	*Grand Larousse encyclopédique.* 10 vols. plus 2 suppl. Paris: Librairie Larousse, 1960–1964.
Lond. Hosp. Clin. Lect. Rep.	*London Hospital Clinical Lectures and Reports*
Math. Ann.	*Mathematische Annalen*
McGDcArt	R. S. Meyers (ed.). *McGraw-Hill Dictionary of Art.* 5 vols. New York: McGraw-Hill, 1969.
McGMSE	*McGraw-Hill Modern Scientists and Engineers.* 3 vols. New York: McGraw-Hill, 1980.
Med. Classics	*Medical Classics*
Med. Surg. Rep.	*Medical and Surgical Reporter*
	Memoirs of the Literary and

Manchester	Philosophical Society of Manchester
Mem. Regia accad. sci. lett. art. Modena	Memorie della Regia accademia delle scienze, lettere ed arti in Modena
Mem. Regia accad. sci. Torino	Memorie della Regia accademia delle scienze di Torino
Mhef. Math. Phys.	Monatshefte für Mathematik und Physik
MIT Technol. Rev.	MIT Technology Review
Mschr. Kinderheilk.	Monatsschrift für Kinderheilkunde
Mschr. Psychiat. Neurol.	Monatsschrift für Psychiatrie und Neurologie
Münch. med. Wschr.	Münchener medizinische Wochenschrift
Mus. Ed. J.	Musical Education Journal
Naturwiss.	Naturwissenschaften
Naturwiss. Rundsch.	Naturwissenschaftliche Rundschau
NCAB	The National Cyclopedia of American Biography. 53 vols. plus 11 suppl. New York: White, 1893—.
NDB	Neue deutsche Biographie. 9 vols. to date. Berlin: Duncker & Humboldt, 1953—.
Ned. Lancet	Nederlandsche Lancet
Nerv. Ment. Dis. Monog.	Nervous and Mental Disease Monographs
Neue psychol. Stud.	Neue psychologische Studien
Neurol. Zbl.	Neurologisches Zentralblatt
New Engl. J. Med.	New England Journal of Medicine
Nissl Beitr. Nerv. Geisteskr.	Nissl Beiträge zu Nerven- und Geisteskrankheiten
Nord. Med. Ark.	Nordisk Medicinsk Arkiv
Not. Rec. Roy. Soc.	Notes and Records of the Royal Society of London
NY Med. J.	New York Medical Journal
NYT	New York Times
Obit. Not.	Royal Society of London. Obituary Notices of Fellows. 8 vols. Cambridge: The Society, 1932–1952.
ObitOF	F. Levy (comp.). Obituaries on File. 2 vols. New York: Facts on File, 1979.
Ophthal. Bibl.	Ophthalmologische Bibliothek
Pagel, Biog. Lex.	J. Pagel. Biographisches Lexikon hervorragender Ärzte des neunzehnten Jahrhunderts. Berlin: Urban & Schwarzenberg, 1901.
Ped. Semin. J. Genet. Psychol.	Pedagogical Seminary and Journal of Genetical Psychology
Perc. Mot. Skills	Perceptual and Motor Skills
Personnel Guid. J.	Personnel Guidance Journal
Personnel J.	Personnel Journal
Personnel Psych.	Personnel Psychology
Persp. Biol. Med.	Perspectives in Biology and Medicine
Pflüg. Arch. ges. Physiol.	Pflügers Archiv der gesamten Physiologie
Phi Beta Phi Quart.	Phi Beta Phi Quarterly
Phil. Mag.	Philosophisches Magazin
Phil. Stud.	Philosophische Studien
Phil. Trans. Roy. Soc.	Philosophical Transactions of the Royal Society of London

Photog. J.	*Photographic Journal*
Pogg. Ann. Phys. Chem.	*Poggendorffs Annalen der Physik und Chemie*
Pop. Sci. Mon.	*Popular Science Monthly*
PR	C. Murchison (ed.). *The Psychological Register.* Vol. 3. Worcester, Mass.: Clark University Press, 1932.
Prag. med. Wschr.	*Prager medizinische Wochenschrift*
Proc. Amer. Acad. Arts Sci.	*Proceedings of the American Academy of Arts and Sciences*
Proc. Amer. Ass. Anatomists, Anat. Rec.	*Proceedings of the American Association of Anatomists, Anatomical Record*
Proc. London Math. Soc.	*Proceedings of the London Mathematical Society*
Proc. Nat. Acad. Sci.	*Proceedings of the National Academy of Science*
Proc. Nat. Inst. Sci. India	*Proceedings of the National Institute of Sciences of India*
Proc. Phys. Soc.	*Proceedings of the Physical Society*
Proc. Roy. Soc.	*Proceedings of the Royal Society of London*
Proc. Roy. Soc. Edinb.	*Proceedings of the Royal Society of Edinburgh*
Proc. Roy. Soc. Med.	*Proceedings of the Royal Society of Medicine*
Proc. R. Virchow Med. Soc.	*Proceedings of the Rudolf Virchow Medical Society*
Proc. Soc. Psychical Res.	*Proceedings of the Society for Psychical Research*
Progr. méd.	*Progrés de médecine*
Psychiat. Quart. Suppl.	*Psychiatric Quarterly Supplement*
Psychoanal. Quart.	*Psychoanalytical Quarterly*
Psychobiol.	*Psychobiology*
Psychol. Beitr.	*Psychologische Beiträge*
Psychol. belg.	*Psychologica belgica*
Psychol. Bull.	*Psychological Bulletin*
Psychol. Forsch.	*Psychologische Forschung*
Psychol. franç.	*Psychologie française*
Psychol. Monog.	*Psychological Monographs*
Psychol. Rep.	*Psychological Reports*
Psychol. Rev.	*Psychological Review*
Psychol. Rev. Monog. Suppl.	*Psychological Review Monograph Supplements*
Psychosom. Med.	*Psychosomatic Medicine*
Publ. Mass. Med. Sci.	*Publications of Massachusetts Medical Society*
Quart. J. Exp. Psychol.	*Quarterly Journal of Experimental Psychology*
Racc. fis.-chim. ital.	*Raccolta fisico-chimica italiana*
Rendic. Accad. med. Torino	*Rendiconti dell'Accademia de medicina Torino*
Rev. franç. pédiat.	*Revue française de pédiatrie*
Rev. Intern. Stat. Inst.	*Review of the International Statistical Institute*
Rev. neurol.	*Revue neurologique*
Rev. Neurol. Psychiat.	*Review of Neurology and Psychiatry*
Riv. pat. nerv. ment.	*Rivista di patologia nervosa e mentale*
Rorschach Res. Exch.	*Rorschach Research Exchange*
Rothschuh	K. E. Rothschuh. *History of Physiology.* New York: Krieger, 1972.
Sat. Eve. Post	*Saturday Evening Post*

Scand. Sci. Rev.	*Scandinavian Scientific Review*
School & Soc.	*School and Society*
Sci. Amer.	*Scientific American*
Sci. Mon.	*Scientific Monthly*
Scripta math.	*Scripta mathematica*
Shepard	L. A. Shepard (ed.). *Encyclopedia of Occultism and Parapsychology.* 2d ed. 3 vols. Detroit: Gale Research Co., 1984.
Sitzber. Akad. wiss. Wien, math.-naturwiss. Cl.	*Sitzungsberichte der Akademie der Wissenschaften in Wien, mathematisch-wissenschaftliche Classe*
Sitzber. kön. böhm. Ges. Wiss. Prag, math.-naturwiss. Cl.	*Sitzungsberichte der königlichen böhmischen Gesellschaft der Wissenschaften in Prag, mathematisch-naturwissenschaftliche Classe*
Sitzber. math.-wiss. Cl. Kais. Akad. Wiss.	*Sitzungsberichte mathematisch-wissenschaftlicher Classe der Kaiserlichen Akademie der Wissenschaften*
Smithson. Inst. Annu. Rep.	*Smithsonian Institute Annual Report*
Soc. biol. Paris, Mém.	*Societé de biologie de Paris, Mémoires*
Soc. clin. méd. psychol.	*Societé de clinique médicale et psychologique*
Soc. franç. ophthal., Bull. mém.	*Societé française d'ophthalmologie, Bulletin et mémoires*
Sociol. Soc. Res.	*Sociological and Social Research*
Soc. Res.	*Social Research*
Soviet	*Great Soviet Encyclopedia.* 31 vols. plus index. Transl. 3d ed. New York: Macmillan, 1973–1983.
Talbot	J. H. Talbot. *A Biographical History of Medicine.* New York: Grune & Stratton, 1970.
Teach. Coll. Contr. Educ.	*Teachers College Contributions to Education*
Teach. Coll. Rec.	*Teachers College Record*
Times	*Times* (London)
Trans. Amer. Soc. Mech. Eng.	*Transactions of the American Society of Mechanical Engineers*
Trans. Edinb. Geol. Soc.	*Transactions of the Edinburgh Geological Society*
Trans. Ophthal. Soc. UK	*Transactions of the Ophthalmological Society of United Kingdom*
Trans. Roy. Soc. Edinb.	*Transactions of the Royal Society of Edinburgh*
Univ. Hawaii Bull.	*University of Hawaii Bulletin*
Upsala Läk. för. Förh.	*Upsala Läkare förening Förhandlingar*
Verh. naturforsch. Ver. Brünn	*Verhandlungen des naturforschenden Vereins in Brünn*
Vision Res.	*Vision Research*
Vopr. Psikhol.	*Voprosy Psikhologii*
Vtljschr. wiss. Philos.	*Vierteljahrsschrift wissenschaftlicher Philosophie*
Webster's	*Webster's Biographical Dictionary.* Springfield, Mass.: G. & C. Merriam Co., 1980.
Wh	*Who Was Who.* London: Adam & Charles Black; New York: St. Martin's Press.

WhAm	*Who Was Who in America*. Chicago: Marquis Who's Who.
WhE&EA	*Who Was Who of English and European Authors 1931–1949*. 3 vols. Detroit: Gale Research Co., 1970.
WhNAA	*Who Was Who among North American Authors, 1929–1939*. 2 vols. Detroit: Gale Research Co., 1976.
Who	*Who's Who*. London: Adam & Charles Black; New York: St. Martin's Press.
WhoAm	*Who's Who in America*. Chicago: Marquis Who's Who.
WhoAmArt	*Who's Who in American Art*. New York: R. R. Bowker.
WhoAmEd	*Who's Who in American Education*. Hattiesburg, Miss.: Who's Who in American Education.
WhoAmWom	*Who's Who of American Women*. Chicago: Marquis Who's Who.
WhoMW	*Who's Who in the Midwest*. Chicago: Marquis Who's Who.
WhoSSW	*Who's Who in the South and Southwest*. Chicago: Marquis Who's Who.
WhoUSSR	*Who's Who in the USSR*. Metuchen, NJ: Scarecrow Press, 1972.
WhoWo	*Who's Who in the World*. Chicago: Marquis Who's Who.
WhoWoJ	I. J. Carmin Karpman (ed.). *Who's Who in World Jewry*. New York: Pitman Publishing Co., 1976.
WhUSSR	*Who Was Who in the USSR*. Munich: Institute for the Study of the USSR, 1972.
Wien. klin. Wschr.	*Wiener klinische Wochenschrift*
WoWhoSci	*World Who's Who in Science*. Chicago: Marquis Who's Who, 1968.
Yale J. Biol. Med.	*Yale Journal of Biology and Medicine*
Yearb. Amer. Philos. Soc.	*Yearbook of the American Philosophical Society*
Z. Biol.	*Zeitschrift für Biologie*
Zbl. med. Wiss.	*Zentralblatt für die medizinischen Wissenschaften*
Z. ges. Neurol. Psychiat.	*Zeitschrift für die gesamte Neurologie und Psychiatrie*
Z. Instrumentenk.	*Zeitschrift für Instrumentenkunde*
Z. Kinderheilk.	*Zeitschrift für Kinderheilkunde*
Z. Psychol.	*Zeitschrift für Psychologie*
Z. Psychol. Physiol. Sinnesorg.	*Zeitschrift für Psychologie und Physiologie der Sinnesorgane*
Z. Sinnesphysiol.	*Zeitschrift für Sinnesphysiologie*
Z. wiss. Zool.	*Zeitschrift für wissenschaftliche Zoologie*

Eponyms in Psychology

A

ABADIE'S SIGN. The absence of pain when the Achilles tendon is pressed, a sign of tabes dorsalis.

Abadie, Joseph Louis Irenée Jean. French neurosurgeon (b. Tarbes, Hautes Pyrénées, December 15, 1873, d. 1946). Abadie received a doctorate in medicine from the University of Bordeaux (1900). After several hospital appointments, he taught, beginning in 1904, at the University of Bordeaux. Abadie published papers on brain lesions, tabes dorsalis, childhood disorders, alcoholism, and toxic psychoses. The sign was described in 1905 (*Gaz. hebd. sci. méd. Bordeaux,* 26, 408).

Biographies: Fischer, *Biog. Lex.*

ABNEY'S EFFECT. 1. The time-related growth and decay of brightness within the contours of a form. When a large surface is suddenly illuminated, its brightness is seen first in the middle of the surface and then spreads out to the contours. The phenomenon is reversed in direction when illumination suddenly ceases. 2. A shift in hue of a chromatic light that is a function of a shift in the purity of the light.

ABNEY'S LAW. The luminance of a mixture of differently colored lights is equal to the sum of the luminances of the components.

Abney, Sir William de Wiveleslie. English chemist (b. Derby, Derbyshire, July 24, 1843, d. Folkestone, Kent, December 3, 1920). Abney was born at about the same time as photography was invented, and he achieved a measure of distinction in his research on photochemical processes and color measurement. He obtained a commission in the Royal Engineers before he was twenty and taught chemistry and photography at the Chatham School of Military Engineering, advancing subsequently to a number of academic and administrative positions. Abney has to his credit several inventions and discoveries in the area of photography. The brightness effect was first described in 1897 (*Phil. Trans. Roy Soc., 190A,* 155–93), the hue effect in 1913 (*Researches in Color Vision and the Trichromatic Theory*), and the law in 1886 (with E. R. Festing, *Phil. Trans. Roy. Soc., 177,* 423–56).

  Biographies: DNB, 3d Suppl.; *DSB,* 1; *EB,* 1.

ACHILLES JERK. The reflex elicited by a tap on the Achilles tendon.

Achilles. Achilles, the greatest Greek warrior of the Trojan War and the central figure of the Iliad, was the son of Peleus and the sea goddess Thetis. Thetis had made Achilles invulnerable by immersing him in the water of the River Styx, forgetting, however, to immerse also the part of the foot by which she was holding him, the tendon of Achilles. Achilles was killed by Paris during the siege of Troy when Apollo guided Paris's arrow to the one spot where Achilles could be wounded.

ADLERIAN PSYCHOLOGY. Also known as individual psychology, Adlerian psychology is a form of psychoanalysis. While retaining many of Freud's concepts, Adler's psychology differs from Freud's in its deemphasis on sex and the unconscious and its emphasis on social relations and conscious ego functions. The basis of neuroses is seen in children's reactions to their feeling inferior to and dependent upon adults. Feelings of inferiority may lead to overcompensation or submissiveness. A person's major goal is to strive for superiority. When inferiority is used to give up attempts at compensation ("inferiority complex"), neurosis results. People are motivated more by goals and future expectations than by their biology. They therefore create their own personalities.

Adler, Alfred. Austrian psychiatrist (b. Vienna, February 7, 1870, d. Aberdeen, Scotland, May 28, 1937). Adler received his medical degree from the University of Vienna in 1895. He became acquainted with Freud's ideas and joined Freud's group, becoming one of its leading members. Adler's own views, however, developed along lines different from Freud's. He made the first public statement of his views in 1911 in a presentation to the Vienna Psychoanalytical Society, the occasion also marking his parting of the ways with Freud. During World War I Adler worked as physican in the Austrian army. His fame spread during the 1920s, and he traveled to many countries on lecture tours. He came to the United States in 1926 and was given an appointment at the Long Island College of Medicine in 1932. Books by Adler include *The Neurotic Constitution* (1917), *The Practice and Theory of Individual Psychology* (1927), and *What Life Should Mean to You* (1937), but his views are largely contained in his numerous papers.

Biographies: A. Adler, *Amer. J. Psychiat.*, 1970, *127*, 771–72; *Asimov;* P. Bottome, *Alfred Adler, a Biography*, 1939; P. Bottome, *Alfred Adler: Apostle of Freedom*, 1957; *EB*, 1; *EP*, 1; *EJ*, 2; *IESS*, 1; H. Orgler, *Alfred Adler: The Man and His Work*, 1939.

AHLFELD BREATHING MOVEMENTS. Also known as Ahlfeld's sign, these are rhythmic movements of the fetus' chest that begin in about the fourth month of gestation and can be felt through the abdominal walls of the mother's body.

Ahlfeld, Friedrich. German pediatrician (b. Alsleben, Saxony, October 16, 1843, d. Marburg, Hesse, May 25, 1929). A Tübingen M.D. (1868), Ahlfeld taught at Leipzig, Giessen, and Marburg from 1876 to 1894, was named Geheimer Medizin-Rat (Privy Medical Councilor) in 1894, and retired in 1909. Ahlfeld was the author of several books on obstetrics and infant development.
   Biographies: EUI, 3; Hirsch, *Biog. Lex.;* Pagel, *Biog. Lex.*

ALEXANDERISM. Overwhelming urge to conquer or to destroy nations, also know as agriothymia ambitiosa.

Alexander III, more often called Alexander the Great. Macedonian king (b. Pella, Macedonia, 356 B.C., d. Mesopotamia, June 13, 323 B.C.). After many conquests, including that of the Persian empire, Alexander became the head of an empire himself, one that extended from Macedonia and Thrace through Asia Minor, Egypt, Syria, all of the Middle East, and Persia, up to the Indus River. Growing emotionally unstable toward the end of his reign, he demanded that he be recognized as a god.
   Biographies: EB, 1.

ALEXANDER'S LAW. A nystagmus, produced either by rotation or thermally, can be accentuated voluntarily by moving the eyes in the direction of the jerky component of the nystagmus (the rapid return movement of the eyes in a direction opposite to the initial, slow movement).

Alexander, Gustav. Austrian otologist (b. Vienna, December 18, 1873, d. Vienna, April 12, 1932). Alexander received the M.D. degree from the University of Vienna in 1898, specialized in ear disorders, and taught at the University of Vienna from 1909 to 1932, when he was murdered. He wrote a large number of articles on inner ear functions and ear disorders, especially the effects of venereal disease.
   Biographies: Fisher, *Biog. Lex.*

ALEXANDER TECHNIQUE. A technique for relearning simple motor acts, such as locomotion, breathing, eating, speaking, lifting, carrying, reading, and writing and for breaking unconscious bad habits associated with these activities. It is based on the proposition that physical, mental, and spiritual processes are translated into muscular tension and that affecting muscular tension will affect not only one's physical but also mental well-being.

Alexander, Frederick Matthias. Australian educator (b. Wyngard, Tasmania, January 20, 1869, d. London, England, October 10, 1955). Alexander was self-educated and trained as an actor, but a voice problem interfered with his career. He corrected the problem himself and in 1894 began teaching his technique in Australia. He went to London in 1904, publishing his first book, *Man's Supreme Inheritance*, in 1910. From 1914 to 1924 he worked in England and the United States, aided by his brother, A. R. Alexander. His second book, *Constructive Conscious Control of the Individual* (1924), had an introduction by the philosopher John Dewey, one of the many famous people who endorsed Alexander's method. Alexander started training courses for teachers of his method and opened schools for children. He also wrote *The Use of the Self* in 1932 and *The Universal Constant in Living* in 1942. The years 1940 to 1943 Alexander spent in Stow, Massachusetts, and then returned to England.

Biographies: C. Stevens, in A. Hill (ed.), *A Visual Encyclopedia of Unconventional Medicine*, 1978; *Wh*, 1951–1960.

"ALICE IN WONDERLAND" SYNDROME. Depersonalization and hallucinations, especially Lilliputian hallucinations, that occur in certain altered states of consciousness, for instance, the hypnagogic state, drug states, high fever, and schizophrenia.

Alice in Wonderland. Lewis Carroll's classic story (1865) in which the heroine, Alice, finds herself shrinking and growing in her dream after partaking of certain cakes, drinks, and mushrooms.

ALLPORT A-S REACTION STUDY. A psychological inventory that measures the personality traits of ascendance and submission as they manifest themselves in an individual's everyday behavior. Gordon Allport first published this test in 1928 (*J. Abn. Soc. Psychol.*, 23, 118–36). With his brother, Floyd Allport, as coauthor, he revised it in 1939.

ALLPORT-VERNON STUDY OF VALUES. A psychological inventory that yields a profile of the strength of interest in six areas of human endeavor: theoretical, economic, aesthetic, social, political, and religious. The instrument was first published by Philip Vernon and Gordon Allport in 1931 (*J. Abn. Soc. Psychol.*, 26, 231–48). It was revised in 1951, becoming the Allport-Vernon-Lindzey Study of Values, and revised once again in 1970 simply as Study of Values.

Allport, Gordon Willard. American psychologist (b. Montezuma, Indiana, November 11, 1897, d. Cambridge, Massachusetts, October 9, 1967). One of the premier American psychologists of personality and the social process, Allport received his undergraduate and graduate degrees (Ph.D. in 1922) from Harvard University and spent most of his professional life (1924–1926, 1930–1967) there. His work was dedicated to the study of human individuality. He viewed human personality as an evolving system of habits, attitudes, and traits that was determined more by social than biological factors. *Personality: A Psychological Interpretation* (1937) was his most important work. Allport was counted among the "third force" or humanistic psychologists. He influenced psychology greatly through his many writings (12 books, 228 other publications), his teaching, and his personality.

Biographies: Brit. J. Psychol., 1968, *59,* 99–103; *ConAu,* 1R; *CurBio,* 1960; *EB,* 1; *HPA,* 5; *IESS,* 18; *NCAB,* J; T. F. Pettigrew, *J. Pers. Soc. Psychol.,* 1969, *12,* 1–5.

Vernon, Philip Ewart. English psychologist (b. Oxford, June 6, 1905). Vernon's doctoral dissertation (Cambridge, 1928) was on individual differences in the appreciation of music. While his musical interest remained avocational, his interest in individual differences continued, and most of Vernon's life work was concerned with psychometric issues. He read Gordon Allport, obtained a scholarship, and spent the years 1929 through 1931 at Yale and Harvard Universities. It was then that his collaboration with Allport led to the coauthorship of *Studies in Expressive Movement* (1933) and the Study of Values, with Vernon doing the research and Allport providing the theory. Vernon held several academic positions in England and Scotland between 1931 and 1968. He was president of the British Psychological Society in 1954 and then left for Canada, where he is at the University of Calgary. Vernon has written a dozen major books that survey current theory and research and offer critique and integration of viewpoints in the area of abilities and their measurement.

Biographies: Blue B., 1976; P. E. Vernon, The Making of an Applied Psychologist, in T. S. Krawiec (ed.), *The Psychologists,* vol. 3, 1978.

ALZHEIMER'S DISEASE. A progressive degenerative disease of the central nervous system that affects especially the aged. It tends to run in families, but several other, nongenetic factors are also involved. It results in the dying off of brain cells and the formation of characteristic neuritic plaques. The atrophy of the brain leads to progressive abnormalities of memory, cognition, speech, and other behaviors and coincides with what used to be called senility.

Alzheimer, Alois. German neuropathologist (b. Marktbreit-am-Main, Bavaria, June 14, 1864, d. Breslau (now Wroclaw), Silesia, December 19, 1915). Alzheimer's name is inextricably associated with a particular form of pathological changes in the brain, but he also produced classical descriptions of general paresis, arteriosclerosis, acute delirium, and many other conditions as well. He described the form of brain pathology that bears his name in 1907 (*Allg. Z. Psychiat.,* 64, 146–48). In 1920 Emil Kraepelin's* proposed that the disease be named after Alzheimer. Several other medical eponyms contain Alzheimer's name. Alzheimer received his M.D. degree from the University of Würzburg in

1887. In his first position at the Städtische Irrenanstalt in Frankfurt-am-Main, Alzheimer became acquainted with the neuropathologist Franz Nissl.* Nissl's ideas and Alzheimer's lucid description of pathological conditions of the nervous system appeared in a six-volume work, *Histological and Histopathological Studies of the Cerebral Cortex* (1904–1918). In 1902, Alzheimer went to Heidelberg to work with Kraepelin and followed him to Munich in 1903. He did his finest work in Munich until 1912, when he was appointed chair of psychiatry at the University of Breslau.

Biographies: Rothschuh; Talbot.

AMES DEMONSTRATION. Devices such as the distorted room, the rotating trapezoidal window, the "thereness-thatness" apparatus, and the aniseikonic lenses that demonstrate the power of assumptions that we make about the world based on past experience, on the perception of the world, by making them conflict with the information provided by the physical properties of objects.

Ames, Adelbert, Jr. American ophthalmologist (b. Lowell, Massachusetts, August 19, 1880, d. Hanover, New Hampshire, July 3, 1955). Ames studied law at Harvard University (LL.B., 1906). Dissatisfied with the practice of law, he turned to painting, which led to the analysis of vision and ophthalmology. In 1936 he established the Dartmouth Eye Clinic, where he discovered and researched the phenomenon of aniseikonia and invented the aniseikonic lenses to correct it. A study of the effects of these lenses in persons with normal vision and other unique conditions of vision led Ames to the formulation of the view of transactional functionalism in perception. The empirical evidence came from the demonstrations Ames devised to show how individuals experience the consequences of their own actions ("transact" with their environment). The first demonstrations were prepared in 1938 and set up at the Hanover Institute for Associated Research. They were then removed to the Perception Demonstration Center, Princeton University.

Biographies: J. Opt. Soc. Amer., 1955, 45, 333–37; NCAB, 44; WhAm, 3.

AMMON'S HORN. The hippocampus, so named because of its curved, tapering appearance.

Ammon. Egyptian god represented with a ram's head.

ANSBACHER EFFECT. A lighted arc, placed at the edge of a disc and rotated in a dark room, will appear to be the shorter the greater is the velocity of the rotation. The phenomenon is also known as the Ansbacher shrinkage effect.

Ansbacher, Heinz Ludwig. American psychologist (b. Frankfurt-am-Main, October 21, 1904). Ansbacher came to the United States in 1924, obtained his Ph.D. in experimental psychology from Columbia University in 1937, did research on his own, and held various business, government, and teaching positions between 1937 and 1946. He took a position with the University of Vermont in 1946, becoming professor emeritus in 1970. The paper in which the shrinkage effect is described was Ansbacher's last experimental publication. He had heard Alfred Adler's* lectures in 1930 and from then on gravitated increasingly toward the Adlerian position, becoming eventually one of the foremost exponents of Adlerian psychology. The effect, which Ansbacher himself called the Harold C. Brown shrinkage phenomenon (to give credit to a fellow graduate student who was first to observe it) was first described by Ansbacher in 1938 (*Psychol. Bull.*, *35*, 701). A second, more complete account of a series of experiments was presented in 1944 (*J. Exp. Psychol.*, *34*, 1–23). The phenomenon was named the Ansbacher shrinkage effect by Gordon Stanley (*Acta Psychol.*, 1964, *22*, 109–18).

   Biographies: AM&WS, 1973S; H. L. Ansbacher. Psychology: A Way of Living, in T. S. Krawiec (ed.), *The Psychologists* (Vol. 2), 1974; *APA Dir.*, 1985; *ConAu*, Pl.

ANTIGONE COMPLEX. A psychological complex described by Benjamin B. Wolman as ''an extreme case of non-sexual love and sacrifice of one's own life for the sake of a beloved person.''

Antigone. Antigone was the daughter of Oedipus.* She buried the body of her brother Polynices, slain in battle, though King Creon had forbidden it under penalty of death. Antigone was ordered to be buried alive. The term was introduced by Benjamin Wolman in 1965 (*Amer. Imago, 22*, 186–201).

ANTON'S SYMPTON. Unawareness on the part of an individual with brain damage of the resulting deficit in mental or physical functioning. It is observed particularly in patients with impaired capacity for abstraction and in patients in whom the incapacity is total.

Anton, Gabriel. Austrian psychiatrist (b. Saaz, Bohemia, July 28, 1858, d. 1933). Anton studied medicine at the University of Prague; obtaining the M.D. degree in 1882. He specialized in psychiatry, became assistant to the neurologist Theodor Meynert in Vienna in 1887, and then went to teach at Innsbruck in 1891, to Graz in 1894, and to Halle in 1905.

   Biographies: Fischer, *Biog. Lex.*

APERT'S SYNDROME. A dominant-gene hereditary condition combining acrocephaly with hypertelorism and syndactilia. It is associated with severe mental deficiency.

Apert, Eugene Charles. French pediatrician (b. Paris, July 27, 1868, d. 1940). A University of Paris doctor of medicine (1897), Apert practiced at the Hôpital des enfants-malades in Paris from 1902, specializing in congenital defects.

   Biographies: Fischer, *Biog. Lex.; WhE&EA, 1.*

APGAR SCORE. A physician's rating of the physical condition of a neonate (within sixty seconds after birth). The signs considered are heart rate, respiration, muscle tone, reflexes, and color, each rated on a scale from 0 to 2, for a maximum of 10 points.

Apgar, Virginia. American physician (b. Westfield, New Jersey, June 7, 1909 d. Westfield, New Jersey, August 7, 1974). Apgar, who received her M.D. from Columbia University (1933), taught at the university from 1936 to 1959 and practiced at the Presbyterian Medical Center from 1938 to 1959. From then until her death, she held a position with the March of Dimes National Foundation, teaching concurrently at Cornell University from 1965 to 1974. She specialized in teratology and anesthesiology. The scoring system was presented at a special meeting of the International Anesthesia Research Society in 1952.

Biographies: AM&WS, 1971P; *ConAu,* 1973; *CurBio,* 1968; *WhAm,* 6.

APPUN'S LAMELLA. A thin strip of flexible graduated steel, tipped with a disc (to reduce the higher harmonics), that is used to produce tones at the lower extreme of the audible range.

Appun, Anton. German acoustician (b. Hanau, Hesse, June 20, 1839 d. Hanau, Hesse, January 13, 1900). Appun studied at the Leipzig Conservatory and worked as a music teacher in Hanau. At the conservatory, Appun continued the work of his father, Georg August Appun.* He worked on the determination of cycles of vibrating bodies, published papers on the determination of very high frequencies, on a natural harmonical system. His one paper on experiments with low tones describes the lamella (*Ber. wetterau. Ges. ges. Naturk.,* 1889, 37–68). Appun claimed to be able to hear tones as low as 8 cycles and as high as 50,000.

Biographies: F. Blume (ed.), *Die Musik in Geschichte und Gegenwart,* Vol. 15, 1973; S. Sadie (ed.), *The New Grove Dictionary of Music and Musicians,* 1980.

APPUN'S TONOMETER. A windchest (harmonium) containing many vibrating reeds that cover a range of two or three octaves but differ in vibration from each other by only 4 cycles.

Appun, Georg August Ignaz. German musical theorist and acoustician (b. Hanau, Hesse, January 27, 1816, d. Hanau, Hesse, January 14, 1885). Appun studied several musical instruments and could play almost all. He taught voice and theory in Hanau and Frankfurt-am-Main until 1860, after which he engaged in acoustic research. The tonometer and other instruments were invented for the purpose of conducting the research.

Biographies: F. Blume (ed.), *Die Musik in Geschichte und Gegenwart,* Vol. 15, 1973; S. Sadie (ed.), *The New Grove Dictionary of Music and Musicians,* 1980.

ARCHES OF CORTI. See RODS OF CORTI.

ARGYLL ROBERTSON PUPIL. A pupil that has lost its reflex to light but does respond to accommodation of the lens to near objects and the convergence of the eyes. It is a sign of neurological damage, as in tabes dorsalis and general paresis.

Robertson, Argyll. Scottish ophthalmic surgeon (b. Edinburgh, 1837, d. Gondal, India, 1909). Robertson obtained his M.D. from St. Andrews University, practiced ophthalmology in Edinburgh, lectured at the university there, and was ophthalmic surgeon to the Royal Infirmary. He published some fifty papers on the physiology of the eyes and their diseases. Of these, the best known concern the effects on the pupil of such substances as belladonna and the Calabar bean. His description of the pupillary response that bears his name was presented in two papers published in 1869 (*Edinb. Med. J.*, *14*, 696–708; *15*, 487–493). The eponym includes Robertson's first name to avoid confusion with his father, John Argyll Robertson, who was also a surgeon.

Biographies: Brit. Med. J., 1909, *1*, 191–93; *Edinb. Med. J.*, 1909, *2*, 159–62; *Havmaker; Talbot.*

ARISTOTLE'S ILLUSION. The illusion that when an object is held between the tips of the two crossed middle fingers, two objects instead of one are felt. Also referred to as Aristotle's experiment.

Aristotle. Greek philosopher (b. Stagira, Chalcidice, 384 B.C., d. Chalcis, Euboea, 323 B.C.). Aristotle probably studied with Plato* in the latter's academy. Not much is known about Aristotle until the age of thirty-seven except that he spent the last twenty years of this period in Athens. He was a teacher, writer, and scientific collector, tutor to Alexander the Great between 342 and 336, then again teacher in Athens for the last twelve years of his life. In Athens he established his famous school of philosophy, the Lyceum. Regarded by many as the greatest mind that ever lived, Aristotle contributed to prescientific psychology in both quantity and quality more than anybody else. His main psychological work is *De anima*. Shorter works are included under the common Latin name of *Parva naturalia*. *De anima* was the first systematic treatise on psychology. The illusion that bears Aristotle's name is described in *Parva naturalia (On Dreams*, II).

Biographies: Asimov; DSB, 1; EB, 1; EP, 1; IESS, 1.

ARTHUR POINT SCALE OF PERFORMANCE TESTS. A performance test of intelligence for children who may be deaf or speak no English. It contains such tests as block and stencil design, form boards, and picture assembly. The test was first published in 1930 and is also known as Arthur Performance Scale.

Arthur, (Mary) Grace. American psychologist (b. May 22, 1883, d. July 1967). After obtaining a Ph.D. in psychology from the University of Minnesota in 1924, Arthur worked as a psychologist at the Amherst H. Wilder Child Guidance Clinic, becoming a consulting psychologist in private practice in St. Paul in 1942. Her specialty was nonverbal tests, remedial teaching, and the measurement of intelligence of American Indians.

Biographies: APA Dir., 1965; *WhoAmWo*, 1961.

ASCH SITUATION. An experimental situation of contrived group pressure under which the target person's judgment is markedly changed. The group consists of the experimenter's confederates, who have conspired to agree that an erroneous judgment is the correct one, thereby influencing the judgment of the group member who is not in on the conspiracy in the same direction, thus evidencing social conformity.

Asch, Solomon Eliot. American psychologist (b. Warsaw, Poland, September 14, 1907). Asch came to the United States at age thirteen. He received the Ph.D. degree from Columbia University in 1932 and afterward held academic positions at Brooklyn College (1932–1943), the New School for Social Research (1943–1947), Swarthmore College (1947–1966), Rutgers University (1966–1973), and the University of Pennsylvania. An award citation mentions Asch's work on "forming impressions of personality and on group conformity pressures" that had become two of the "most imitated research designs in our generation." The basic Asch situation is described in a chapter by Asch in H. Geutzkow (ed.), *Groups, Leadership, and Men* (1951).

Biographies: Amer. Psychologist, 1967, 22, 1128–30; APA Dir., 1968; AMS, 1962S; IESS, 18.

AUBERT-FLEISCHL PARADOX. A moving object appears to move more slowly when the observer fixates the object than when he or she fixates the background.

AUBERT-FORSTER PHENOMENON. Small objects nearby are discriminated over a larger area of the retina than large objects farther away that subtend the same visual angle as the smaller objects.

AUBERT PHENOMENON. A vertical line in an otherwise empty visual field appears to be tilted in the direction opposite to which the observer's head is tilted.

AUBERT'S DIAPHRAGM. A type of adjustable opening for controlling the amount of light in vision experiments. The opening is formed by two overlapping leaves with right-angle notches in them. By sliding one leaf against the other, a square opening varying in size is achieved.

Aubert, Hermann. German physiologist (b. Frankfurt-am-Main, November 1826, d. Rostock, Mecklenburg, February 12, 1892). Along with Hermann von Helmholtz,* Aubert was a pioneer in the area of physiological optics. After receiving the M.D. degree from the University of Berlin in 1850, Aubert studied visual space perception in the 1850s, as well as cutaneous space perception, and, in the 1860s, psychophysics. The first complete understanding of dark and light adaptation is found in Aubert, as well as the first thorough experimental measurement of the retinal color zones. His last contribution was to the understanding of bodily orientation. His 1888 book, *Physiologische Studien über die Orientierung,* contains a description of the Aubert phenomenon. The Aubert-Forster phenomenon is mentioned briefly in a joint paper by Aubert and Forster in 1856 (*Jber. schles. Ges. vaterl. Kult., 43,* pp. 33ff.), and more fully in 1857 (*Albrecht v.*

Graefes Arch. Ophthalm., 3, 1–37). Aubert described the movement paradox in 1886 (*Arch. ges. Physiol., 39,* 347–70).
  Biographies: ADB, 46; *EUI,* 6; Hirsch, *Biog. Lex.;* Pagel, *Biog. Lex.*

Fleischl von Marxow, Ernst von. Austrian physiologist (b. Vienna, August 5, 1846, d. Vienna, October 22, 1891). Fleischl, who received his M.D. from the University of Leipzig in 1870, taught at the University of Vienna from 1873 to 1891. His work was on the physiology of circulation, but he also invented various pieces of apparatus for research in physiology, optics, and physiological optics. His contribution to the movement paradox was published in 1882 (*Sitzber. Akad. wiss. Wien, Math.-naturwiss. Cl.,* Abt. III, 86, 17).
  Biographies: Pagel, *Biog. Lex.*

Förster, Richard. German ophthalmologist (b. Lissa [now Lisa], Bohemia, November 15, 1925, d. Breslau [now Wroclaw], Silesia, July 7, 1902). Förster's M.D. was from the University of Berlin (1849). He spent most of his professional life at the University of Breslau (1857–1899). His published work was largely on eye diseases, myopia, and other ophthalmological topics.
  Biographies: Hirsch, *Biog. Lex.;* Pagel, *Biog. Lex.*

AUSTRIAN SCHOOL OF PSYCHOLOGY. Also known as the Graz school of psychology, it is so named not only because several of its members were active at the University of Graz, which is in Austria, but also because others who shared the view of the Graz group were at various other universities in Austria or the Austro-Hungarian Empire. Known by its full name as the Austrian school of act psychology, its first ideas came from Franz Brentano (at Vienna 1874–1894), who stressed the mental act as the key psychological phenomenon and thus gave a phenomenological orientation to the Austrian school. Ernest Mach* (at Graz 1864–1867, at Prague 1867–1895, at Vienna 1895–1901) stressed the primacy of sensory processes in scientific observation, spoke of space sensations, and thus established a link between himself and the Austrian school, especially that branch of it known as the form-quality school. The principal members of the form-quality school, a forerunner of the Gestalt school, were Christian von Ehrenfels* (at Graz 1885–1888, at Vienna 1889–1896, at Prague 1896–1929), who introduced the concept of form quality, and Alexius von Meinong (at Vienna 1878–1882, at Graz 1882–1920), the leader of the Austrian school at Graz. Additional figures who may be counted as belonging to the Austrian school were Vittorio Benussi, Theodor Lipps,* and Stephan Witasek.

AUTOEROTICISM, AUTOEROTISM. Sexual behavior or thinking that is self-initiated or reverts on oneself, as in masturbation.

Eros. See EROS.

B

BABINSKI REFLEX. The upward flexion of the big toe and the splaying of the rest when the sole of the foot is tickled. It is seen in infants, with decreasing strength, up to the age of about twenty-four months, when it is replaced by the plantar response (curling of the toes). The reflex is normal in infants, indicating only immaturity of the nervous system. In older individuals it is a sign of neurological damage, specifically to the upper motor neurons (the pyramidal tract). The reflex is also referred to as the Babinski sign.

Babinski, Joseph François Felix. French neurologist (b. Paris, November 17, 1857, d. Paris, October 29, 1932). Babinski's parents were political refugees who fled from Poland to France in 1848. Babinski obtained his medical degree from the University of Paris in 1885. He never taught at a university but was a highly regarded clinical neurologist who, after a few years' work under Jean-Martin Charcot* at the la Salpêtrière clinic,* spent most of his professional life as the head of the neurological clinic of the Hôpital de la Pitié in Paris. Babinski published extensively (288 published items) on neurology, neurosurgery, physiology, endocrinology, psychiatry, and other medical topics. He first described the reflex briefly at an 1896 meeting (*C. r. hebd. séances mém. Soc. biol.*, 10e serie, t. III, 1896, 207–8). It had been described before, but it was Babinski who recognized its diagnostic significance. He described it more fully in 1903 (*Rev. neurol., 11,* 728–29), referring to its diagnostic characteristic as the *signe de l'eventail* (''fan sign''). There are at least eight other neurological signs and syndromes that bear Babinski's name.

Biographies: Arch. Neurol. Psychiat., 1933, *29,* 168–74; *Haymaker; J. Nerv. Ment. Dis.,* 1933, *77,* 121–31; *J. Hist. Med.,* 1958, *13,* 544–46; *Proc. Roy. Soc. Med.,* 1967, *60,* 399–405; *Talbot.*

BABINSKI SIGN. See BABINSKI REFLEX

BABKIN REFLEX. When an infant's palms are pressed, its mouth opens reflexively.

Babkin, Boris Petrovich. Russian-Canadian physiologist (b. Kursk, January 4, 1877, d. May 3, 1950). Educated at the Military Academy of St. Petersburg (M.D., 1904), Babkin taught physiology at the University of Odessa from 1915 to 1922. He went to England and, in 1924, to Canada, where he became professor of physiology at the University of Dalhousie and research professor of physiology at McGill University in 1928. Among his books are *Secretory Mechanisms of the Digestive Glands* (1944, 1950) and *Pavlov: A Biography* (1949).
   Biographies: Canad. Biog., 1963; *Canad. Who*, 1948; A. J. Carson, *J. Neurophysiol.*, 1950, *13*, 389–90.

BAER'S LAW. See VON BAER'S LAW

BALDWIN'S FIGURE. A bisected line segment, with one of its ends connected to a small square, the other to a larger one. The two halves of the bisected line do not appear to be of the same length.

Baldwin, James Mark. American psychologist (b. Columbia, South Carolina, January 12, 1861, d. Paris, France, November 8, 1934). Baldwin, who received his Ph.D. in philosophy from Princeton University in 1889, was a writer and speculative psychological theorist. He taught at Toronto, Princeton, and Johns Hopkins universities, as well as in Mexico and France. His contributions were in the area of textbook writing, the popularization of the evolutionary theory, and developmental psychology. Baldwin's books emphasized the importance of the evolutionary theory to the human sciences. He applied the evolutionary concept in his pioneering studies of child development. With G. Stanley Hall, Baldwin was a cofounder of the American Psychological Association, the founder of early psychological laboratories at Toronto and Princeton, and the founder of *Psychological Review, Psychological Bulletin, Psychological Monographs,* and *Psychological Index.* He was also well known for having edited the four-volume *Dictionary of Philosophy and Psychology* (1901–1902). His illusion appeared in 1896 (*Science, 4*, 774).
   Biographies: J. M. Baldwin, *Between Two Wars,* 1926; *DAB,* 21; *EB,* 2; *HPA,* 1; *IESS,* 1; J. Jastrow, *Science,* 1934, *80,* 497–98; J. R. Kantor, *Psychol. Bull.,* 1935, *32,* 1–3; *Nature,* 1934, *134,* 840–41; *NCAB,* 25; W. M. Urban, *Psychol. Rev.,* 1935, *42,* 303–306; *WhAm,* 1.

BALES CATEGORY SYSTEM. Part of Bales' interaction process analysis, the category system is a list of twelve behaviors that range from positive social-emotional ones to negative ones by way of neutral or task-oriented behaviors. The categories are used by observers of social interaction in a group, who keep a record of the source and addressee of each expressive act and sort the acts into the twelve categories.

Bales, Robert Freed. American psychologist (b. Ellington, Missouri, March 9, 1916). Bales joined the Harvard University faculty in 1945, the same year he received his Ph.D. in social psychology from that institution. He became professor of social relations in 1957 and headed the Laboratory of Social Relations from 1960 to 1967. Bales also headed the social psychology program of the Department of Psychology and Social Relations at various times. He pioneered in the study of small group behavior, specializing in the development of observational methodology. This included the computer-based Systematic Multiple Level Observation of Groups (SYMLOG), developed in 1979. The category system was first described in Bales's 1950 book, *Interaction Process Analysis: A Method for the Study of Small Groups*.
  Biographies: *Amer. Psychologist*, 1985, *40*, 343–44; *APA Dir.*, 1985.

BALINT'S SYNDROME. A disorder of spatial analysis characterized by visual disorientation, optic ataxia (deficit of visual reaching), and ocular apraxia (deficit of visual scanning). It is caused by bilateral brain damage in the occipitoparietal region.

Balint, Rezsö. Hungarian physician (b. 1874, d. 1929). Balint had the M.D. degree and at the time he described the syndrome that bears his name held an appointment at the First Medical Clinic in Budapest. The syndrome was described in 1909 (*Mschr. Psychiat. Neurol.*, *25*, 51–81).
  Biographies: Hirsch, *Biog. Lex.*

BARANY CHAIR. A chair that allows rotation in all three planes for tests of labyrinthine functioning.

BARANY POINTING TEST. The subject points with a finger at an object, alternately with eyes open and closed. Repeated failure to return the arm to the original position suggests unilateral cerebellar damage.

BARANY TEST. A test that assesses separately the functioning of each of the three semicircular canals. Seated in the Bárány chair, the testee is rotated in each of the three planes in which the semicircular canals lie.

Bárány, Robert. Austrian-Swedish physiologist (b. Vienna, April 22, 1876 d. Uppsala, Sweden, April 8, 1936). A clinical neurophysiologist and otologist, Bárány received his M.D. from the University of Vienna in 1900. From 1905 until World War I, Bárány worked in the world-famous ear clinic of Adam Politzer.* For his work on the factors that govern labyrinthine functioning, he was awarded the Nobel Prize in 1915. He served in the Austrian army during the war, was captured by the Russians, released through the intervention of the Swedish government and scientists, and in 1917 accepted a faculty appointment at the University of Uppsala. His work concerned vestibular functioning, the nystagmus, diagnosis of labyrinthine malfunctioning, and the functioning of the cerebellum. His most important discovery was that of caloric nystagmus. The chair was described in 1906 (*Arch. Ohrenheilk., 68,* 1–30) and the pointing tests in 1913 (*Deutsch. med. Wschr., 39,* 637–42).

 Biographies: DSB, 1; *EB,* 3; *Haymaker; PR,* 3; *Talbot.*

BARRON-WELSH ART SCALE. A subscale of the Welsh Figure Preference Test,* it is based on the finding that in a task requiring the sorting of various designs into preferred and nonpreferred categories, artists and nonartists differ in that the former prefer complex designs while the latter prefer the simpler forms.

Barron, Frank X. American psychologist (b. Lansford, Pennsylvania, June 17, 1922). Barron, who received a Ph.D. from the University of California at Berkeley (1950), has taught at a number of universities, but mostly at Berkeley (1952–1969) and the University of California at Santa Cruz (since 1969). His research has been on personality traits, mainly creativity, an area in which he has achieved prominence. His major works are *Scientific Creativity* (1963, with C. W. Taylor), *Creativity and Psychological Health* (1963), *Creativity and Personal Freedom* (1968), *Creative Person and Creative Process* (1969), and *Artists in the Making* (1972). The scale first appeared in 1952 (F. Barron & G. S. Welsh, *J. Psychol., 33,* 199–203).

 Biographies: AM&WS, 1978S; *Amer. Psychologist,* 1969, *24,* 94–95; *APA Dir.,* 1985; *ConAu,* 5R.

Welsh, G. S. See WELSH FIGURE PREFERENCE TEST.

BARTLETT'S TEST. A statistical test of the hypothesis of homogeneity of variance when there are marked differences among the variances of the treatment groups.

Bartlett, Maurice Stevenson. English mathematician (b. June 18, 1910). Bartlett graduated from Cambridge University in 1932, received a D.Sc. degree from the University of London, and held teaching positions at several British universities, including Cambridge (1938–1947), Manchester (1947–1960), London (1960–1967), and Oxford (1967–1975, professor emeritus since 1975). Bartlett wrote several books on probability and statistics, as well as many papers. Bartlett described the test in 1937 (*Proc. Roy. Soc., A901, 160,* 268–82).

 Biographies: Who, 1986–1987.

BAYES' ESTIMATOR. A principle of statistical estimation. Associated with the different estimators of parameter Θ, Θ_i, is a loss function, proportional to $(\Theta_i - \Theta_i)^2$ and called the risk. A Bayes' estimator is some function of the sample observations that minimizes the expected value of the risk. When the sample size is large, the values of Bayes' estimator differ little from maximum likelihood estimators.

BAYES' THEOREM. Also known as Bayes' principle or Bayes' rule, Bayes' theorem provides for the calculations of backward probabilities, the revision of previously assumed probabilities in the light of the actual probabilities of subsequently observed events. If A is a future probable event and B is a relevant observed event that has a bearing on A's occurrence, then the revised probability of A, given that B has occurred, is computed by

$$p(B|A) = \frac{p(A|B)p(B)}{p(A)}$$

provided $p(A/B)$ and $p(A)$ are known.

Bayes, Thomas. English mathematician (b. London, 1702, d. Tunbridge Wells, Kent, April 17, 1761). Bayes was educated privately. He was ordained and became one of the first Nonconformist ministers in England. In the 1720s, he went to Tunbridge Wells, where he was minister at the Presbyterian chapel. He retired from the ministry in 1752, having been elected to the Royal Society ten years earlier for his work on the mathematics of probability. The paper that contains his theorem was published in 1763 (*Phil. Trans. Roy. Soc., 53,* 370–418) by his friend Richard Price.
Biographies: DSB, 1; EB, 3.

BAYLE'S DISEASE. An obsolete name for general paresis.

Bayle, Antoine Laurent Jesse. French physician (b. Vernet, Pyrenées Orientales, January 13, 1799, d. Paris, March 1858). Bayle had an M.D. from the University of Paris (1822). He worked as a librarian in the Faculty of Medicine in Paris (1824–1827) and then taught medicine at the University of Charenton. He was the author of seven books and the editor of a forty-volume encyclopedia of medical sciences (1835–1846). He presented a description of general paresis in 1822 as part of his doctoral dissertation.
Biographies: WoWhoSci.

BAYLEY SCALES OF INFANT DEVELOPMENT. A psychological instrument for assessing infant development, the scales cover the ages two to thirty months. There are two scales, a motor and a mental scale, plus thirty behavioral rating items.

Bayley, Nancy. American psychologist (b. The Dalles, Oregon, September 28, 1899). After receiving a Ph.D. in psychology from the State University of Iowa in 1926, Bayley became a research associate at the Institute of Child Welfare of the University of California at Berkeley, initiating a study of child development. The Berkeley growth study was a pioneer longitudinal developmental study that followed the subjects for thirty-six years, from infancy onward. In 1954, Bayley became chief of the Section on Child Development, Laboratory of Psychology of the National Institutes of Mental Health, Bethesda, Maryland. She returned to Berkeley ten years later, retiring in 1968. The scales were first published in 1969.

Biographies: AM&WS, 1978S; Amer. Psychologist, 1966, 21, 1190–94; Amer. Psychologist, 1983, 38, 61–62; APA Dir., 1985.

BEARD'S DISEASE. A parallel name for neurasthenia.

Beard, George Miller. American physician (b. Montville, Connecticut, May 8, 1839, d. New York City, June 23, 1883). A graduate of the College of Physicians of New York (1866), Beard practiced medicine privately and was also on the staff of Demilt Dispensary after about 1870. Beard coined the term *neurasthenia* and described the disorder in an 1869 paper (*Boston Med. Surg. J., 80,* 217–21), but his writings were more in the popular vein, dealing with such topics as psychiatry, psychology, and the medical uses of electricity. He was even better known to the general public through his works on electrology and, later, on animal magnetism, clairvoyance, and spiritualism. He was a pioneer in the medical use of electricity in the United States.

Biographies: NCAB, 8; WhAm, HS.

BECK SYSTEM. A system for interpreting Rorschach protocols, characterized by empiricism and conservatism in making predictions. It was the first systematic approach to the Rorschach test* after Rorschach's* death.

Beck, Samuel J. American psychologist (b. Tecuci, Rumania, July 19, 1896, d. Chicago, Illinois, June 10, 1980). Beck's doctorate was in psychology (Columbia University, 1932). He held positions in various medical settings, the longest at Michael Reese Hospital, Chicago (since 1936), and lectured at Northwestern University (1943–1960) and the University of Chicago (after 1949). Beck started writing on the Rorschach test before 1932, developing the new approach to the test in three articles published in 1933. He continued to elaborate it for the rest of his life. The first monograph appeared in 1937 (*Introduction to the Rorschach Technique*). A critique of it by Bruno Klopfer* led to a sharp disagreement and controversy over the next few years. Beck's three-volume series on the Rorschach (1944, 1945, 1952) became the standard manual for users of the test. Beck wrote three other books on the Rorschach.

Biographies: APA Dir., 1981; J. E. Exner, Jr., Amer. Psychologist, 1981, 36, 986–87; WoWhoSci.

BEHRENS-FISHER DISTRIBUTION. Sampling distribution of the t* statistic (for sample numbers smaller than 30). The Behrens-Fisher problem is the problem of finding an exact method for testing the difference between the means of two distributions having unknown and unequal variances.

Behrens, W. U. German statistician. Behrens made the first attempt to solve the Behrens-Fisher problem in 1929 (*Landw. Jb., 68,* 807–37). He was at that time at the Institut für Pflanzenbau of the University of Konigsberg. The solution was further developed by R. A. Fisher in 1935 (*Ann. Eugen., 6,* 391–98).
    Biographies: Unavailable.

Fisher, Ronald Aylmer. See under eponyms that begin with FISHER.

BEKESY AUDIOMETER. A device to measure the absolute threshold of hearing. Upon first hearing a tone, the listener pushes a button and releases it when the tone disappears. The listener's response controls a servomotor that automatically increases or decreases stimulus intensity and records it. By this method, a complete audiogram may be obtained in less than half an hour.

Békésy, Georg von. Hungarian-American physicist (b. Budapest, Hungary, June 3, 1899, d. Honolulu, Hawaii, June 15, 1972). With a Ph.D. in physics obtained from the University of Budapest in 1923, Békésy worked as an acoustics researcher for the Hungarian telephone system for the next twenty-three years. For fourteen of these years, he also taught at the University of Budapest. From 1947 to 1966 Békésy was at Harvard University as a senior research fellow in psychophysics and from 1966 to 1972 as professor of sensory sciences at the University of Hawaii. Békésy spent his life studying the physics of sensory perception, especially that of hearing. His major achievement was the direct observation of the operation of the basilar membrane as it was being stimulated by tones of different frequencies. Békésy's achievements were recognized by the award of the 1961 Nobel Prize in Medicine and Physiology. Békésy published over 120 papers, as well as *Experiments in Hearing* (1960) and *Sensory Inhibition* (1967). Békésy introduced the audiometer in 1946.
    Biographies: AM&WS, 1970P; *Asimov; CurBio,* 1962, 1972N; E. B. Newman, *Amer. J. Psychol.,* 1973, *86,* 855–57; F. Ratliff, in J. Wirgin (ed.), *The Georg von Békésy Collection,* 1974.

BEKHTEREV'S NUCLEUS. One of the four major vestibular nuclei in the medulla, the first synaptic connection for vestibular neurons.

BEKHTEREV'S NYSTAGMUS. The nystagmic eye movements observed upon the removal or one or both labyrinths (also the removal of the cortex or the cerebellum). The central compensation that causes the nystagmus originates in the vestibular nuclei, of which Bekhterev's nucleus is one.

Bekhterev, Vladimir Mikhailovich. Russian psychiatrist and neuropathologist (b. Sorali [now Bekhterovo], Vyatka province, February 2, 1857, d. Moscow, December 24, 1927). Bekhterev acquired his medical degree from the St. Petersburg Medical and Surgical Academy in 1881. Four years later, having done research at the same institution and having spent a year abroad, Bekhterev was appointed professor and occupied the chair of psychiatry at the University of Kazan'. In 1894, he returned to St. Petersburg, holding positions at the Military Medical Academy, the Psychoneurological Institute, and the Brain Research Institute. Bekhterev contributed to the areas of neurophysiology, neuropathology, and the objective study of psychological phenomena. Bekhterev's psychology was based on the reflex (reflexology). In distinction from Pavlov,* Bekhterev preferred to condition motor responses, and he applied the concept of the conditioned reflex to both individuals (*General Principles of Human Reflexology*, 1917) and societal groups (*Collective Reflexology*, 1921). Bekhterev was enormously productive, publishing more than 600 papers and books. The first two psychological laboratories in Russia were founded by Bekhterev, as well as the Psychoneurological Institute at St. Petersburg and two neurological and psychiatric journals. Bekhterev's nucleus and nystagmus were described in 1885 (*Neurol. Zbl., 3*, 145–47). There are six other neurological signs and reflexes named after Bekhterev.

Biographies: DSB, 1; EB, 3; Haymaker; IESS, 2; L. Pines, Arch. Psychiat., 1928, 83, 677–87; Soviet, 3.

BEL. See DECIBEL.

BELL ADJUSTMENT INVENTORY. The Student Form of the inventory measured adjustment in four areas: home, health, social, and emotional. The Adult Form added an occupational adjustment score. The more widely used Student Form was used principally to identify students in need of counseling. The Student Form was published in 1934. Neither form of the inventory is currently in use.

Bell, Hugh McKee. American psychologist (b. Frostburg, Pennsylvania, July 9, 1902, d. Chico, California, December 25, 1967). Bell's main interest was in counseling (Ph.D., Stanford University, 1941), personality inventories, and motor learning. He spent most of his professional life at Chico State College, California (1928–1967). He was dean of students from 1946 to 1956 and professor of psychology after 1956. Bell published many articles on counseling and related topics.

Biographies: APA Dir., 1965; WhAm, 5.

BELLEVUE SCALE. See WECHSLER-BELLEVUE INTELLIGENCE SCALE.

BELL-MAGENDIE LAW. The dorsal nerve roots of the spinal cord carry afferent (sensory) impulses to the brain whereas the ventral roots carry efferent (motor) impulses to the muscles. Also known as Bell's law.

BELL'S CIRCLE OF NERVES. "Between the brain and the muscles, there is a circle of nerves; one nerve conveys the influence from the brain to the muscle; and another gives the sense of the condition of the muscle to the brain. If this circle be broken by the division of the motive nerve, motion ceases; if it be broken by the division of the other nerve there is no longer a sense of the condition of the muscle, and therefore no regulation of it actively'' (Bell, 1826, p. 170).

Bell, Sir Charles. Scottish anatomist (b. Edinburgh, November 1774, d. Hallow Park near Worcester, Worcestershire, England, April 28, 1842). A physician by training (University of Edinburgh, 1799), Bell became one of the greatest neuranatomists of the early nineteenth century. His greatest discovery was the existence of two kinds of nerves, motor and sensory. Bell described this discovery in a privately published monograph (*Idea of a New Anatomy of the Brain: Submitted for the Observations of His Friends*) in 1811. Few people read it, and its significance was not appreciated at the time, one reason being that the results and their implications were not stated very clearly. François Magendie* performed elegant experiments and stated the distinction between the two kinds of nerves later but independently of Bell. The controversy between the two men over priority was resolved by naming the discovery the Bell-Magendie law. Bell described the circle of nerves in an 1826 paper (*Phil. Trans. Roy. Soc., 2,* 163–73). Five other eponyms in medicine bear Bell's name.
   Biographies: E. Bramwell, *Edinb. Med. J.,* 1935, *42,* 252–64; L. Carmichael, *Psychol. Rev.,* 1926, *33,* 188–217; *DNB,* 1; *DSB,* 1; *EB,* 3; G. Gordon-Taylor & E. W. Walls, *Sir Charles Bell, His Life and Times,* 1958; *Haymaker;* H. Paskind, *Bull. Soc. Med. Hist.,* 1937, *5,* 34–43; B. Spector, *Bull. Hist. Med.,* 1942, *12,* 314–22; *Talbot.*

Magendie, François. French physiologist (b. Bordeaux, October 15, 1783, d. Sannois, near Paris, October 17, 1855). After obtaining his medical degree (University of Paris, 1808), Magendie remained for the rest of his life a practicing hospital physician. He taught physiology both privately and at the Collége de France (1831–1855) and did much research in this field. His best work was the experiments on the spinal nerves of eight puppies, experiments that clearly established the distinction between sensory and motor nerves. He did this work without a knowledge of Bell's, and it was of superior quality. It was published in two papers in 1822 (*J. physiol. exp. pathol., 2,* 276–79, 366–71). Three other eponyms of medical significance bear Magendie's name.
   Biographies: Asimov; L. Carmichael, *Psychol. Rev.,* 1926, *33,* 188–217; *DSB,* 9; *EB,* 14, *Haymaker;* J. M. D. Olmsted, *François Magendie,* 1944; *Talbot.*

BELL'S MANIA. A form of acute mania that was first described by Luther Bell.

Bell, Luther Vose. American physician and politician (b. Francestown, New Hampshire, December 20, 1806, d. Budd's Ferry, Maryland, February 11, 1862). Bell received his medical degree from Dartmouth College in 1826, practiced medicine in Chester, New Hampshire, and served in the state legislature in 1835 and 1836. He then took the post of superintendent of the McLean Hospital for the Insane at Charlestown, Massachusetts, resigning in 1856. He was active politically during this time and participated in the Civil War as well. Bell died in an army camp near Washington, D.C., where he served as medical inspector. He

described the mania that bears his name in an 1848 pamphlet, *On a Form of Disease Resembling Some Advanced Stages of Mania and Fever*.
   Biographies: DAB, 2; *NCAB*, 22; *WhAm*, HS.

BEM SEX-ROLE INVENTORY. A self-rating scale in which subjects describe themselves by endorsing, on a seven-point scale, statements that describe masculine and feminine characteristics. The subject is then described as masculine, feminine, or androgynous depending on the size and director of the difference between the feminine and masculine item scores.

Bem, Sandra L. American psychologist (b. Pittsburgh, Pennsylvania, June 22, 1944). Bem's Ph.D. (University of Michigan, 1968) was in developmental psychology. Her major field is personality psychology, in which she specializes in sex roles and sex differences. She has taught at Carnegie-Mellon and Stanford universities and is now at Cornell University. She was the recipient of the Early Career Award of the American Psychological Association for 1976. The inventory was published in 1974 (*J. Consult. Clin. Psychol.*, 42, 155–62).
   Biographies: AM&WS, 1978S; *Amer. Psychologist*, 1977, 32, 88–91; *APA Dir.*, 1985.

BENDER GESTALT TEST. A test that consists of copying nine simple designs. The quality of the reproduction is substandard in those who are neurologically immature (children) or impaired (brain-damaged adults). The test is also used to assess personality deviations, especially those involving regression. The test designs and the rules for the evaluation of the reproductions are based on Gestalt principles, such as good continuation, and on principles of psychomotor differentation.

Bender, Lauretta. American neurologist and psychiatrist (b. Butte, Montana, August 9, 1897). Bender, who received her M.D. from the State University of Iowa, has held appointments at a number of hospitals and universities in New York State and New York City, notably Bellevue Hospital (1930–1956) and New York University (1930–1958). She has been at the University of Maryland since 1975. The test was published in 1938 (*Amer. Orthopsychiat. Ass., Res. Monog.*, No. 3, p. 176).
   Biographies: AM&WS, 1971P; *Biog. Dir. APA*, 1977; *WhoAm*, 1976–1977.

BENEDIKT SYNDROME. Midbrain disease in which there is palsy of the ipsilateral eye muscles, contralateral involuntary movements, and sometimes hemiplegia that precedes the syndrome.

Benedikt, Moritz. Austrian neurologist (b. Eisenstadt, Hungary, July 6, 1835, d. Vienna, Austria, April 14, 1920). Benedikt was a pioneer in neurology, psychiatry, electrotherapy, and criminology. A productive researcher and writer, he published articles and books in these and other areas. Before the advent of psychoanalysis, Benedikt anticipated some of its ideas. After obtaining his medical degree from the University of Vienna in 1859, Benedikt was a military surgeon; he then taught and did research at the University of Vienna (after 1861) while maintaining a lucrative private practice. He traveled widely and was held to be one of the leaders of Austrian medicine. In 1899 he occupied the newly created chair of electrotherapy. He described the syndrome that bears his name in an 1899 paper (*Bull. méd., 3,* 547–48).

   Biographies: M. Benedikt, *Au meinem Leben,* 1906; *Bonin; Haymaker.*

BENHAM'S TOP. A disk with a black pattern that, when rotated at the proper speed, produces color sensations of orange and blue. The disk is half black and half white, the white half containing segments of concentric circles of different diameters.

Benham, Charles Edwin. English writer and amateur scientist (b. Colchester, Essex, April 15, 1860, d. Colchester, Essex, April 1, 1929). Benham was part proprietor (with his elder brother Gurney, the compiler of *Benham's Book of Quotations*) of the *Essex Country Standard* and a writer. He wrote a column for the newspaper for forty-five years and became well known for his poems written in dialect (*Essex Ballads,* 1895). Benham had attended the Colchester Royal Grammar School and engaged in scientific experimentation. He invented the top as a toy for children, meant to be spun by hand. He called it the artificial spectrum top. It was manufactured and sold by Messrs. Newton & Co. The top was described in an anonymous note in 1894 (*Nature, 51,* 113). It was followed by an exchange of letters in *Nature* between people who had experimented with the top and Benham.

   Biographies: H. Benham, preface to C. E. Benham, *Essex Ballads,* 1960; obituary, *Essex County Standard,* April 6, 1929.

BENNETT HAND-TOOL DEXTERITY TEST. Provides a measure of proficiency in the use of ordinary mechanical tools. The subject's task is to remove all nuts and bolts from an upright board and install them on another board in a given order.

BENNETT TEST OF MECHANICAL COMPREHENSION. A combination of pictures and questions that measures mechanical aptitude in high school students and adults. The test has several forms varying in difficulty.

Bennett, George Kettner. American psychologist (b. New York City, February 26, 1904, d. Bronxville, New York, February 2, 1975). After receiving a Ph.D. from Yale University (1935), Bennett took a position with the Psychological Corporation, remaining with that firm until his death. He was elected president of the corporation in 1947. From 1939 to 1946, Bennett taught concurrently at Columbia University. His main interest was test preparation and evaluation. The dexterity test appeared in 1947, the comprehension test in 1948.

   Biographies: AM&WS, 1973S; *APA Dir.,* 1975; *WhAm,* 6.

BENTON VISUAL RETENTION TEST. A visual memory test in which the testee copies a series of designs of increasing complexity, each design being exposed for ten seconds.

Benton, Arthur Lester. (American psychologist, b. New York City, October 16, 1909). With a doctorate (Columbia University, 1935) in clinical psychology, Benton taught and worked as a psychologist at several universities, medical schools, and psychiatric facilities until 1948 (between 1941 and 1946, he served in the U.S. Naval Reserves). He has been at the University of Iowa as professor of neurology since 1948 and is now professor emeritus. Benton's research has been in the areas of psychodiagnostics, psychoneurology, and brain lesions. The test first appeared in 1945 (*Arch. Neurol. Psychiat., 54,* 212–16).
   Biographies: AM&WS, 1982P; *APA Dir.,* 1985.

BERGER RHYTHM. The alpha or 10 herz frequency component of the electroencephalogram, usually signifying a resting but alert brain.

Berger, Hans. German psychiatrist (b. Nauses, near Coburn, Bavaria, May 21, 1873, d. Bad Blankenburg, Thuringia, June 1, 1941). Berger received his medical degree from the University of Jena (1897) and spent his professional life there. He was always intensely interested in the physical basis of mental phenomena and in 1924 succeeded in obtaining a continuous record of the electrical activity of the intact brain of a human subject, as well as in observing changes in this activity as a function of sensory stimulation. He was secretive about his work and did not publish his results until 1929 (*Arch. Psychiat. Nervenkr., 87,* 527–70). Berger's work came at a time when the organic view in psychiatry was in eclipse, and he was met by opposition. It was not until Lord Adrian in England was able to duplicate Berger's results (in 1934) that electroencephalography came into general use.
   Biographies: Asimov; DSB, 2; F. A. Gibbs, *Arch. Neurol. Psychiat.,* September 1941, 514–16; *Haymaker.* ·

BERGSONISM. Henri Bergson led a movement against evolutionary theory, arguing that the complexities of organic life could not have resulted from random processes and that creative evolution was necessary. In psychology, Bergson opposed both associationism and Wundtian structuralism to the point of denying the possibility of a scientifically based psychology. Inner experience and the outside world of facts are incommensurable, Bergson said, and inner experience cannot be described using the methods of acquisition of knowledge. Although human intelligence can analyze the world and synthesize it again, it is inadequate to comprehend the inner world of experience. The mechanism whereby the stream of consciousness is apprehended is intuition, which differs totally from intelligence. Intuition permits humans to "live" inner reality instead of just representing it cognitively. The experience of time is made central in Bergson's philosophy.

Bergson, Henri. French philosopher (b. Paris, October 18, 1859, d. Paris, January 4, 1941). Bergson was born of parents of Anglo-Jewish ancestry and acquired French citizenship as an adult before entering the Ecole normale supérieure. He obtained the doctorate in philosophy from that school in 1881. Bergson's philosophical views had considerable influence on European thought before World War I. *Creative Evolution,* first published in 1907, was Bergson's main work. He taught at the Ecole normale for two years and then at the Collége de France for fourteen years. He withdrew from teaching after the outbreak of World War I, receiving the Nobel Prize in Literature for 1927. In 1932, he published *Two Sources of Morality and Religion,* which went beyond the natural-istic limits of *Creative Evolution* by proposing two kinds of morality, unrelated to each other, and two kinds of religion, also unrelated.

   Biographies: DSB, 2; *EB,* 3; *EP,* 1; H. M. Kallen, *William James and Henri Bergson,* 1914; A. Ruhe & N. M. Paul, *Henri Bergson: An Account of His Life and Philosophy,* 1914.

BERLIN GESTALT SCHOOL. The (original) Gestalt psychology school of Max Wertheimer, Wolfgang Köhler,* and Kurt Koffka. Wertheimer and Köhler, though not Koffka, were at the University of Berlin (1916–1929, 1920–1935, respectively) during the period of the school's greatest flourishing, as were other important figures in the Gestalt school: Adhemar Gelb (1909–1912), Kurt Lewin (1922–1932), and Karl Duncker (1929–1937). Another school that bore the Gestalt name was formed at Leipzig.

BERNHEIM'S THERAPY. A historical term for the use of hypnosis in the treatment of neuroses, introduced by Hippolyte Bernheim.

Bernheim, Hippolyte. French neurologist and hypnotist (b. Mulhouse, Haut Rhin, April 17, 1840, d. Nancy, Meurthe et Moselle, 1919). Bernheim remained at the University of Strasbourg after receiving his M.D. there in 1867. He joined the faculty of the University of Nancy in 1872 and in 1882 began private practice there. He was already a well-known physician when Ambroise-Auguste Liébeault, a country physician, happened to cure one of Bernheim's patients of sciatica using hypnosis. Bernheim, whose own orthodox treatment had failed, became a pupil of Liébeault in 1882. Together they established a clinic at Nancy, making hypnosis the treatment of choice. Bernheim induced hypnotic sleep using suggestion of sleepiness and treated his patients on the assumption that medical cures could be achieved in a state of suggestibility. He was thus first to treat neurotic disorders hypnotically.

   Biographies: DSB, 2; *EJ,* 4; M. Goldsmith, *Franz Anton Mesmer: The History of an Idea,* 1934; *Jewish,* 2.

BERNOULLI DISTRIBUTION. The expected probability distribution for a binomial event. The distribution specifies the probability of obtaining one or the other outcome on a given trial as a function of the number of events, such as the expected number of heads or tails when coins are tossed simultaneously.

BERNOULLI TRIALS. One of the trials in a binomial event that leads to the Bernoulli distribution of probabilities for one or the other of the two possible outcomes of the event.

Bernoulli, Daniel. Swiss mathematician, physician, and physicist (b. Groningen, Netherlands, February 8, 1700, d. Basel, Switzerland, March 17, 1782). Bernoulli obtained a Master's degree in philosophy in 1716 and a doctorate in medicine in 1721 from the University of Basel. He worked at the St. Petersburg Academy from 1725 to 1733 and from 1733 to 1767 at the University of Basel. A precursor of game and decision-making theorists, Bernoulli gave, in a monograph on "a new theory of the measurement of risk" ("Specimen theoriae novae de mensura sortis," *Comentarii Academiae Scientarium Imperialis Petropolitanae,* 1738, 5, 175–92), a mathematical formulation of a value theory whereby the hope of a gain could be evaluated. The distribution that bears his name is described in this monograph. Bernoulli made other significant contributions to probability theory and introduced the calculus of probability into epidemiology and insurance.
   Biographies: DSB, 2; *IESS,* 2.

BERNREUTER PERSONAL ADJUSTMENT INVENTORY. A personality inventory that yields scores for six traits: neurotic tendency, self-sufficiency, introversion-extroversion, dominance-submission, self-confidence, and sociability. The inventory was formerly called the Bernreuter Personality Inventory.

Bernreuter, Robert Gibbon. American psychologist (b. Tampico, Illinois, December 9, 1901). After receiving a Ph.D. in 1931 in general psychology from Stanford University, Bernreuter taught and directed the psychological clinic at Pennsylvania State College until 1957, when he went into administrative work at the same institution. He held various concurrent positions, both civilian and military. Bernreuter retired in 1966. His main field has been clinical psychology, with specialization in personality assessment and aptitude testing. The inventory was first published in 1935.
   Biographies: AM&WS, 1973S; *APA Dir.,* 1985.

BETZ CELLS. The pyramid-shaped bodies of certain large cells in the fifth layer of the motor cortex of the brain.

Betz, Vladimir Aleksandrovich. Russian anatomist (b. 1834, d. September 30, 1894). Betz had a medical degree from the University of Kiev (1860), and he taught at that institution from 1868 to 1889, becoming afterward chief physician of the Southwest Railroad (1889–1894). The cells were announced by Betz in

1874 (*Zbl. med. Wiss.*, *12*, 578–80ff.) and 1881 (*Zbl. med. Wiss.*, *19*, 193–195ff.).

Biographies: Fischer, *Biog. Lex.*

BEZOLD-BRUCKE PHENOMENON. Except for certain invariable points, with increasing intensity of light, all colors shift slightly toward yellow or blue: yellow if they are toward the red end of the spectrum and blue if they are in the green region.

Bezold, Wilhelm von. German meteorologist (b. Munich, June 21, 1837, d. Berlin, February 17, 1907). Bezold organized the Bavarian network of meteorological stations from 1879 to 1885. He directed the Prussian Meteorological Institute and was professor at the University of Berlin from 1885. In meteorology, Bezold made contributions in explaining the source of energy of atmospheric movements and the origin and dynamics of cyclones and anticyclones. His interest in color arose in connection with color changes at sunrise. He described the phenomenon briefly in 1873 (*Ann. Phys. Chem., 150*, 221–47).

Biographies: Soviet, 3.

Brücke, Ernst Wilhelm von. German-Austrian physiologist (b. Berlin, June 6, 1819, d. Vienna, January 7, 1892). As a professor of physiology (M.D., University of Berlin, 1842), Brücke spent the last forty-two years of his life at the University of Vienna, where he directed his Physiological Institute. He passed his strictly physicalistic physiology on to his students, one of whom was Sigmund Freud.* Brücke did also work in psychophysics. Of enduring value was the thorough study of change in hue as a function of light intensity that he performed in 1878 (*Sitzber. Akad. wiss. Wien, math.-naturwiss. Cl., 77*(3), 39–71). It earned him the honor of a coeponym with Bezold.

Biographies: DSB, 2; ED, 4; W. A. Stewart, *Psychoanalysis: The First Ten Years,* 1962.

BIDWELL'S GHOST. See PURKINJE AFTERIMAGE.

Bidwell, Shelford. English physicist (b. Thetford, Norfolk, March 6, 1848, d. Weybridge, near London, December 18, 1909). Bidwell studied mathematics (B.A., Cambridge University, 1870) and law and history (M.A., Cambridge, 1873) and was called to the bar at Lincoln's Inn in 1873. He practiced law for a year and then began to do science: electricity, magnetism, and physiological optics. Bidwell was first to propose the use of selenium for the transmission of pictures by wire. The afterimage that is now often named after Purkinje was described by Bidwell in 1901 (*Proc. Roy. Soc., 68*, 262–85).

Biographies: DNB, 2d suppl. vol. 1.

BINET-SIMON SCALE. The first instrument ever devised to measure intelligence. It contained a single scale, a long series of problems of increasing difficulty. In its first revision, published in 1908, Binet introduced the age scale, arranging test items according to the different ages at which they were to be passed by normal children. In 1911, Binet's last revision of the test appeared. It contained the new idea of mental age, a score of problem-solving ability expressed as years and months.

Binet, Alfred. French psychologist (b. Nice, Alpes Maritimes, July 8, 1857, d. Paris, October 18, 1911) Binet first obtained a law degree (in 1878) and only later became interested in psychology through private study. He did not obtain a Ph.D. in science until 1894 (University of Paris). By that time he was already the most prominent French psychologist. He and Henri Beaunis had founded the first French psychological laboratory and, with Victor Henri, the first French psychological journal. Binet also published papers and books on hypnotism, but he turned to other matters in the 1890s, the most important of which was intelligence. He published several important papers on the subject before the fall of 1904 when the minister of public instruction appointed a committee to study the problem of educating retarded children. Binet and Simon wrote a paper in 1905 criticizing the medical approach to the assessment of intelligence and proposed a different one. Another paper followed the same year (*L'Année psychol.*, *11*, 191–244) in which the new Binet-Simon scale was proposed. The test inaugurated the objective measurement of mental processes and became the prototype for all subsequent intelligence tests. The Binet-Simon test has been called most important innovation in psychology.
   Biographies: Asimov; DSB, 2; *EB,* 3; 1; *IESS,* 2; R. H. Pollack & M. W. Brenner, in *The Experimental Psychology of Alfred Binet: Selected Papers,* 1969; H. L. Silverman & K. Krenzel, *Psychiat. Quart. Suppl.,* 1964, *38,* 323–35; T. H. Wolf, *Amer. Psychologist,* 1961, *16,* 245–48; T. H. Wolf, *Alfred Binet,* 1973.

Simon, Theodore. (b. Dijon, Côte d'Or, July 10, 1873, d. Paris, September 4, 1961). Although he was a psychiatrist by training (M.D., University of Paris, 1900) and held various medical positions at hospitals until 1936, Simon always had an interest in philosophy and psychology. He initiated a collaboration with Binet in 1899 when Binet learned of the ready availability to Simon of child subjects, his patients. Simon not only joined Binet in producing the world's first intelligence test but wrote with him some twenty-eight papers and a book (*Les enfants anormaux,* 1907). Simon failed to develop the test after Binet's death, but he devised two scales of his own. He sought to advance Binet's goal to understand human nature, as well as to rectify the overuse and abuse of the Binet-Simon scale. He was also responsible for creating the first medico-psychological consultation for delinquent children brought before the courts.
   Biographies: I. Rapaport, *Amer. J. Ment. Defic.,* 1962, *67,* 367–68; T. H. Wolf, *Amer. Psychologist,* 1961, *15,* 245–48; T. H. Wolf, *Alfred Binet,* 1973.

BLACKY PICTURES. A projective test for children originated by G. S. Blum (*The Blacky Pictures: A Technique for the Exploration of Personality Dynamics: Manual*, Psychological Corp., 1950). It consists of eleven cartoon-like pictures showing a dog named Blacky in various situations involving his parents and siblings. The child is invited to tell a story about each picture. The stories and answers to questions are analyzed to determine the stage of development of certain dynamic personality processes, such as the Oedipus conflict.

BLAKEMAN'S TEST. A test for the linearity of regression. If $N(\eta^2 - r^2)$ is smaller than 11.37, the regression is linear (Blakeman's criterion).

Blakeman, J. English statistician. Blakeman (M.Sc.) worked with R. A. Fisher* on statistical problems. He published the test in 1905 (*Biometrika, 4,* 124–60).
   Biographies: Unavailable.

BLOCH'S LAW. The Bunsen-Roscoe law,* or the photographic law, as applied to the human eye.

Bloch, A. M. (b. n.a., d. n.a.) Bloch's formulation of the intensity-duration relationship for light in the case of the human eye appeared in 1885 (*Soc. Biol. Paris, Mém.,* 37, 493–95).
   Biographies: Unavailable.

BLUMENFELD ALLEYS. An experimental setup in space perception in which the observer arranges two rows of point lights so that the apparent distance between frontally coplanar points is equal or so that the points are parallel. The finding that the observer places the lights of the parallel alleys closer to the median than the lights of the distance alleys is taken to support Luneburg's theory* that visual space is non-Euclidean.*

Blumenfeld, Walter Georg. German psychologist (b. Neuruppin, Brandenburg, July 12, 1882, d. Lima, Peru, June 17, 1967). Blumenfeld earned an engineering degree from the Technische Hochschule Charlottenburg in 1906 and a Ph.D. in psychology from the University of Berlin in 1913. He was at the Technische Hochschule Dresden from 1920 to 1935. His main work is *Zur kritischen Grundlegung der Psychologie* (1920), but he wrote twelve other books. Blumenfeld emigrated to Peru in 1935. He held positions at the San Marcos University in Lima until his death. The alleys were described in 1913 (*Z. Psychol., 65,* 241–404).
   Biographies: F. Baumgarten-Tramer, *Psychol. Beitr.,* 1968, *10,* 484–93; *PR,* 3; *WhE&EA,* 1.

BOGARDUS SOCIAL DISTANCE SCALE. The subject is given a list of ethnic, social, and other groups and is asked to mark, with respect to each, the degree to which he or she would be willing to engage in seven types of social relationship.

Bogardus, Emory Stephen. American sociologist (b. near Belvidere, Illinois, February 21, 1882, d. Los Angeles, California, August 21, 1973). Bogardus earned his Ph.D. in sociology from the University of Chicago in 1911. He worked at the University of Southern California from 1911 to 1949 as professor, director of the Division of Social Work, and dean. He was author of many books, including *Fundamentals of Sociology* (several editions), *The Making of Public Opinion* (1951), *Principles of Cooperation* (several editions), and *Social Distance* (1959). The scale was published in 1933 (*Sociol. Soc. Res., 17,* 265–71).
   Biographies: ConAu, 116; *IESS,* 18; *WhAm,* 6.

BOGEN CAGE. An intelligence test consisting of a single item, a glass-covered maze through which a ball is driven toward the goal box by means of a stick.

Bogen, Hellmuth Arnold. German psychologist (b. Berlin, February 2, 1893, d. n.a.). Bogen was self-taught. He was assistant at the Institut fur angewandte Psychologie in Berlin from 1919 to 1922, headed the Arbeitsamt Berlin-Mitte from 1923, and taught at the Deutsche Hochschule für Politik from 1927. Bogen wrote papers on ability testing and vocational counseling. The cage is described (with O. Lipmann) in a monograph, *"Naive Physik." Theoretische und experimentelle Untersuchungen über die Fähigkeit zu intelligentem Handeln,* which appeared in 1923.
   Biographies: PR, 3.

BOOLEAN ALGEBRA. The calculus associated with symbolic logic, a branch of mathematics in which symbols are used to represent logical operations. The calculus is derived not from mathematics but from the nature of logical thinking, and the mathematical symbols used represent not numbers but objects of thought.

Boole, George. English mathematician (b. Lincoln, Lincolnshire, November 2, 1815, d. Cork, Ireland, December 8, 1864). Although mostly self-educated, Boole was able to secure a teaching appointment in mathematics at Queen's College, Cork, at the age of thirty-five. He remained there for the rest of his life. His greatest achievement was to show how symbols and operations that resemble those of algebra can be used to represent the operations of logic. In *Mathematical Analysis of Logic* (1847), Boole demonstrated that logic belongs with mathematics rather than metaphysics. Then, in *An Investigation of the Laws of Thought on Which Are Founded the Mathematical Theories of Logic and Probabilities* (1854), his principal work, Boole established a new branch of mathematics, symbolic logic. Boole also showed that the symbols of his calculus could be made to take only two values, zero and one, to perform all necessary operations. Today the binary system of logic underlies the operation of electronic computers.

Biographies: Asimov; DNB, 2; *DSB,* 2; *EB,* 3; *EP,* 1; W. Kneele, *Mind,* 1948, *57,* 149–75; G. Taylor, *Not. Rec. Roy. Soc.,* 1956, *12,* 44–52.

BORG SCALE. A psychophysical scaling technique for evaluating perceived exertion.

Borg, Gunnar Anders Waldemar. Swedish psychologist (b. Stockholm, November 28, 1927). Borg, who received his Ph.D. from the University of Lund in 1962, has held positions at the University of Umea Medical School (1962–1966) and the University of Stockholm (since 1968). Borg published his scale in 1962 (*Physical Performance Ratings of Perceived Exertion*).
   Biographies: WhoWo, 1980–1981.

BOULDER MODEL. The model for training professional psychologists developed at a 1949 conference, held in Boulder, Colorado, sponsored by the American Psychological Association and under a grant from the U.S. Public Health Service. The seventy-one conferees, leaders in clinical training in various settings, issued several recommendations. The main one was that students being trained for professional work in psychology should be trained as scientist-practitioners, with equal emphasis on proficiency in research and service. Uniformity in training was to be achieved by introducing a basic core curriculum that combined general and clinical psychology.

BOURDON EFFECT. If two triangles, ABD and BCE, with angles A and C of 90 degrees and angle B of about 10 degrees, are placed so that they touch at point B, and the sides AB and BC are made colinear and the line ABC is made to tilt about 10 degrees, the line ABC will appear not straight but bent inward toward points E and D. The effect is also known as the Bourdon illusion.

Bourdon, Benjamin Bienaimé. French psychologist (b. Montmartin-sur-mer, Manche, August 5, 1869, d. Rennes, Ille-et-Vilaine, July 11, 1943). Bourdon received an *agregé* in philosophy from the University of Paris in 1885 and the degree of doctor of letters in 1892. He remained for most of his career at the University of Rennes (1890–1930). Bourdon established one of the earliest experimental laboratories in France soon after his arrival at Rennes. He did a large number of experimental studies, most of them on sensation and perception, but also on intelligence, memory, and language. He wrote chapters on sensation and perception for G. Dumas' treatise on psychology, and several books on language, space perception, and intelligence. The illusion appears in his *La perception visuelle de l'espace* (1902).
   Biographies: HPA, 2; H. Piéron, *Psychol. franç.,* 1961, *6,* 163–72.

BOVARISM. Failure to tell daydreams and reality apart.

Bovary, Emma. The heroine of Gustave Flaubert's novel, *Madame Bovary* (1856), one of the most famous novels in world literature. An uneventful youth disposes Emma to daydreaming, which is fostered by the reading of romantic novels. She marries a humdrum physician, Charles Bovary, and is depressed by the monotony of their lives. She takes on a lover, but the relationship only emphasizes the discrepancy between Emma's daydreams of a happy life and reality. Distraught by the thought of court action for the recovery of money she has borrowed from a loan shark and squandered on luxuries, Emma poisons herself.

BOWDITCH'S LAW. The principle that the nerves cannot be fatigued; they will keep transmitting impulses no matter how many times consecutively they are stimulated.

Bowditch, Henry Pickering. American physiologist (b. Boston, Massachusetts, April 4, 1840, d. Boston, Massachusetts, March 13, 1911). An eclectic physiologist of international repute (M.D., Harvard University, 1868), Bowditch opened the first physiological laboratory in the United States in 1971. He got a late start in his medical education because of military service throughout the Civil War and in his professional career because of his three-year stay at various physiological laboratories in Europe. He received a teaching appointment at the Harvard Medical School in 1871, remaining there until 1893. He did not publish much, his main topic of research being nerve conduction, especially in relation to the cardiovascular system. He was first to demonstrate the all-or-none law of nerve impulse transmission in heart fiber muscles (*Ber. ü. Verh. kön. sächs. Ges. Wiss. Leipzig, math.-phys. Cl.*, 1871, *23*, 652–89). Bowditch retired early because he was afflicted with paralysis agitans.
   Biographies: W. B. Cannon, *Science*, 1938, *87*, 471–74; *DSB*, 2; F. W. Ellis, *New Engl. J. Med.*, 1938, *219*, 819–28; G. S. Minot, *Science*, 1911, *33*, 598–601; *NCAB*, 12; G. Roser, *Bull. Hist. Med.*, 1936, *4*, 609–50; *Talbot*.

BRAIDISM. An old name for hypnotism. James Braid coined the term *hypnotism*, but after the study and use of hypnotism in clinical settings had spread to France, the French called it braidism for some time (about 1860 to 1875).

Braid, James. Scottish physician (b. Rylow House, Fife, c. 1795, d. Manchester, England, March 25, 1860). Braid received his medical education at the University of Edinburgh, but he went into private practice in Manchester, England. Within five weeks after a mesmerist had given a stage demonstration at Manchester, Braid had developed his own theory of the nature of mesmerism.* He was a moderate, seeking the middle ground between the mesmerists and the medical profession. Braid continued experimenting and writing, providing a scientific foundation for the phenomenon he named hypnotism. He published several books and many articles on the topic. These eventually resulted in the acceptance, by the scientific world, of hypnotism as a valid phenomenon, as well as of Braid's explanation of the phenomenon.

Biographies: J. M. Bramwell, *Brain,* 1896, *73,* 90–116; *DNB,* Suppl. 5, 2; *EB,* 4; M. Goldsmith, *Franz Anton Mesmer: The History of an Idea,* 1934; G. Newbold, *Brit. J. Med. Hypn.,* 1950, *1,* 3–7.

BRAILLE. A system for representing alphanumeric characters with patterns of raised dots that can be read by touch. Each character is represented by dots in a matrix or cell of two by three dot spaces.

Braille, Louis. French educator (b. Coupray, near Paris, January 4, 1809, d. Paris, March 28, 1852). Braille blinded himself as a child while playing with an awl. Although he injured only one eye, he later became blind in the other as well. In school, he read by feeling twigs twisted in the shape of letters or, at the Institut national des jeunes aveugles, large embossed letters. Braille got the idea for his system from an army officer, Charles Barbier, who had devised a touch system of reading using dots and dashes, punched in thick paper, to convey messages in the dark. Braille improved and developed Barbier's letters and published his system in 1829. Braille was also a musician and organist and adapted his system for musical notation.

Biographies: Collier's; DE; EB, 4.

BRAWNER DECISION. A 1972 legal decision concerning the use of the insanity defense. It was held that "a person is not responsible for criminal conduct if at the time of such conduct as a result of mental disease or defect he lacks substantial capacity either to appreciate the wrongfulness of his conduct or to conform his conduct to the requirements of law." In doing so the District of Columbia Court of Appeals rejected the *Durham* decision.*

Brawner, Archie W. After being assaulted in a barroom brawl, Brawner fired five shots at his assailants through a door, killing one person. Brawner suffered from epilepsy and associated memory disturbances. He appealed his second-degree murder conviction, which resulted in the *Brawner* decision.

Biographies: U.S. v. Brawner, 471 F.2d 969 (1979).

BREMERMANN'S LIMIT. The absolute limit of the amount of information that one gram of matter can process in one second: 1.5×10^{47} bits.

Bremermann, Hans Joachim. German-American mathematician and biophysicist (b. Bremen, Germany, September 14, 1926). Bremermann's Ph.D. was from the University of Münster (1951). He taught at that university and at Stanford, Princeton, and Washington Universities between 1951 and 1958. He has been at the University of California at Berkeley since 1959, becoming a naturalized U.S. citizen in 1965. Bremermann's work has been on information

theory, self-organizing systems, and mathematical models of biological processes.
Biographies: AM&WS, 1982P; WhoAm, 1976; WoWhoSci.

BREWSTER EFFECT. See BROCA-SULZER EFFECT.

BREWSTER STEREOSCOPE. First stereoscope to use the principle of refraction with lenticular prisms to achieve fusion of the sterogram.

Brewster, Sir David. Scottish physicist (b. Jedburgh, Roxburgh County, December 11, 1781, d. Allerly, Melrose, Roxburgh County, February 10, 1868). Although he trained for the ministry, Brewster turned to science in his twenties. His scientific work concerned mostly light and the reflection and refraction of light. In 1815 he demonstrated the polarization of light, for which he received the Rumford Medal. A year later he invented the kaleidoscope. He described the prism stereoscope first in 1843, constructing one in 1849. Some of Brewster's other activities included the editorship of the *Edinburgh Encyclopedia* and the founding of the British Association for the Advancement of Science.
Biographies: Asimov; DNB, 2; EB, 4.

BRIGNER-KAUFFMAN ILLUSION. Contours that vary across space according to the Mach pattern show an increment and a decrement in apparent extent of a position corresponding to the position of Mach bands,* that is, inflection points of the pattern.

Brigner, Willard Leon. American psychologist (b. Portland, Indiana, March 19, 1932). Brigner earned the master's degree from Purdue University in 1954, held a position with the North Carolina Board of Juvenile Correction from 1958 to 1963, and then obtained the Ph.D. degree in experimental psychology from Duke University. He has been with Appalachian State University since 1968. His research has been in the area of visual perception. The illusion was described by Brigner and Kauffman in 1974 (*Perc. Mot. Skills, 38,* 919–32).
Biographies: AM&WS, 1978s; APA Dir., 1985.

Kauffman, Irvin. American psychologist (b. Wilmington, Delaware, December 1937). Kauffman obtained his master's degree from the University of Alabama in 1983 and the psychology specialist degree in 1984. After teaching in colleges in Alabama and North Carolina, Kauffman took a position with the Alabama Department of Youth Services in 1985. His research has been on the organizational factors in human memory and the extinction of aversively motivated behavior.
Biographies: Unavailable.

BRIQUET'S SYNDROME. A behavior disorder, loosely characterized by a set of vague somatic complaints and poorly articulated feelings of unease.

Briquet, Paul B. French physician (b. Châlons-sur-Marne, Marne, 1796, d. Paris, November 25, 1881). Briquet received the M.D. degree from the University of Paris (1824) and taught medicine there. He was also attending physician at various Paris hospitals, and in 1860 became member of the Academie de médecine. Briquet wrote a number of medical papers but is best known for his book, *Traité clinique et thérapeutique de l'hystérie* (1859), in which he described the syndrome.

   Biographies: Fischer, *Biog. Lex.;* Hirsch, *Biog. Lex.*

BROADBENT FILTERING EFFECT. In a dichotic listening task, the phenomenon of not hearing the message in the unattended ear when the hearer complies with instructions to listen only to the message presented to the other ear.

Broadbent, Donald Eric. English psychologist (b. Birmingham, May 6, 1926). Broadbent is an applied psychologist with an interest in engineering psychology. He studied psychology at Cambridge University between 1947 and 1949, with a short course in aeronautical engineering and pilot training in the United States just preceding. Upon graduation, Broadbent remained at Cambridge as a staff member of the Applied Psychology Unit of the Medical Research Council. He was its director from 1958 to 1974, remaining on its external staff afterward. Broadbent never held an academic appointment but was awarded the D.Sc. degree by Cambridge in 1965. His *Perception and Communication* (1958) was the first systematic treatment of humans as information processing systems, and *Decision and Stress* (1971) treated selectivity in information processing, perceptual biases, and the effects of noise. The filtering effect was described in three papers in 1952 (*J. Exp. Psychol., 43,* 267–73; *44,* 51–55, 428–33).

   Biographies: Amer. Psychologist, 1976, *31,* 53–59; *HPA, 7; Who,* 1986–1987.

BROCA'S APHASIA. An aphasia in which the person is unable to name objects or to repeat verbal materials due to temporary damage or destruction of Broca's area in the brain.

BROCA'S AREA. The inferior frontal gyrus of the left cerebral hemisphere in right-handed persons that serves as the speech center. It is one of several speech centers, serving mainly the motor aspects of speech. Also known as Broca's convolution.

Broca, Paul. French surgeon and anthropologist (b. Sainte-Foy-la-Grande, Gironde, June 28, 1824, d. Paris, July 9, 1880). From 1853 to 1880, Broca taught at the University of Paris (M.D., University of Paris, 1849) and held various hospital appointments. On the basis of his theory of the cerebral localization of functions, Broca predicted that a certain patient with a disorder in speech articulation would have a lesion in the third left frontal convolution of the brain. When the patient died, a postmortem confirmed Broca's prediction, and Broca took the brain to the Société d'anthropologie for a demonstration (*Bull. Soc. anthrop.,* 1861, *2,* 235–38; *Bull. Soc. anat.,* 1861, *36,* 330–57). The demonstration impressed scientists greatly, made a case for the exact localization of brain functions, and made Broca famous. The area of the brain involved was later named after him by David Ferrier.* Broca is even better known for his work in physical anthropology, which occupied him later in life. He founded the world's first anthropological society.

Biographies: Asimov; DSB, 2; *EB,* 4; *Haymaker;* B. Hollander, *In Search of the Soul and the Mechanism of Thought, Emotion, and Conduct,* c. 1920; *IESS,* 2; Riese, *Bull. Hist. Med.,* 1947, *21,* 322–34.

BROCA-SULZER EFFECT. A flash of light appears brighter than a steady light of the same intensity. While the apparent brightness of a flash increases during the first 50 to 100 msec, it then decreases up to the 250 msec point, after which no further changes take place. The phenomenon is evident only with fairly strong stimuli.

Broca, André. French physicist and physician (b. Paris, November 2, 1863, d. Paris, February 23, 1925). André Broca, one of Paul Broca's* two sons, achieved distinction in his own right as researcher in medical physics. He obtained an M.D. in 1893 and from 1895 to 1925 taught medical physics at the University of Paris. He and D. Sulzer described the phenomenon that bears their names in 1902 (*J. physiol. path. gén.,* 4, 632–40). The phenomenon was first described by David Brewster* in 1934 and is therefore sometimes called the Brewster effect.* It is also know as the Brücke effect.

Biographies: Fischer, *Biog. Lex.*

Sulzer, David Emile. French ophthalmologist (b. 1858, d. 1918).
Biographies: Unavailable.

BRODMANN'S AREAS. Histologically differentiated areas of the cerebral cortex that have been outlined and numbered by K. Brodmann. It is the commonly used reference system for identifying cortical areas.

Brodmann, Korbinian. German neuranatomist (b. Liggersdorf, Württemberg, November 17, 1868, d. Munich, August 22, 1918). Brodmann, who in 1898 received his M.D. from the University of Leipzig, did all of his important work between 1901 and 1910 at the Neurobiological Institute in Berlin. The institute was directed by Oskar Vogt, who had earlier inspired Brodmann to study neurology and psychiatry. Contact with Aloys Alzheimer* a year before Brodmann's move to Berlin led him to devote the rest of his life to anatomical problems. He mapped the human cortex by recognizing that it is organized anatomically the same way as the cortex of all other mammals, and he classified cortical types and layers on the basis of the morphogenesis of the cortex. His work culminated with the publication of *Vergleichende Lokalisationslehre der Grosshirnrinde* in 1909. The medical establishment at the University of Berlin, however, resisted his ideas and denied him the opportunity to teach there. He moved to Tübingen in 1910, to a psychiatric clinic near Halle in 1916, and to Munich in 1918 to join the Deutsche Forschunganstalt für Psychiatrie.

Biographies: Haymaker.

BROGDEN UTILITY MODEL. A procedure for estimating the monetary value of interventions.

Brogden, Hubert E. American psychologist (b. Sydney, Australia, October 9, 1913). Brogden earned a Ph.D. in general psychology from the University of Illinois in 1939. He held positions with the Ohio State University and the Louisiana State Public Health Bureau before joining the Personnel Research Branch of the U.S. Department of the Army in 1942. In 1964, Brogden left that post to teach at Purdue University. His research has been in the area of personnel psychology and psychometrics. The utility model was presented in 1949 (*Personnel Psychol., 2,* 171–83) and 1950 (with E. Taylor, *Personnel Psychol., 3,* 133–54).

Biographies: AM&WS, 78S; *APA Dir.,* 1985.

BROWN-SEQUARD SYNDROME. Paralysis of one side of the body, accompanied by heightened sensitivity, and anaesthesis on the opposite side. The syndrome is produced by a lesion or sectioning of the lateral half of the spinal cord.

Brown-Séquard, Charles-Edouard. French neurologist (b. Port-Louis, Mauritius, April 8, 1817, d. Sceaux, near Paris, April 2, 1894). Brown-Séquard was born of a French mother and an Irish-American father on an island that was a British protectorate. His father was lost with his ship soon after marriage, and his mother died suddenly in 1843. At age twenty-nine, Brown added his mother's maiden name to his surname. Although he was a British subject, he felt more at home in Paris and became a naturalized French citizen. He was married three times, two of his wives dying. He originally wanted to become a dramatic author and then switched to medicine (M.D., University of Paris, 1846). He did not practice, however, and was much more interested in physiological research. He held various medical and teaching appointments and traveled frequently among Mauritius, France, England, and the United States. He spent his last sixteen years at the Collége de France in Paris. Brown-Séquard's reputation as a neurophysiologist started with his M.D. thesis that foreshadowed the discovery of the phenomenon that bears his name (*J. physiol. l'homme anim.,* 1863, *6,* 124–45, 232–48, 581–646). His major contribution was the demonstration of the crossing over of sensory fibers in the spinal cord and the study of the consequences of experimental lesions in the nervous system. Brown-Séquard founded three physiological journals and published hundreds of articles.

Biographies: E. B. Carmichael, *AL J. Med. Sci.,* 1972, *9,* 224–37; *DSB,* 2; W. Goddy, *Proc. Roy. Soc. Med.,* 1964, *57,* 189–92; *Haymaker;* J. M. Olmsted, *Charles-Edouard Brown-Séquard, a Nineteenth Century Neurologist and Endocrinologist,* 1946; T. C. Ruch, *Yale J. Biol. Med.,* 1946, *18,* 227–38; J. Schiller, *J. Hist. Med., 1966, 21,* 260–70; *Talbot.*

BROWN-SPEARMAN FORMULA. See SPEARMAN-BROWN PROPHECY FORMULA.

BRÜCKE EFFECT. See BROCA-SULZER EFFECT.

BRUNSWIK FACES. A series of schematic faces whose only features are lines for the eyes, nose, and mouth, used in the study of categorization and discrimination.

BRUNSWIK RATIO. The degree of an observer's perceptual constancy with respect to lightness can be expressed by the formula $R - S/A - S$, where S is the percentage reflectance for a stimulus match, A is the percentage reflectance of the object to be matched, and R is the percentage reflectance of the observer's matching sample when the task is to match two grays seen under different illuminations. If the observer matches strictly according to the intensity of the stimulus, he or she shows no lightness constancy; if he or she responds strictly according to reflectance, constancy is perfect. The actual match or the degree of lightness constancy is some percentage figure between these two extremes.

Brunswik, Egon. Austrian-American psychologist (b. Budapest, Hungary, March 18, 1903, d. Berkeley, California, July 7, 1955). Brunswik obtained a Ph.D. in psychology from the University of Vienna in 1927 and taught there until 1935. After a year in Ankara, Turkey, he came to the United States. He held a position at the University of California at Berkeley until he died by his own hand. Brunswik's theoretical approach to psychology received the name of probabilistic functionalism. Brunswik was the author of *Wahrnehmung und Gegenstandswelt* (1934), *Experimentelle Psychologie in Demonstrationen* (1935), and *Perception and the Representative Design of Psychological Experiments* (1956). Brunswik's faces were published in 1937 (*Z. Psychol., 142*, 67–134) and the ratio in 1929 (*Z. Psychol., 109*, 40–115).
   Biographies: IESS, 2; *PR*, 3; E. C. Tolman, *Amer. J. Psychol.*, 1956, *69*, 315–24.

BUNSEN-ROSCOE LAW. The trade-off relationship between the intensity of light and its duration: $T \times I = c$. It applies to visual threshold measurements and to the effect of light on photographic emulsion (hence also known as the photographic law). It holds only for values of T of 50 milliseconds or less. In visual science, the relationship is known as Bloch's law.

Bunsen, Robert Wilhelm Eberhard. German chemist (b. Göttingen, March 31, 1811, d. Heidelberg, August 16, 1899). Bunsen was a noted chemist, with several important discoveries and inventions to his credit. He studied at the University of Göttingen (Ph.D., 1830) and held positions at the universities of Kassel, Marburg, and, the longest, at Heidelberg (1852–1899). He never married, dedicating his life entirely to chemistry, mostly inorganic. He suggested methods for cutting heat losses in blast furnaces through gasses, invented several calorimeters, a zinc-carbon battery, a grease-spot photometer, and the Bunsen burner. Most celebrated was his introduction, together with Gustav Kirchhoff, of the technique of spectroscopy. The Bunsen-Roscoe law was described by Bunsen and Henry E. Roscoe in *Photochemical Researches* (1858–1863).

Biographies: Asimov; DSB, 2; EB, 4.

Roscoe, Sir Henry Enfield. English chemist (b. London, January 7, 1833, d. Woodcote, near Leatherhead, Surrey, December 18, 1915). Roscoe had a B.A. in chemistry (1852) from University College, London, and a Ph.D. from the University of Heidelberg (1854), where he studied under Bunsen. He took a position at Owens College in Manchester in 1857, became a member of Parliament for South Manchester in 1885, and resigned his Owens College chair. In 1896 Roscoe became the vice-chancellor of the University of London. Among his achievements in chemistry was the preparation of pure vanadium.

Biographies: DNB, 1912–1921.

BURIDAN'S ASS. An illustration of the approach-approach type of conflict that takes the form of an ass poised exactly in the middle between two identical haystacks. Torn between two equal but opposite tendencies, the ass presumably starves. In actual situations this type of conflict is the easiest to solve, however, because momentary fluctuations in the motivational state will incline a person to approach one of the two goals first.

Buridan, Jean. French philosopher (b. Nethune, Artois, about 1300 [or 1295], d. Paris, about 1385 [or 1366]). Buridan was rector of the University of Paris in 1328 and again in 1340. He is most famous for the point he is supposed to have made concerning the impossibility of taking freely willed action when motivated by two equal but opposed motives; however, there is no mention of the ass in Buridan's writings. He does make the point concerning indecision in a commentary on Aristotle's *De caelo,* but the animal he uses as an example is a dog, not an ass.

Biographies: Asimov; DE.

BURMESE PYRAMID. See TOWER OF HANOI

C

CAIN COMPLEX. Rivalry, competition, and destructive feelings toward a brother.

Cain. In the biblical story of Cain and Abel (Genesis 4:1–16), Cain, envious of the favor shown his brother, Abel, by God, slays Abel.

CALIFORNIA ACHIEVEMENT TESTS. The CATs are a standard achievement test battery in reading vocabulary, reading comprehension, arithmetic reasoning, arithmetic fundamentals, arithmetic total, mechanics of English, spelling, and handwriting for grades one through fourteen. First published in 1933 under the name of Progressive Achievement Test, the tests have been amplified and revised many times since, acquiring the present name in 1951. They are published by the California Test Bureau.

CALIFORNIA PSYCHOLOGICAL INVENTORY. A widely used personality inventory that yields scores on either eighteen or twenty-four trait scales. The author of the test is Harrison G. Gough. The test was first published in 1956–1957 by the Consulting Psychologists Press.

CALIFORNIA TEST OF PERSONALITY. A multilevel, self-administering personality questionnaire for children and adults that yields scores on fifteen trait scales. The authors are Louis P. Thorpe, Willis W. Clark, and Ernest W. Tiegs. It was first published by the California Test Bureau in 1939.

California. All tests that are California eponyms are named after the state of California (rather than the university) and are published either by the California Test Bureau or the Consulting Psychologists Press, both located in California.

CANNON-BARD THEORY OF EMOTION. A modification of the James-Lange theory of emotion* that involves, on the one hand, decision making concerning the nature of stimuli prior to the cortex's giving commands to the muscles to contract and, on the other, the hypothalamus, which sends messages to the cortex rather than the muscles themselves, as in the James-Lange theory, and thereby causes the conscious experience of emotion as a consequence of action.

CANNON-WASHBURN EXPERIMENT. A classical experiment (also referred to as technique) in which the hunger contractions of the stomach in a human subject were recorded by having the subject swallow a balloon attached to a rubber tube and a manometer, inflating the balloon, and recording changes in its pressure on a kymograph. The subject pressed a key every time he felt hunger pangs. There was an exact coincidence between felt hunger pangs and stomach contractions.

Cannon, Walter Bradford. American physiologist (b. Prairie du Chien, Wisconsin, October 19, 1871, d. Franklin, New Hampshire, October 1, 1945). An internationally famous physiologist, Cannon earned his medical degree at Harvard University in 1900, where he then taught until his retirement as emeritus professor in 1942. Cannon first studied the physiology of thirst and hunger, demonstrating the movements of the alimentary tract by means of X-rays and the simultaneity of felt hunger pangs and stomach contractions. His study of digestive activities led Cannon to the discovery of the effects of strong emotion on digestion and the study of the autonomic nervous system. Further research led him to a broadened concept that included diverse adaptive changes in the physiology of the body under emotion, stress, and tissue need. It was presented in a widely read book, *Bodily Changes in Pain, Hunger, Fear and Rage* (1915). Cannon also studied traumatic shock, the effects of endocrine secretion on the functioning of the nervous system, and the autonomic nervous system. His concept of homeostasis was presented in *The Wisdom of the Body* (1932). Cannon's modification of the James-Lange theory was presented in 1927 (*Amer. J. Psychol.*, 39, 106–24) and the Cannon-Washburn experiment in 1912 (*Amer. J. Physiol.*, U29, 441–54).

Biographies: Asimov; W. B. Cannon, *The Way of an Investigator,* 1945; C. K. Drinker, *Science,* 1945, *102,* 470–72; *DSB,* 15, *EB,* 4; *Haymaker; IESS,* 2; *NCAB,* 15, 34; *WhAm,* 2.

Bard, Philip. American physiologist (b. Hueneme, California, October 25, 1898, d. Ojai, California, April 5, 1977). Bard's Ph.D. was from Harvard University (1927). He was at Harvard from 1931 to 1933, having previously

(1928–1931) taught at Princeton University. For most of his career (1933–1964), however, Bard was at Johns Hopkins University. His contribution to the revision of the James-Lange theory of emotion appeared in 1934: The neurohumoral basis of emotional reaction. In C. A. Murchison (ed.), *Handbook of General Experimental Psychology*.

Biographies: AM&WS, 1976P; WhAm, 7.

Washburn, Albert L. (b. n.a., d. n.a.). In the Cannon-Washburn experiment, Washburn, a student of Cannon, was both the subject of the experiment and the coauthor, with Cannon, of the paper in which the experiment was described. Over a period of several weeks and on a daily basis, Washburn would introduce the balloon into his stomach. After carrying it around for several hours to get used to it, Washburn had the balloon inflated, and the experiment took place. Washburn does not appear to have obtained an advanced degree or made any further contribution to psychology. Nothing else is known about him.

Biographies: Unavailable.

CAPGRAS' SYNDROME. A delusion marked by the belief that familiar persons have been replaced by doubles.

Capgras, Jean-Marie-Joseph. French psychiatrist (b. 1873, d. 1950). The delusion that bears Capgras' name appeared in a 1923 paper, published with J. Reboul-Lachaux (*Soc. clin. méd. psychol.*, 81, 186).

Biographies: Unavailable

CATTELL INFANT INTELLIGENCE SCALE. A downward extension of the Stanford-Binet scale* to cover the ages three months through thirty months.

Cattell, Psyche. American psychologist (b. Garrison, New York, August 2, 1893). Psyche Cattell, daughter of James McKeen Cattell,* obtained an Ed.D. from Harvard University in 1927. She held research and clinical positions at Harvard from 1922 through 1936, was chief psychologist at the Lancaster Guidance Clinic in Pennsylvania from 1939 to 1963, engaged in private practice during the period 1939–1972, and directed the Cattell School from 1941. She retired in 1974. Her main research interests have been the mental and physical growth of infants and children, intelligence, school standing, and physical traits. She wrote *Dentition as a Measure of Maturity* (1927), *The Measurement of Intelligence in Infants and Young Children* (1940), *Raising Children With Love and Limits* (1972), and over twenty other publications, including a column, ''Children under Eight.'' The scale appeared in her 1940 book.

Biographies: AM&WS, 1978s; APA Dir., 1985; ConAu, 41–44R.

CHADDOCK REFLEX. 1. A reflex present in pyramidal tract lesion cases, consisting of the extension of the big toe when the external malleolus is stimulated. 2. In hemiplegia, the flexion of the wrist and fanning of the fingers when the ulna is stimulated.

Chaddock, Charles Gilbert. American neurologist (b. Jonesville, Michigan, November 14, 1861, d. St. Louis, Missouri, July 20, 1893). Chaddock's M.D. was from the University of Michigan (1885). He was with the Northern Michigan Asylum from 1889 to 1892 and with St. Louis University from 1892 onward, spending the years 1888–1889 and 1896–1900 abroad. He was the author of several books and the translator of such authors as Krafft-Ebing.
   Biographies: WhAm, 1.

CHARCOT TRIAD. The three symptoms of intention tremor, nystagmus, and staccato speech that are due to brain stem involvement in multiple sclerosis.

Charcot, Jean-Martin. French neurologist (b. Paris, November 29, 1825, d. Paris, August 16, 1893). After receiving the M.D. degree from the University of Paris in 1853, Charcot was physician at the Central Hospital Bureau from 1856 to 1860 and taught at the University of Paris from 1860 to 1862. He spent the rest of his life as a senior physician at the Salpêtrière hospital* in Paris. Charcot is often called the Father of Neurology because of his skill in relating patients' symptoms to the anatomy of the nervous system (*Leçons sur les maladies du système nerveux,* 5 vols., 1872–1893). He was famous as both a physician and a teacher. The neurological clinic that he established at the La Salpêtrière hospital was the best in the nineteenth century, attracting students from all over the world. Charcot's views of the nature of hypnosis and its relation to hysteria constituted the Salpêtrière school. In medicine, at least ten processes and syndromes are named after Charcot.
   Biographies: Beeson, *Ann. Med. Hist.,* 1928, *10,* 126–32; *DSB,* 3; *EB,* 5; Garrison et al., *Bull. NY Acad. Med.,* 1926, ser. 2 (suppl.), *2,* 1–32; *Haymaker;* G. Guillain, *J. M. Charcot, 1825–1893: His Life—His Work,* 1959; *IESS,* 2; J.-L. Langlois, *Bull. Isaac Ray Med. Libr.,* 1954, *2,* 1–14; F. H. Mackay & E. LeGrand, *Arch. Neurol. Psychiat.,* 1935, *34,* 390–400; *Talbot.*

CHARLIER'S CHECKS. Checks on the accuracy of computations of certain statistics, such as the standard deviation, when these are performed by hand using grouped data.

Charlier, Carl Wilhelm Ludwig. Swedish astronomer (b. Ostersund, April 1, 1862, d. Lund, November 4, 1934). Charlier was a professor at the University of Lund and director of the Lund Observatory. He made contributions to celestial mechanics, mathematical optics, stellar statistics, and probability calculus. His main work was *Celestial Mechanics* in two volumes (1902–1907).
   Biographies: Brockhaus, 3.

CHARPENTIER'S BANDS. Dark bands that appear against the light background of an annulus produced by an illuminated radial slit rotating against a dark background. The bands are recurrent afterimages of the slit.

CHARPENTIER'S ILLUSION. 1. Synonym for autokinetic illusion, or the apparent movement of a small, low-intensity light in the dark. 2. Synonym for size-weight illusion or the illusion that, of two equal masses, the one having the greater volume will be judged to be lighter than the one with the smaller volume.

CHARPENTIER'S LAW. In the retinal fovea, the product of the area of a stimulus and its intensity is constant for stimuli at threshold intensities.

Charpentier, Augustin. French biophysicist (b. Argenton-sur-Creuse, Indre, June 14, 1852, d. Argenton-sur-Creuse, Indre, August 4, 1916). Charpentier obtained a medical degree from the University of Paris in 1877, taught biophysics there for a year, and then went to the University of Nancy in 1879. He produced a series of important works in physiological optics. Charpentier described the bands in 1892 (*C. r. hebd. séances mém. Soc. biol.*, 114, 1423–26) and the autokinetic illusion in 1886 (*C. r. hebd. séances Acad. sci.*, 102, 1155–57). He formulated the law that bears his name in 1880 (*C. r. hebd. séances mém. Soc. biol.*, 91, 995).
   Biographies: Fischer, *Biog. Lex.*

CHERNOFF FACES. Cartoon-like schematic faces that vary along eighteen dimensions, used to study multidimensional discrimination.

Chernoff, Herman. American mathematician (b. New York City, July 1, 1923). Chernoff's Ph.D. was in applied mathematics (Brown University, 1948). He filled positions at the University of Illinois (1949–1952) and Stanford (1952–1974) before moving to MIT in 1974. He has done research on statistical problems in econometrics, sequential design of experiments, large sample theory, and pattern recognition. The faces were presented in 1973 (*J. Amer. Stat. Ass.*, 68, 361–68).
   Biographies: AM&WS, 1982P; WhoAm, 1982.

CHEYNE-STOKES PSYCHOSIS. Psychosis in which there is anxiety, restlessness, and Cheynes-Stokes respiration.*

CHEYNE-STOKES RESPIRATION. Labored respiration characterized by alternating rapid increases and decreases in its rate. It is found in certain diseases and in prematurely born infants.

Cheyne, John. Scottish physician (b. Edinburgh, 1777, d. Sherington near Newport Pagnel, Buckinghamshire, January 31, 1836). Cheyne began to assist his physician father in the care of the sick at the age of thirteen and obtained his medical degree at the age of eighteen. During the following fours years as a military surgeon Cheyne's activities were mostly non-medical, but then Cheyne began to study medicine again and practice it seriously. He made careful observations and published papers. In 1809 he moved to Dublin. The eponymous respiration was first described by Cheynes in the case report of a man who had a fatal heart attack (*Dublin Hosp. Rep. Comm. Med. Surg.*, 1818, *2*, 216–23).

Biographies: DNB, 10; T. J. Pettigrew, *Memoir of John Cheyne,* 1839; *Talbot.*

Stokes, William. Irish physician (b. Dublin, July 1804, d. Dublin, January 10, 1878). Stokes studied medicine at the University of Edinburgh (M.D., 1825). He returned to Dublin and soon became a physician at Meath Hospital. He reorganized clinical teaching at the hospital, wrote some 140 scientific publications, and in general became the leader of the Irish school of medicine, following Cheyne. Outstanding among his publications are *Treatise on the Diagnosis and Treatment of Diseases of the Chest* (1837) and *The Diseases of the Heart* (1854). In the former publication Stokes gives a fuller description of the type of breathing first described by Cheyne and recognizes its connection with heart dysfunction, which Cheyne had not done. Stokes received many honors, and additional syndromes, signs, and medicaments bear his name.

Biographies: G. T. Bettany, *Eminent Doctors: Their Lives and Their Work,* 1885, vol. 2, pp. 188–93; *DNB,* 54; *Med. Classics,* March 1939, *3,* 711–46; *Talbot.*

CHICAGO SCHOOL. 1. The Chicago school of functionalism. Functionalism as a self-conscious school of psychology centered on the University of Chicago and its Department of Psychology. The paper that introduced the school was written in 1896 by a Chicago philosopher, John Dewey. The most notable psychologists in the Chicago school were James Rowland Angell, Harvey Carr, and Edward Stevens Robinson. 2. The neo-Freudian Chicago school of psychoanalysis that centered around the Chicago Institute for Psychoanalysis. Franz Gabriel Alexander, founder of the institute, was the most important representative of the school.

Chicago, University of. It is the University of Chicago, founded in 1891, rather than the city of Chicago, Illinois, that lends its name to the functionalist school.

Chicago Institute for Psychoanalysis. Founded by Franz Alexander in 1932, the institute was an entity unrelated to the University of Chicago; the psychoanalytic institute is named after the city.

CHVOSTEK REFLEX. Spasm of the ipsilateral facial muscles produced by tapping the face in front of the ear. It is due to hyperirritability of facial nerves and is seen in tetany and anxiety states.

Chvostek, Franz. Austrian surgeon (b. May 21, 1835, d. November 16, 1884). Chvostek graduated in medicine from the Josephs-Akademie in 1861 and held a position at the Duchek Clinic. He did research and therapy of spinal cord and nervous system diseases. He described the reflex in 1876.

Biographies: WoWhoSci.

CLERAMBAULT-KANDINSKY COMPLEX. In some psychotic states, the psychotic's feeling that his mind is being controlled by somebody or something outside him.

Clérambault, Gaétan-Henri-Alfred-Edouard-León-Marie Gatian de. French psychiatrist (b. Bourges, Cher, July 2, 1872, d. Paris, November 17, 1934). Clérambault obtained his medical degree in 1899. He was physician of the special clinic of the Prefecture de police of Paris from 1905 to 1914. After military service during World War I, he returned to police work, ending it in the 1920s. Clérambault described the complex in 1927 (*Ann. méd.-psychol., 85,* 398–413).
  Biographies: DBN, 8; *Larousse,* 3.

Kandinsky, Viktor Khrisanfovich. Russian psychiatrist (b. Nerchinsk raĭon [now Chita oblast'], April 18, 1849, d. St. Petersburg, August 15, 1899). Kandinsky graduated from the medical faculty of the University of Moscow in 1872. From 1882 to 1899 he was staff physician at St. Nicholas Mental Hospital, St. Petersburg. Kandinsky was the first psychiatrist in Russia to propose a classification of mental illnesses. He formulated a theory of mental automatisms and was first to define pseudohallucinations. A description of the complex appears in his book on pseudohallucinations (*O psevdogallyutsinatsiyakh,* 1890).
  Biographies: Soviet, 11.

CLEVER HANS PHENOMENON. Animals seemingly performing high-level mental feats when in fact their performance is owing to their having become sensitive to very slight cues given unconsciously by the trainer.

Clever Hans. Clever Hans, one of the Elberfeld horses,* was originally owned and trained by Mr. von Osten in Berlin. The horse could allegedly read, do arithmetic, and answer various kinds of questions by tapping his foot and shaking his head. In the summer of 1904, Clever Hans became a phenomenon, and thousands of people came to see von Osten demonstrate Clever Hans' abilities. There were also allegations of fraud. In order to clear his name, von Osten appealed to the Berlin Board of Education. The board appointed a committee under the direction of the psychologist Carl Stumpf. The committee at first was unable to explain how the horse got the answers and conducted a second series of tests. This time, Stumpf had selected a graduate student, Oskar Pfungst, to conduct the investigation in his absence. Pfungst determined that Clever Hans was acting on very slight cues von Osten supplied, such as nodding his head when the horse had made the correct number of taps. When the trainer was out of sight, the horse's performance fell to chance. Pfungst was able to produce results identical to those of von Osten by supplying the cues to the horse himself.
  Biographies: D. Fernald, *The Hans Legacy,* 1984.

CLYTEMNESTRA COMPLEX. The dynamics of the psychological complex involved in a wife's killing her husband.

Clytemnestra. Clytemnestra was the wife of Agamemnon, one of the principals of Homer's epic, the *Iliad*. She took a lover, Aegisthus, when Agamemnon went to the Trojan war. Upon his return, she and her lover killed Agamemnon.

COCHRAN Q TEST. A nonparametric statistic for testing the hypothesis of no difference between *k* related samples.

COCHRAN TEST. A test of homogeneity of variance that yields the statistic *C*, the ratio of the largest treatment variance and the sum of all treatment variances.

Cochran, William Gemell. American mathematician (b. Rutherglen, Scotland, July 1909, d. Orleans, Massachusetts, March 29, 1980). Cochran received the M.S. degree from Glasgow (1931) and Cambridge Universities (1938). He was at the Rothamsted Experimental Station from 1934 to 1939, then at several American universities, and finally, from 1957 to 1976, at Harvard University. Cochran was the author of several statistical texts and more than 100 articles. The *Q* test was published in 1950 (*Biometrika, 37,* 256–66) and the homogeneity test in 1947 (*Biometrics, 3,* 22–38).
    Biographies: AM&WS, 1979P; A. P. Dempster, *Amer. Statistician,* 1981, *35,* 38; *WhoAm,* 1976–1977.

COLUMNS OF GOLL. Nerve tracts (spinobulbar tracts) located on either side of the posterior median fissure of the spinal cord that conduct impulses from the legs and the lower trunk to the brain.

Goll, Friedrich G. Swiss physician (b. Zofingen, Aargau, March 1, 1825, d. Zurich, November 12, 1903). Goll obtained his M.D. from the University of Zurich in 1853, returning in 1863 as director of the university clinic. He was also professor at that university, his research being mostly pharmacological, but he did work also in other areas. His *Beiträge zur feineren Anatomie des menschlichen Rückenmarks* (1860) contains the description of the nerve tracts that bear his name.
    Biographies: La S. Archambault, *Albany Med. Ann.,* 1907, *28,* 228; Hirsch, *Biog. Lex.*

COMREY PERSONALITY SCALES. A personality inventory for normal persons aged sixteen or older, consisting of eight bipolar scales, such as trust versus defensiveness, orderliness versus lack of compulsion, and introversion versus extroversion. Testees respond to each item (160 total) using two seven-point scales. The final result is graphed as a profile of standard scores.

Comrey, Andrew Laurence. American psychologist (b. Charleston, West Virginia, April 14, 1923). Comrey had a Ph.D. in psychometrics from the University of Southern California (1949). He specialized in factor analysis and related techniques. He has been professor of psychology at the University of

California at Los Angeles since 1951 and a consulting psychologist in private practice. The scales were first published in 1970.

Biographies: AM&WS, 1978S; *APA Dir.,* 1985.

COMTIAN POSITIVISM. The view that the basic data of science are those that are immediately observable, basic, nonspeculative, preinferential, and therefore undebatable. Such basic data are social in addition: one can investigate others but not oneself. Therefore, although societal laws are like the laws of physics and make the science of sociology possible, by this view psychology as a science becomes impossible.

Comte, Auguste. French philosopher (b. Montpellier, Hérault, January 19, 1978, d. Paris, September 5, 1857). Comte studied science at the École polytechnique in Paris. He taught mathematics there and then held the position of tutor from 1832 to 1842. In 1838, Comte coined the term *sociology* and attempted to systematize a new science under that name. He believed that individual behavior is largely the product of society and not of the individual's experience or personality. Humans can be understood only in relation to each other. Through his main work, *Cours de philosophie positive* (1830–1842), Comte exercised a powerful influence on the development of thinking in the social sciences.

Biographies: DSB, 3; *EP,* 2; *IESS,* 3; F. S. Marvin, *Comte: The Founder of Sociology,* 1937.

COOLIDGE EFFECT. In animals, the need of the male for variety in female sex partners. In rats, the initial high rate of copulation with a receptive female eventually decreases to almost zero, and rams and bulls are unwilling to mate repeatedly with the same female. The phenomenon is less pronounced in primates and even less so in humans, but some vestiges remain.

Coolidge, Calvin. American president (b. Plymouth Notch, Vermont, July 4, 1872, d. Northampton, Massachusetts, January 5, 1933). The eponym derives from a story told about the thirtieth president of the United States. Once, when visiting a government farm, he and his wife were taken on separate tours. On inspecting some chicken coops, Mrs. Coolidge was prompted to inquire concerning the frequency with which the rooster was expected to perform his duty each day. The figure of dozens of times a day impressed Mrs. Coolidge, and she said, "Please tell that to the president." As the president himself inspected the chickens, he was offered this information. Coolidge's response was to ask whether the rooster mated with the same hen each time. On being told that it was with a different hen, Coolidge nodded slowly and said, "Tell that to Mrs. Coolidge." The story is given in a chapter "Sexual behavior: Hard times with the Coolidge effect" by G. Berman (in M. H. Siegel & H. P. Zeigler [eds.], *Psychological Research: The Inside Story,* 1976) and by Glenn Wilson in *The Coolidge Effect* (1981).

Biographies: DAB, 21; *NCAB,* 24; *WhAm,* 1.

COOPERSMITH SELF-ESTEEM INVENTORIES. Three self-report questionnaires that measure "the evaluations a person makes and customarily maintains with regard to him or herself." The three forms are the School Form, School Short Form, and Adult Form.

Coopersmith, Stanley. American psychologist (b. New York City, July 15, 1926). Coopersmith, who received his Ph.D. in psychology from Cornell University in 1957, taught at Wesleyan University from 1957 to 1963 and then moved to the University of California at Davis, where he was chairman of the Psychology Department. Coopersmith is the author of *Antecedents of Self-Esteem* (1967) and other books. The present (1981) inventories are based on an earlier inventory designed for research purposes and published in his 1967 book.
    Biographies: AM&WS, 1978s; *APA Dir.,* 1975; *ConAu,* 21R.

CORI CYCLE. A series of chemical reactions showing the passage of lactic acid, formed during muscular activity from glycogen, to glucose and again to glycogen.

Cori, Carl Ferdinand. Czech-American biochemist (b. Prague, December 5, 1896). Cori obtained the M.D. degree from the German University in Prague in 1920. He came to the United States in 1922 and became naturalized. From 1922 to 1931 Cori was employed by the State Institute for Study of Malignant Diseases. He held positions at Washington University from 1931 to 1966 and has been a visiting lecturer and consultant with the Massachusetts General Hospital and Harvard Medical School and director of the Enzyme Research Laboratory since 1966. Cori and his wife began their work on the metabolism of lactic acid in 1923. They were both awarded the Nobel Prize for their work in 1947.
    Biographies: AM&WS, 1982p; *Asimov; CurBio,* 1947; *McGMSE,* 1; *Who,* 1982; *WhoAm,* 1984–1985.

Cori, Gerty Theresa Radnitz. Czech-American biochemist (b. Prague, August 15, 1896, d. St. Louis, Missouri, October 26, 1957). Carl Cori and Gerty Radnitz were married in Prague. Gerty Cori shared with her husband an identical career, except that hers was cut short in 1957 while at the Washington University Medical School.
    Biographies: Asimov; CurBio, 1947, 1958; *DAB,* Sup. 6; *DAB,* 3; *McGMSE,* 1; *NCAB,* 48; *WhAm,* 3.

CORNELIA DE LANGE SYNDROME. A complex of congenital malformations of unknown origin. The infant is microbrachycephalic and suffers from mild to usually severe mental and physical retardation.

de Lange, Cornelia Catharina. Dutch pediatrician (b. 1871, d. 1950). De Lange graduated from the University of Amsterdam in 1897. She was professor of pediatrics at the University of Amsterdam from 1927 to 1938, the first woman on the medical faculty of this university. She described the syndrome in 1934 (*Amer.*

J. Dis. Ch., 48, 243–68).
   Biographies: E. P. Lovejoy, *Woman Doctors of the World,* 1957; *WoWhoSci.*

CORNELL-COXE PERFORMANCE ABILITY SCALE. A performance test used to supplement verbal intelligence tests in cases of language difficulty. The test employed many of the items of the Army Performance Scale, which, in turn, had borrowed from the Pintner-Paterson Performance Scale.* The scale was replaced by the Arthur Performance Scale,* and this scale, in turn, by others.

Cornell, Ethel Letitia. American psychologist (b. New York City, November 28, 1892, d. Hyannis, Massachusetts, December 8, 1963). With a Ph.D. in psychology from Columbia University (1919), Cornell held various mental health positions and was associate education supervisor for the New York State Education Department from 1920. Her research concerned learning difficulties, individual differences, and school psychology. Ethel Cornell and Warren Coxe published the scale in 1934 (*A Performance Ability Scale: Examination Manual,* World Book Co.).
   Biographies: AMS, 1949; *APA Dir.,* 1948; *NYT,* December 9, 1963, p. 35, col. 1.

Coxe, Warren Winfred. American psychologist (b. Belvidere, Illinois, July 19, 1886, d. May 1971). Coxe was primarily interested in tests and educational measurement. He received his Ph.D. from Ohio State University in 1923 and from 1923 to 1929 headed the Bureau of Educational Measurement in Albany, New York, becoming the director of the Division of Research in Albany in 1929. He remained in that position until his retirement in 1956.
   Biographies: AMS, 1968S; *APA Dir.,* 1965.

CORNELL CRITICAL THINKING TEST. A seventy-one-item, four-part test of the ability to evaluate the bearing of information on a hypothesis, to judge the reliability of information, to judge whether a statement follows from a premise, and to identify assumptions. The test was prepared in 1961 by Robert H. Ennis and Jason Millman, then at Cornell University.

CORNELL TECHNIQUE. Another term for the Guttman scale.* When the technique was published in 1944, Louis Guttman,* author of the scale, was at Cornell University, hence the alternate name.

Cornell University. Founded in 1865, the university is located in Ithaca, New York, and is named after Ezra Cornell (1807–1874), founder of Western Union Telegraph, who led in the establishment of the university by taking the initial steps under the Morill Act and by providing its initial monetary and land endowment.

CORNFIELD-TUKEY ALGORITHM. In the factorial design of experiments, a set of rules for deriving the expected mean values of mean squares.

Cornfield, Jerome. American statistician (b. New York City, October 30, 1912, d. Great Falls, Virginia, September 17, 1979). Cornfield received a B.S. from New York University (1933), and he was in graduate school at Columbia University. He worked as a statistician in various federal government offices from 1936 to 1967 and taught at Johns Hopkins University, the University of Pittsburgh, and George Washington University from 1958 to 1979.
   Biographies: WhAm, 7.

Tukey, John Wilder. See under TUKEY TEST.

CORTI'S TEETH. Also known as auditory teeth, these are miscroscopic elevations on the surface of the vestibular lip of the internal spiral sulcus of the cochlear duct.

Corti, Alfonso Giacomo Gaspare. Italian anatomist (b. Gambrana, near Pavia, June 22, 1822, d. Corvino San Quirico, near Castaggio, October 2, 1876). Corti received the doctoral degree from the University of Vienna in 1847. He spent the next three years in postdoctoral studies at various universities, until family business forced his return to Italy in 1851. After 1854, Corti spent his time managing his estate and educating his children. He described the structures of the inner ear that now bear his name in 1851 (*Z. wiss. Zool., 3,* 109–69). The name *organ of Corti** was proposed by Albert Kolliker, under whom Corti had studied histology at Würzburg.
   Biographies: DSB, 3; E. von Ullman, Arch. Otolaryng., 1951, 54, 1–28.

COTARD'S SYNDROME. Paranoia, accompanied by delusions of negation, sensory disorders, and suicidal tendency.

Cotard, Jules. French neurologist (b. 1840, d. Paris, August 19, 1889). Cotard received his medical education at the University of Paris (M.D., 1866). He was physician at the Maison de Santé at Vanves, Paris. He was elected president of the Societé médico-psychologique in 1888. He described the syndrome in 1880 (*Ann. méd.-psychol., 4,* 168–74).
   Biographies: Leopoldina, 1889, 25, 70–171.

COUEISM. A method of psychotherapy through autosuggestion that involves the repetition of such phrases as, "every day in every way I am getting better and better." The effective agent of change in this method is imagery rather than motivation.

Coué, Emile. French hypnotist (b. Troyes, Aube, February 26, 1857, d. Nancy, Meurthe-et-Moselle, July 2, 1926). Coué was educated at a lycée (B.A. and B.S.). He worked as a druggist between 1882 and 1891 and from 1910 to 1926 operated a hypnotic clinic. He became interested in suggestion and hypnotism in 1901 and took up their study with Ambroise-Auguste Liébeault and Hippolyte Bernheim* Nancy. In 1910 he opened his own clinic at Nancy. Unlike other hypnotists, Coué taught his clients self-help. He thought that even organic disorders could be cured by the power of imagination, but he disclaimed any miraculous processes. Coué became famous, published a number of books (among them *Self-mastery Through Conscious Autosuggestion* (1922) and *My System* (1932), and went on lecture tours in England and the United States.

Biographies: C. Caudouin et al., *Emile Coué and His Life-Work,* 1923; *EB,* 6; E. B. Kirk, *My Pilgrimage to Coué,* 1922; H. Macnaghten, *Emile Coué: The Man and His work,* 1922; *NYT,* July 3, 1926, p. 13, col. 3; *Shepard,* 1.

COULOMB FRICTION. With reference to mechanical control system, it is the friction that does not depend on the speed of the control motion. If significant, it may adversely affect the performance of the operator.

Coulomb, Charles Augustin. French physicist (b. Angoulême, Charente, June 14, 1736, d. Paris, August 23, 1806). Coulomb made major contributions in the fields of electricity, magnetism, applied mechanics, friction studies, and torsion. In his twenties, Coulomb worked as a military engineer. Several years on the island of Martinique damaged his health. He returned to Paris in 1776, began doing scientific experiments, and spent the years of the French Revolution quietly in the provinces. In 1777 he invented the torsion balance and later used the invention to measure the magnitude of electric charges. In 1785 he formulated the relationship between the strength of attraction or repulsion of two charged spheres in terms of the amount of electricity on them and their distance. It became known as Coulomb's law. A unit of electric charge is also named after Coulomb. Coulomb's studies in ergonomics are the most significant before those of F. W. Taylor.* He read the first of his several memoirs on the subject before the French Academy of Sciences in 1778. These studies were published in 1799 as *Résultats de plusieurs expériences.*

Biographies: Asimov; DSB, 3; *EB,* 6.

CRAIK-O'BRIEN-CORNSWEET ILLUSION. When two fields of equal luminance meet at a border whose luminance profile is shaped like a double spur, all of one of the two fields appears brighter than all of the other.

Craik, Kenneth J. W. English psychologist (b. 1914, d. May 7, 1945). Craik received his Ph.D. in psychology from Cambridge University (1940). From 1939 to 1945 he was on the vision, personnel, target tracking, and similar committees of the British armed forces. He was director of the research in the applied psychology unit of the Cambridge Psychology Department from 1944 to 1945. Craik designed the Cambridge experimental cockpit, which showed the difference between skill fatigue from muscles and mental fatigue. Between 1937 and 1945 he wrote seventy-seven papers and a monograph, *The Nature of Explanation*

(1943), reissued posthumously as *The Nature of Psychology*. His description of the illusion appears in this volume.

Biographies: Brit. J. Psychol., 1946, *36*, 109–16.

O'Brien, Vivian. American physicist (b. Baltimore, Maryland, February 1, 1924). O'Brien received her Ph.D. in physics from Johns Hopkins University in 1960. She worked for Martin Company from 1945 to 1947 and has been on the Johns Hopkins faculty since 1947, now as physicist of fluid dynamics in the Applied Physics Laboratory. Her description of the illusion appeared in 1958 (*J. Opt. Soc. Amer.*, *48*, 112–19).

Biographies: AM&WS, 1982P.

Cornsweet, Tom Norman. American psychologist (b. Cleveland, Ohio, April 29, 1929). Cornsweet has a Ph.D. in experimental psychology from Brown University (1955). He has held positions at several universities and research institutes and has been with the University of California at Irvine since 1976. Cornsweet's main research areas have been vision and ophthalmic instrumentation. His contribution to the research on the luminance illusion appears in his book *Visual Perception* (1970).

Biographies: AM&WS, 1982P.

CRESPI EFFECT. In animal learning, when the amount of reward is increased, there is a disproportionate increase in response rate, to a level higher than it is for an animal trained on the same higher level from the beginning. The finding led Clark Hull to reformulate his learning theory to include the concept of incentive.

Crespi, Leo Paul. American psychologist (b. Aurora, Illinois, July 23, 1916). Crespi received the Ph.D. degree in psychology from Princeton University in 1942. He remained at Princeton until 1948, was on the staff of the U.S. military government in Germany from 1949 to 1954, and then joined the U.S. Information Agency, becoming deputy chief of public opinion research in 1970 and senior research adviser to the International Communications Agency in 1974. His major area of interest is social psychology with specialization in attitudes and opinions and cross-cultural psychology. He described the effect in 1942 (*Amer. J. Psychol.*, *55*, 467–517).

Biographies: AM&WS, 1973s; *APA Dir.*, 1985.

CROCKER-HENDERSON ODOR SYSTEM. A system for specifying smells. The strength of each of four basic components—fragrant, acid, burned, and caprylic—is rated on a scale from zero to eight, which produces a four-digit number that describes a given smell.

Crocker, Ernest Charlton. American chemist (b. Boston, June 11, 1888). Crocker graduated from MIT with a B.S. in chemistry (1914). He worked as a chemist for different companies, taught at MIT from 1919 to 1922, and then took a position as chemist with the Authur D. Little Company, Cambridge, Massachusetts. An exceptional olfactory memory—he could remember several thousand smells—aided Crocker in his work. Crocker and Henderson proposed the odor system in a 1927 article (*Amer. Perfumer Essent. Oil Rev., 22*, 325–27, 356).

Biographies: AMS, 1927; Sat. Eve. Post, Sept. 29, 1951, 224:27 +.

Henderson, Lloyd C. American chemist (b., n.a., d., n.a.).

Biographies: Unavailable

CRONBACH'S COEFFICIENT ALPHA. A coefficient that measures interitem reliability in a test and is numerically equal to the coefficient obtained by the Kuder-Richardson coefficient of equivalence.* Cronbach provided a new derivation for it using simpler assumptions.

Cronbach, Lee Joseph. American psychologist (b. Fresno, California, April 22, 1916). Cronbach received his doctorate in educational psychology from the University of Chicago. He taught at several colleges and universities, the longest at Stanford University (1964–1980), from which he retired. All of his work has been in educational psychology, evaluation and measurement, individual differences, and methodology. Cronbach's paper on the concept of construct validity, written with Paul Meehl in 1955, and the 1957 paper on the two disciplines of scientific psychology were influential. His 1949 text, *Essentials of Psychological Testing*, was widely used and saw several editions. The coefficient alpha was described in 1951 (*Psychometrika, 16*, 297–334).

Biographies: AM&WS, 1978S; APA Dir., 1985; Amer. Psychologist, 1974, 29, 27–32; *WhoAm, 1984–1985.*

CROVITZ ILLUSION. A line-length analog of the Craik-O'Brien-Cornsweet illusion.*

Crovitz, Herbert F. American psychologist (b. Providence, Rhode Island, May 21, 1932). Crovitz is an experimental psychologist (Ph.D., Duke University, 1960). He has been a research psychologist at the Veteran's Administration Medical Center, Durham, and lecturer in psychology at Duke University since 1961. He has been professor of medical psychology at the Duke University Medical School since 1973. Crovitz works in the areas of vision and memory. He has written the book *Galton's Walk* (1970) and many articles. The illusion was described in 1976 (*Vision Res., 16*, 435).

Biographies: AM&WS, 1978s; APA Dir., 1985.

CULLER'S PHI PROCESS. An obsolete method for determining the difference threshold in which the difference thresholds obtained on each trial are taken to be equal to the probable errors of the ogive distribution of the threshold measurements.

Culler, Elmer Augustin Kurtz. American psychologist (b. Louisville, Ohio, October 11, 1889, d. Columbus, Ohio, June 30, 1961). With a Ph.D. from the

University of Chicago (1922), Culler taught at several universities, mostly at the University of Illinois (1923–1938) and the University of Rochester (1938–1954). At Rochester, he was also the director of the hearing laboratory. Culler's main areas of research were conditioning, temperature sensitivity, hearing, and psychophysics. He described the phi process in 1927 (*J. Exp. Psychol., 10,* 463–77).

Biographies: APA Dir., 1960; W. J. Brogden, *Amer. J. Psychol.,* 1962, *75,* 155–60.

CURRENS FORMULA. The 1961 ruling by the Third Circuit Court of Appeals that a person is not to be held responsible for a crime if that person did not have "adequate capacity to conform his conduct to the requirements of the law" because of a mental disorder. The ruling rejected the "to appreciate the wrongfulness of his conduct" phrase in the *Brawner* decision* because of its overemphasis on the cognitive element in criminal responsibility. It is applied only in certain federal courts.

Currens, Donald Kenneth. Currens, born about 1936, was the appellant in a case of transportation of a stolen vehicle across state lines. Currens, at the time about twenty-two years old, took a vehicle from a car dealer for a tryout but never returned it, having driven it to a different state. He later claimed poor memory of the events subsequent to the theft. Currens had several prior convictions for minor offenses, was of average intelligence, but was diagnosed as being an undifferentiated schizophrenic with sociopathic tendencies.

Biographies: U.S. v. Currens, 290 F.2d 751 (1961).

CURTIS CLASSIFICATION FORM. A projective sentence-completion test for children aged eleven and older.

Curtis, James Wylie. American psychologist (b. Madison, Indiana, July 3, 1913). Curtis obtained the master's degree from the University of Kentucky in 1938 and then did two years of postgraduate work at Princeton University and the University of Panama. He has held a number of university and government positions and has been staff psychologist at the Memorial Hospital School of Nursing, Springfield, Illinois, since 1951. Curtis has produced seven other tests and has written seven books on numismatics. The test was first published in 1951.

Biographies: AM&WS, 1973S; *WhoSSW,* 1985–1986; *WoWhoSci.*

D

DALE'S PRINCIPLE. The principle that only one kind of neurotransmitter substance is produced by a given neuron.

Dale, Sir Henry Hallett. English neuropharmacologist (b. London, June 9, 1875, d. Cambridge, July 23, 1968). Dale completed his medical training at St. Bartholomew's Hospital (M.D., 1909). He was director of the Wellcome Physiological Research Laboratory (1904–1914), on the scientific staff of the Medical Research Committee (1914–1927), a member of the General Medical Council (1927–1937), director of the National Institute for Medical Research at Hampstead (1928–1942), and Crown nominee to the City of London University (1939–1950). For his work on the neurotransmitters (he isolated acetylcholine in 1914 and coined such terms as *cholinergic* and *adrenergic*), Dale was awarded the Nobel Prize in 1936.

    Biographies: Asimov; H. H. Dale, *Perspect. Biol. Med.,* 1957–58, *1,* 125–37; *DSB,* Suppl. 1; *McGMSE,* 1; *Talbot; WhAm,* 5.

DALTONISM. For a time after 1827, red-green color blindness was called daltonism and is still so called in some languages.

Dalton, John. English chemist (b. Eaglesfield, Cumberland, September 6, 1766, d. Manchester, Lancashire, July 27, 1844). Dalton was largely self-taught. He taught at New College at Manchester for six years but was a poor speaker, and he engaged in private tutoring after 1799. At age twenty-one, Dalton began meteorological observations that he continued throughout his life, and he is considered one of the pioneers in meteorology. This led to an interest in gases, vapors, and steam, areas in which he also did important work. This work, in turn, led to his formulation of the atomic theory of matter (1803), which he published in his *New*

System of Chemical Philosophy (1808). In psychology, Dalton is known for his study and description of color blindness. In a presentation to the Manchester Literary and Philosophical Society on October 31, 1794 (*Mem. Lit. Phil. Soc. Manchester,* 1798, *5,* pt. 1, 28–45), Dalton described his own inability to see reds and greens, as well as some other cases of color blindness. The study and understanding of color blindness dates from 1794.

Biographies: Asimov; DNB, 5; *DSB,* 3, 15; *EB,* 7; F. Greenway, *John Dalton and the Atom,* 1966; E. C. Patterson, *John Dalton and the Atomic Theory,* 1970; A. Thackray, *John Dalton,* 1972.

DARWINIAN FITNESS. The extent to which an organism is capable of producing viable offspring.

DARWINIAN REFLEX. Observable in premature infants and infants up to the age of four months, it is the involuntary closing of the hand over objects that stimulate the palm. It decreases in strength over the first four months of life and is replaced by the voluntary grasp.

DARWINISM. The theory of evolution, especially its aspects of natural selection or survival of the fittest (Herbert Spencer's phrase), as in social darwinism.

Darwin, Charles. English naturalist (b. Shrewsbury, Shropshire, February 12, 1809, d. Down, Kent, April 19, 1882). Darwin first studied medicine at Edinburgh and then went to Cambridge to study for the ministry, graduating in 1831. He spent the next five years as a naturalist on the H. M. S. Beagle, making a large number of systematic, comparative observations and collecting specimens. Soon after his return, Darwin read Malthus'* *Essay on the Principle of Population,* which furnished him with the idea that the struggle for existence would favor the survival of the favorable variations of plants and animals while unfavorable ones would perish. Darwin marshaled the evidence for evolution as no one else had done and provided a theory of how evolution happens in his *Origin of Species* (1859). He spent the rest of his life developing and defending his ideas.

Biographies: P. Appelman (ed.), *Darwin,* 1970; *Asimov;* G. De Beer, *Charles Darwin: A Scientific Biography,* 1965; *DNB,* 5; *DSB,* 3; *EB,* 7; *IESS,* 4; R. Olby, *Charles Darwin,* 1967; W. Wichler, *Charles Darwin,* 1961.

DASHIELL MAZE. A maze with several correct paths to the goal.

Dashiell, John Frederick. American psychologist (b. Indianapolis, Indiana, April 30, 1888, d. Alexandria, Virginia, May 3, 1975). After receiving his Ph.D. in psychology from Columbia University (1913), Dashiell taught at several universities before settling down at the University of North Carolina (1919–1958). From 1920 to 1949, he was chairman of the Psychology Department, which he had organized. Here, psychology was taught to undergraduates as a natural science, with a full laboratory, the first such program in the United States.

Dashiell was an experimentalist who worked in a wide variety of areas. After retirement in 1958, he continued teaching at Wake Forest College and the University of Florida until 1974. He described the new maze in 1919 (with R. H. Stetson, *Psychol. Bull.*, *16*, 223–30).
   Biographies: Amer. Psychologist, 1960, *15*, 798–99; *HPA*, 5; *NCAB*, F; *WhAm*, 6.

DAVIS-EELLS GAMES. A test of general intelligence for children in grades one through six. The test requires no reading; all instructions are given orally. It consists of pictures with multiple choice answers in the areas of verbal problems, money problems, best-way problems, and analogies.

Davis, Allison. American social anthropologist (b. Washington, D.C., October 14, 1902, d. Chicago, Illinois, November 21, 1983). Davis did field research in social anthropology at Harvard University in the mid-1930s and taught at other universities. Most of his career was at the University of Chicago (1939–1970). Davis was the author or coauthor of eight books in the field. He and Eells published the test in 1953.
   Biographies: WhAm, 8.

Eells, Kenneth Walter. American psychologist (b. Seattle, Washington, August 31, 1913). Eells obtained the Ph.D. degree in educational psychology from the University of Chicago (1948), holding positions as research psychologist and instructor at various universities and in the U.S. Navy from 1945 to 1955. He was at the University of Illinois from 1955 to 1961 and at California Institute of Technology from 1961 to 1972. His research has been in the areas of student counseling, psychological testing, and student use of drugs.
   Biographies: AM&WS, 1973S; *APA Dir.*, 1969.

DAZZLE REFLEX OF PEIPER. When a bright light is applied to an infant's eyes, the eyelids close immediately and remain closed as long as the stimulus lasts.

Peiper, Albrecht. German pediatrician (b. Greifswald, Rostock, October 23, 1889, d. Leipzig, October 7, 1968). Peiper worked in Berlin from 1930 to 1943, in Greifswald from 1943 to 1948, and in Leipzig from 1948 to 1958. He wrote five books on infants, the infant nervous system, and the history of pediatrics.
   Biographies: Brockhaus, 14; A. Peiper, *Erinnerungen eines Kinderarztes*, 1967.

DECIBEL. A unit of sound pressure, equal to one-tenth of a bel, a less-often-used measure. Bels are obtained by taking the common logarithm of the ratio of two intensities or energies. Because energy in a sound wave is proportional to the square of the pressure, the number of decibels is obtained by taking ten times the logarithm of the ratio of the two pressures squared, or twenty logarithms of the ratio of the simple pressures.

Bell, Alexander Graham. Scottish-American inventor (b. Edinburgh, Scotland, March 3, 1847, d. Baddeck, Nova Scotia, August 2, 1922). Between 1868 and 1870, Bell worked with his father, a pioneer in teaching speech to the deaf. The family went to Canada in 1870. Bell left Canada for the United States in 1871 and in 1873 was teaching vocal physiology at Boston University. Bell had conceived of the idea of electrical voice transmission as early as 1865. He patented the telephone in 1876, and in 1877 the Bell Telephone Company was founded. He also invented the carbon microphone, the photophone, the first practical sound record, the audiometer, the metal locator, and many other devices. He founded the journal *Science,* still the official organ of the American Association for the Advancement of Science.

  Biographies: Asimov; DAB, 2; *DE; DSB,* 1; *EB,* 3; *NCAB,* 6.

DECROLY METHOD. A set of educational principles based on psychological insights that deviate considerably from traditional pedagogical prescriptions. The main principles are that the school should be a simple and natural environment that resembles real life and that school activities should be based on real life; children should prepare themselves to live in the real world by experiencing it in the school through mental and physical exercises, play, and games that lead to easy and natural concept acquisition. Formal drill in reading, writing, and arithmetic is subordinated to this goal.

Decroly, Ovide Jean. Belgian psychologist (b. Ronse [Renaix], Belgium, July 23, 1871, d. Brussels, September 12, 1932). Although Decroly was a *Dr. en médecine* (University of Ghent, 1896), his main interest was in educational psychology. Between 1901 and 1919 he held a variety of positions with schools and institutions for children. A 1910 paper, written with J. Degand, introduced the relationship between social class and intelligence as an area of study. Decroly published eight books in the area of child psychology, and some 130 additional titles in this and the areas of intelligence, educational psychology, and the exceptional child. He was at the University of Brussels from 1919 to 1932.

  Biographies: CE, 4; J. Nuttin, *Psychology in Belgium,* 1961; M. Peers, *Ovide Decroly,* 1942; *PR,* 3.

DEITERS'S CELLS. Elongated cells that support the hair cells in the outer portion of the organ of Corti.*

DEITERS'S NUCLEUS. The lateral vestibular nucleus of the brain.

Deiters, Otto Friedrich Karl. German physician (b. Bonn, November 15, 1834, d. Bonn, December 5, 1863). Deiters published an article on cells as early as 1849. He was in military service in Berlin in 1859 and also worked in Wirchow's Pathological Institute. He obtained his medical degree from the University of Bonn a year later and started work at that university in 1858 but died of typhus five years later. His studies on the nervous system were published posthumously by Max Schultze in *Untersuchungen über Gehirn und Rückenmark der Menschen und Saugtiere* (1865).

Biographies: Pagel, *Biog. Lex.; EI*, 12.

DE LANGE SYNDROME. See CORNELIA DE LANGE SYNDROME

DELBOEUF ILLUSION. The apparent change in size in one of two adjacent circles of identical size if another, larger concentric circle is placed around it.

Delboeuf, Joseph Remi Leopold. Belgian psychologist (b. Liège, September 30, 1831, d. Bonn, Germany, August 14, 1896). Delboeuf obtained a Ph.D. and taught at the universities of Ghent (1863–1866) and Liège (1866–1896). Under the influence of G. T. Fechner,* Delboeuf began psychophysical experimentation on brightness in 1865. In this field, his contributions rank right after those of Fechner himself and Georg Müller.* Delboeuf published several critical monographs on psychophysics between 1873 and 1883. During the last years of his life, Delboeuf turned his attention to hypnotism and wrote a volume on this subject. He presented the illusion in 1893 (*Bull. Acad. roy. belge*, 24, 545–58).

Biographies: G. S. Hall, *Amer. J. Psychol.*, 1896, 8, 312; J. Nuttin, *Psychology in Belgium*, 1961.

DELPHI METHOD. A method for predicting future events in which the opinions of a number of experts are pooled to arrive at a single prediction.

Delphi. A place in ancient Greece considered by the Greeks to be the center of the earth and site of a famous temple to Apollo and his most renowned oracle. The prestige of the oracle reached a peak in the sixth century B.C. It was consulted on matters both private and public, its utterances determining such national decisions as the sites of new Greek colonies and the waging of wars.

DEMOSTHENES COMPLEX. The neurotic need to master feelings of inferiority through the use of words in oral discourse.

Demosthenes. Greek statesman and orator (b. Athens, 384 or 383 B.C., d. island of Calauria, 322 B.C.). Demosthenes began as a speech writer for private litigants, and then became involved in Athenian political life; he eventually became the leading politician in Athens. He was also the greatest of Greek orators. His three speeches against the Macedonian king Philip gave rise to the eponym *philippic*. Initially, however, Demosthenes had to fight hard to overcome physical defects that interfered with his speech. According to one legend, in order to strengthen his voice to make it understandable before a noisy audience, he practiced speaking amid the noise of a beating surf while holding pebbles in his mouth.

Biographies: EB, 7.

DENNIE-MARFAN SYNDROME. Spastic paraplegia accompanied by mental retardation in children suffering from congenital syphilis.

Dennie, Charles Clayton. American dermatologist (b. Excelsior Springs, Missouri, October 20, 1883, d. Kansas City, Missouri, January 13, 1971). Dennie received the M.D. degree from the University of Kansas in 1912. He was in private practice in Kansas City from 1914 to 1917 and held various hospital appointments there from 1918 to 1968. Dennie also taught at the University of Kansas (from 1937) and the University of Missouri (from 1966). His main work was on syphilis, in which area he wrote three books. He described the syndrome in 1929 (*Amer. J. Syph.*, *13*, 157–63).
  Biographies: NCAB, 57; *WhAm*, 5.

Marfan, Jean-Bernard-Antoine. French pediatrician (b. Castelnaudary, Aude, June 23, 1858, d. Paris, 1942). Marfan's medical degree was from the University of Paris (1887), and he held various positions in the medical school and hospital of that university from 1889 until his retirement. Marfan wrote several volumes on childhood diseases. His description of the syndrome appeared in 1936 (*Rev. franc. pédiat.*, *12*, 1–16).
  Biographies: Fischer, *Biog. Lex.*; Pagel, *Biog. Lex.*

DENVER DEVELOPMENTAL SCREENING TEST. Evaluates the motor, language, social, and adaptive abilities of children through age six by the use of various objects supplied with the test and parental observations of behavior.

Denver. The test was first constructed by William K. Frankenburg in 1968 and published by Ladoca Publishing Company, Denver, Colorado.

DERCUM'S DISEASE. A rare disease, adiposis dolorosa, with onset at about midlife. The person becomes obese, and there is sharp pain in areas of abnormal fat accumulation. The disorder is accompanied by mental deterioration, loss of memory, and emotional disturbance. Epileptic convulsions may also be present.

Dercum, Francis Xavier. American neurologist (b. Philadelphia, August 10, 1856, d. Philadelphia, April 23, 1931). Dercum had an M.D. and a Ph.D. from the University of Pennsylvania, both obtained in 1877. He began practice in Philadelphia in 1877 and was on the faculties of the University of Philadelphia (1879–1892) and the Jefferson Medical College (1892–1925). Dercum was first to photograph people having convulsions, some of which were obtained by suggesting seizures hypnotically. Dercum wrote five books and a number of papers on medical subjects. The disease was described in 1892.
  Biographies: DAB, Suppl. 1; *NCAB*, 22; *WhAm*, 1; *WoWhoSci*.

DESPERT FABLES. English version of the fables used by the French psychoanalyst L. Duss in 1950 as a projective test for children. The test consists of the child's solutions to problems represented in each of ten short fables.

Despert, Juliette Louise. American psychiatrist (b. Versailles, France, June 9, 1892). Despert became an American citizen in 1930 and obtained the M.D. degree from New York University in 1932. After her internship and residency years, she was a research associate and professor at Cornell University from 1937 to 1960, going into private practice in 1960. Despert has written eight books on emotional problems in children, including *Children of Divorce* (1953). She is also an artist.

    Biographies: Biog. Dir. APA, 1977; *ConAu,* 69; *WhoAmWom,* 1972.

DEVELOPMENTAL GERSTMANN'S SYNDROME. A complex of symptoms that includes difficulty in learning to read, to write, to do arithmetic, and to make right-left discriminations. It is present in children with minimal brain damage.

Gerstmann, Josef. See under GERSTMANN'S SYNDROME.

DEVEREUX ELEMENTARY SCHOOL RATING SCALE. A scale used with emotionally disturbed and retarded children, aged eight to twelve, to assess behavior in seventeen areas, such as distractibility, self-care, emotional detachment, and sociability.

Devereux Foundation. The foundation is an institution for study, education, and research in medicine and psychology concerning children with emotional and learning problems. It operates the Devereux Schools, the largest school system of its kind in the world. It was founded by Helena Trafford Devereux (1885–1975), with campuses in Devon and other places in Pennsylvania and in five other states. The rating scale was constructed by George Spivack and Jules Spotts in 1967 and published by the Devereux Foundation.

DIANA COMPLEX. In psychoanalysis, the repressed desire of a woman to be a man.

Diana. In ancient Greece, Diana was the goddess of the hunt, a predominantly male pursuit.

DITCHBURN-RIGGS EFFECT. The name initially given to the phenomenon of the rapid cessation of vision of contours when the image of the contours, cast upon the retina by the lens of the eye, undergoes prolonged stabilization with respect to the retina. The stabilization is achieved optically by having the retinal image undergo the same physiological tremor experienced by the eyeball.

Ditchburn, Robert William. English physicist (b. January 14, 1903). Ditchburn graduated from Cambridge University. He was a fellow at Trinity College in Dublin from 1928 to 1946 and professor of natural and experimental philosophy at the University of Dublin from 1929 to 1946. He went to the University of Reading in 1946, becoming emeritus professor in 1968. Ditchburn wrote *Light* in 1952 and *Eye-Movements and Visual Perception* in 1973. In 1952, Ditchburn and B. L. Ginsborg described the first experiments in which the retinal image was optically stopped (*Nature*, 170, 36–37).
   Biographies: Who, 1986–1987.

Riggs, Lorrin A. American psychologist (b. Harput, Turkey, June 11, 1912). Riggs' Ph.D. was from Clark University (1936). He taught for four years at the University of Vermont and went to Brown University in 1941. His work has been devoted to the study of events in the visual system. He developed a more effective way of recording the human electroretinogram and studied eye movements in relation to visual acuity. It was in connection with this work that he developed a method for stabilizing the retinal image a year after Ditchburn and independently of him (with F. Ratliff, J. C. Cornsweet, and T. N. Cornsweet,* *J. Opt. Soc. Amer.*, 1953, *43*, 495–501). Riggs' latest work concerns the interaction between color and form perception and the investigation of color, form, movement, and spatial frequency channels.
   Biographies: AM&WS, 1982P; Amer. Psychologist, 1975, 30, 54–58.

DODGE MIRROR TACHISTOSCOPE. One of the early forms of a device for brief presentations of visual stimuli. It had no moving parts, both the fixation and exposure fields being successively presented in the same spot of a half-silvered mirror at 45 degrees to the line of sight by the turning on and off of two light bulbs.

Dodge, Raymond. American psychologist (b. Woburn, Massachusetts, February 20, 1871, d. Tryon, North Carolina, April 8, 1942). Dodge was a versatile and productive experimental psychologist (Ph.D., University of Halle, 1896). He was at Wesleyan University from 1898 to 1924. While in the military service during World War I, Dodge invented a device for recording gun pointing by navy trainees that was used by all U.S. Navy training stations and by the British Navy. At Yale University from 1924 to 1936, he was one of the founders of the Institute of Human Relations. Dodge's main areas of research were motor performance, vestibular reactions, and vision and visual perception, particularly eye move-ments. He was first to measure and classify eye movements. He described the mirror tachistoscope in 1907 (*Psychol. Bull.*, *4*, 10–13). Dodge had earlier (1901) invented an apparatus for recording horizontal and vertical eye movement and had been coinventor of the Erdmann-Dodge tachistoscope.*
   Biographies: EB, 7; HPA, 1; NCAB, 32, E; C. E. Seashore, Science, 1942, 95, 472–73; R. S. Woodworth, Psychol. Rev., 49, 395–402.

DOGIEL CORPUSCLE. A transitional or developmental form of nerve ending, either of the Krause end bulb or of the Meissner corpuscle,* found in the mucous membranes of the nose, mouth, eyes, and so on.

Dogiel (Dogel'), Aleksandr Stanislavovich. Russian histologist (b. Panevežys, Lithuania, January 27, 1852, d. Petrograd, November 19, 1922). Dogiel studied medicine at the University of Kazan', obtaining his M.D. in 1883. He taught embryology there from 1885 to 1888, moving to the University of Tomsk and, again, to St. Petersburg in 1895, where he held positions at the Women's Medical Institute. He organized a histological laboratory there that eventually attracted worldwide attention. Dogiel was considered the most distinguished Russian neurohistologist. His work centered on the histological structure of nerve fibers, especially sensory nerve endings, and their distribution.
Biographies: Haymaker; Soviet.

DONATISM. An early stage of the hypnotic state in which the subject follows suggestions while being still aware of them and is able to remember them later.

Donato (pseudonym of Alfred d'Hondt). Belgian stage hypnotist (b. 1845, d. 1900). Donato was one of the best-known stage hypnotists of his time. He called this early stage of the hypnotic state "fascination." It was named cataplexy by medical researchers.
Biographies: Unavailable.

DONDERS' LAW. Every line of regard with respect to an object fixated is independent of the prior eye movements executed to arrive at this position and corresponds to a definite and invariable angle of torsion of the eyes.

DONDERS' METHOD. The method of subtracting discrimination reaction time from choice reaction time to measure the time taken by a choice decision and of subtracting simple reaction time from discrimination reaction time to measure the time required to make a discrimination.

Donders, Franciscus Cornelis. Dutch ophthalmologist (b. Tilburg, May 27, 1818, d. Utrecht, March 24, 1889). Donders, who received his M.D. from the University of Utrecht in 1842, taught at a military school in Utrecht (1842–1852) and the University of Utrecht (1852–1889). He did some work in areas of interest to psychology: eye movements, accommodation, the formation of vowel sounds, and reaction time, the last being by far the most important. He published his first report on reaction time in 1865. It linked reaction time to the speed of thought and inaugurated the so-called age of mental chronometry. The principle concerning lines of regard was published in 1846 (*Ned. Lancet, 2,* 104–38, 345–80, 432–63, 537–68, 641–55), and the subtraction procedure was first described in 1868 (*Arch. Anat. Physiol., 6,* 657–81).

Biographies: W. Bowman, *Acta Psychologica,* 1969, *30,* 389–408; *DSB,* 4; *EB,* 7; E. C. v. Leersum (ed.), *The Life Work of Franciscus Cornelis Donders,* 1932; R. L. Pfeiffer, *Bull. NY Acad. Med.,* 1936, *12,* 566–81; H. W. Williams, *Proc. Amer. Acad. Arts Sci.,* 1889, *24,* 465–70.

DON JUANISM. Another term for satyriasis or inordinate sexual urge in the human male.

Don Juan. Originally a folklore figure, or possibly a real one (fourteenth-century Spanish nobleman Don Juan Tenorio), Don Juan was made a literary persona in Tirso de Molina's drama, *El Burlador de Sevilla,* written in 1630, after which the character received numerous treatments in plays, poems, and dramas in Spain, Italy, France, Germany, England, and other countries, becoming a symbol of licentiousness and libertinism. The central plot of all Don Juan stories tells of how, after many affairs and amorous adventures, Don Juan dishonors a girl from a noble family, kills her father who tries to avenge her, invites to dinner the stone effigy of the father placed on his tomb, and the stone visitor actually arriving for dinner, which leads to Don Juan's death.

DOPPLER EFFECT. Also referred to as the Doppler principle or Doppler shift, it is the heightening and lowering of the pitch of a moving sound source as perceived by a stationary listener, depending on whether the sound source approaches or recedes from the listener. The phenomenon is also observed with light. If the light source moves with sufficient speed, a shift may be observed in its spectrum.

Doppler, Johann Christian. Austrian physicist (b. Salzburg, November 29, 1803, d. Venice, Italy [then part of Austria], March 17, 1853). From 1822 to 1829 Doppler received both public and private education. He was a mathematics assistant in Vienna from 1829 to 1833. He taught mathematics in Prague from 1835 to 1841 and became a professor of mathematics at the State Technical Academy in 1841. In 1842, Doppler stated the mathematical relationship between the pitch of the sound produced by a moving sound source and its position relative to the perceiver. Doppler's paper, read on May 25 (and published in *Abh. Kön. böhm. Ges. Wiss.,* 5th ser., *2,* 465), actually concerned the change in color of a moving light source, but he also applied the principle to acoustic waves. A few years later, the relationship was confirmed experimentally by Buy Ballot. Doppler moved to the Mining Academy at Chemnitz in 1847 but soon returned to Vienna, to become professor of experimental physics (first in the world) at the University of Vienna in 1850.

Biographies: Asimov; DSB, 4; *EB,* 7.

DOWN'S SYNDROME. A congenital disorder, formerly known as mongolism, caused by the failure of chromosome 21 to separate in meiosis. Children born of germ cells with an extra chromosome 21 have a physical appearance characterized by a flattened face, Oriental eye-fold pattern, straight hair, and thick, fissured tongue. They also have internal disorders and are usually, but not invariably, mentally retarded.

Down, John Langdon Haydon. English physician (b. Torpoint, Cornwall, 1828, d. 1896). With a University of London doctorate in medicine (1859), Down taught medicine at various hospitals and was superintendent of the Earlwood Asylum from 1858 to 1868. He wrote *Nature's Balance* and medical papers, most of them on mental disorders, feeblemindedness, and the accompanying physical changes. Down described the syndrome in 1866 (*London Hosp. Clin. Lect. Rep., 3,* 224–36, 259–62).
  Biographies: Allibone, Suppl. 1; Hirsch, *Biog. Lex.*

DUNCAN'S MULTIPLE RANGE TEST. An a posteriori multiple comparison procedure for all pairwise comparisons between means.

Duncan, David Beattie. Australian-American statistician (b. Sydney, Australia, June 16, 1916). Duncan came to reside in the United States in 1950. He had already obtained his Ph.D. in mathematical statistics from Iowa State College in 1947. He had been at the University of Sydney from 1938 to 1950 and held positions at various American universities from 1950 onward. He went to Johns Hopkins University in 1961 and became professor emeritus in 1977. The test was presented in 1955 (*Biometrics, 11,* 1–42).
  Biographies: AM&WS, 1979P; *WhoAm,* 1980–1981.

DUNLAP CHRONOSCOPE. Also known as the Johns Hopkins chronoscope, it was driven by a ten-pole synchronous motor, with a double magnetic clutch for stopping and starting the hands of the clock.

Dunlap, Knight. American psychologist (b. Diamond Springs, California, November 21, 1875, d. Columbus, South Carolina, August 14, 1949). Dunlap was a versatile general psychologist (Ph.D. from Harvard University, 1903) who worked and published in a wide variety of areas, from ocular nystagmus to the social psychology of religion. In addition to the chronoscope, developed before 1914, Dunlap invented such pieces of apparatus as a chair for vestibular investigations and a steadiness plate. Dunlap spent most of his professional life at Johns Hopkins University (1906–1936) and the University of California at Los Angeles (1936–1946).
  Biographies: R. M. Dorcus, *Amer. J. Psychol.,* 1950, *63,* 114–19; *HPA,* 2; K. G. Moore, *Psychol. Rev.,* 1949, *56,* 309–10; *NCAB,* 39; *WhAm,* 2.

DUNNETT TEST. A statistical test of significance between k treatments and a control. A single level of significance is set for all comparisons, the decision being considered a single decision that summarizes the outcomes.

Dunnett, Charles William. Canadian mathematician (b. Windsor, Ontario, August 24, 1921). Dunnett received the M.A. degree from the University of Toronto in 1946, subsequently holding positions at various Canadian and American universities. He was with Lederle Laboratories from 1953 to 1974 and has been with McMaster University since 1977. Dunnett received a D.Sc. from the University of Aberdeen in 1960. His field has been the design and analysis of experiments and medical statistics. The test was published in 1955 (*J. Amer. Stat. Ass.*, *50*, 1096–1121).
   Biographies: AM&WS, 1982P.

DUNN'S MULTIPLE COMPARISON PROCEDURE. A statistical procedure that makes a priori comparisons among all planned means, not just those that are orthogonal.

Dunn, Olive Jean. American mathematician and biostatistician (b. Winnipeg, Canada, September 1, 1915). Dunn received the Ph.D. in mathematics from the University of California at Los Angeles (1956). She taught biostatistics and biomathematics at the UCLA School of Public Health and School of Medicine from 1957 onward. The author of the multiple comparison procedure is unknown. Dunn examined it in detail and prepared tables for ease in its use (*J. Amer. Stat. Ass.*, 1961, *56*, 52–64).
   Biographies: AM&WS, 1982P.

***DURHAM* DECISION.** The decision made by the U.S. Court of Appeals for the District of Columbia in 1954 to the effect that "an accused is not criminally responsible if his unlawful act was the product of mental disease or mental defect." The difficulties that have arisen in the application of this decision center on the precise meanings of *product, mental disease,* and *mental defect.* The *Durham* test has not been adopted by any other U.S. court.

Durham, Monte. Durham was discharged from the U.S. Navy as unfit for naval service because of "profound personality disorder." It was 1945, and Durham was seventeen years old. In the following years he generated a history of repeated thefts and burglaries, psychiatric diagnoses of psychosis and psychopathic personality, psychiatric hospitalization, and repeated releases as "improved." *Durham* arose from his having been caught burglarizing an apartment in 1951.
   Biographies: Durham v. U.S., 214 F.2d 862 (1954).

DVORINE COLOR PERCEPTION TESTING CHARTS. First American-made test for color blindness that was based on the same principle as the Stilling* and Ishihara* color-blindness tests. It differs from the Ishihara test in that the arrangement of dots prevents the recognition of patterns of dots by the color-blind and in the number of pseudoisochromatic plates used (seventy training, sixty test).

Dvorine, Israel. American optometrist (b. 1900). Dvorine wrote *Theory and Practice of Analytical Refraction and Orthoptics* in 1939 and published the first edition of the color blindness test in 1944. It was renamed *Dvorine Pseudoisochromatic Plates* in its second edition (1953).
   Biographies: Unavailable.

DWYER ALGORITHM. In factorial designs, a least-squares solution used with unequal numbers per cell. The procedure is also applied to inverting small, symmetric matrices in the process of obtaining regression weights for multiple prediction schemes.

Dwyer, Paul Sumner. American statistician (b. Chester, Pennsylvania, December 8, 1901). Dwyer received the Ph.D. degree from the University of Michigan in 1936. He was at Pennsylvania State University from 1921 to 1926, Antioch College from 1926 to 1936, and the University of Michigan from 1936 to 1971. The algorithm appears in his *Linear Computations* (1951).
   Biographies: AM&WS, 1972P; *WhoMW,* 1982–1983.

E

EBBINGHAUS COLOR PYRAMID. A forerunner of the color spindle, the color pyramid consisted of two pyramids with a common base of rounded corners, in which hues were located on the periphery of the base, gray in its middle, and black and white at the two apexes.

EBBINGHAUS CURVE. A curve that shows the course of forgetting of non-meaningful materials, such as nonsense syllables. The amount retained decreases sharply immediately after learning, with relatively little loss over the following days and weeks.

EBBINGHAUS FIGURE. Synonymous with Titchener circles,* this is a geometric illusion in which the one of two circles of the same size that is surrounded by other, smaller circles appears larger than the circle surrounded by circles larger than itself.

EBBINGHAUS TEST. A recall test consisting of sentences in which a word or words are left blank, to be filled in by the person tested. It is also known as the completion test.

Ebbinghaus, Hermann. German psychologist (b. Barmen [now part of Wuppertal], North Rhine-Westphalia, January 24, 1850, d. Halle, February 26, 1909). After obtaining a Ph.D. in philosophy from the University of Bonn in 1873, Ebbinghaus studied independently for seven years. He subsequently held appointments at the universities of Berlin (1880–1893), Breslau (1894–1905), and Halle (1905–1908). It was during the period of independent research that Ebbinghaus decided to study memory, devised the methodology to do so, including the invention of nonsense syllables as the material to be memorized, and conducted a series of experiments. The experimental study of human learning and memory begins with Ebbinghaus. The color pyramid appears in his *Grundzüge der Psychologie* (1902, vol. 1, p. 184). The forgetting curve was published in his classic 1885 monograph, *Memory*. The Ebbinghaus figure was probably first presented in his *Grundzüge*. It is also called Titchener circles because E. B. Titchener* used it in his *Experimental Psychology* (1901–1905). The completion test technique was introduced by Ebbinghaus while at the University of Breslau (*Z. Psychol.*, 1897, *13*, 401–59).

Biographies: EB, 7; *IESS,* 4; L. Postman, *Amer. Psychologist,* 1968, *23,* 149–57; D. Shakow, *Amer. J. Psychol.,* 1930, *42,* 505–18; R. S. Woodworth, *J. Phil.,* 1909, *6,* 253–56.

EDWARDS PERSONAL PREFERENCE SCHEDULE. A personality inventory that measures the strength of fifteen manifest needs, taken from Henry Murray's system of needs. The needs are represented by statements of experiences or activities, each paired with another statement of equal social desirability, a total of 225 items.

Edwards, Allen Louis. American psychologist (b. Houston, Texas, April 15, 1914). Edwards' work has centered on the application of statistical methods to psychological problems, specifically the design of experiments and the measurement of personality variables. With a Ph.D. in general psychology from Northwestern University (1940), Edwards worked for the War Department during World War II and held academic appointments at several universities. He was at the University of Washington from 1944 until his retirement as emeritus professor in 1984. Among his works are *Techniques of Attitude Scale Construction* (1957), *The Measurement of Personality Traits by Scales and Inventories* (1970), *Experimental Design in Psychological Research* (4th ed. 1972), and several texts on statistics. The test was published in 1954.

Biographies: AM&WS, 1978S; *APA Dir.,* 1985.

EGAN EFFECT. The loudness of speech in one ear is increased if noise is applied to the opposite ear.

Egan, James Pendleton. American psychologist (b. Missouri Valley, Iowa, August 4, 1917). Egan received a Ph.D. in psychoacoustics from Harvard University in 1947, and psychoacoustics has remained his main area of interest and research. Egan has held positions at the universities of Wisconsin (1947–1951), Indiana (1951–1968), Washington (1968–1970), Texas at Austin (1970–1974), and Washington State University (since 1974). He first described the effect in 1948 (*J. Acoust. Soc. Amer.,* 20, 58–62).

Biographies: AM&WS, 1978S.

EHRENSTEIN FIGURE. A geometric illusion in which a square, placed in a sheaf of lines radiating from a common point, appears to assume a trapezoidal shape, with the base facing that point.

EHRENSTEIN ILLUSION. If, in a square grid of lines, the ends of the four lines that converge to form a node are removed so that a blank spot results, the spot assumes a circular shape and its brightness is apparently enhanced.

Ehrenstein, Walter. German psychologist (b. 1899). Ehrenstein belonged to the Leipzig Gestalt school of psychology and wrote books on holistic psychology (*Ganzheitspsychologie*), such as *Probleme der ganzheitspsychologischen Wahrnehmungslehre* (1954), and on mass psychology. The Ehrenstein figure appeared in 1924 (*Z. Psychol., 95,* 305–52) and the illusion in 1941 (*Z. Psychol., 150,* 83–91).
  Biographies: Unavailable.

ELBERFELD HORSES. A group of horses trained to respond to very slight cues, unnoticeable to the audience, seemingly to perform high-caliber mental operations, such as arithmetic. They tapped out their answers to questions with their hoofs. The most famous of these horses, Clever Hans,* was trained by Herr von Osten and exhibited in Berlin, later in Elberfeld by Karl Krall, who trained the other Elberfeld horses.

Elberfeld. A town in North Rhine-Westphalia, first mentioned in the twelfth century. Independent until 1929, it was joined with Barmen and other smaller towns into a complex that a year later was named Wuppertal.

ELECTRA COMPLEX. In Freudian theory, the repressed desire of the girl for a love relationship with her father and the consequent anxiety over the possible loss of her mother's love and nurturance. It is the female counterpart of the Oedipus complex.*

Electra. In Greek mythology, Electra was the daughter of Agamemnon and Clytemnestra. Clytemnestra took a lover, and together they killed Agamemnon. Out of her love for her father, Electra arranged for Orestes,* her brother, to kill their mother and her lover.

ELGIN CHECK LIST. A list of behavior items found more frequently among psychotic than among normal individuals.

Elgin. The name derives from Elgin State Hospital, Elgin, Illinois. The checklist was developed by M. P. Wittman in 1941 (*Elgin State Hospital Papers, 4,* 20–33).

ELLIS HARMONICAL. A specially tuned harmonium for demonstrating pitches not found in the ordinary harmonium.

Ellis, Alexander John. English philologist (b. Hoxton, Middlesex, June 14, 1814, d. West Kensington, London, October 28, 1890). A bequest from a relative enabled Ellis to go to school and devote his life to study and research. He graduated from Trinity College, Cambridge, in 1837. Ellis first wrote on mathematics, then took interest in phonetic reform and, with Isaac Pitman, devised a phonetic alphabet for English. Beginning with 1860 and for the rest of his life Ellis' interest was in the history of English pronunciation. He produced *On Early English Pronunciation* from 1869 to 1889. His interest in musical theory arose in this connection. Ellis described the harmonical in his 1875 translation of Hermann von Helmholtz's *Sensations of Tone*. About one-third of the work was Ellis' original contribution.

Biographies: DNB, Suppl. vol. 2.

EMMERT'S LAW. If l is the linear size of an object, d its distance from the observer, L the linear size of the object's afterimage (or eidetic image), and D the distance between the observer and the surface on which the afterimage is seen, then $l/L = d/D$.

Emmert, Emil. Swiss ophthalmologist (b. Bern, December 1, 1844, d. Bern, October 10, 1911). In the 1870s, having just obtained his M.D. from the University of Bern (1868), Emmert published five books on vision, visual perception, and the eye. His one lasting contribution to psychology, the law of afterimage size, was made in an 1881 article (*Klin. Mittbl. Augenheilk., 19,* 443–50).

Biographies: Fischer, Biog. Lex.; Pagel, *Biog. Lex.*

ERDMANN-DODGE TACHISTOSCOPE. A tachistoscope that recorded both the direction and the reaction time of the eyes as they moved to look at a briefly exposed peripheral stimulus.

Erdmann, Benno. German philosopher and psychologist (b. Guhren near Glogau, Silesia, May 30, 1851, d. Berlin, June 7, 1921). Erdmann had a Ph.D. in philosophy (University of Berlin, 1873) and held positions at the universities of Kiel (1878–1884), Breslau (1884–1890), Halle (1890–1898), Bonn (1898–1901), and Berlin (1876–1878, 1909–1921). As a psychologist, Erdmann was interested in thinking. Between 1900 and 1920 he wrote three books on this subject. The tachistoscope was developed in the 1890s when Raymond Dodge was studying with Erdmann at Halle. They jointly published a book on reading and eye movements (1898).

Biographies: R. Dodge, Amer. J. Psychol., 1922, *33,* 155–56.

Dodge, Raymond. See under DODGE MIRROR TACHISTOSCOPE.

EST. Acronym for Erhard Seminars Training, the name of a mind training movement and the Latin word for *is,* intended to reflect the central idea of Erhard's philosophy. The seminars are conducted on two consecutive weekends and include elements of the various disciplines that Erhard had tried himself, especially Mind Dynamics, Silva mind control,* zen, motivational courses for salesmen, and the conditioning phenomena observed in the state of transmarginal inhibition. The est adage of "what is, is; what isn't, isn't" is as old as philosophy itself, but the success of est is attributable to the modern package in which the idea is presented.

Erhard, Werner. American businessman and leader of consciousness movement (b. Philadelphia, Pennsylvania, September 5, 1935). Born John Paul Rosenberg, Erhard graduated from high school in 1952, married, held a variety of jobs, and abandoned his wife and four children around 1959, changing his name to Werner Erhard. When he moved to the West Coast in the 1960s, Erhard began taking consciousness-enhancement courses and following disciplines in the human potential movement. He was most attracted to mind dynamics, becoming its most successful teacher. He quit mind dynamics, and, with the help of some of the instructors he had trained at mind dynamics, started an organization of his own, est, on October 4, 1971. The est seminars have since become a great success, with centers in many U.S. and foreign cities and associated commercial enterprises.
   Biographies: W. W. Bartley III, *The Transformation of Man,* 1978; M. Brewer, *Psychol. Today,* August 1975, 35–40, 82, 88–89; *CurBio,* 1977; *WhoAm,* 1982–1983.

EROS. In Freud's* theory, the collective name for all life-sustaining drives, including the sex drive.

EROTIC APATHY. Sexual apathy; abnormally low level of sexual interest.

EROTICISM. Sexual excitement; higher than average disposition to become interested or excited sexually; sexual excitement arising from areas other than the genitals, such as anal eroticism.

EROTIZATION. In psychoanalysis, the process whereby a part of the body or a bodily function becomes a source of sexual feelings.

EROTOGENIC ZONE. Also erogenous zone. Bodily area in which sexual sensations arise when it is stimulated.

EROTOMANIA. Inordinate sexual desire. The term encompasses both satyriasis and nymphomania.

Eros. The god of love in ancient Greece. The adjectival and nominal derivations come from the possessive form of Eros, Erotos.

ESHMUN COMPLEX. In psychoanalysis, castration complex.

Eshmun. According to some Greek sources, Eshmun of Sidon was a Phoenician deity. He was first a beautiful youth who, being amorously pursued by Astronoe, a Phoenician goddess and mother of the gods, cut off his own genitals with an axe. In remorse, the goddess turned the youth into a god by generative heat, and

Eshmun became a deity of healing and vital force. The term was introduced by N.D.C. Lewis (*Psychoanal. Rev.*, 1928, *15*, 174).

EUSTACHIAN TUBE. A valved tube that connects the middle ear and the pharynx. Swallowing opens it and produces equalization of air pressure between the middle ear and outside air.

Eustachio, Bartolommeo. Italian anatomist (b. San Severino, near Salerno, Ancona, c. 1500–1510, d. Via Flaminia, en route to Fossombrone, August 27, 1574). Eustachio practiced medicine, serving as physician-in-ordinary to the pope for a time. In 1562 he was appointed to a teaching position in the Collegio della Sapienza in Rome. He distinguished himself with his descriptions of numerous anatomical structures of the human body. Eustachio published many of them in 1564, but his main achievement was the detailed anatomical tables prepared on copper plates. He was poor all his life, however, and could not publish the plates. They were not discovered and published until 1714. The Eustachian tube was discovered not by Eustachio but by Alcmaeon of Croton two thousand years earlier. Eustachio, however, provided the first clear description of this structure in an essay on the organ of hearing in 1564 (*Opuscula anatomica*).
   Biographies: Asimov; DSB, 4; Talbot.

EYSENCK PERSONALITY INVENTORY. A revision of the Maudsley Personality Inventory,* this instrument contains three scales: extroversion, neuroticism, and lie.

EYSENCK PERSONALITY QUESTIONNAIRE. A revision of the Eysenck Personality Inventory,* which is still in print. To the three scales of the latter it adds a fourth, psychoticism.

Eysenck, Hans-Jürgen. German-English psychologist (b. Berlin, March 4, 1916). Eysenck left Germany at the age of eighteen. He obtained his Ph.D. from the University of London in 1940. During World War II, he worked at the Mill Hill Emergency Hospital and then, until 1947, at Maudsley Hospital. In 1950, he established at the University of London the first psychology department in England to offer training in clinical psychology. He is professor emeritus at the University of London and also senior psychiatrist at Maudsley Hospital and Bethlehem Royal Hospital. Eysenck's main interest lies in the area of personality measurement and individual differences. He is also a best-selling author in psychology. He is the author or editor of at least two dozen books. The inventory was first published in 1963, the questionnaire in 1975.
   Biographies: ConAu, 9R; CurBio, 1972; H. B. Gibson, Hans Eysenck, 1981; Who, 1986–1987.

F

FECHNER-HELMHOLTZ LAW. A visual stimulus reduces the excitability of the visual system so that the effect of an equal subsequent stimulus is diminished by approximately the same amount as would have been the case had the stimulus intensity itself been diminished proportionately.

FECHNER WEIGHT HOLDERS. Containers with lids and handles used in threshold experiments for lifted weights. The standard and comparison containers are identical except for a small difference in weight fastened to the lid of the comparison container.

FECHNER'S COLORS. Subjective colors generated by black and white patterns rotated at a certain speed.

FECHNER'S LAW. The law of psychophysics that states that the intensity of sensation is directly proportional to the logarithm of the intensity of the stimulus: $S = k \log R$, where S is sensation, R stimulus (*Reiz* in German), and k a coefficient of proportionality.

FECHNER'S PARADOX. The increase in the brightness of a visual stimulus when, after experiencing it binocularly, one eye is suddenly covered up.

FECHNER'S SHADOW EXPERIMENT. An experimental setup for demonstrating Weber's law.* The observer compares the intensity of the two shadows cast by a single pole illuminated by two light sources whose intensities may be varied independently.

Fechner, Gustav Theodor. German physicist, philosopher, and psychologist (b. Gross-Särchen, Lower Lusatia, April 19, 1801, d. Leipzig, November 18, 1887). Fechner spent all of his professional life at the University of Leipzig, beginning with his M.D. in 1822. He taught physics from 1824 to 1840 and was pensioned in 1844 because of poor eyesight but continued to engage in philosophy. All of his contributions to psychology date from 1850. Scientific psychology begins with Fechner. Motivated to prove that mind and body are aspects of the same unity, Fechner on October 22, 1850, experienced an insight of how to measure sensation, a mental event. He presented a program of psychophysics in 1851 in a treatise called *Zend-Avesta*. He then proceeded to verify the stimulus-sensation relationship experimentally, developing the three classical methods of psychophysics in the process. He described his theory and experimental findings in *Elements of Psychophysics* (1860). The psychophysical law is stated and the shadow experiment described in Fechner's *Elements*. The subjective colors were described by Fechner in 1838 (*Pogg. Ann. Phys. Chem.*, *44*, 221–45, 513–35; *45*, 227–32).
  Biographies: Asimov; DSB, 4; *EB,* 9; *IESS,* 5.

Helmholtz, Hermann von. See under eponyms that begin with HELMHOLTZ.

FELDENKRAIS FUNCTIONAL INTEGRATION. A method for achieving psychological wholeness through bodily movements. Based on ideas from Oriental self-defense systems, it postulates interdependence of body posture and psychological expression. Body posture is taken to be a dynamic expression of energy rather than a static spatial form.

Feldenkrais, Moshe Pinchas. Israeli engineer (b. Baranowicze, Poland, May 6, 1904). Feldenkrais had a doctorate in engineering from the Sorbonne (1935). He held various engineering positions in France, England, and Israel between 1935 and 1952. In 1952, Feldenkrais founded the Feldenkrais Institute in Tel-Aviv. He was lecturer in psychology at the Tel-Aviv University from 1963 to 1967. Feldenkrais, holder of the black belt in judo, wrote eight books on jiu-jitsu and *Body and Mature Behavior* (1949), *Awareness Through Movement* (1952), and *Basic Feldenkrais* (1978).
  Biographies: ConAu, 73R; *WhoWoJ,* 1978.

FERE METHOD. See FERE PHENOMENON.

FERE PHENOMENON. The galvanic skin response,* especially when measured as a change in the resistance of the skin to the passage of electric current (Féré method).

Féré, Charles Samson. French psychiatrist (b. Auffay, Seine-Maritime, June 13, 1852, d. Paris, April 22, 1907). Upon graduating from the University of Paris with a degree in medicine in 1882, Féré held just one medical appointment, which was at the Bicêtre Hospital in Paris. He wrote many books on psychiatry, psychopathology, heredity, and criminality. He collaborated with Alfred Binet* on a book on animal magnetism and one on the psychology of reasoning. He also studied fatigue, built the first ergograph, and formulated a teaching of dynamogenesis, presented in the 1887 book *Sensation and Movement*. In 1888, Féré described the changes that take place in the electrical conductance of the skin during emotional arousal (*C. r. Soc. biol., Mém., 40,* 217–19). It was named the psychogalvanic reflex and renamed the galvanic skin response later.

Biographies: Fischer, *Biog. Lex.; EUI,* 23.

FERREE-RAND DOUBLE BROKEN CIRCLES. A visual acuity test chart containing circles of varying size, with two gaps in each instead of one, as in the Landolt circle.*

FERREE ROTARY CAMPIMETER. An apparatus for mapping the visual field up to 92 degrees of excentricity. It differs from other instruments of this type in that in it, it is the fixation point that is movable while the stimulus is fixed. This permits the use of bulky apparatus for stimulus presentation.

Ferree, Clarence Errol. American psychologist (b. Sidney, Ohio, March 11, 1877, d. Baltimore, Maryland, July 26, 1942). Ferree had a Ph.D. in psychology from Cornell University (1909). He spent the next eighteen years at Bryn Mawr College and the rest of his career at Johns Hopkins University Medical School, where he was the director of the Research Laboratory of Physiological Optics and lecturer in ophthalmology. Ferree did a large amount of work on vision. He introduced the measurement of spectral energies in the study of vision and did considerable work on visual perimetry, lighting, reading, and vision in industrial settings. There are 249 titles in his total scientific output. The campimeter was described in 1912 (*Amer. J. Psychol., 23,* 449–53).

Biographies: DAB, Suppl. 3; F. L. Dimmick, *Amer. J. Psychol.,* 1943, *56,* 137–40; L. G. H. Hardy, *Arch. Ophthal.,* 1943, *29,* 668–69; *NCAB,* 33; *WhAm,* 2.

Rand, Gertrude. American psychologist (b. October 29, 1886, d. Stony Brook, Long Island, New York, June 30, 1970). Gertrude Rand was the wife of Clarence Ferree and the coauthor of most of his papers on vision. She had a Ph.D. in psychology from Bryn Mawr (1911), where she stayed with her husband until 1927, when both moved to Johns Hopkins. From 1936 to 1943 she was associate director of the Research Laboratory of Physiological Optics and research associate in ophthalmology at Columbia University College of Physicians and Surgeons from 1943 to 1957. She was consultant at the Knapp Memorial Library at Columbia from 1957 to 1970. Her main work was *Studies in Physiological Optics* in two volumes (1934), written with C. Ferree. She was the inventor of many optical and vision instruments.

Biographies: APA Dir., 1965; *NYT,* July 2, 1970, p. 35; *WhAm,* 5.

FERRIER'S EXPERIMENT. An experiment designed to show that efferent nerve impulses do not cause sensations. The experimental subject is instructed to place a finger on a button or lever and to imagine vividly pressing on it but without actually executing any movements. It can be shown in this manner that the accompanying sensations are kinesthetic sensations from neighboring muscles, feedback from breathing, and the like.

Ferrier, Sir David. Scottish neurophysiologist (b. near Aberdeen, January 1843, d. London, March 19, 1928). After receiving an M.A. from Aberdeen in 1863, Ferrier went to Heidelberg, where he studied psychology for a year. He then studied medicine and obtained the M.D. degree from the University of Edinburgh in 1870. Ferrier moved to London, where he held positions with the National Hospital (1880–1907) and the Medical School of King's College (1871-1908). Ferrier is noted for his pioneering work in neurophysiology, particularly the experiments that established the idea of localization of brain functions. His defense of animal experimentation against the antivivisectionists made him famous throughout England. His experiments are described in *West Riding Lunatic Asylum Medical Reports* (1873, *3,* 30–96) and in his *Functions of the Brain* (1876).
    Biographies: DSB, 4; *Haymaker;* C. S. Sherrington, *Proc. Roy. Soc.,* 1928, Ser. B, *103,* vii–xvi; G. Stewart, *J. Ment. Sci.,* 1928, *74,* 375–80.

FERRY-PORTER LAW. Critical fusion frequency (the frequency of an intermittent light at which the dark and light phases fuse to produce the impression of a steady light) increases as a function of the logarithm of stimulus intensity ($F = a \log L + b$). The relationship holds for only a portion of the range in which critical fusion frequency and luminance are related.

Ferry, Ervin Sidney. American physicist (b. Croydon, New Hampshire, June 14, 1868, d. Lafayette, Indiana, October 8, 1956). Ferry studied physics at Cornell (1891–1893), Johns Hopkins (1893–1894), and Upsala (1897–1898) universities. He then taught physics at Purdue University beginning in 1899. Ferry was the author of several volumes on physical subjects. The law, originally presented in 1892 (*Amer. J. Sci.,* 44, 192–207), was based on a limited amount of data (one log unit range).
    Biographies: WhAm, 3.

Porter, Thomas Cunningham. English scientist (b. Bristol, February 16, 1860, d. Slough, Buckinghamshire, March 31, 1933). Porter studied mathematics and science at Oxford University and held the M.A. degree (1885) from that university; he then taught mathematics and science at Eton. In 1902 (*Proc. Roy. Soc.,* 70A, 313, 329), Porter presented a broader range of measurements (five log units) than had Ferry to support the relationship between critical fusion frequency and luminance stated by Ferry.
    Biographies: Wh, 1929–1940.

F TEST (F RATIO, F STATISTIC). The ratio of two variances, either the larger/smaller of two variances for a test of homogeneity of variance, or the ratio of "between"/"within" variances in an analysis of variance context.

FISHER EXACT PROBABILITY TEST. A nonparametric test of statistical signifiance of the difference between two small independent samples when the scores belong to one or the other of two mutually exclusive classes.

FISHER'S Z STATISTIC. A logarithmic transformation of the correlation coefficient, r, that has a normal distribution. This makes possible the testing of the statistical significance of a difference between two r's.

Fisher, Ronald Aylmer. English statistician (b. London, February 17, 1890, d. Adelaide, Australia, July 29, 1962). Fisher studied mathematics and physics at Cambridge, graduating in 1912. He was awarded the Sc.D. degree by Cambridge fourteen years later. Most of Fisher's important contributions to statistics and genetics were made during his stay at the Rothamsted Experimental Agricultural Station (1919–1933). He was professor of eugenics at University College from 1938 to 1943 and professor of genetics at Cambridge from 1943 to 1957. Fisher spent his retirement years at the University of Adelaide. Fisher made important contributions to the mathematical theory of statistics, to the application of statistical theory to agriculture and the design of experiments, and to genetics. Contemporary analytical statistics begins with Fisher. He wrote three texts on statistics, two on genetics, 294 papers on statistics and genetics, several hundred miscellaneous papers and reviews, and prepared a famous book of statistical tables. The F and z statistics were presented in *Statistical Methods for Research Workers* (1925), but the use of the symbol F was introduced later by G. G. Snedcor.

  Biographies: *DSB*, 5; J. Fisher Box, *The Life of a Scientist*, 1978; *IESS*, 5; M. G. Kendall, *Biometrika*, 1963, *50*, 1–15; G. A. Miller, *Amer. J. Psychol.*, 1963, *76*, 157–58; J. Neyman, *Science*, 1968, 156, 1456–60; *Biog. Mem. Fellows Roy. Soc.*, 1963, *9*, 91–130; F. Yates, *Nature*, 1962, *195*, 1151–52.

FISSURE OF SYLVIUS. See SYLVIAN FISSURE.

FITTS' LAW. An equation that describes the relationship between movement time, *MT*, the distance moved, *D*, and the width of the target moved toward, *W*: $MT = a + (b \log_2 2D/W)$, where a and b are constants.

Fitts, Paul Morris. American psychologist (b. Martin, Tennessee, May 5, 1912, d. Ann Arbor, Michigan, May 2, 1965). Fitts obtained the Ph.D. degree from the University of Rochester in 1938, taught at the University of Tennessee (1938–1941), was with the U.S. Army Air Force from 1942 to 1949, and then with Ohio State University (1948–1958) and the University of Michigan

(1958–1965). Fitts' work was in human engineering, particularly equipment design. It helped define the new field of engineering psychology. Fitts wrote chapters for edited books on human engineering and equipment design and edited several volumes. The eponymous law was first presented in 1954 (*J. Exp. Psychol., 47,* 381–91).

Biographies: *AM&WS,* 1960P; *NCAB,* 54.

FLANAGAN TABLE. A table for the rapid estimation of the biserial correlation coefficient using only the upper and lower 27 percent of a distribution. If the distribution is that of test scores, the correlation is a measure of how well a test item discriminates between the high and the low scorers on the test.

Flanagan, John Clemans. American psychologist (b. Armour, South Dakota, January 7, 1906). Flanagan's Ph.D. was in mental measurement (Harvard, 1934). He became the director of the Cooperative Test Service of the American Council on Education in New York, lectured at Columbia (1936–1941), worked in aviation psychology for the U.S. Army Air Force (1941–1946), taught at the University of Pittsburgh (1946–1972), and was president of the American Institute for Research (1942–1972) and has been chairman of its board of directors since 1967. As a psychometrician, Flanagan has worked in the areas of research methodology and the measurement of aptitudes, abilities, and performance. He is the author of *Aptitude Classification Tests* (1953), *Measuring Human Performance* (1959), and close to 300 other publications. He prepared the table in January 1936.

Biographies: *AM&WS,* 1978S; *APA Dir.,* 1965, 1985; *WhoAm,* 1984–1985.

FLESCH INDEX. A number that indicates the difficulty level of a reading material.

Flesch, Rudolf F. Austrian-American psychologist (b. Vienna, Austria, May 8, 1911, d. Dobbs Ferry, New York, October 5, 1986). Educated in Austria (LL.D., University of Vienna, 1933) and the United States (Ph.D., Columbia University, 1943), Flesch concerned himself with the psychology of language and thinking and the measurement of readability. He held various academic and government positions and was a writer and editorial consultant after 1946. Among his many books on reading and language, the best known are *Why Johnny Can't Read* (1955) and *Why Johnny Still Can't Read* (1981). Flesch presented the index in 1948 (*J. Appl. Psychol., 32,* 221–33).

Biographies: *AM&WS,* 1978S; *ConAu,* 9R; *CurBio,* 1948; *NYT,* October 7, 1986, 49; *WhoAm,* 1984–1985.

FOOTLAMBERT. Brightness of a perfectly reflecting surface at one foot from a standard candle.

Lambert, J. H. See LAMBERT.

FORBES-GREGG HYPOTHESIS. The hypothesis that stimulus strength is translated by nerve fibers into frequency of discharge. The hypothesis was offered to explain how the nervous system handles varying stimulus intensities in spite of the all-or-none law, which precludes variability of the strength of discharge in a nerve fiber.

Forbes, Alexander. American physiologist (b. Milton, Massachusetts, May 14, 1882, d. Milton, Massachusetts, March 27, 1965). Forbes had an M.D. from Harvard University (1910), and he was associated with that university from 1910 to 1948, but he did little teaching, engaging in science as an amateur. Forbes was also an outdoorsman and once mapped the coast of Labrador using aerial photography. His physiological contributions came early in his life. He was first to use an electronic amplifier in physiological experiments and first to use the string galvanometer to measure accurately spinal reflexes. In 1915, he used it in an experiment, performed with Alan Gregg, that gave rise to the Forbes-Gregg hypothesis (*Amer. J. Physiol., 37,* 118–76).
  Biographies: AMS, 1960P; *DSB,* 5; *NCAB,* 52; *WhAm,* 4.

Gregg, Alan. American physician (b. Colorado Springs, Colorado, July 11, 1890, d. Big Sur, California, June 19, 1957). Like Forbes, Gregg also had an M.D. from Harvard (1916). Unlike Forbes, he went into foundation work. From 1919 until his retirement in 1954, Gregg held various positions with the Rockefeller Foundation, the last as vice-president.
  Biographies: CurBio, 1950; *DAB,* 26; W. Penfield, *The Difficult Art of Giving: The Epic of Alan Gregg,* 1967; *WhAm,* 3.

FOURIER'S LAW (FOURIER'S THEOREM). Any complex periodic vibration, such as sound, light, or spatial frequencies, may be broken down into simple sine wave components in frequency ratios of 1, 2, 3, 4, and so on. Such a breakdown is called Fourier analysis, and the components constitute a Fourier series.

Fourier, Jean-Baptiste-Joseph, baron. French mathematician (b. Auxerre, Yonne, March 21, 1768, d. Paris, May 16, 1830). Although of working-class origins and orphaned at an early age, Fourier's ambition was to become an artillery officer and to work in mathematics. The French Revolution made this possible. He graduated from a military school, taught there, then joined Napoleon on his campaign in Egypt, and was made governor of part of Egypt. He returned to France in 1801 to follow scientific pursuits. He made his greatest discovery, the Fourier theorem, in 1807, but the paper he wrote on it was never published. A revised 1810 paper, however, won a prize for him. For his achievements, Napoleon made Fourier a baron. He flourished even after Napoleon's downfall and was elected secretary of the Academy of Sciences in 1822, along with Baron Georges Cuvier. In that year he also published *Analytical Theory of Heat,* in which he applied his theorem to the analysis of the flow of heat in bodies.
  Biographies: Asimov; DSB, 5; *EB,* 9.

FRANKFURT SCHOOL. Common term for the Institut für Sozialforschung (Institute of Social Research), established in Frankfurt-am-Main, Germany, in 1923. Its key figures were the philosopher and social psychologist Max Horkheim, the economist Friedrich Pollack, the philosopher and sociologist Theodor Adorno, the psychoanalyst and social psychologist Erich Fromm, the philosopher Herbert Marcuse, the political scientist Franz Neumann, and the literary critic Walter Benjamin. They worked primarily in the area of ideology critique, drawing on Kant, Hegel, Marx, Weber, and Lukács. Fromm and Marcuse in particular employed Freudian concepts extensively in a philosophical analysis of the impact of advanced industrial society on psychological functioning. The school went into exile during the Nazi years, returning in the 1950s. A contemporary figure in the Frankfurt tradition is Jürgen Habermas.

FRANKLIN EXPERIMENT. Benjamin Franklin's demonstration that a visual afterimage may be positive when seen against a light background with one's eyes closed but positive when the background is darkened.

Franklin, Benjamin. American philosopher, printer, diplomat, and scientist (b. Boston, Massachusetts, January 6, 1706 d. Philadelphia, Pennsylvania, April 17, 1790). Although Franklin received only two years of formal education, his inventions and scientific discoveries made him the only American of colonial times to achieve a European reputation. The recognition came mostly for his work on electricity. In addition to the afterimage experiment, described in Franklin's latter to Lord Kames of June 2, 1765, Franklin's name enters the history of psychology because of his participation in the work of the commission that investigated Franz Anton Mesmer* during Franklin's stay in France as U.S. ambassador.

   Biographies: Asimov, DAB, 6; DSB, 5; EB, 9, EP, 3; B. Franklin, Benjamin Franklin: A Biography in His Own Words, 1972; R. L. Ketcham, Benjamin Franklin, 1965; NCAB, 1.

FRASER SPIRAL. A set of specially constructed concentric circles that look like a spiral.

Fraser, James. b., n.a., d., n.a. Fraser published the spiral in 1908 (*Brit. J. Psychol., 2*, 307–20 + plates), at which time he was deputy medical superintendent of the Central London Sick Asylum.
   Biographies: Unavailable.

FREEMAN RULE. A standard of legal sanity recommended under the Model Penal Code of the American Law Institute: ''A person is not responsible for criminal conduct if at the time of such conduct as a result of mental disease or mental defect he lacked substantial capacity either to appreciate the wrongfulness of his conduct or to conform his conduct to the requirements of law.'' The rule arose from a decision made in 1966 by the Second Circuit Court.

Freeman, Charles F. Freeman (b. c. 1930) was found guilty of selling narcotics but claimed diminished mental capacity as a defense.
Biographies: U.S. v. Freeman, 357 F.2d 606 (1966).

FREEMAN TIME UNIT. In the cinematography of writing movements, the 0.04 second time interval between two successive film frames. It is abbreviated FTU or FU.

Freeman, Frank Nugent. American psychologist (b. Rockwood, Ontario, April 17, 1880, d. El Cerrito, California, October 17, 1961). Freeman, who in 1908 received his Ph.D. from Yale University, was an educational psychologist (University of Chicago, 1909–1939; University of California at Berkeley, 1939–1948) who did research and published half a dozen books and a number of papers in the area. Of these, the best known is *Twins—A Study of Heredity and Environment* (1937, with H. H. Newman and K. J. Holzinger). Freeman also pioneered in the study of hand movements in writing. The eponym was suggested by Robert Saudek, an English psychologist who specialized in handwriting analysis.
Biographies: R. H. Beck, *Phi Delta Kappan,* 1956, *37,* 161; *PR,* 3; *WhAm,* 4.

FREUDIANISM (FREUDISM). Psychoanalytic theory, especially as originally propounded by Sigmund Freud. Psychoanalysis as theory and school of thought in the broad sense.

FREUDIAN SLIP. An error in speaking or writing that is the unconscious expression of the true feelings of the speaker or writer. It is also known by the name *parapraxis.*

Freud, Sigmund. Austrian psychoanalyst (b. Freiberg, Moravia, May 6, 1856, d. London, England, September 23, 1939). As the founder of psychoanalysis, Freud contributed to psychological thought more than any other single individual in the twentieth century. After receiving an M.D. from the University of Vienna (1881), Freud spent a few years searching for a professional identity. The study of one of the patients of his mentor, Joseph Breuer,* convinced him that sexual problems underlie hysteria. In 1895 he and Breuer published *Studies in Hysteria,* a book that laid the foundation of psychoanalysis. The role that Freud assigned to the unconscious counts as his greatest contribution to psychology. In 1900, Freud published his greatest work, *Interpretation of Dreams.* International recognition of Freud began when G. Stanley Hall invited Freud to the United States in 1909. Although his most important disciples broke off their relationship with Freud a few years later, Freud's fame grew from here on as he elaborated his theory and kept publishing additional works. The content of the twenty-four volumes of Freud's collected works not only has produced thousands of titles of research, observation, and theory but has become part of the heritage of Western culture.
Biographies: DSB, 5; *EB,* 9; *EP,* 3; S. Freud, *An Autobiographical Study,* 1935; M.

Freud, *Glory Reflected: Sigmund Freud: Man and Father*, 1957; *IESS*, 6; E. Jones, *The Life and Work of Sigmund Freud*, 1953–1957; R. Wollheim, *Sigmund Freud*, 1971.

FRIEDMAN TEST. A statistical test that uses the chi-square statistic to test in an analysis of variance format the hypothesis of no difference among *k* matched samples when the data are ranked data.

FRIEDMAN TWO-WAY ANOVA. See FRIEDMAN TEST.

Friedman, Milton. American economist (b. Brooklyn, New York, July 31, 1912). Friedman obtained the M.A. degree in economics from the University of Chicago in 1933. He taught at that university from 1933 to 1935 and from 1935 to 1940 served in Washington, D.C., with several government agencies. He was at Columbia University from 1943 to 1945, receiving his Ph.D. in 1946. Friedman went back to Chicago that year, retiring in 1983 as emeritus professor of economics. A conservative economist, Friedman is a prolific author and an important contributor to economic theory. He received the Nobel Prize in Economics in 1976. The test was published in 1937 (*J. Amer. Stat. Ass., 32*, 675–701).
Biographies: ConAu, 1R, 1NR; CurBio, 1969; WhoAm, 1984–1985.

FROEBELISM. Fröbel's educational philosophy, determined by his belief that life, nature, and spirit each have an inner unity. The development of nature shows itself in the development of the individual mind, and the educational process should reflect the natural inner development of the pupil. Education should unfold the whole person: religion unfolds the individual's emotions, natural science reveals God, and mathematics shows the order that reigns in the universe. Self-activity and instructive play were to be the basic features of the kindergarten, an educational stage Fröbel introduced. Fröbel introduced toys and devices ("gifts") to stimulate learning through play.

Fröbel, Friedrich Wilhelm August. German educator (b. Oberweissbach, Thuringia, April 21, 1782, d. Marienthal, Brunswick, June 21, 1852). It was not until Fröbel was thirty-four that, having pursued a variety of occupations, he entered the field of education, establishing schools and training others in his method of education. He had had only a few university courses at Jena and Göttingen. Fröbel developed the idea of the kindergarten in 1836, establishing the first one in Blankenburg in 1837. He spent the rest of his life as an educator of both children and future kindergarten teachers. *The Education of Man* (1826) is Fröbel's most important book.
Biographies: EB, 9; EP, 3; F. Fröbel, Autobiography of Friedrich Fröbel, 1889 (reprinted 1971); I. M. Lilley, in *Friedrich Fröbel: A Selection from His Writings*, 1967, pp. 1–30.

FROIS-WITTMANN POSES. A series of emotional expressions posed by an actor. Seventy-two of the best were used by Harold Schlosberg to plot his circle of emotions with the cardinal points marked pleasant-unpleasant, rejection-attention.

Frois-Wittmann, Jean. French psychoanalyst (b. 1892, d. n.a.). Frois-Wittmann produced the poses as part of his 1929 Ph.D. dissertation, done at Princeton University. The work was published the following year (*J. Exp. Psychol.*, 1930, *13*, 113–51).
  Biographies: Unavailable.

FUCHS PHENOMENON. A phenomenon observed when viewing an object through a transparent filter against a homogeneous background. If the object's contours are all inside the contours of the filter and the contours of the filter all inside the contours of the background, the filter will be perceived as transparent both on the background and the object. (If the object is displaced completely outside the contours of the filter, the filter will appear opaque.)

Fuchs, Wilhelm. German psychologist. (b. n.a., d. n.a.) Fuchs obtained his Ph.D. degree from the University of Frankfurt in 1923. He described the phenomenon in his dissertation, and it was published in the same year (*Z. Psychol.*, *91*, 145–235).
  Biographies: Unavailable.

FULLERTON-CATTELL LAW. Observation errors and just noticeable differences between stimuli vary directly with the square root of the reference stimulus. This relationship was proposed as a substitute for Weber's law,* but it does not work any better.

FULLERTON-CATTELL PRINCIPLE. Equally often noticed differences are equal, unless always or never noticed.

Fullerton, George Stuart. American philosopher (b. Fategarh, India, August 18, 1859, d. Poughkeepsie, New York, March 23, 1925). Fullerton graduated from the University of Pennsylvania with a master's degree in philosophy in 1882 but got involved in psychology enough to be elected president of the American Psychological Association in 1896. He was at the University of Pennsylvania from 1883 to 1904 and at Columbia University from 1904 to 1917. It was at Pennsylvania that Fullerton collaborated with Cattell on some psychophysical experiments and wrote with him an important monograph, *On the Perception of Small Differences, with Special Reference to the Extent, Force, and Time of Movement* (1892). The Fullerton-Cattell law appears stated in this publication. F. Nowell Jones (*Amer. Psychologist*, 1974, *29*, p. 272) notes that the Fullerton-Cattell principle does not appear there and that Leon Thurstone* was the first (in

1932) to attribute the principle to Fullerton and Cattell, whereas in fact it was Edward Lee Thorndike* who in a 1910 paper on handwriting (*Teachers College Record, 11*[2]) first stated it.

Biographies: AMS, 1921; *NCAB,* 12; *WhAm,* 1.

Cattell, James McKeen. American psychologist (b. Easton, Pennsylvania, May 25, 1860, d. Lancaster, Pennsylvania, January 20, 1944). Cattell was the first American to receive a doctorate from Wilhelm Wundt* (1886). At the University of Pennsylvania (1887–1891), Cattell came to occupy the world's first chair in psychology. He also established there the first formally recognized psychological laboratory in the United States. On his arrival at Columbia University in 1891, Cattell started promoting the idea of mental tests, and his time at Columbia is associated with the mental test movement. Cattell was dismissed from Columbia for pacifism in 1917, which led to his organizing the American Association of University Professors. He then founded the Psychological Corporation for the promotion of applied psychology. Throughout his career, Cattell founded, published, and edited many periodical publications, but he never wrote a text and was the author of relatively few papers. He was elected president of the American Psychological Association in 1895.

Biographies: P. S. Achilles, *J. Appl. Psychol.,* 1941, *25,* 609–18; E. G. Conklin et al., *Science,* 1944, *99,* 151–65, 232–33; *DAB,* 23; *DSB,* 3; *EB,* 5; *IESS,* 2; *NCAB,* 34; M. M. Sokal, *Amer. Psychologist,* 1971, *26,* 626–35; F. L. Wells, *Amer. J. Psychol.,* 1944, *57,* 270–75; R. S. Woodworth, *Psychol. Rev.,* 1944, *51,* 201–9.

G

GABOR TEXTURE. An image containing a number of Gabor signals. A two-dimensional Gabor signal is a bivariate Gaussian waveform (for example, a circular patch of gray that is darkest in the center, with grayness diminishing concentrically and in a Gaussian fashion).

Gabor, Dennis. Hungarian-British physicist (b. Budapest, June 5, 1900, d. London, England, February 9, 1979). Gabor obtained the doctorate in engineering from the Technische Hochschule at Berlin-Charlottenburg in 1927 and was employed by Siemens and Halske, Berlin, from 1927 to 1933. He worked for the British Thomson-Houston Company in Rugby from 1934 to 1948 and taught at the University of London until 1967. He is best known as the inventor of holography, the flat television tube, and speech compression. Gabor was the author of five books and about one hundred articles. The Gabor signal and texture concepts were presented in 1946 (*J. IEE, 93,* 429–57).
   Biographies: AM&WS, 1973P; *ConAu,* 17R; *CurBio,* 1972; *Wh,* 1971–1980.

GALANT'S REFLEX. In an infant in the first month of life, the scratching of skin along the spinal cord from the shoulders to the buttocks causes the curving of the trunk so that it is concave toward the region stimulated. If there is a transverse lesion in the spinal cord, no response can be elicited if stimulation is applied below the level of the lesion.

Galant, Ivan Borisovich. Russian psychiatrist (b. 1893). Galant graduated from the medical faculty of the University of Basel in 1917. He interned at the university's psychiatric clinic from 1917 to 1920 and served at psychiatric clinics in Moscow, Smolensk, and Leningrad from 1921 to 1935. In 1935 he became chief psychiatrist of the Khabarovsk Kraĭ. Galant worked on psychoses and encephalitis and described a number of other reflexes. Galant described the spinal reflex in a 1917 monograph, *Refleks pozvonochnika—novyĭ refleks v detskom vozraste*.

Biographies: Prominent Personalities in the USSR, 1968; *WoWhoSci*, 1968.

GALENIC TEMPERAMENTS. The sanguine, melancholic, choleric, and phlegmatic temperaments, the fourfold basis of a personality theory that predominated in Europe and the Arab world until replaced by phrenology in the nineteenth century. Galen saw the four humors of Hippocrates—blood, black bile, yellow bile, and phlegm—as the physiological basis of the temperaments. He used them primarily to explain medical pathology and only secondarily behavior, but in the hands of his epigones, the temperaments became the first and longest-lasting personality theory.

Galen. Greek-Roman physician (b. Pergamum, Asia Minor, 130 A.D., d. possibly in Sicily, c. 200 A.D.). In his twenties, Galen traveled and studied, completing his education at the famous Alexandrian library. He became surgeon to the gladiators at Pergamum but in 161 was appointed physician to the emperors of Rome. Galen did physiological experiments, had wide and good knowledge of anatomy, and his medical work was so impressive that it was held as valid for fourteen centuries. He wrote many treatises on medicine. These were translated into Arabic and Latin and served as the main medical manuals until the time of Vesalius and Harvey. His statement on temperaments appears in his treatise *Hippocratis de natura hominis libri II et Galeni in eos commentarius*.

Biographies: Asimov; DSB, 5; EB, 9; EP, 3; L. Clendening, Source Book of Medical History, 1960; *Talbot*.

GALTON BAR. A square bar used in psychophysical experiments to determine thresholds for perceived length. It is one meter long, usually mounted on legs, graduated in millimeters on one side and blank on the opposite side, and has three riders on top. The middle and one lateral rider are used by the experimenter to set a predetermined distance that the subject attempts to reproduce using the other lateral rider.

GALTON WHISTLE. A whistle of very small diameter and an air column of variable length, used to produce very high frequency (6500 to 84,000 hertz) tones, including tones beyond the audible range for humans. It was used to produce tones to test the upper limits of hearing, but it is not very accurate. Galton had such a whistle built into his cane. Like all other such whistles, it was operated by squeezing a rubber bulb. Its sound, inaudible to humans, would readily summon dogs.

GALTON'S LAWS. The law of ancestral inheritance states that, on the average, one-fourth of the individual characteristics are derived from each parent, one-sixteenth from each grandparent, and so on. This law has been superseded by the Mendelian ratio.* The law of filial regression, now more often referred to as the law of the regression to the mean, states that the offspring of parents who represent very high or very low values of some quantitative characteristic will tend to be more like the mean value of that characteristic for the group to which the parents belong. For instance, very tall parents will tend to produce children who are shorter than they are.

GALTON'S QUESTIONNARY. A questionnaire that Galton sent out in 1883 to obtain data on mental imagery. It was the first large-scale use of the questionnaire method in a psychological investigation.

Galton, Sir Francis. English scientist (b. Birmingham, February 16, 1822, d. Haslemere, Surrey, January 17, 1911). Galton, who in 1844 received a B.A. from Cambridge University, was a man of independent means and never held an academic or official position. Although primarily a scientist-at-large, Galton became one of the founding fathers of psychology. He established the study and measurement of individual differences by uniting psychological methods of measurement and evolutionary theory. In 1869, *Hereditary Genius* appeared, a study of the variability of human intellect through the biographies of eminent individuals. Galton applied the normal law of error to behavior measurements and concluded that statistical treatment of psychological measures in general was appropriate. His most important contribution here was the development of the measure of correlation. In 1882, Galton established a laboratory in London where physical and mental measurements were taken. It was the first mental test center in the world. Galton's psychological contributions were published in 1883 in *Inquiries into Human Faculty and Its Development.* In addition to psychology and statistics, Galton pioneered also in eugenics and meteorology and developed a system of identification by means of fingerprints. The bar was constructed by Galton before 1884 (*Outfit for an Anthropometric Laboratory,* 1883, privately printed) when he used it in his Anthropometric Laboratory at the International Health Exhibition held in South Kensington. After the exhibition, he published its description in a paper (*J. Anthrop. Inst.,* 1885, *14,* 205–18). The description of the whistle appeared first in *South Kensington Museum Conference Held in Connection with the Special Loan Collection of Scientific Apparatus, 1876, Physics and Mechanics Volume,* p. 61, published in London by Chapman and Hall in 1876. In the same year Tisley & Co. issued a pamphlet, *Galton's Whistle,* that reproduced Galton's paper. The company was manufacturing the whistle commercially. Galton's two laws were presented in *Hereditary Genius* and the use of the questionnary described in *Inquiries.*

Biographies: Asimov; DNB, Suppl. 1; *DSB,* 5; *EB,* 9; D. Forrest, *Francis Galton,*

1973; F. Galton, *Memories of My Life*, 1908; *IESS*, 6; K. Pearson, *The Life, Letters, and Labours of Francis Galton*, 1914–1930.

GALVANIC SKIN RESPONSE. Also known as the electrodermal reponse and the psychogalvanic reflex, it is most often referred to as the GSR, the changes in the amount of direct (galvanic) current that is passed between two points on the skin surface (Féré phenomenon)*, or changes in the strength of the very weak currents generated by the body at the surface of the skin (Tarchanoff phenomenon).* The change is brought about by arousal or activation of the nervous system, as in emotional arousal.

GALVANOTROPISM. The orientation of a whole organism toward or away from a source of electrical stimulation.

Galvani, Luigi. Italian physiologist (b. Bologna, September 9, 1737, d. Bologna, December 4, 1798). Galvani obtained a degree in medicine and philosophy from the University of Bologna in 1762. He lectured on medicine and was professor of anatomy at that university from 1762 to 1791. In 1771, Galvani noticed that a frog's leg would twitch when an electric spark was generated nearby as well as when a nerve in the frog's leg was connected to its outside by two pieces of different metals. Galvani believed that it was animal tissue that generated the electricity when in fact he had constructed the first wet battery. Galvani described his experiment in 1791 ("De viribus electricitatis in motu musculari commentarius"). Although his idea about animal electricity was soon proved to be wrong by Alessandro Volta, Galvani's name eventually became part of some two dozen additional eponyms related to direct current.
Biographies: Asimov; DSB, 5; EB, 9.

GANSER SYNDROME. A factitious disorder with psychological symptoms that include memory loss, hallucinations, dissociative and conversion symptoms, and giving inaccurate, bizarre, or irrelevant answers to even the simplest questions. The syndrome is largely under the voluntary control of the patient, the goal being to assume the patient role. It is not malingering, it is pathological, and it often involves severe personality disturbance. Synonymous terms are *pseudopsychosis* and *pseudodementia*.

Ganser, Sigbert. German psychiatrist (b. Rhaunen, Rhineland-Palatinate, January 24, 1853, d. Dresden, January 4, 1931). After obtaining the M.D. degree from the University of Munich in 1876, Ganser worked in various mental hospitals until 1884 but also engaged in work on brain anatomy. In 1884, Ganser became an asylum administrator. He described the syndrome in 1898 (*Arch. Psychiat. Nervenkr., 30*, 633–40).
Biographies: Fischer, Biog. Lex.; Pagel, Biog. Lex.

GARCIA EFFECT. Conditioned taste aversion, or toxicosis. The learning to avoid a particular food because the smell or the taste of the food has been linked to such reflexive alimentary reactions as nausea or to ionizing radiation.

Garcia, John. American psychologist (b. Santa Rosa, California, June 12, 1917). Garcia obtained the M.A. (1949) and the Ph.D. (1965) degrees from the University of California at Berkeley. He taught at Berkeley from 1949 to 1951, worked at the U.S. Naval Radiological Defense Laboratory in San Francisco from 1959 to 1965, lectured at Harvard University (1965–1968) and the State University of New York at Stony Brook (1968–1972), spent a year at the University of Utah, and became professor of psychiatry and psychology at University of California at Los Angeles in 1973. His main area of research has been on the effects of ionizing radiation on behavior and the physiological correlates of behavior. The first paper on conditioned taste aversion was published by Garcia with D. J. Kimeldorf and R. A. Koelling in 1955 (*Science, 122*, 157–158).
  Biographies: AM&WS, 1978S; Amer. Psychologist, 1980, 35, 37–43; APA Dir., 1968.

GATTI ILLUSION. The illusion consists of a number of equally spaced, concentric equilateral triangles upon which is superimposed a square. The side of the square that faces one of the apexes of the triangle appears longer than the side that is parallel with one of the sides of the triangle.

Gatti, Alessandro. Italian scientist (b. n.a., d. n.a.) Gatti had a doctorate in natural sciences from the University of Torino (1923). He held positions at the universities of Torino (1923–1924, 1929–   ) and Milan (1924–1927).
  Biographies: PR, 3.

GAUSSIAN CURVE. A curve showing the frequencies with which the values of a variable occur when nothing but chance controls the occurrence of the variable. Also known as Gaussian distribution, normal curve of distribution, normal curve, normal distribution, normal frequency curve, normal probability curve, curve of error, and bell-shaped curve. Although no natural variable follows the exact mathematical shape of the curve, if a sufficiently large number of observations is made, many biological and behavioral variables approximate this distribution. The curve is extremely important because the sampling distributions of various statistics are normal. It plays a crucial role in sampling statistics and statistical inference.

Gauss, Karl Friedrich. German mathematician and astronomer (b. Braunschweig, Lower Saxony, April 30, 1777, d. Göttingen, February 23, 1855). A mathematical prodigy, Gauss obtained a Ph.D. in mathematics at the University of Göttingen. He was first sponsored by the Duke Ferdinand of Brunswick. Upon the latter's death, he was appointed director of the Göttingen Observatory. Gauss made important mathematical discoveries while still in his teens. He worked on the construction of polygons, theory of numbers, and many other branches of mathematics. To psychology, his most important work involves the normal curve. Although it was Pierre Simon Laplace and Abraham de Moivre who pioneered in the mathematical theory of errors, Gauss' development of it was so important that the law of errors and the curve that goes with it were named after him. Gauss expanded the theory of errors in his 1809 astronomical work, *Theoria motus corporum coelestium*. Gauss worked also on terrestrial magnetism, and the unit of magnetic flux density is named after him.

Biographies: Asimov; E. T. Bell, in J. R. Newman (ed.), *The World of Mathematics,* 1956, vol. 1, pp. 295–339; *DSB,* 5; G. W. Dunnington, *Carl Friedrich Gauss, Titan of Science,* 1955; *EB,* 10; T. Hall, *Carl Friedrich Gauss: A Biography,* 1970; *IESS,* 6.

GELB-GOLDSTEIN COLOR SORTING TEST. One of the five Goldstein-Scheerer Tests of Abstract and Concrete Reasoning.* It is a sorting test in which a large number of skeins of wool differing in hue, brightness, and saturation are sorted according to two criteria, hue and brightness.

GELB PHENOMENON. A spot of colored light has a higher threshold when projected inside a figure than when projected upon adjacent ground.

Gelb, Adhemar Maximilian Maurice. German psychologist (b. Moscow, Russia, November 18, 1887, d. Schömberg, Baden-Württemberg, August 7, 1936). Gelb first worked at the University of Berlin, where he had obtained his Ph.D. in 1910. After 1912, he was at Frankfurt, mainly at the University of Frankfurt (1919–1933) and from 1931 to 1933 at the University of Halle. Gelb was a Gestalt-oriented psychologist whose work with Kurt Goldstein on soldiers with brain lesions resulted in numerous papers on the effects of brain damage on perception, speech, and color vision, as well as the book, written with Goldstein, *Psychological Analysis of Cases of Brain Pathology* (1920). Gelb and Ragnar Granit described the epnymous phenomenon in 1923 (*Z. Psychol., 93,* 83–118).

Biographies: R. Bergius, *Psychol. Beitr.,* 1963, *7,* 360–39; *NDB,* 6; *PR,* 3.

Goldstein, Kurt. See under eponyms that begin with GOLDSTEIN.

GELLERMAN SEQUENCES. Chance orders for alternating stimuli in discrimination experiments, originally constructed for visual discrimination experiments with animals. The purpose was to avoid scores due to position habits, simple right-left alternation, and double alternation.

Gellerman, Louis Wanger. American psychologist (b. Gig Harbor, Washington, January 18, 1901). Gellerman, who received his Ph.D. from Clark University (1930), held positions at Yale University, Connecticut State College, Blackborn College, and the University of Southern Illinois between 1930 and 1942. From 1942 to 1947 he was with Boeing Aircraft Co. Beginning with 1945,

Gellerman was also the director of the Human Relations Counseling Center, Seattle, Washington. Gellerman's work was in the areas of personality, group counseling, psychotherapy, and hypnotherapy. The sequences of trials were presented in 1933 in connection with form discrimination in chimpanzees and young children (*J. Genet. Psychol., 42*, 207–8).

    Biographies: APA Dir., 1948.

GERSTMANN'S SYNDROME. A complex of dysfunctions occasioned by lesions in the left angular gyrus and the middle occipital gyri. These include the inability to write and calculate, sometimes to read, finger agnosia, inability to discriminate right from left, construction apraxia, and homonymous hemionopsis.

Gerstmann, Josef. Austrian-American neuropsychiatrist (b. Lemberg, Austria, July 17, 1887, d. New York City, March 23, 1969). Gerstmann received his M.D. from the University of Vienna in 1912. For the next eighteen years, he was with the Psychiatric and Neurological Clinic, Vienna, and with the University of Vienna from 1927 to 1938. From 1930 to 1938 he was also the head of the Maria-Theresien-Schlössel Nerve Clinic in Vienna. Gerstmann came to the United States in 1938. He held hospital appointments until 1946, when he went into private practice. Gerstmann worked on brain pathology, motor dysfunctions, and other medical problems. He described the elements of the syndrome over a period of several years (*Wien. klin. Wschr.*, 1924, *31*, 1010–12; *Nervenarzt*, 1931, *3*, 691–95). He received the 1927 Nobel Prize in Physiology and Medicine.

    Biographies: Fischer, Biog. Lex.; EUI, Suppl. 1969–1970; *NYT*, March 24, 1969, 45.

GESELL DEVELOPMENTAL SCHEDULES. Scales for the assessment of the developmental status of infants and children aged four weeks to six years. Scores in the form of the developmental level attained by the child, expressed in months, are obtained in four areas: motor, adaptive, language, and personal-social behavior.

GESELL OBSERVATION DOME. A domelike structure, made of half-silvered material, for one-way observation and filming of infant behavior.

Gesell, Arnold Lucius. American psychologist (b. Alma, Wisconsin, June 21, 1880, d. New Haven, Connecticut, May 29, 1961). After receiving his doctorate in psychology (Clark University, 1906), Gesell became interested in the growth and development of children and obtained a medical degree as well (Yale University, 1915). He established the Clinic of Child Development at Yale (Gesell Institute of Child Development since 1950) and spent all of his career (1911–1961) at Yale, devoting it to the study of child development. He published some thirty books on the subject, including the three-volume *Atlas of Infant Behavior* (1934). The Developmental Schedules were published in 1949 and have served as models for many subsequent infant development tests, including some that bear Gesell's own name: the Gesell Preschool Test (1980), an abbreviated adaptation of the Gesell Developmental Schedules, and the Gesell Developmental Tests (1964), now called the Gesell School Readiness Test (1980). The dome was introduced in 1928 in *Infancy and Human Growth*.

Biographies: L. B. Ames, *Science*, 1961, *134*, 266–67; *DSB*, 5; *HPA*, 4; *IESS*, 6; *NCAB*, 49; *WhAm*, 4.

GIBSON EFFECT. Viewed through a wedge prism, vertical lines appear curved. The apparent curvature diminishes with prolonged inspection, but when the prism is removed, vertical lines again appear to be curved but in the opposite direction. The effect is also achieved without the prisms by inspecting truly curved lines.

Gibson, James Jerome. American psychologist (b. McConnelsville, Ohio, January 27, 1904, d. Ithaca, New York, December 11, 1979). From 1928, when he obtained his Ph.D. at Princeton University, to 1949, Gibson was at Smith College. His five years (1941–1946) with the U.S. Air Force were most fruitful in providing him with the ideas that went into the construction of his approach to visual perception. During the years 1949 to 1979 Gibson was associated with Cornell University. Gibson offered a view of how we perceive the world that differed radically from the traditional. In his first and most influential book, *The Perception of the Visual World* (1950), Gibson showed that the most significant aspect of the perception of the real, three-dimensional world is the variety of optical gradients present in the retinal projection of the world. Gibson extended his approach to vision to other sense modalities in *The Senses Considered as Perceptual Systems* (1966). In his last book, *The Ecological Approach to Visual Perception* (1979), Gibson once again emphasized the need to study vision in terms of people behaving in the real world performing meaningful tasks. Gibson described the curvature aftereffect in 1933 (*J. Exp. Psychol., 16*, 1–31).

Biographies: AM&WS, 1979P; *Amer. Psychologist*, 1961, *16*, 799–802; *ConAu*, 85; *HPA*, 5; V. J. Nordby & C. S. Hall, *A Guide to Psychologists and Their Concepts*, 1974; A. D. Pick et al., *Amer. J. Psychol.*, 1982, *95*, 693–700.

GILLES DE LA TOURETTE SYNDROME. Repeated bodily and vocal tics, such as barks, grunts, clicks, and yelps, and, in some 60 percent of cases, explosive utterance of obscenities. The disorder appears before adolescence and is lifelong. The symptoms disappear in sleep and may be voluntarily suppressed for brief periods. The disorder is three times more common in males than in females.

Gilles de la Tourette, Georges. French neurologist (b. Saint-Gervais-lès-Trois-Clochers, Vienne, October 30, 1857, d. Lausanne, Switzerland, May 26, 1904). Tourette's medical doctorate was from the University of Paris (1885). He was cofounder of *Nouvelle iconographie de la Salpêtrière,* an outlet for medical articles concerning art works. His main work was the book *Traité clinique et thérapeutique de l'hystérie* (1891). The syndrome that bears his name was described in 1885 (*Arch. neurol., 9,* 19–42, 158–200).

Biographies: Fischer, *Biog. Lex.; The New Century Cyclopedia of Names,* vol. 1, 1954.

GJESSINGS'S SYNDROME. Recurring catatonic and manic episodes in schizophrenia related to variations in the amounts of nitrogen in the patient's body that are caused by deficient protein metabolism.

Gjessing, Rolv. Norwegian physician (b. Norway, 1887, d. Lom, Norway, 1959). In 1941, Gjessing was at the Dikemark Mental Hospital, actively resisting attempts to disorganize Norwegian medical services during the German occupation of Norway. He had described the eponymous syndrome in 1938 (*J. Ment. Sci., 84,* 608–621).

Biographies: Canad. Med. Ass. J., 1959, *80,* 848.

GÖDEL'S PROOF. The proof of the theorem (Gödel's theorem) that "all consistent axiomatic formulations of number theory include undecidable propositions." This means that although all mathematics is based on a set of axioms, some mathematical truths cannot be derived from these axioms and the set of axioms is therefore incomplete. Gödel's proof has a bearing not only on formal logic and mathematics but also on psychology and artificial intelligence: computers must be programmed, but there is only a finite number of programs. Humans, however, are capable of an infinite variety of behaviors. It follows that any set of existing computer programs will be incomplete, and, hence, it will be impossible to construct a machine that will behave like a human being.

Gödel, Kurt. Austrian-American mathematician (b. Brünn, Austria-Hungary [now Brno, Czechoslovakia], April 28, 1906, d. Princeton, New Jersey, January 14, 1977). Gödel obtained his Ph.D. at the University of Vienna in 1930 and a year later published the paper that contained the theorem and the proof that bear his name (*Mhef. Math. Phys.,* 1931, *38,* 173–98). Gödel was on the faculty of the University of Vienna from 1933 to 1938. He became a member of the Institute for Advanced Study at Princeton in 1938 (with earlier stays in 1933 and 1935) and came to stay in the United States in 1940, becoming a citizen in 1948.

Biographies: AM&WS, 1976P; *Asimov; McGMSE,* 1980; *WhAm,* 7.

GOLDSTEIN CATASTROPHIC REACTION. Extreme agitation, anger, and resistance seen in patients who have lost such skills as language or arithmetic when they attempt to engage in tasks requiring the use of the lost functions. Otherwise normal behavior is observed.

GOLDSTEIN-SCHEERER CUBE TEST. A modified version of the Kohs' Block Design Test.*

GOLDSTEIN-SCHEERER OBJECT SORTING TEST. A number of everyday objects are sorted into categories according to as many criteria as possible.

GOLDSTEIN-SCHEERER STICK TEST. A test in which the subject copies patterns using plastic sticks or reproduces them from memory.

GOLDSTEIN-SCHEERER TESTS OF ABSTRACT AND CONCRETE THINKING. A set of five tests that measure impairment in thinking caused by brain damage. Each of the subtests has also been used as an independent test. The subtests are: Goldstein-Scheerer Cube Test, Gelb-Goldstein Color Sorting Test, Goldstein-Scheerer Object Sorting Test, Weigl-Goldstein-Scheerer Color Form Sorting Test, and Goldstein-Scheerer Stick Test.

Goldstein, Kurt. German-American neurologist (b. Kattowitz, Upper Silesia, November 6, 1878, d. New York City, September 19, 1965). Goldstein, who received his M.D. from the University of Breslau (1903), held various academic and medical positions in Germany and, after 1936, in the United States. Influenced by both the Gestalt theory and the holistic tradition of German science, Goldstein began using Gestalt concepts in his clinical neurology work. His experience with cases of brain injury during World War I led him to postulate that an organism must be considered as a whole whenever a particular aspect of its functioning is evaluated. He presented the holistic-organismic theory in his major work, *The Organism* (1934). Goldstein's total output of publications was some 250 items. The catastrophic reaction is described in *The Organism*. The Goldstein-Scheerer tests were first presented in 1941 (*Psychol. Monog., 53*, No. 2).
   Biographies: EJ, 7; W. Eliasberg, *Proc. R. Virchow Med. Soc.,* 1965, *24,* 185–94; *IESS,* 6; *Jewish,* 5; H. Jonas, *Soc. Res.,* 1965, *32,* 351–56; J. Meiers, *J. Indiv. Psychol.,* 1966, *22,* 116–25; M. L. Simmer (ed.), *The Reach of Mind: Essays in Memory of Kurt Goldstein,* 1968; M. L. Simmel, *J. Hist. Behav. Sci.,* 1966, *2,* 186–91; D. Shakow, *Amer. J. Psychol.,* 1966, *79,* 150–54.

Scheerer, Martin. American psychologist (b. New York City, June 10, 1900, d. Lawrence, Kansas, October 19, 1961). Scheerer obtained his Ph.D. from the University of Hamburg in 1927, after which he taught briefly there and at half a dozen universities in the United States, his last position being at the University of Kansas (after 1948). Influenced by Gestalt psychology, Scheerer wrote *The Gestalt Doctrine* in 1931 and a few papers. His major contribution was the development, with Kurt Goldstein, of several tests of concept formation.
   Biographies: NYT, Oct. 20, 1961, 30; C. Scheerer, *Bull. Menninger Clin.,* 1966, *30,* 85–86.

GOLGI-MAZZONI CORPUSCLES. One type of encapsulated nerve ending found in the skin. There is some evidence that it may be a receptor organ for pressure.

GOLGI TENDON ORGAN. A type of nerve ending found near the point of attachment of tendon and muscle. It is thought to be a receptor organ that registers changes in tension and therefore serves as a proprioceptor.

Golgi, Camillo. Italian neurohistologist and pathologist (b. Corteno [now Corteno Golgi], Lombardy, July 7, 1843, d. Pavia, January 21, 1926). With an M.D. from the University of Pavia (1865), Golgi held hospital appointments near and in Pavia from 1865 to 1875. He was called to the University of Pavia in 1875 and remained there until 1918. In 1873, Golgi used silver nitrate to stain nerve cells. It was a cornerstone in the study of the nervous system. He studied and described many structures of the nervous system and of the neuron and developed a theory of the nervous system as a network of axons and dendrites. His studies were important enough to have a dozen nervous system structures named after him. In 1906 he (and Santiago Ramón y Cajal) received the Nobel Prize in Physiology and Medicine. Golgi's work of importance to sensory psychology is described in his *Studi sulla fina anatomia degli organi centrali del sistema nervoso* (1886). In the 1890s, Golgi shifted his attention to other topics, making important contributions to malaria research, for instance.

    Biographies: DSB, 5; *EB,* 10; *Haymaker;* T. Stevenson, *Nobel Prize Winners in Medicine and Physiology, 1901–1950,* 1953, pp. 32–40; *Talbot.*

Mazzoni, Vittorio. Italian physiologist (b. 1880, d. 1940).
    Biographies: Unavailable.

GOMPERTZ CURVE. A doubly inflected curve of the form $y = vg^{c^x}$, where x is time, c rate of growth, g initial growth, and v a limiting value of y or asymptote specifying amount of growth at maturity. The constants g and c have values of between 0 and 1. The curve was originally used as a life expectancy curve (x being age), but it is of interest to psychologists because it is also a more general growth curve that depicts the growth of an organism, or of a cell in a developing organism, as well as the learning process.

Gompertz, Benjamin. English mathematician (b. London, March 5, 1779, d. London, July 14, 1865). As a son of a Jewish merchant family that had emigrated to England from Holland, Gompertz was denied admission to British universities. He educated himself and by associating with learned societies, such as the Spitalfields Society of Mathematicians. He worked on mathematical problems, especially those of astronomy and statistics, and was elected a fellow of the Royal Society. Gompertz was a pioneer in actuarial science. He developed the curve named after him as a result of his interest in life contingencies and the application of Newtonian fluxions to such contingencies. The pertinent paper was published in 1825 (*Phil. Trans. Royal Soc., 115*, 513–85).

Biographies: DNB, 22; *DSB,* 5; P. F. Hooker, *J. Inst. Actuaries,* 1965, *91,* pt. 2, No. 389, 203–12.

GOODENOUGH DRAW-A-MAN TEST. An intelligence test for ages three to fifteen. It consists of a single item, the drawing of a person. Presence or absence of specified items of clothing or bodily parts adds up to a score that is converted to mental age equivalent, from which IQ can be computed.

Goodenough, Florence L. American psychologist (b. Honesdale, Pennsylvania, August 6, 1886, d. Saint Paul, Minnesota, April 4, 1959). Goodenough was a prominent worker in the area of child psychology and child development. She received her Ph.D. from Stanford University in 1924. She presented the Draw-A-Man Test in her book, *Measurement of Intelligence by Drawing,* in 1926. In the 1940s, the test was the third most widely used intelligence test (after the Binet* and Wechsler* tests). It was renamed the Goodenough-Harris Drawing Test in 1963.

Biographies: D. B. Harris, *Child Dev.,* 1959, *30,* 305–6; *PR,* 3; *AMS,* 1956S; *APA Dir.,* 1958.

GORDON HOLMES REBOUND PHENOMENON. See HOLMES PHENOMENON.

GORDON PERSONAL PROFILE INVENTORY. An inventory that measures eight aspects of personality: ascendancy, responsibility, emotional stability, sociability, cautiousness, original thinking, personal relations, and vigor. It was the result of combining the Gordon Personal Profile and Gordon Personal Inventory.

Gordon, Leonard V. American psychologist (b. Montreal, Canada, August 15, 1917). Gordon received the Ph.D. degree from Ohio State University in 1950. From 1952 to 1962 he did personnel work for the U.S. Navy and from 1962 to 1966 for the army. He has been on the faculty of the State University of New York at Albany since 1966. Gordon's work has been primarily in industrial/organizational psychology and the measurement and evaluation of personnel. The Personal Profile Inventory dates from 1978.

Biographies: AM&WS, 1978S; *APA Dir.,* 1985; *WhoAm,* 1984–1985.

GORDON REFLEX (GORDON SIGN). 1. A variant of the Babinski reflex:* as the calf muscle is compressed, the big toe or all toes extend. Also known as the Gordon leg sign, it is observed in cases of lesion to the pyramidal tract. 2. The flexion of the thumb and the index finger or of all fingers when the forearm muscle is compressed. Also known as Gordon's finger sign, it is observed in cases of damage to the pyramidal tract.

Gordon, Alfred. American neurologist (b. Paris, France, November 2, 1874, d. 1953). Gordon received his medical education at the University of Paris (M.D., 1895). He came to the United States a year later, was at Jefferson College in Philadelphia from 1899 to 1908, the Philadelphia General Hospital from 1904 to 1908, and several other hospitals afterward. His main work is *Diseases of the Nervous System* (1908).

   Biographies: WhAm, 5.

GOTTSCHALDT FIGURES. Simple figures embedded in more complex designs and used in tests of figure-ground perception.

Gottschaldt, Kurt Bruno. German psychologist (b. Dresden, April 25, 1902). Gottschaldt, after receiving a Ph.D. from Friedrich-Wilhelms University in 1926, taught at the universities of Bonn (1929–1933), Berlin (1926–1929, 1938–1944, 1948–1962), and Göttingen (after 1962). His work has been mainly in the area of developmental psychology but also the psychology of personality and the psychology of learning. In the 1920s, Gottschaldt concerned himself with the question of the influence of experience on the Gestalt laws of organization. He showed that when figures were presented in embedding contexts, experience did not help in their detection (*Psychol. Forsch.,* 1926, *8,* 261–317; 1929, *12,* 1–87). Although his contention was disproved, the figures continue to be used in tests designed for other purposes.

   Biographies: Bonin; W. Hehlman, *Wörterbuch der Psychologie,* 4th ed., 1965; *PR,* 3; *Wer ist Wer?* 1951; *Who's Who in Science in Europe,* 1967.

GRACE ARTHUR PERFORMANCE SCALE. See ARTHUR POINT SCALE OF PERFORMANCE TESTS.

GRAM-CHARLIER SERIES. See POISSON DISTRIBUTION.

GRAM-SCHMIDT PROCESS. In mathematical statistics, the Gram-Schmidt orthogonalization process that yields uncorrelated variables. For the case of three variables, $X_1, X_2,$ and $X_3,$ if $X_2 = b_{20} + b_{21} X_1,$ and $X_3 = b_{30} + b_{31} X_1 + b_{32} X_2$ are prediction equations with the weights determined using the least-squares criterion, then the transformations $X_1 = X_1, X_{2.1} = X_2 - X_2,$ and $X_{3.21} = X_3 - X_3$ constitute the Gram-Schmidt orthogonalization process.

Gram, Jorgen Pedersen. Danish mathematician (b. Nustrup, Haderslev, June 27, 1850, d. 1916). Gram received the Ph.D. degree in mathematics from the University of Copenhagen in 1879. He applied mathematics in his work for life insurance companies and in forestry and also engaged in theoretical mathematics.

   Biographies: C. F. Bricka (ed.), *Dansk Biografisk Leksikon.* Copenhagen: Gyldenhal, 1887–1905.

Charlier, C. W. See under CHARLIER'S CHECKS.

Schmidt, Erhard. German mathematician (b. Dorpat [now Tartu], Estonia, January 13, 1876, d. Berlin, December 6, 1959). Schmidt's Ph.D. in mathematics was from the University of Göttingen (1905). He taught for short periods at several universities from 1905 to 1917, holding positions at the University of Berlin from 1917 to 1959. Schmidt's most significant contributions were in integral equations and Hilbert space theory. The Gram-Schmidt process is part of his work on the integral equations that is the basis for Schmidt's fame. It appeared in 1907 (*Math. Ann., 63*, 433–76; *64*, 161–74).
   Biographies: DSB, 12.

GRANIT-HARPER LAW. The generalization that critical fusion frequency and the logarithm of the areas of the stimulus are linearly related over a luminance range of 1,000 to 1 and circular stimulus areas ranging from 0.98 to 5.0 degrees in diameter for retinal locations up to 10 degrees away from the fovea.

Granit, Ragnar. Finnish-Swedish neurophysiologist (b. Helsinki, Finland, October 30, 1900). Granit received the M.D. degree from the University of Helsinki in 1927. From 1929 to 1931 he was a fellow in medical physics at the Johnson Foundation, University of Pennsylvania. He was appointed docent of physiology at the University of Helsinki in 1932 and went from there to the Institute of Neurophysiology at the Karolinska Institute, Stockholm, in 1940, becoming its director in 1945 and retiring in 1967. The main thrust of Granit's work has been to establish the role of the interplay of excitatory and inhibitory processes in the retina and the nervous system. He has made pioneering contributions to the knowledge of how information about motion, color, and form is encoded in the retina and transmitted to the visual cortex. For his work Granit received the Nobel Prize in 1967. The Granit-Harper law was published in 1930 (R. Granit & P. Harper, *Amer. J. Physiol., 95*, 211–27).
   Biographies: Asimov; F. Ratliff, *Science*, 1967, *158*, 469–71; *Who*, 1986–1987; *WhoAm*, 1984–1985.

Harper, Phyllis. (b. n.a.). In 1930, when she collaborated with Granit in research on the critical fusion frequency, Harper was a graduate student at the Johnson Foundation for Medical Physics, University of Pennsylvania.
   Biographies: Unavailable.

GRASSMANN'S LAWS. Laws of color mixture when colored lights are used (1) when lights equivalent in color are added to equivalent lights, their sums are also equivalent; (2) when equivalent lights are subtracted from equivalent lights, the differences are also equivalent; and (3) lights equivalent to the same light are equivalent to each other.

Grassmann, Hermann Günther. German mathematician (b. Stettin [now Szczecin], Germany, April 15, 1809, d. Stettin, September 26, 1877). Grassman studied at the University of Berlin, but although his work made it possible for him to become a member of scientific societies, he was never able to obtain an academic teaching position. He taught high school in Stettin and Berlin, holding a position at the Otto Schule in Stettin after 1835. While teaching, Grassmann also worked on mathematics, his most notable achievement being the development of a calculus of extension. Because his work was far ahead of its time, Grassmann never achieved the recognition that he deserved and turned to linguistics. He learned several languages and became a Sanskrit scholar. In this area, recognition of his work was prompt. He also studied light, his laws of color mixture being published in 1853 (*Ann. Phys. Chem., 165, 69–84*).
   Biographies: DSB, 15.

GRAVES DESIGN JUDGMENT TEST. A test of artistic aptitude that uses abstract designs exclusively. A test item consists of one design that is in accord with certain aesthetic principles, such as symmetry, proportion, and rhythm, and one or more other designs that violate one or more of these principles. The testee indicates which of the designs is preferred.

Graves, Morris Cole. American artist (b. Fox Valley, Oregon, August 28, 1910). Graves has had many American and international retrospective exhibitions and one-man shows in art galleries and museums. His works are exhibited in several permanent collections in the United States, Dublin, and London. The test was published in 1946.
   Biographies: Britannica Encyclopedia of American Art, 1973; Contemporary Artists, 1983; Dictionary of American Artists, Sculptors, and Engravers, 1968; WhoAm, 1984–1985.

GRAY'S MODIFICATION. Gray modified Helmholtz's theory of hearing* by stating that a given tone excites not only the fibers on the basilar membrane that are specifically in tune with that tone but also neighboring cells. These, however, are excited to a progressively lesser extent as their distance from the maximally excited cells increases. Gray called this the principle of maximum stimulation.

Gray, Albert Alexander. English aural surgeon and pathologist (b. Glasgow, October 8, 1868, d. London, January 4, 1936). Gray was educated at the universities of Glasgow, Leipzig, and Munich; he received an M.D. in 1897. He wrote *The Labyrinth of Animals, Textbook of Diseases of the Ear,* and *The Mechanism of the Cochlea* (with G. Wilkinson). His modification of Helmholtz's theory was published in 1900 (*J. Anat. Physiol., 34, 324–50*).
   Biographies: Wh, 1929–1940; WhE&EA, 3.

GRAY STANDARDIZED ORAL READING PARAGRAPHS. A pioneering instrument widely used since 1915. It includes text samples of increasing difficulty that are scored for eight types of errors in reading them. The Paragraphs test was replaced by the Gray Oral Reading Test. Although it bears Gray's name, the publisher does not consider it a revised edition.

Gray, William Scott. American educator (b. Coatburg, Illinois, June 5, 1885, d. Chicago, Illinois, September 8, 1960). Gray received his Ph.D. from the University of Chicago in 1916 and remained at that institution until 1950. From 1917 to 1930 he was dean of the College of Education. Gray wrote several books and a number of papers on reading.
   Biographies: DAB, Suppl. 6; W. J. Moore, in *Pioneers in Reading, I, Elementary English,* 1957; *NCAB,* 48; *WhAm,* 4.

GRAZ SCHOOL OF PSYCHOLOGY. See AUSTRIAN SCHOOL OF PSYCHOLOGY.

GREENSPOON EFFECT. Covert conditioning of a verbal reponse. The frequency of use of specified verbal categories may be increased without the speaker's awareness if these categories are reinforced, as they occur, by the listener's assent in the form of nods, uh-huhs, or mm-mms.

Greenspoon, Joel. American psychologist (b. Charleston, West Virginia, October 11, 1921). Greenspoon, who received a Ph.D. from Indiana University in 1952, has been on the faculties of Pomona College (1951–1955), Florida State University (1955–1963), Arizona State University (1963–1967), Temple Buell College (1967–1973), the University of North Carolina at Charlotte (1974–1976), and the University of Texas at Permian Basin (since 1976). Greenspoon is an experimental analyst of behavior who has concentrated on verbal behavior and behavior modification and the behavioristic approach to therapy. Greenspoon described the effect in 1955 (*Amer. J. Psychol., 68,* 409–16).
   Biographies: AM&WS, 1978S; *APA Dir.,* 1985.

GREIG SYNDROME. Hypertelorism, or anbormally increased interocular distance, associated with mental retardation.

Greig, David Middleton. Scottish scientist (b. Dundee, 1864, d. Edinburgh, May 4, 1936). Greig obtained the M.B. degree from the University of Edinburgh in 1885. He served in the army until 1901 but spent much of his professional life in Dundee at the Royal Dundee Infirmary, where he was also a lecturer in clinical surgery. From 1921 to 1936 Greig was conservator at the Museum of the Royal College of Surgeons of Edinburgh. Greig left a bibliography of 140 items. He described hypertelorism in 1924 (*Edinb. Med. J., 31,* 560).
   Biographies: Edinb. Med. J., 1936, *43,* 531–39.

GRISELDA COMPLEX. A father's desire to keep his daughter to himself because of unresolved Oedipus conflict* (in which the subject of desire was his mother).

Griselda. Paragon of womanly virtue in medieval romance. Of long-suffering patience, she endures the abuses of her husband to prove her love. The character was used later by Chaucer, Boccaccio, Petrarch, and others. The term was coined by the American psychiatrist James Jackson Putnam (*Intern. Z. ärztl. Psychoanal.*, 1913, *1*, 205–18).

GUILFORD-ZIMMERMAN TEMPERAMENT SURVEY. A 300-item personality inventory that assesses ten traits established by means of factor analysis. It revises and condenses the Guilford-Martin Inventory of Factors, Guilford-Martin Personnel Inventory, and the Inventory of Factors STDCR.

Guilford, Joy Paul. American psychologist (b. Marquette, Nebraska, March 7, 1897).

Guilford's Ph.D. was in experimental psychology (Cornell University, 1927). He taught at the universities of Illinois, Kansas, and Nebraska but was the longest at the University of Southern California (1940–1967). Guilford made important contributions to a variety of fields by applying quantitative methods to them: sensory processes, psychophysical judgment, attention, interests, personality traits, intelligence, and creativity. He published more than 300 articles, developed more than 30 psychological tests, and wrote such well-known books as *Psychometric Methods* (1936, 1954), *Fundamental Statistics in Psychology and Education* (six editions between 1942 and 1978), and *The Nature of Human Intelligence* (1967). The Temperament Survey was first published in 1949.

Biographies: AM&WS, 1978S; Amer. Psychologist, 1964, 19, 947–54; 1984, 39, 310–11; APA Dir., 1985; ConAu, 1R; HPA, 5; IESS, 18.

Zimmerman, Wayne Seaton. American psychologist (b. Davison, Michigan, January 10, 1916). Educated at the University of Southern California (Ph.D. in psychometrics, 1949), Zimmerman has dedicated his career to psychometrics. He taught at Brandeis University (1949–1953) and San Diego State College (1953–1956) and was a human factors scientist with Systems Development Corporation (1956–1961), a testing officer at the California State University at Los Angeles (1961–1980), and a consultant to the Aptitude Research Project, University of Southern California from 1961, among other positions. He published ten articles with Guilford, including a 1956 monograph on the fourteen dimensions of temperament.

Biographies: AM&WS, 1978S; APA Dir., 1983.

GUTTMAN SCALE. A scale, typically an attitude scale, in which the items are ordered so that a testee's response to any item may be taken as indicative of the kind of response that will be given to all items of lower rank. The method of obtaining such a scale, scalogram analysis, is intended to ensure that all test items of the same kind measure the same thing. The technique is also known as Guttman scaling, cumulative scale, or Cornell technique.

Guttman, Louis. American psychologist (b. New York City, January 10, 1916). A social psychologist, Guttman specialized in social and psychological measurement. He obtained the Ph.D. degree from the University of Minnesota in 1942. He consulted to the secretary of war from 1941 to 1945, taught at Cornell University from 1941 to 1950, and has been at the Israel Institute of Applied Social Research since 1947 and the Hebrew University in Jerusalem since 1955. Guttman has done research on the integration of theory construction and research design for the social sciences, nonmetric techniques for data analysis, social problem indicators, and attitudes and intergroup relations. He has published some 120 papers, monographs, and book chapters in these areas. The Guttman scale was presented in 1944 (*Amer. Sociol. Rev., 9,* 139–50).

Biographies: AM&WS, 1978S; *APA Dir.,* 1985.

H

HAAB'S PUPIL REFLEX. The contraction of both pupils when a bright object in a darkened room is fixated. The reflex is mediated by the cerebral cortex rather than the pretectal region, as in the ordinary pupillary reflex.

Haab, Otto. Swiss ophthalmologist (b. Wülflingen, Zurich, April 19, 1850, d. Zurich, October 17, 1931). After receiving an M.D. from the University of Zurich (1875), Haab specialized in ophthalmology. He taught at the University of Zurich from 1878 to 1919. Haab wrote several volumes on ophthalmology, including three atlases on ophthalmoscopy, eye diseases, and eye operations. The pupillary reflex was described in 1886 (*Korrespbl. schw. Arzte, 16,* 153).
   Biographies: Fischer, *Biog. Lex.*

HAIDINGER'S BRUSHES. If one looks at the sky through a Nicol prism (which polarizes light), a small, yellow, hourglass-shaped figure appears at the point of fixation, its axis parallel to the electric vector of the light transmitted by the prism. It can be seen in lights that are absorbed by the macular pigment and is in fact produced by it. At any point in the retina, this pigment mostly absorbs polarized light whose electric vector is parallel to the line that connects that point and the fovea.

Haidinger, Wilhelm Karl. Austrian mineralogist (b. Vienna, February 5, 1795, d. Dornbach, near Vienna, March 19, 1871). At age seventeen, Haidinger became assistant to the mineralogist Friedrich Mohs at Graz. He spent the years 1823 to 1827 arranging a mineral collection for a banker and then worked in a china factory at Elbogen (1827–1840). He became an inspector of mines and in 1849 director of the Reichsanstalt for geological survey, retiring in 1866. His observation of the brushes came as a result of his working with crystals, especially

those that polarize light, such as fluorspar. His theory was published in 1844 (*Ann. Phys.*, Leipzig, *63*, 29–39).
  Biographies: DSB, 6.

HALSTEAD-REITAN NEUROPSYCHOLOGICAL TEST BATTERY. An instrument for assessing brain damage. There are two forms for children and one for adults. The adult battery consists of eleven tests, some yielding more than one score. The combined score is called the Halstead impairment index.

Halstead, Ward Campbell. American psychologist (b. Sciotoville, Ohio, December 31, 1908, d. Chicago, Illinois, March 25, 1969). Halstead, who received a Ph.D. in psychology from Northwestern University (1935), spent all his academic career (1936–1969) at the University of Chicago. He became internationally known for his work on the brain. The Halstead Laboratory of Medical Psychology was the first laboratory in the world devoted to full-time study of brain functioning in humans. In 1950 he and J. Katz proposed the first formal theory of biochemistry of learning, suggesting that RNA and protein molecules might be the place to look for the memory engram. Halstead wrote *Brain and Intelligence* (1947), *Cerebellar Functions* (1935), *Medicine and the War* (1945, with W. H. Taliaferro), and *Brain and Behavior* (1958, with J. Katz). He developed the test battery in 1950 to measure "biological intelligence," as articulated in *Brain and Intelligence*. Reitan did extensive work on the battery. It now includes several of Halstead's original tests, a number of tests added by Reitan, as well as subtests taken from other test batteries.
  Biographies: APA Dir., 1968; NCAB, 55; WhAm, 5.

Reitan, Ralph Meldahl. American psychologist (b. Beresford, South Dakota, August 29, 1922). Reitan obtained the Ph.D. degree in physiological psychology from the University of Chicago in 1950. He continued working in the area of brain functions at the University of Indiana Medical Center (1951–1970), the University of Washington (1970–1977), and, since 1977, the University of Arizona. While at Indiana, Reitan undertook the task of establishing correlations between psychological test performance and damage in specific brain sites confirmed by postmortem diagnoses. The work led to a refinement of the Halstead test battery. The battery makes it possible to distinguish brain lesions from psychiatric involvement and to specify the location of the lesion even when a neurological examination may fail to diagnose brain dysfunction.
  Biographies: AM&WS, 1982P; APA Dir., 1985.

HAMPSTEAD INDEX. A system for classifying data obtained in psychoanalytic therapy sessions to make them more readily usable for research or teaching.

Hampstead. A neighborhood in greater London, location of the Hampstead Child Therapy Clinic whose workers developed the Hampstead Index in 1955.

HAMPTON COURT MAZE. A six-by-eight-foot rectangular replica of the pattern of a complicated trapezoidal maze made by Willard Stanton Small for the study of learning in the white rat. It was built of wire mesh and placed on a floor covered with sawdust, the first instance (1901) of the use of a maze in the study of animal learning.

Hampton Court. A Tudor palace located on the Thames River in greater London, fifteen miles southwest of St. Paul's Cathedral. It was built by Cardinal Wolsey and presented by him to Henry VIII in 1528. The maze in the gardens was planted during the reign of William III (1689–1702) and consists of alleys enclosed by walls of hollies, yews, and other shrubs taller than a person's height. The way to get to the center of the maze (it has only one entrance/exit) is to turn left on entering, then turn right the first two times there is a choice, but turn left every time after that.

HANFMANN-KASANIN CONCEPT FORMATION TEST. A variant of the Vygotskiĭ blocks* test in which the task is to classify twenty-two wooden blocks varying in color, shape, height, and surface size into four groups, each having a single name. The name of each block is printed on its underside.

Hanfmann, Eugenia. German-American psychologist (b. St. Petersburg, Russia, March 3, 1905, d. Waltham, Massachusetts, September 14, 1983). Hanfmann obtained the doctor of natural philosophy degree from Jena in 1927. She was at that institution from 1928 to 1930 and then held teaching and research positions at a number of colleges, hospitals, and private institutions in the United States. She was at Brandeis University from 1952. Hanfmann's work was on the development and pathology of thinking, personality assessment methods, projective techniques, and national character. The test was published by Hanfmann and Kasanin in 1942 (*Nerv. Ment. Dis. Monog.*, No. 67).
  Biographies: AM&WS, 1973S; *APA Dir.*, 1981; M. L. Simme, *J. Hist. Behav. Sci.*, 1986, *22*, 348–356; *WhoAmW*, 1972.

Kasanin, Jacob Sergi. American psychiatrist (b. Slavgorod, Russia, May 11, 1897, d. San Francisco, California, May 4, 1946). Kasanin came to the United States in 1915. He obtained the M.D. degree from the University of Michigan six years later and then held positions at various universities and hospitals from 1923 to 1939. He was chief of psychiatric services at Mount Zion Hospital, San Francisco, beginning in 1939 and taught at the University of California Medical School beginning in 1940. Kasanin wrote books and papers on schizophrenia.
  Biographies: AMA J., 1946, *131*, 475; *NYT*, May 6, 1946, 21; *WhAm*, 2.

H-R-R PLATES. Hardy-Rand-Rittler Plates. A test for color blindness that includes tritanopia and tetartanopia, usually not included in other color-blindness tests.

Hardy, LeGrand Haven. American ophthalmologist (b. Provo City, Utah, June 13, 1894, d. New York City, April 14, 1954). After his medical studies at Columbia University (M.D. 1921), Hardy began practicing ophthalmology in New York City. He held positions in a number of hospitals and, after 1941, directed the Knapp Memorial Laboratories of the Columbia University College of

Physicians and Surgeons. Hardy studied defects of color vision, the effects of illumination, and space perception (*The Geometry of Binocular Space Perception*, 1953, with others). The color vision test was published by Hardy, Rand, and Rittler in 1955 (*H-R-R Pseudoisochromatic Plates*).
  Biographies: AMA J., 1954, *155*, 503; *AMS*, 1949; *WhAm*, 3.

Rand, Gertrude. See under FERREE-RAND DOUBLE BROKEN CIRCLES.

Rittler, J. M. C.
  Biographies: Unavailable.

HARROWER'S GROUP RORSCHACH. Also called the Harrower's Multiple Choice Test, it is a set of inkblots that parallel the Rorschach* inkblots and used in group administration of the test.

Harrower, Molly R. American psychologist (b. Johannesburg, South Africa, January 25, 1906). Harrower studied psychology at the University of London but received the Ph.D. from Smith College in experimental psychology (1934). She developed an interest in clinical psychology and psychopathology and has held numerous clinical and research appointments in university and clinical settings, worked as a government consultant, and engaged in private practice (1945–1967). She was at the University of Florida from 1967 until she retired in 1975. Harrower has published some fifteen books and around one-hundred articles. The group Rorschach was published by her and M. E. Steiner in 1945 (*Large Scale Rorschach Techniques*).
  Biographies: AM&WS, 1973S; *APA Dir.*, 1985; *ConAu*, 5R; M. Harrower, in T. S. Krawiec (ed.), *The Psychologists*, vol. 3, 1978; *WhoAm*, 1976–1977; *WhoAmW*, 1974–1975.

HARTLEY'S TEST. A test for homogeneity of variance for k treatments in an experiment if n is the same for all. The test statistic, *F max*, is obtained by obtaining the ratio of the largest to the smallest of the k treatment variances.

Hartley, Hermann Otto. American statistician (b. Berlin, Germany, April 13, 1912, d. Durham, North Carolina, December 30, 1980). Hartley left Germany in 1934, the same year he obtained his Ph.D. in mathematics from the University of Berlin. He also received a Ph.D. in statistics from Cambridge University (1940) and a D.Sc. in statistics from the University of London in 1954. Hartley held university and business appointments in England from 1936 to 1953. He was at Iowa State University from 1953 to 1963, Texas A&M University from 1963 to 1979, and Duke University in 1979 and 1980. Harvey worked in statistical methodology, sample survey theory and methods, estimation theory of mathematical techniques, and operations research. The test was published in 1940 (*Biometrika, 31*, 249–55) and 1950 (*Biometrika, 37*, 308–12).
  Biographies: AM&WS, 1979P; W. B. Smith, *Amer. Statistician*, 1981, *35*, 142–143.

HARTNUP DISEASE. A rare form of aminoaciduria, associated with mental retardation and transient mental abnormalities. It is thought to be transmitted as a homozygous autosomal recessive trait.

Hartnup. Hartnup was the name of the family for whom the disease was first described.

HAWTHORNE EFFECT. The increase in productivity observed among industrial workers following the introduction of any innovation or change, regardless of its nature. The increase is at least temporary and is thought to be produced by the increased motivation experienced by the workers as they realize that attention is being paid to them.

Hawthorne. A population center near Chicago, Illinois, location of the Hawthorne Works of the Western Electric Company. The Hawthorne Works was the site of some famous experiments and studies performed around 1930 by Elton Mayo and others on the effects of social organization on productivity (*Human Factor,* 1930, *6,* No. 1).

HEAD'S AREAS. Also called Head's zones, these are areas of the skin that show excessive sensitivity or lack of sensitivity as a result of visceral disease.

Head, Henry. English neurologist (b. Stamford Hill, Lincolnshire, August 4, 1861, d. Reading, Berkshire, October 8, 1940). After receiving an M.D. from University College, London, in 1892, Head held various medical appointments at hospitals, the longest at London Hospital (1898–1925). His main contributions were in the area of sensory physiology, especially the physiology of pain. His neurological work was summarized in 1920 in *Studies in Neurology.* After 1910, Head became interested in aphasia and made important contributions in this area as well (*Aphasia and Kindred Disorders of Speech,* 1926). The eponym originated with Head's doctoral thesis. It was published as a book in German translation in 1898 (*Die Sensibilitätsstörungen der Haut bei Visceralerkrankungen*).
   Biographies: R. Brain, *Brain,* 1961, *84,* 561–66; M. Critchley, in *The Black Hole and Other Essays,* 1964, pp. 98–107; K. W. Cross et al., *Henry Head Century: Essays and Bibliography,* 1961; *DNB,* Suppl. 4; *Haymaker;* K. E. McBride, *Amer. J. Psychol.,* 1941, *54,* 444–46; C. S. Meyers, *Brit. J. Psychol.,* 1941, *32,* 5–14; *Obit. Not.,* 3.

HEALY-FERNALD TEST SERIES. A series of twenty-three performance tests devised to supplement the more verbal tasks of the Binet-Simon scale.* Some of these tests were incorporated in later intelligence tests.

HEALY PICTURE COMPLETION TEST. One of the tests in the Healy-Fernald series consisting of a scene that the testee completes by inserting the appropriate square in the place where it is missing. The completion depends on the testee's understanding of the entire situation depicted. The test was later incorporated into such instruments as the Arthur Performance Scale* and the Pintner-Paterson Scale of Performance.*

Healy, William. American psychiatrist (b. Buckinghamshire, England, January 20, 1869, d. Clearwater, Florida, March 15, 1963). Healy received his medical education at the University of Chicago (M.D., 1900) and held various medical and teaching appointments between 1900 and 1909. In 1909, he became the director of the Juvenile Psychopathic Institute in Chicago, the first child guidance clinic. In collaboration with his first wife, Grace Fernald, and later with his second wife, Augusta Bronner, both psychologists, Healy pioneered in the study of childhood delinquency. In Boston, where he was the director of the Judge Baker Foundation from 1917 to 1947, Healy conducted extensive research on delinquency. Healy wrote many articles and fourteen books. Of the latter, the most significant was *The Individual Delinquent* (1915). The Healy-Fernald test series appeared in 1911 (*Psychol. Monog., 13,* No. 2).

Biographies: G. E. Gardner, *J. Amer. Acad. Child Psychiat.,* 1972, *11,* 1–29; D. M. Levy, *Amer. J. Orthopsychiat.,* 1968, *38,* 799–804; H. Meltzer, *Psychol. Rep.,* 1967, *20,* 1028–30.

Fernald, Grace Maxwell. American psychologist (b. Clyde, Ohio, November 29, 1879, d. Los Angeles, California, January 16, 1950). Grace Fernald liked to point out that her Ph.D. had been conferred on her under the direction of James Rowland Angell (University of Chicago, 1907). She taught at Bryn Mawr and in 1909 went to Chicago, where she was the first psychologist to work in the Juvenile Psychopathic Institute. It was here that the Healy-Fernald test series was produced in 1911. In the same year Grace Fernald moved to Los Angeles, where she remained for the rest of her life working at the State Normal School and the University of California. She published many articles in the fields of educational and child psychology, juvenile delinquency, and mental measurement. Among her books, *Remedial Techniques in Basic School Subjects* (1943) was the best received.

Biographies: NYT, June 18, 1950, 32; *Psychol. Rev.,* 1950, *57,* 319–321; *School & Soc.,* January 28, 1950.

HECHT-SHLAER ANOMALOSCOPE. An instrument that measures the Rayleigh equation* (the amounts of green and red needed to match a given yellow) for purposes of screening for color blindness. It uses narrow-band color filters to generate lights of the appropriate wavelength.

Hecht, Selig. American physiologist (b. Glogau, Silesia, February 8, 1892, d. New York City, September 18, 1947). Upon receiving the doctorate in physiology from Harvard University in 1917, Hecht, one of the principal contributors to modern vision theory, went to Creighton University (1917–1925) and then Columbia University (1926–1947). His special contribution lay in the study and theoretical formulation of photopigment processes in the retina. Hecht and his coworkers contributed numerous papers to the field of retinal photochemistry, many of which are classics. Hecht's books include *The Retinal Processes Concerned with Visual Acuity and Color Vision* (1931) and *La bas chimique et structurale de la vision* (1938).

Biographies: DAB, Suppl. 4; C. H. Graham, *Amer. J. Psychol.*, 1948, *61*, 126–28; R. Kingslake, *J. Opt. Soc. Amer.*, 1942, *32*, 37–39; B. O'Brien et al., *Science*, 1948, *107*, 105–6; *NCAB*, 38; *WhAm*, 2.

Shlaer, Simon. American physiologist (b. Lubar, Russia, July 15, 1902). Shlaer became naturalized in 1929 and obtained his Ph.D. in physiology from Columbia University in 1937. He was at Columbia from 1928 to 1947 and at the Los Alamos Scientific Laboratory after 1947, where he engaged in work on radiation physiology.

Biographies: AMS, 1967P.

HEINIS CONSTANT. Because mental age units are not equal, the ratio of mental age to chronological age, or IQ, does not represent equal units either. In Heinis constant, mental age units are first converted to a scale that represents theoretically equal mental growth units and then divided by chronological age.

HEINIS LAW OF MENTAL GROWTH. If y is intelligence at a given age, CA, and e the base of natural logarithms, according to Heinis law,

$$y = 429(1 - e^{\frac{ca}{6.675}}).$$

Heinis, Hugo. Swiss psychologist (b. Basel, October 9, 1889, d. n.a.). Heinis received a Ph.D. from the University of Basel (1913), and he taught at the University of Geneva after 1925.

Biographies: Documents pour servir a l'histoire de l'Université de Genève, 1938, *8*, 415.

HEISS-SANDERS ILLUSION. See SANDERS PARALLELOGRAM.

Heiss, Alfred. German psychologist (b. n.a., d. n.a.). It is not clear why the Sanders parallelogram should have been named after Heiss as well. Heiss did some experiments with the parallelogram (*Neue psychol. Stud.*, 1930, *4*, 285–318) but acknowledged that Sanders was its originator.

Biographies: Unavailable.

HELLER'S SYNDROME. Also called Heller's dementia, it is a degenerative disease of the neurons of the cerebral cortex. The onset of the disease occurs around the age of three and leads to loss of speech, as well as some motor impairment.

Heller, Theodor. German psychologist (b. Vienna, June 3, 1869 d. n.a.). Heller studied at the universities of Vienna and Leipzig from 1889 to 1894 and obtained the Ph.D. degree from the latter in either 1895 or 1904 (the sources differ). His specialty was therapeutic education, and he worked at the Heilpädagogische Anstalt, Vienna, from 1906. Heller published several books and a number of papers on exceptional children. The syndrome was named after Heller by J. Zappert (*Mschr. Kinderheilk.*, 1921–1922, 389–97).

Biographies: PR, 3.

HELMHOLTZ COLOR MIXER. All possible mixtures of the spectral colors are obtained by viewing, through a telescope, two complete spectra, superimposed at right angles to each other.

HELMHOLTZ COLOR TRIANGLE. One of the early representations of the color diagram in a triangular rather than a circular form, showing that the spectral colors are located at different distances from white, which lies inside the triangle.

HELMHOLTZ LIGAMENT. The portion of the anterior ligament of the malleus, one of the three ossicles of the middle ear, which is attached to the greater tympanic spine.

HELMHOLTZ LINES. Lines normal to the plane of the axis of rotation of the eyes.

HELMHOLTZ RESONATORS. A series, graded in size, of spherical brass bottles, used to produce tones by blowing air across the top of the neck of the bottle. This makes the air column within resonate at a specific frequency.

HELMHOLTZ'S CHESSBOARD. A hyperbolic chessboard for demonstrating the curving of ocular direction lines in the visual globe.

HELMHOLTZ'S THEORY OF ACCOMMODATION. The lens of the eye becomes more convex by its own elasticity as the ciliary muscle relaxes; a flattening of the lens occurs as the ciliary muscle contracts.

HELMHOLTZ'S THEORY OF HEARING. The theory (1863) that the ear is a resonating organ, the resonators proper being the rods of Corti.* In 1869, Helholtz substituted the transverse fibers of the basilar membrane for the rods of Corti as the resonators, making the basilar membrane the main organ of hearing. Because the basilar membrane tapers from its apex to its base, the graded series of its fibers were thought to resonate each to a particular frequency of sound.

Helmholtz, Hermann Ludwig Ferdinand von. German physicist and physiologist (b. Potsdam, Brandenburg, August 31, 1821, d. Charlottenburg, Brandenburg, September 8, 1894). Helmholtz obtained free medical education (M.D. 1842) from the state-supported Medico-Surgical Friedrich-Wilhelm Institute in Berlin, but he had to pay for it later by working as an army surgeon. He spent much of his time on research, however, publishing his statement on the first law of thermodynamics in 1847. This prompted his appointment as professor of physiology at the University of Königsberg before his ten-year army stint was over. He was at the University of Bonn from 1855 to 1858, and he spent the rest of his life at the University of Berlin. Helmholtz is one of the great names in science. His genius encompassed theoretical physics, physiology, optics, vision, acoustics, and the psychology of the senses. His *Handbook of Physiological Optics* (1867) is a classic in science, as is his *Sensations of Tone* (1863). At his death, Helmholtz had 217 major publications to his credit. His research and strong empirical position aided greatly in the emergence of experimental psychology. Helmholtz described the color mixer in 1855 (*Ann. Phys. Chem., 170,* 1–28). The three auditory eponyms were first described in *Sensations of Tone;* all the remaining ones may be found in Helmholtz's *Handbook of Physiological Optics.*

   Biographies: Asimov; A. C. Crombie, *Sci. Amer.,* 1958, *198*(3), 94–102; *DSB,* 6; *EB,* 11; *EP,* 3; R. Kahl, in *Selected Writings of Hermann von Helmholtz,* 1971, pp. xii–xlv; L. Konigsberger, *Hermann von Helmholtz,* 1906, reprinted 1956; R. M. Warren & R. P. Warren, in *Helmholtz on Perception,* 1968, pp. 3–15; *Talbot.*

HENMON-NELSON TEST OF MENTAL ABILITY. A verbal group test of mental ability of the spiral omnibus variety for persons beginning with the third grade through college, used mostly as a scholastic aptitude test.

Henmon, Vivian Allen Charles. American psychologist (b. Centralia, Wisconsin, November 27, 1877, d. Wichita, Kansas, January 10, 1950). After receiving a Ph.D. in psychology from Columbia University (1905), Henmon taught briefly there. He then taught at the University of Colorado and in the School of Education of the University of Wisconsin. After a year at Yale University, he returned to Wisconsin, this time as the first chairman of its psychology department. He remained there until his retirement in 1948. Henmon did research on different topics in educational psychology, but most of his papers and books dealt with individual differences and psychological measurement. The Henmon-Nelson tests were first published in 1931.

   Biographies: H. F. Harlow, *Amer. J. Psychol.,* 1950, *63,* 462–63; *PR,* 3; *Science,* 1950, *111,* 348; *WhAm,* 3.

Nelson, Marjory J. American physician (b. 1906).
   Biographies: Unavailable.

HENNING'S SMELL PRISM. A classificatory scheme for smells in which the six primary smells are located at the six corners of the prism: spicy, resinous, and burned at one end of the prism and fragrant, ethereal, and putrid at the other. Intermediate smells are represented along the edges of the prism or on the surfaces but not inside.

HENNING'S TASTE TETRAHEDRON. A four-sided solid with the four primary tastes—sweet, sour, salty, and bitter—located at the apexes. Other tastes, if located on an edge, can be analyzed into two primaries, three primaries if they are on one of the surfaces, and four if located inside the solid.

Henning, Hans Karl Ferdinand. German psychologist (b. Strasbourg, February 15, 1885, d. 1946). Henning, who received his Ph.D. in 1910 from the university of Strasbourg, held academic appointments at the University of Frankfurt (1914–1922) and the Technische Hochschule in Danzig (1922–1944?). He is known for his research on taste and smell. Until 1915, the classification of smells was that of Linnaeus and Zwaardemaker. Henning introduced a systematic conceptual change by placing all smells on the edges and surfaces of a geometric solid (*Der Geruch,* 1916, pp. 51–98). He proposed a similar solution for the classification of tastes (*Z. Psychol.,* 1916, 74, 203–19).
   Biographies: PR, 3.

HERBARTIAN PSYCHOLOGY (HERBARTISM). Herbart's psychology was based on observation, metaphysics, and mathematics. He specifically denied that it could be experimental. Neither was it analytic (he denied the existence of mental faculties) or physiological. It was, however, scientific in that mental processes could be described in mathematical terms. Mental states are the result of interaction of ideas. Ideas are forces, however, and combine dynamically in a complicated manner. Ideas differ in quality and intensity. When ideas do not resist each other, they coalesce in the way stated by the British associationists. When ideas clash or contrast, they may not only fail to associate but one idea may expel another from consciousness. Inhibited ideas do not vanish, however, but remain as tendencies. The force of existing ideas Herbart called apperceptive mass. When this force changes, a previously inhibited idea may return to consciousness. Herbart thus postulated the notion of a threshold of consciousness and the existence of conscious and unconscious mental processes. His theory of the apperceptive mass had the greatest influence in educational psychology. Herbart argued that because new ideas that enter the mind have to contend with the existing apperceptive mass, for learning to take place in the easiest and most efficient way, new ideas must be introduced so that they are related to what is already known.

Herbart, Johann Friedrich. German philosopher (b. Oldenburg, Lower Saxony, May 4, 1776, d. Göttingen, August 4, 1841). Herbart's career began at the University of Göttingen, where in 1804 he obtained his doctorate in philosophy. He stayed there until 1809 when he was called to the University of Königsberg to occupy the chair of philosophy that had been previously Kant's. In 1833, Herbart returned to Göttingen. Herbart's psychological views are found in his *Lehrbuch zur Psychologie* (1816) and particularly his *Psychologie als Wissenschaft neu gegründet auf Erfahrung, Metaphysik und Mathematik* (1824–1825).
   Biographies: DSB, 6; EB, 11; EP, 3.

HERING AFTERIMAGE. The first positive afterimage that follows the exposure of the eye to a brief, bright stimulus. The afterimage has the same hue and saturation as the color of the stimulus. Its latency is about 0.05 second and its duration also about .05 second.

HERING GRAYS. A graded series of fifty gray papers, ranging from white to black, in which each gray differs from its neighbors by the same, subjectively equal amount.

HERING ILLUSION. Two parallel lines, placed upon two sheafs of lines radiating from the same point but in opposite directions, will appear curved, the direction of the curvature being away from the point from which the lines radiate.

HERING THEORY OF COLOR VISION. Hering proposed that there are three visual pigments, which, depending on whether they are metabolically broken down or reconstituted, produce the sensations of six primaries. These, however, always function in opponent pairs: black-white, red-green, and blue-yellow. Color mixtures arise when processes in nonantagonistic pairs are aroused simultaneously, whereas the simultaneous arousal of both processes in a single pair produces grays.

HERING WINDOW. A device for demonstrating simultaneous color contrast in the form of colored shadows. Light is admitted to a darkened room through two openings in an opaque screen that covers a window. One opening has ground glass in it; the other has colored glass. The two openings serve as light sources that throw shadows of a black rod on a milk-glass screen where their colors can be compared.

Hering, Ewald. German physiologist (b. Altgersdorf, Saxony, August 5, 1834, d. Leipzig, January 26, 1918). Hering began practicing medicine after graduating from the University of Leipzig in 1858 with an M.D. Soon, however, he was devoting more time to science than to his practice. He returned to the University of Leipzig, remaining there until 1865 and then moving to Vienna where he taught at the Josephs-Akademie until 1870. Hering spent the first ten years of his scientific career studying space perception. He published two monographs in this area. The illusion that bears his name appeared in his *Beiträge zur Physiologie* (1861–1864). Hering moved to the University of Prague in 1870 and returned to Leipzig in 1895. The second decade of Hering's scientific life was dedicated to vision. His color vision theory, the afterimage, and his window were described in his book *Zur Lehre vom Lichtsinne* (1872–1875). Hering invented or modified a large number of pieces of apparatus and materials. These, through their use in other laboratories, did much to earn the new experimental psychology the nickname ''brass-instrument psychology.''

Biographies: *DSB*, 6; *EB*, 11; L. M. Hurvich, *Amer. Psychologist*, 1969, *24*, 497–514; *IESS*, 6.

HERMANN GRID. A square pattern of dark squares with narrow white "streets" between them. When viewed, dark spots appear at the intersections of the streets.

Hermann, Ludimar. German physiologist (b. Berlin, October 21, 1838, d. Königsberg, June 5, 1914). Hermann, who in 1859 received his Ph.D. from the University of Berlin, taught physiology there from 1865 to 1868. He was at the University of Zurich from 1868 to 1884 and at the University of Königsberg afterward. Hermann was the author of many works in physiology, chemistry, and physics. With others, he wrote a handbook of physiology in six volumes (1879–1882). He was the author of *Lehrbuch der Physiologie,* which saw twelve editions between 1863 and 1899 and was translated into all major languages. His grid appeared in 1870 (*Pflüg. Arch. ges. Physiol., 3,* 13–15).
   Biographies: H. Boruttan, *Deutsch. med. Wschr.,* 1914, *40;* Pagel, *Biog. Lex.*

HERMAPHRODITE. With reference to humans, one whose reproductive organs are not clearly either male or female.

Hemaphroditos. In Greek mythology, Hermaphroditos was the son of the gods Hermes and Aphrodite. He was loved by the nymph Salmacis so much that she wished to join him and become one person, which is what happened.

HERRING-BINET TEST. An early modification of the Binet-Simon Scale.* The main differences between the two scales were that instead of being an age scale, the Herring modification was a point scale, and its items were arranged in five groups, there being no necessity to take all of them.

Herring, John Peabody. American psychologist (b. Haverhill, Massachusetts, June 30, 1882, d. c. 1933). Herring received a Ph.D. in 1942 from Columbia University Teachers College. He was at Columbia from 1922 to 1929 and with the National Council of the YMCA after 1929. He revised the Binet-Simon Scale in 1922.
   Biographies: PR, 3.

Binet, Alfred. See BINET-SIMON SCALE.

HERTZ. The number of cycles a sound wave (or any other waveform energy) completes in one second. It is usually written as an abbreviation, Hz.

Hertz, Heinrich Rudolf. German physicist (b. Hamburg, February 22, 1857, d. Bonn, January 1, 1894). Hertz, a German scientist of Jewish extraction, first studied engineering and then switched to physics, studying under Helmholtz* and Kirchhoff at the University of Berlin. He obtained a Ph.D. in 1880. Hertz held positions at the universities of Kiel, Karlsruhe, and, after 1889, Bonn. He died of chronic blood poisoning. Hertz's major achievement was the demonstration of the presence of radiation produced by an oscillating electric circuit, as predicted by

Maxwell. He showed that the radiation was electromagnetic and measured its wavelength.

Biographies: Asimov; DSB, 6; EB, 11.

HESS EFFECT. When viewed with one eye, of two laterally moving targets the target whose luminance is reduced relative to the other will appear to lag behind the other. Like the binocular Pulfrich effect,* the Hess effect depends on the greater latency of the dimmer target.

HESS IMAGE. The third positive phase of an afterimage of a primary stimulus that is relatively bright and of brief duration. This stage is less bright than the Purkinje afterimage* or second positive phase and is enhanced if the primary stimulus is red.

Hess, Carl von. German ophthalmologist (b. Mainz, March 7, 1863, d. Munich, June 28, 1923). Hess earned his medical degree at the University of Heidelberg (1886). From 1887 to 1923 he held teaching positions at the universities of Prague, Leipzig, Marburg, Würzburg, and Munich. He was the author of books and papers on vision and opthalmology. He described the movement effect in 1904 (*Pflüg. Arch. ges. Physiol., 101*, 226–62) and the image in 1890 (*Arch. Ophthal., 36*, 1–32).

Biographies: Biog. Lex.

HETEROEROTIC. Descriptive of sexual attraction toward another person (as opposed to oneself).

Eros. See under EROS and following eponyms.

HEYMANS LAW. The threshold for one visual stimulus is raised in direct proportion to the magnitude of another, inhibitory stimulus acting simultaneously: $T_a = T_o + K_a$, where T_o is the normal threshold and K_a a coefficient of inhibition for an inhibiting stimulus of strength a. Heymans considered this relationship to be the general law of which Weber's law* was a special case.

Heymans, Gerardus. Dutch psychologist (b. Ferrwerd, April 17, 1857, d. Groningen, February 18, 1930). Heymans obtained the doctorate in philosophy from the University of Freiburg in 1890 and then held teaching positions at the University of Groningen for the next thirty-six years. He was a philosophically inclined psychologist who established the first psychological laboratory in Holland and did some empirical research in a variety of areas. In psychology, Heymans wrote three monographs and a number of papers. His law was presented in a paper on mental inhibition (*Z. Psychol. Physiol. Sinnesorg.*, 1901, *26*, 305–82).

Biographies: HPA, 2; PR, 3.

HICK-HYMAN LAW. See HICK'S LAW.

Hyman, Ray. American psychologist (b. Chelsea, Massachusetts, June 23, 1928). After receiving a Ph.D. in experimental psychology from Johns Hopkins University, Hyman taught at Harvard University (1953–1958), was a consultant with the General Electric Company (1958–1961), and has been at the University of Oregon since 1961. His research has been in the areas of perception and thinking processes. The classical research on the relationship between reaction time and amount of information processed appeared in 1953 (*J. Exp. Psychol., 45*, 188–96).
   Biographies: AM&WS, 1978S; APA Dir., 1985.

HICK'S LAW. Reaction time increases as a linear function of the binary logarithm of the number of stimulus alternatives, or the amount of information in bits: $RT = a + bH$, where a and b are constants and H is the binary logarithm of equally likely stimulus alternatives.

Hick, William Edmund. English psychologist (b. Tynemouth, Northumberland, August 1, 1912). Hick received an M.D. from the University of Durham (1949) and an M.A. from Cambridge University (1954). He was reader in experimental psychology at Cambridge and held a position with the Medical Research Council Applied Psychology Research Unit, Cambridge. Hick's research has been on skills and ergonomics, fatigue and accidents, and psychotherapy with hallucinogens. He presented the principle governing information processing in 1952 (*Quart. J. Exp. Psychol., 4*, 11–26).
   Biographies: IDP, 1966.

HIPP CHRONOSCOPE. Although driven by a clockwork, this chronoscope was started and stopped by means of an electromagnetic clutch and measured elapsed time in seconds, tenths, hundredths, and thousandths of a second. First used by astronomers, it was introduced in the early psychological laboratories to measure reaction times and later other brief events, such as those occurring in learning experiments.

Hipp, Matthäus. German inventor and entrepreneur (b. Blaubeuren, Württemberg, October 25, 1813, d. Zurich-Fluntern, May 3, 1893). Hipp apprenticed watchmaking, working with V. Stoss, a well-known watchmaker in Ulm, from 1832 to 1834. He spent most of the rest of his life in Switzerland, although he never became a Swiss citizen. In St. Gallen in 1834, Hipp conceived the idea of an electrically pulsed pendulum, an invention still in use. He worked in a clock factory in Saint-Aubin am Neuenburger See from 1835 to 1840 and then opened his own shop in Reutlingen in 1840. Hipp invented several electric telegraph systems, the teletype, and other devices. The chronoscope was made in 1843 and greatly improved in 1849. Hipp directed the Swiss telegraph between 1852 and

1860. His telegraph system was used in other countries, Hipp supplying them with electric clock systems as well.

Biographies: W. Keller & H. R. Schmid, in *Schweizer Pioniere der Wirtschaft und Technik,* 12, 1961, pp. 9–39; *NDB,* 9.

HIPPEL-LINDAU'S DISEASE. Also known as retinocerebellar angiomatosis, it is a dominant gene disorder characterized by retinal and cerebellar angiomata. Mental deficiency is often present.

Hippel, Eugen von. German ophthalmologist (b. Königsberg, August 3, 1867, d. 1939). Hippel, who received his M.D. in 1889 from Göttingen, held positions at the universities of Heidelberg (1889–1909), Halle (1909–1910), and Göttingen (after 1910). His description of the disease appeared in 1895 (*Bericht über die 24. Versammlung der Ophthalmologischen Gesellschaft,* 1895, p. 269).

Biographies: Fischer, Biog. Lex.

Lindau, Arvid Vilhelm. Swedish pathologist (b. Malmö, July 23, 1892). Lindau received his medical education at Lund University (Med. kand. 1914, Med. lic. 1923, Med. dr. 1926) and taught at this university beginning in 1923. His contribution to the understanding of retinocerebellar angiomatosis was presented in 1926 (*Acta path. microb. scand., 3,* Suppl., 1–128).

Biographies: Svenska Maen Och Kvinnor: Biografisk Uppslagsbook. Stockholm: Bonniers, 1942–1955).

HITZIG'S CENTER. Motor area of the cortex, especially in monkeys and dogs.

HITZIG'S GIRDLE. Lack of sensitivity to pain in the region of the breast. It is one of the symptoms of tabes dorsalis.

Hitzig, Eduard. German psychiatrist (b. Berlin, February 6, 1838, d. St. Blasien, Baden, August 21, 1907). Hitzig's M.D. was from the University of Berlin (1862). He was in private practice in Berlin from 1862 to 1875 and then directed the Burghölzli asylum of the University of Zurich until 1879, moving to the University of Halle and directing the asylum at Nietleben. Hitzig is known for the famous experiment, performed with Gustav Fritsch, that established the electrical excitability of brain tissue in 1870. Applying electric current to a dog's brain, Fritsch and Hitzig also established that muscular contractions were controlled by certain areas of the brain only, as well as the location of some of the more specific motor centers (G. Fritsch & E. Hitzig, *Arch. Anat. Physiol.,* 1870, 300–32).

Biographies: DSB, 6; H. Grundfest, *J. Hist. Med.,* 1963, *18,* 125–29; *Haymaker.*

HOBSON'S CHOICE. A choice such that of the several alternatives nominally available, it is possible to choose only one. A choice that is no choice at all is of interest in the social-psychological study of choice behavior.

Hobson, Thomas. Hobson was a liveryman, described by the English essayist Sir Richard Steele in 1712 in *The Spectator* (No. 509) and by Jonathan Swift in two epitaphs in verse. Hobson kept a stable of some forty horses for rent, but he would lend out only the horse that was nearest the stable door because that horse had had the most rest.

HOFFDING STEP. The mediating mental step assumed to be necessary for connecting present perception to a memory trace. When a present stimulus, A, leads to the recall of another, associated stimulus, B, it occurs only when the present stimulus comes in connection with the memory trace of a similar stimulus, A_1, that has been experienced in the past in conjunction with stimulus B. The importance of this concept for pattern perception and recognition has been realized only recently.

Höffding, Harald. Danish philosopher (b. Copenhagen, March 11, 1843, d. Copenhagen, July 2, 1931). Höffding received both his degrees (in theology, 1865; Ph.D. in philosophy, 1870) from the University of Copenhagen and spent his professional life there (1871–1915). His psychology was "without soul," concerned with mental phenomena and their introspective investigation. He wrote the first psychology text in Danish in 1882, as well as 392 other publications. The concept of the mediating mental step was presented in 1889 (*Vtljschr. wiss. Philos., 13,* 420–58).
   Biographies: EP, 4; *HPA,* 2; *PR,* 3.

HOLMES PHENOMENON (HOLMES SIGN, GORDON HOLMES RE-BOUND PHENOMENON). In cases of cerebellar lesions, the forcible bounding of a limb in the direction of the pressure exerted by the patient when a strong counterpressure is suddenly removed.

Holmes, Sir Gordon Morgan. English neurologist (b. Dublin, Ireland, 1876, d. Farnham, Surrey, December 28, 1965). Holmes had an M.B. from Trinity College (1897) and an M.D. He maintained a lifelong association with the National Hospital for Nervous Disease in London. His most important contributions were in clinical neurology. Holmes described the rebound phenomenon in 1918 (*Brit. J. Ophthal., 2,* 449–68, 506–16).
   Biographies: W. Penfield, *J. Neurol. Sci.,* 1967, *5,* 185–90; *Talbot; Wh,* 1961–1970.

HOLMGREN TEST (HOLMGREN WORSTEDS). A test of color blindness in which the testee sorts skeins of colored wool into three categories, matching the skeins with samples.

Holmgren, Alarik Frithiof. Swedish physiologist (b. Linköping, October 22, 1831, d. Uppsala, August 14, 1897). Holmgren graduated with an M.D. from the University of Uppsala in 1861. Sent abroad, he studied with the eminent physiologists of the day (1861–1864) in preparation for establishing the first physiological laboratory in Sweden. From 1864 to 1897, Holmgren served as professor of physiology at Uppsala, becoming well known for his studies of retinal electric

potentials, color vision, and color blindness. Holmgren at Uppsala and C. Loven at the University of Stockholm headed the two Swedish schools of physiology that produced the majority of all later Swedish physiologists. Holmgren began to develop the color-blindness test in 1871. The first mention of it is found in 1874 (*Nord. Med. Ark., 6,* 24–28) and a fuller discussion in 1878 (*Upsala Läk. för. Förh., 13,* 193–226).
    Biographies: DSB, 6; *Rothschuh.*

HOLTZMAN INKBLOT TECHNIQUE. A projective technique that, like the Rorschach test,* utilizes inkblots but uses more of them, forty-five. Only one response is given to an inkblot. The response may be scaled on several dimensions, however, of which there are twenty-two. The test is similar to the Rorschach in that it is based on the same fundamental conceptions. Unlike the Rorschach, however, the test is constructed following standard psychometric criteria and may be administered to groups.

Holtzman, Wayne Harold. American psychologist (b. Chicago, Illinois, January 16, 1923). After graduating with a Ph.D. from Stanford University in 1950, Holtzman went to the University of Texas in Austin, where he has remained to the present time. Besides being a professor of psychology, he was dean of the College of Education from 1964 to 1970 and associate director (1955–1964) and president (since 1970) of the Hogg Foundation for Mental Health. Holtzman has done research on the cross-cultural development of personality, computer applications in psychology, social experiments in community mental health, and measurement and evaluation in psychology and education. He is the author and coauthor of a number of books, among them *Inkblot Perception and Personality* (1961, with others). The test was first published in 1958.
    Biographies: AM&WS, 1978S; *APA Dir.,* 1985; *ConAu,* 37R; *WhoAm,* 1984–1985.

HOLZINGER-CROWDER UNI-FACTOR TEST. A group intelligence test based on factor-analytical findings. Intended for vocational and educational counseling in grades seven through twelve, it measures a verbal, spatial, numerical, and reasoning factor. The score may be translated into an IQ.

Holzinger, Karl John. American psychologist (b. Washington, D.C., August 9, 1892, d. Chicago, Illinois, January 15, 1954). Holzinger graduated from the University of Chicago with a Ph.D. in mathematics and education (1922), and he was on its faculty from 1923 to 1954. Holzinger contributed to psychology in the area of factor analysis (*Factor Analysis,* 1941, with H. H. Harman). In addition to the many papers and monographs that Holzinger wrote on statistical topics, he was a coauthor (with H. H. Newman and F. N. Freeman) of a well-known developmental study, *Twins: A Study of Heredity and Environment* (1937). The Uni-Factor Test was published by World Book Company in 1952.
    Biographies: H. H. Harman, *Psychometrika,* 1954, *19,* 95–96; *PR,* 3; *WhAm,* 3.

Crowder, Norman Allison. American educator (b. Raymond, Washington, April 6, 1921). After receiving the M.A. degree from the University of Chicago in 1948, Crowder stayed at that institution until 1951, when he took a position with the U.S. Air Force. After 1958, Crowder held various training positions in industry. His work has been mainly in the area of programmed learning. He developed the branching program or intrinsic programming (his term) and has written several programmed books for teaching mathematics.

Biographies: WhoAmEd, 1961–1962.

HONI PHENOMENON. In one of the Ames demonstrations,* the distorted room, a person walking along the back wall of the room appears to shrink and grow in size. In 1949, Hadley Cantril observed that to a woman, nicknamed Honi, her husband failed to appear distorted when in the Ames room. Cantril named it the Honi phenomenon. The main factor that appears to determine whether a person will or will not seem distorted in the Ames room is whether that person does or does not produce anxiety in the observer. Anxiety-producing persons appear less distorted.

HORN ART APTITUDE INVENTORY. A test of artistic aptitude (or achievement) for use in grades twelve to sixteen and with art school applicants. The test includes a scribble exercise, a doodle exercise, and an imagery exercise (making a complete drawing while incorporating the few stimulus lines already present on the sheet of paper). The inventory was first published in 1944.

Horn, Charles C. American psychologist (b., n.a., d. n.a.).

Biographies: Unavailable.

HORSLEY-CLARKE STEREOTAXIC INSTRUMENT. An instrument used for precise localization of points inside the brain for purposes of electrical stimulation or electrolytic ablation of focal points within the brain. It consists of a frame that is fastened to the animal's head at the outer ears and the inferior margin of the orbits. A system of racks, pinions, and micrometric scales allows the movement and precisely measured insertion of electrodes in any point in the interior of the brain.

Horsley, Sir Victor Alexander Haden. English neurosurgeon (b. Kensington, London, 1857, d. Amara, Mesopotamia, July 16, 1916). Horsley graduated with a B.S. and a B.M. from the Royal College of Surgeons in 1881. He held various medical appointments, including a professorship of pathology at the University College in London, and became the most renowned neurosurgeon in England. He was first to produce myxedema experimentally by the extirpation of the thyroid gland, worked on the localization of motor functions in the cortex using electrical stimulation, and pioneered in neurosurgery by performing full-fledged brain surgery where previous intervention in the brain had been limited to trephining.

The apparatus that Horsley and Clarke constructed for the study of the brain was described in a joint article in 1908 (*Brain, 31,* 45–124).

Biographies: EB, 11; *Haymaker;* J. B. Lyons, *The Citizen Surgeon: A Biography of Sir Victor Horsley,* 1966; *Rothschuh; Talbot.*

Clarke, R. H. English physiologist (b. 1850, d. n.a.). While working at St. George's Hospital in London, Clarke engaged in pure research. He collaborated with Sir Victor Horsley for many years, one result of this collaboration being the construction of the stereotaxic instrument.

Biographies: Unavailable.

HOTELLING'S T^2. In tests of the hypothesis of no difference between means, the multivariate analog of the univariate t test (that is, when the samples whose means are being compared have been drawn from p-variate normal populations).

Hotelling, Harold. American statistician (b. Fulda, Minnesota, September 29, 1895, d. Chapel Hill, North Carolina, December 26, 1973). Hotelling had a Ph.D. in mathematics from Princeton University (1924). He was on the faculties of Stanford (1924–1931), Columbia (1931–1946), and North Carolina (1946–1966) universities. He presented the test in 1931 (*Ann. Math. Stat., 2,* 360–78).

Biographies: AM&WS, 1976P; H. Levene, *Amer. Statistician,* 1974, *28,* 71–73; *IESS,* 18; *WhAm,* 6.

HOWARD-DOLMAN TEST. A test of stereoscopic acuity in which the testee's ability to perceive the separation of two rods staggered in depth (the Howard-Dolman apparatus), but without any monocular depth clues, is measured.

Howard, Harvey J. American ophthalmologist. Howard had an M.D. and also an Oph.D. He published his test for the judgment of distance in 1919 (*Amer. J. Ophthal., 2,* 656–75).

Biographies: Unavailable.

Dolman. No information is available on the eponymous Dolman.

HOYT FORMULA. A formula for computing the reliability coefficient using analysis of variance:

$$r = 1 - \frac{Vr}{Ve} = \frac{Ve - Vr}{Ve}$$

where V_r is the variance of the remainder sum of squares and V_e the variance for examinees.

Hoyt, Cyril Joseph. American psychologist (b. Stewart, Minnesota, November 22, 1905). Hoyt earned a Ph.D. in educational psychology from the University of Minnesota in 1944. He was at the University of Chicago from 1945 to 1948 and

from 1948 to 1974 at the University of Minnesota. Hoyt's work was in psychometrics and educational measurement. He published the formula in 1941 (*Psychometrika, 6,* 153–60).
Biographies: AM&WS, 1978S.

HUMM-WADSWORTH TEMPERAMENT SCALE. A personality inventory designed for the screening of applicants in industrial settings. It yields measures on seven scales—normal, hysteroid, manic, depressive, autistic, paranoid, epileptoid—as well as a scale of response bias and self-mastery. The scale names were originally defined by Aaron Rosanoff.

Humm, Doncaster George. American psychologist (b. Punxsutawney, Pennsylvania, May 21, 1887, d. 1959). Humm obtained the Ph.D. degree in psychology from the University of Southern California in 1932. He had been a school administrator and school psychologist before. He held positions with private companies from 1932 to 1939 and then headed the Humm Personnel Consultants firm, Los Angeles. The scale was first published in 1934.
Biographies: AMS, 1956S.

Humm, Kathryn Elizabeth Avery. American psychologist (b. St. Paul, Minnesota, October 12, 1898). Before obtaining her master's degree in general psychology from the University of Southern California, Kathryn Humm worked as secretary and assistant to Aaron Rosanoff between 1924 and 1933. She was examiner and assistant supervisor in the Los Angeles school system from 1936 to 1942 and then, with her husband, Doncaster Humm, formed a consulting firm, the Humm Personnel Consultants, of which she was the associate director from 1943 to 1959, director from 1959 to 1970, and codirector since 1970. Her work has been in the areas of personality research, industrial employment testing, and vocational counseling.
Biographies: APA Dir., 1975; *WhoAmW,* 1970–1971.

Wadsworth, Guy Woodbridge, Jr. American psychologist (b. January 19, 1901). After receiving a B.A. from Occidental College, Wadsworth went to work as personnel manager for Southern Counties Gas Company of California in 1930, progressing to assistant general manager of the company by 1941.
Biographies: APA Dir., 1955.

HUNTINGTON'S CHOREA. Hereditary, progressive chorea, accompanied by mental deterioration. It sets in between the ages of thirty and forty and eventually leads to death.

Huntington, George. American physician (b. East Hampton, Long Island, New York, 1850, d. Cairo, New York, March 3, 1916). Huntington received his medical training at the College of Physicians and Surgeons of Columbia University (M.D. 1871). He was a private practitioner in Long Island, Pomeroy, Ohio, and Dutchess County, New York, mostly in the last location. Huntington's only medical publication was the detailed description of the symptoms and the course of the chorea that he had observed in East Hampton, one of the few areas in which the disease was concentrated, although he was not the first to mention it (*Med. Surg. Rep.*, Philadelphia, 1872, *26*, 317–21).

Biographies: Haymaker; Talbot.

HUNT-MINNESOTA TEST FOR ORGANIC BRAIN DAMAGE. A test of brain damage, no longer in use, that employed the Stanford-Binet* vocabulary test as a basis for measuring intellectual deterioration. It consisted of six tests of visual and aural memory. The difference in performance levels on the vocabulary test, relatively insensitive to brain damage, and the memory tests, relatively sensitive to such damage, was taken as a measure of intellectual impairment.

Hunt, Howard Francis. American psychologist (b. Morgantown, West Virginia, May 29, 1918). Hunt graduated from the University of Minnesota with a Ph.D. in clinical psychology in 1943. After two years at Minnesota, Hunt worked as a clinical psychologist for the U.S. Navy and taught at Stanford University. He was at the University of Chicago from 1948 to 1962 and at the New York State Psychiatric Institute and Columbia University from 1962 to 1977. Hunt worked in the areas of experimental psychopathology, psychopharmacology, and conditioning and learning. The test was published in 1943 (*The Hunt-Minnesota Test for Organic Brain Damage: Manual*, University of Minnesota Press; H. F. Hunt, *J. Appl. Psychol.*, 27, 375–86).

Biographies: AM&WS, 1982P; APA Dir., 1985; WhoAm, 1984–1985.

HURLER'S SYNDROME. Also known as gargoylism, it is a syndrome of stunted growth, grotesque face, and other physical defects, accompanied by mental retardation. It is due to a single recessive gene.

Hurler, Gertrud. Austrian pediatrician (b. n.a., d. n.a.). Hurler published a description of the syndrome in 1919 (*Z. Kinderheilk.*, 24, 220–34).

Biographies: Unavailable.

I

ICARUS COMPLEX. A behavioral and attitudinal complex whose main features are a lofty but fragile ambition, narcissism, the wish to live forever, fascination with fire, and a history of bedwetting.

Icarus. In the ancient Greek story, Daedalus and his son, Icarus, made themselves wings of wax and feathers to escape from their imprisonment by King Minos on Crete. Daedalus was able to fly to Sicily, but Icarus flew too high and too close to the sun. The wax of his wings melted, he fell into the sea, and he drowned. The complex was introduced by Henry Murray (American Icarus, in A. Burton & R. E. Harris [eds.], *Clinical Studies in Personality* [2d ed.]. New York: Harper & Row, 1955, pp. 615–41).

ILLINOIS TEST OF PSYCHOLINGUISTIC ABILITIES. Intended for children aged two to ten, the test yields ten subtest scores (such as auditory reception, visual sequential memory, and manual expression) and two scores from optional subtests.

Illinois, University of. The authors—Samuel A. Kirk, James J. McCarthy, and Winifred D. Kirk—based the test on one developed by Dorothy Jean Sievers for her doctoral dissertation at the University of Illinois in 1955. Samuel Kirk was at the University of Illinois from 1947 to 1967, and James McCarthy obtained his doctorate there in 1957. The test was published by the University of Illinois Press in 1961.

ISHIHARA PLATES. A modern version of the color-blindness test invented by Stilling* in 1878, which he called the pseudo-isochromatic test. The plates contain patterns of dots, some of the dots forming meaningful patterns, such as geometric figures, because they differ in hue from the rest. Since the background and figure dots do not differ in lightness, only individuals whose color vision is intact are able to see the patterns.

Ishihara, Shinobu. Japanese opthalmologist (b. Tokyo, September 25, 1879, d. 1963). Ishihara graduated from the Tokyo Imperial University in 1906. From 1906 to 1936 he was a military surgeon and also taught at the Military-Medical Academy in Tokyo. He was on the faculty of the University of Tokyo from 1936 to 1940. The test was published, in English, in 1917 (*Test for Colour-Blindness*).
   Biographies: Fischer, *Biog. Lex; Kodansha Encyclopedia of Japan,* 1983, v. 3.

ISLAND OF REIL. Also known as the insula, this is a structure in the cortex of primates, completely concealed inside the Sylvian fissure.* There is evidence that it is involved in motor functions, taste, and visceral sensations.

Reil, Johann Christian. German physician (b. Rhaude, East Friesland, February 20, 1759, d. Halle, November 22, 1813). Upon completing his medical studies (M.D., University of Halle, 1782), Reil went into private practice at Norden. He taught at Halle from 1787 to 1810 and then, until 1813, at the University of Berlin. Originally Reil followed Kant; he then came under the influence of Schelling's philosophy of nature, abandoning mechanical and physical principles in the interpretation and treatment of disease in favor of an idealistic, wholistic view of nature. Reil described the island in an 1809 paper (*Arch. Physiol., 9,* 196).
   Biographies: DSB, 11.

IVANOV-SMOLENSKY TECHNIQUE. An operant conditioning technique in which a child is exposed to the sight of a moving piece of chocolate and instructed to squeeze a rubber bulb. If the squeeze is timed correctly, the chocolate is delivered through a chute. Pairing a conditioned stimulus with the event leads to the child's response anticipating the delivery of the chocolate.

Ivanov-Smolenskiĭ (Smolensky), Anatoliĭ Grigorevich. Russian pathophysiologist (b. St. Petersburg, May 17, 1985, d. Moscow, 1983). Ivanov-Smolenskiĭ obtained a doctorate in medical sciences from the Petrograd Military Medical Academy in 1921. He remained there until 1925 when he went to the Leningrad Pedagogical Institute and then to Pavlov's Institute in 1931. At the latter, he founded the psychiatric laboratory and was its director until 1945. For the next five years he was the head of the Moscow department of the Pavlov Institute of Evolutionary Physiology and director of the Institute of Higher Nervous Activity (1950–1957). Ivanov-Smolenskiĭ produced more than 2000 publications on pathophysiology and therapy of brain trauma cases. He developed and interpreted

Pavlov's* research concerning types of the nervous system and the classification of temperaments. His approach became the basis of Soviet personality theory. Ivanov-Smolenskiĭ also reorganized Soviet psychiatry on the basis of Pavlov's teachings. The conditioning technique was presented in 1927 (*Brain*, *50*,
138–41).

Biographies: InternWho 1982–1983; PR, 3; WhoWo, 1974.

J

JABBERWOCKY. Slang term used by researchers in the field of information processing for sentences constructed to resemble the general structure of an English sentence but using only nonsense words for nouns, adjectives, verbs, and adverbs.

Jabberwocky. The title of a famous nonsense poem by Lewis Carroll featuring a monster by the same name that begins, " 'Twas brillig, and the slithy toves. . . . " It appears in Carroll's *Through the Looking Glass* (1871).

JACKSONIAN EPILEPSY. A form of epilepsy in which only local muscle groups are involved, usually on one side of the body, and the individual does not lose consciousness. In this form of epilepsy, the focus is in the motor cortex.

JACKSON'S LAW. When mental abilities are lost because of a neurological disorder, the abilities that appeared last in the course of evolution are lost first because it is the higher nervous centers (that is, those appearing last phylogenetically) that are first affected; the lower or older centers are the last.

Jackson, John Hughlings. English neurologist (b. Providence Green, Hammerton, Yorkshire, April 4, 1835, d. London, October 7, 1911). Jackson received an M.D. from St. Andrews University in 1860. He held various hospital and medical appointments, the most significant ones at Moorfield's Eye Hospital, the London Hospital, and the National Hospital in Queen Square, London, which was the longest (1860–1905). Jackson is known for his studies of epilepsy, aphasia, and paralysis. He identified sites of motor action, sensation, and language in the cortex and was first to demonstrate the use of the ophthalmoscope in the study of disorders of the nervous system. Because much of his work was advanced for his time, he laid the groundwork for future brain investigation and is sometimes called the Father of British Neurology. He never wrote a book, but he did publish over 300 scientific communications. The form of epilepsy that bears his name is sometimes also called the Bravais-Jackson epilepsy because Bravais, a French medical student, had described it in his graduation thesis in 1827. Jackson's own term was uncinate seizures. It was Jean-Martin Charcot* who began referring to the epilepsy as Jacksonian. Jackson's first report on it appeared in 1870 (*Transactions of the St. Andrew's Medical Graduates' Association, 3,* 162–204). Jackson's law was formulated in 1898 (*Lancet, 1,* 79–87).

   Biographies: DNB, Suppl. 1; *DSB,* 7; *EB,* 12; *Haymaker;* A. M. Lassek, *The Unique Legacy of Doctor Hughlings Jackson,* 1970; *Talbot.*

JACQUET CHRONOMETER. A form of chronometer that measures time intervals down to one-fifth of a second, records them on a kymograph, and shows total elapsed time on two dials. It was used in the early psychological laboratories.

Jacquet, Edouard Auguste. French navigator. Jacquet flourished around 1896, but it is questionable whether he is the real eponym.
   Biographies: Unavailable.

JAMES-LANGE THEORY OF EMOTION. Sensory impressions, after being conducted to the brain, give rise to motor impulses that travel to skeletal and visceral muscles. The feedback from action, such as running or visceral events, causes the experience of emotion when it arrives back at the brain. The notion that emotion is the result of action upset the prevalent, commonsense view that emotion precedes action and is the cause of it.

James, William. American philosopher and psychologist (b. New York City, January 11, 1842, d. Chocorua, New Hampshire, August 26, 1910). Although James received a medical degree from Harvard University in 1868, he never practiced or taught medicine. At Harvard from 1872 to 1907, James taught physiology, psychology, and then philosophy. He was twice elected president of the American Psychological Association, in 1894 and 1904. Many still consider James America's foremost psychologist. His influence on psychology and psychologists occurred mainly through his *Principles of Psychology* (1890) and his numerous personal contacts and lectures. As a result of his philosophical writings that appeared in the early 1900s (*Pragmatism,* 1907; *The Meaning of Truth,* 1909), pragmatism as a philosophical theory became important, and James gained the distinction of being considered America's most important philosopher. Of the two additional books that James wrote, *Talks to Teachers* (1899) and *Varieties of Religious Experience* (1902), the latter is still used as a text. James' theory of emotion was published in 1884 (*Mind, 9,* 188–205) and then in a revised version in his *Principles,* where he takes account of Lange's statement.

   Biographies: G. W. Allen, *William James: A Biography,* 1967; B. P. Brennan, *William James,* 1968; *DAB,* 9; *DSB,* 7; *EB,* 12; *IESS,* 8; E. C. Moore, *William James,* 1965; *NCAB,* 18, 31.

Lange, Carl Georg. Danish physiologist (b. Vordingborg, December 4, 1834, d. Copenhagen, May 29, 1900). Lange held an M.D. from the University of Copenhagen (1859) and had various medical appointments in Denmark from 1859 to 1875. He lectured at the University of Copenhagen from 1869 to 1872 and was a professor of pathological anatomy at the University Hospital from 1875 to 1900. At about the same time as James and independently of him, Lange conceived a similar theory of emotion. In studying the circulatory system, Lange came to the conclusion that emotion was the result of felt changes in the blood vessels. He published his views in 1885 in his *Om Sindsbevoegelser*. Lange's theory was not quite as broad as James' and stressed vascular rather than all visceral changes.

Biographies: DSB, 8; V. Meisen, *Prominent Danish Scientists Through the Ages*, 1932.

JANET'S DISEASE. A synonym for psychasthenia, an obsolete term for a type of neurosis characterized by anxiety and obsessive ideas.

Janet, Pierre. French psychologist (b. Paris, May 30, 1859, d. Paris, February 24, 1947). Janet received a *Docteur des lettres* degree from the University of Paris in 1889 and an M.D. four years later. He was at the La Salpêtrière hospital* from 1890 to 1894 and taught at the Sorbonne from 1895 to 1920 and at the Collège de France from 1920 to 1936. Janet was a systematic psychopathologist. He developed a system of psychology and psychopathology that he called *psychologie de la conduite*. He systematized the existing knowledge about hysteria and related clinical and academic psychology to it. Janet became known to the English-speaking world through the translations of his *Mental States of Hystericals* (1892, trans. 1893) and *The Major Symptoms of Hysteria* (1907, trans. 1924). Janet wrote seventeen books and more than seventy additional titles. The term *psychasthenia* appears in the title of a book that Janet published with F. Raymond in 1903 (*Les obsessions et la psychasthénie*).

Biographies: M. Culpin, *Nature*, 1947, *159*, 357–64; *EB*, 12; H. F. Ellenberger, *Dialogue*, 1973, *12*, 254–87; H. Eye, in B. B. Wolman (ed.), *Historical Roots of Contemporary Psychology*, 1968, pp. 177–95; L. L. Havens, *J. Nerv. Ment. Dis.*, 1966, *143*, 383–98; *HPA*, 1; *IESS*, 8; W. S. Taylor, *Amer. J. Psychol.*, 1947, *60*, 637–45; R. M. Yerkes, *Yearb. Amer. Phil. Soc.*, 1947, 253–58.

JASTROW CYLINDERS. A series of hard rubber cyclinders used in experiments to determine thresholds for weight, passively experienced or lifted. The weight of the cylinders can be adjusted—for example, by inserting or removing birdshot or lead inserts.

JASTROW ILLUSION. The illusion that in a set of concentric annular segments, the inside arcs describing the segments, although physically equal, are not of the same length.

Jastrow, Joseph. American psychologist (b. Warsaw, Poland, January 30, 1863, d. Stockbridge, Massachusetts, January 8, 1944). Jastrow's was the first American doctorate taken specifically in psychology (Johns Hopkins University, 1886).

He taught at the University of Wisconsin (1888–1927) and at the New School for Social Research (1927–1933). At Wisconsin, Jastrow established one of the early American psychological laboratories and published many experimental papers, but he is best known as a popularizer of the "new" psychology. Of his many books, *Wish and Wisdom* (1935, first published in 1900) was the most popular. The illusion was presented in an 1892 article, written with H. West (*Amer. J. Psychol.*, *4*, 382–98).

Biographies: *HPA*, 1; C. L. Hull, *Amer. J. Psychol.*, 1944, *57*, 581–85; *Jewish*, 6; *NCAB*, 11; W. B. Pillsbury, *Psychol. Rev.*, 1944, *51*, 261–65; *PR*, 3; *WhAm*, 2.

JEHOVAH COMPLEX. Identification of oneself with God by a person suffering from a delusion of greatness.

Jehovah. The intended but incorrect transliteration of the Hebrew word for God, Jahweh.

JENDRASSIK REINFORCEMENT. Also known as the Jendrassik maneuver, it is a method for increasing the strength of a reflex, such as the patellar (knee-jerk) reflex, by interlocking one's fingers and pulling hard.

Jendrassik, Ernö. Hungarian physician (b. Klausenburg, Hungary, June 7, 1858, d. Budapest, December 21, 1921). Jendrassik received an M.D. from the University of Budapest (1880). He taught there from 1887 to 1908 and was then the head of a clinic of internal medicine in Budapest (1908–1921). Jendrassik wrote many articles and books on medical subjects. He described the manuever in 1885 (*Neurol. Zbl.*, *4*, 412).

Biographies: *EUI*, 18; Hirsch, *Biog. Lex.*

JOCASTA COMPLEX. The excessive attachment of a mother to her son, part of the Oedipus complex.*

Jocasta. In the ancient Greek story, Jocasta was both the mother and wife of Oedipus.* She was first the wife of Laius, the king of Thebes. It had been prophesied that Laius would be killed by his own son. When a son was born, Laius had him put out on a mountain where he would perish. Oedipus survived, but when he was told the prophecy that he would kill his father, he left his adopted family. On his way to Delphi, he killed a man who would not give him way, not knowing that the man was Laius. He went to Thebes and unknowingly married Jocasta, his mother. They had four children. When they learned the truth, Jocasta killed herself, and Oedipus blinded himself. The term was introduced by Raymond de Saussure in 1920 (*Intern. Z. Psychoanal.*, *6*(2), 118–22).

JOHNS HOPKINS CHRONOSCOPE. See DUNLAP CHRONOSCOPE.

Johns Hopkins University. The chronoscope was named after the university where Knight Dunlap,* its inventor, worked for thirty years. The university took its name from the Quaker merchant and banker of Baltimore, Johns Hopkins.

JORDAN CURVE. A closed curve that does not intersect itself. Kurt Lewin used such curves to represent regions in life space.

Jordan, Camille. French mathematician (b. Lyons, January 5, 1838, d. Paris, January 22, 1921). Jordan received his education at the Ecole polytechnique in Paris and was an engineer until 1885. He taught mathematics at the Ecole polytechnique and the Collège de France from 1873 to 1912. His early work was on geometry, but he changed later to higher algebra. In dealing with the function of bounded variation, Jordan applied it to the topological version of the circle, now known as the Jordan curve.
   Biographies: DSB, 7; EB, 13.

JOST'S LAW. A generalization concerning human learning that states that of two associations of equal strength, the one that was formed earlier will be strengthened more by repetition than the more recent one. The generalization was based on the observation that older associations decay less rapidly than more recent ones, and it served also to explain why learning is improved if learning trials are distributed in time rather than massed.

Jost, Adolph. German psychologist (b. Graz, Austria, August 22, 1874, d. c. 1920, place n.a.). Jost obtained a Ph.D. in psychology at the University of Göttingen in 1896 working under Georg Müller,* but not much more is known about his life. Jost's work on his doctoral dissertation led to the formulation of the eponymous law. Later Jost worked with Müller on human learning using the method of right associates. The method was invented by Müller but published by Jost.
   Biographies: In A. Jost, Die Assoziationsfestigkeit in ihrer Abhängigkeit von der Verteilung der Wiederholungen, 1897. (Ph.D. dissertation, Göttingen).

JULESZ'S STEREOGRAM. A stereogram consisting of computer-produced square arrays of sequences of black and white dots arranged in two identical matrices of rows and columns. A portion of the dots in one of the matrices is shifted laterally by an amount corresponding to binocular disparity. When viewed through a stereoscope, the displaced portion is seen stereoscopically as an object either in front of or behind the plane of the stereogram. A person with deficient stereopsis is unable to see anything except random arrays of dots.

Julesz, Bela. Hungarian-American engineer and psychologist (b. Budapest, Hungary, February 19, 1928). Julesz was a diplomate of the Budapest Technical University in 1950 and received the doctor of engineering degree from the Hungarian Academy of Science in 1956. He was at the Institute of Telecommunications Research in Budapest from 1951 to 1956 and then served as the head of the Sensory and Perceptual Processes Department of the Bell Telephone Laboratories beginning in 1956. Julesz's work has been in vision, physiological optics, optical data processing, the psychophysics and neurophysiology of vision, and depth perception. He presented the stereogram in 1964 (*Science, 145,* 356–62).

Biographies: AM&WS, 1982P.

JUNGIAN PSYCHOLOGY. Jungian or analytic psychology is a form of psychoanalytic theory that, while similar to Freudianism* in that it emphasizes the role of the unconscious in personality dynamics and assumes some of the same components of personality, differs from the latter in its lessened emphasis on the role of sexual factors in the etiology of neuroses and a greater role of the collective aspect of the unconscious. The core of Jung's theory of personality is that every psychological phenomenon implies the opposite of itself—for example, in addition to the opposition between extroversion and introversion, the psychological functions of thinking and feeling (the rational functions) are the opposites of sensation and intuition (the irrational functions). The dominance of one of these (the superior function) further determines the psychological type of an individual. The principle of opposites also implies that both manifest and latent tendencies need to be recognized and dealt with if one is to live in harmony with oneself. The Jungian individual consists of an ego, a persona, the shadow, the animus or anima, the self, and the unconscious, which consists of a personal and a collective layer. The process of attaining a healthy, creative personality—individuation—involves the differentiation as well as the compensatory balancing of the opposing facets of personality in relation to the central core, the self.

Jung, Carl Gustav. Swiss psychiatrist (b. Kesswil, Thurgau, July 26, 1875, d. Küsnacht, Zurich, June 6, 1961). Jung was already an established psychiatrist (M.D., University of Basel, 1900) when he learned of Freud's* approach and began applying his technique to treating patients. He met Freud in 1907 and in 1911 became the first president of the International Psychoanalytic Society and heir apparent to Freud. By 1914, however, his views had grown sufficiently apart from those of Freud for him to sever his connection with Freud and to form his own school. Jung had been with the University of Zurich since 1900. In 1913 he gave up his university position to go into private practice and devote time to the study of the unconscious and its manifestations. Jung reentered the academic field in 1933 when he began to teach at the Federal Polytechnic Institute in Zurich (until 1942). The English edition of Jung's collected works contains 17 volumes.

His *Psychological Types,* first published in 1921, is his best-known and most influential book.

Biographies: E. A. Bennet, *C. G. Jung,* 1961; *DSB,* 7; *EB,* 13; *EP,* 4; *IESS,* 8; A. Jaffe, *From the Life and Work of C. G. Jung,* 1971; C. G. Jung, *Memories, Dreams, Reflections,* 1973; S. T. Seleznick, in F. Alexander et al. (eds.), *Psychoanalytic Pioneers,* 1966, pp. 63–77; G. Wehr, *Portrait of Jung,* 1971.

K

KANNER SYNDROME. Infantile autism, described by Kanner as the "innate inability of certain children to relate to other people."

Kanner, Leo. Austrian-American psychiatrist (b. Klekotow, Austria, June 13, 1894, d. Sykesville, Maryland, April 3, 1981). Kanner received his M.D. from the University of Berlin in 1921, left for the United States in 1924, and became an American citizen in 1930. In 1930 he founded the Johns Hopkins Children's Psychiatric Clinic. He was at Johns Hopkins from 1928 to 1959. Kanner was first to describe infantile autism (*J. Pediat.,* 1944, *25,* 211–17), and he is also considered to be the Father of Child Psychiatry (*Child Psychiatry,* 1935, 1972; 4). His total published output contains more than 250 items.
  Biographies: ConAu, 17R, 103; *WhAm,* 7.

KAUFMAN ASSESSMENT BATTERY FOR CHILDREN. Assesses the intelligence and achievement of children aged two and a half to twelve and a half. The battery is based on research in cognitive psychology and neuropsychology, especially the right-left functional asymmetry of the brain and the neuropsychological theory of A. S. Luria.* It separates problem-solving ability (fluid thinking) from educational achievement (crystallized thinking). The former, measured by the Mental Processing Scale, considers separately the abilities to solve problems sequentially or simultaneously. The Achievement Scale focuses on acquired facts.

Kaufman, Alan Stephen. American psychologist (b. April 21, 1944). Kaufman received a Ph.D. in psychometrics from Columbia University in 1970. He has held various academic appointments and has been professor of education psychology at the University of Alabama since 1984. Kaufman's main field of interest has been educational psychology, with emphasis on intelligence. While working as assistant director of test research for the Psychological Corporation (1968–1974), Kaufman helped develop both the Wechsler Intelligence Scale for Children—Revised* and the McCarthy Scales.* The Kaufman Battery was published in 1983.

Biographies: APA Dir., 1985.

Kaufman, Nadeen Laurie. American psychologist (b. January 17, 1945). Nadeen Kaufman and her husband, Alan Kaufman, are the coauthors of the Kaufman Assessment Battery for Children (KABC). N. Kaufman received an Ed.D. in special education from Columbia University in 1978. Her main field is school psychology, specializing in learning difficulties. She has held various academic appointments and has been at the University of Alabama since 1984.

Biographies: APA Dir., 1985.

KEELER POLYGRAPH. The lie detector, an instrument for measuring changes in blood pressure, respiration rate, heart rate, and the galvanic skin response* that occur when the testee lies in answer to a question (or is aroused for any reason).

Keeler, Leonarde. American psychologist and criminologist (b. Berkeley, California, October 30, 1903, d. Sturgeon Bay, Wisconsin, September 20, 1949). Keeler received an A.B. from Stanford University (1930). He worked as a criminologist from 1929 to 1933 and was assistant professor of law in psychology at Northwestern University (1933–1939). He went into private practice in 1939 and in 1948 established the Keeler Polygraph School. Keeler was granted a U.S. patent for his polygraph in 1931. It was first used as a source of evidence in court in 1935.

Biographies: NCAB, 41; *NYT*, Sept. 21, 1949:31; *WhAm*, 2.

KELLER PLAN. A name for the Personalized System of Instruction devised by Fred Keller. It is based on principles of operant conditioning and applies some of the principles used in the design of teaching machines to the classroom. Materials are presented to students in relatively small amounts. Students take a quiz over a unit on an individual basis when they feel they are ready. They move on to the next unit if they pass the quiz over the previous unit, but there is no penalty for failing a quiz. The amount of time needed to complete a course of study depends on the individual student.

Keller, Fred Simmons. American psychologist (b. Rural Grove, New York, January 2, 1899). Keller received the Ph.D. degree in experimental psychology from Harvard University in 1931. He held positions at Colgate (1931–1938), Columbia (1938–1964), Arizona State (1964–1968), Western Michigan (1968–1973), and Georgetown (1974–1976) universities. Keller, who studied at Harvard University with B. F. Skinner,* became a Skinnerian behaviorist and contributed to the development of the reinforcement theory of learning during his tenure at Columbia. He was instrumental in developing psychology in Brazil in 1961 during his year there as Fulbright-Hayes professor. It was on his return there in 1964 that he developed the personalized system of instruction.

Biographies: AM&WS, 1978S; *Amer. Psychologist*, 1977, *32*, 68–71; F. Keller, in R. Gandelman (ed.), *Autobiographies in Experimental Psychology*, 1985; *ConAu*, 1969; *WhoAm*, 1978–1979.

KELLEY'S CONSTANT PROCESS. In psychophysics, a method of fitting data obtained by the constant stimulus method to the normal ogive by converting the data to z-scores. It is equivalent to the Müller-Urban method* except that it uses the standard deviation instead of steepness of the distribution, *h*.

Kelley, Truman Lee. American psychometrician (b. Whitehall, Michigan, May 25, 1884, d. Santa Barbara, California, May 2, 1961). Kelley graduated with a Ph.D. in psychology from Columbia University in 1914 and then taught a few years at the University of Texas and at Columbia. Most of his career was spent at Stanford (1920–1931) and Harvard (1931–1950). Kelley made important contributions to statistics and psychometrics: scaling, factor analysis of intelligence, canonical correlation, and test construction. He wrote a dozen books and many articles in these areas. The constant process was described in his *Statistical Method* (1924).

Biographies: I. Flanagan, *Psychometrika*, 1961, *26*, 343–45; *IESS*, 8; *NCAB*, 49; *PR*, 3; *WhAm*, 4.

KENDALL COEFFICIENT OF CONCORDANCE. A nonparametric measure of the degree of association among *k* variables that are in the form of rankings. Its symbol is *W*.

KENDALL PARTIAL RANK CORRELATION COEFFICIENT. A nonparametric measure of correlation between two sets of ranked data when the effect of a third variable, also on the ordinal scale, is being kept constant.

KENDALL RANK-ORDER CORRELATION COEFFICIENT. A nonparametric correlation coefficient that shows the degree to which two sets of ranks vary together. It is used with the same kind of data as Spearman's rho,* with the advantage that Kendall's correlation coefficient, tau, can be generalized to a partial correlation coefficient.

Kendall, Sir Maurice George. English statistician (b. Kettering, Northampton, September 6, 1907, d. London, March 29, 1983). Kendall was educated at Cambridge University. He held government jobs as statistician between 1930 and 1949 and then taught at the University of London from 1949 to 1961. He was at Scientific Control Systems, Ltd., from 1961 to 1971. Kendall wrote ten books on statistical subjects. The *W* statistic and the partial correlation coefficient are presented in his *Rank Correlation Methods* (1948), the tau statistic in *Biometrika,* 1938, *30,* 81–93.

Biographies: InternWho, 1982–1983; *Nature,* July 16, 1949, *164,* 96; *Who,* 1982–1983.

KENT E-G-Y TEST. A brief intelligence test for children aged five to fourteen, used for quick, preliminary estimation of intelligence before giving a full-scale test.

KENT-ROSANOFF FREE ASSOCIATION TEST. The authors' original intent was to use the test as a diagnostic tool for various categories of mental disorder, the rationale being that specific mental disorders were reflected in specific types of word association. Their main contribution to the associative technique was to establish statistical norms of frequency of usage of associations to 100 stimulus words using 1,000 normal adults. It was shown later that association depends also on such factors as ethnicity and socioeconomic class, and the test ceased to be used for individual diagnosis. It has retained its use, however, as a measure of defense mechanisms and in the laboratory setting in work on verbal learning.

KENT-SHAKOW INDUSTRIAL FORMBOARDS. A form board with five recesses whose shapes may be reproduced using sets of blocks of the same shape that have been cut along one or more straight lines. The eight sets of blocks constitute tasks of increasing difficulty.

Kent, Grace Helen. American psychologist (b. Michigan City, Indiana, June 6, 1875, d. Silver Springs, Maryland, September 18, 1973). Kent obtained her Ph.D. degree from George Washington University in 1911. She held seven hospital appointments from 1906 through 1946, the longest at Danvers State Hospital (1928–1946). Her name became well known after the publication of the association test (with Rosanoff, *Amer. J. Insanity,* 1910, *67,* 37–96, 317–90). She continued to work in the area of clinical psychometrics, producing additional psychological instruments. The Kent-Shakow Formboards was first developed as a clinical instrument (*Ped. Semin. J. Genet. Psychol.,* 1925, *32,* 599–611) and later, under the name of Kent-Shakow Industrial Formboards, as an industrial instrument (*Personnel J.,* 1928, *7,* 115–20). The E-G-Y Test, or Kent Series of Emergency Scales, was first published in 1946. Kent produced about twenty-five papers and the book *Mental Tests in Clinics for Children* (1950).

Biographies: AMS, 1956S; *PR,* 3; D. Shakow, *J. Hist. Behav. Sci.,* 1974, *10,* 275–80.

Rosanoff, Aaron Joshua. American psychiatrist (b. Pinsk, Russia, June 26, 1878, d. Los Angeles, California, January 7, 1943). Rosanoff's M.D. was from Cornell University (1900). From 1901 through 1922 he was at State Hospital in King's Park, New York, and in private practice from 1923 to 1943. At the same time, Rosanoff lectured at the University of Southern California, and, from 1939 to 1942, he was California state director of institutions. Rosanoff published on the relationship among heredity, constitution, and psychosis, on degenerative brain diseases, on war neuroses, on organic psychoses, and other topics. His work with World War I shell-shock cases merited him a government citation. He also organized a private mental institution and planned two mental hospitals, one in Los Angeles and one in San Francisco (Langley Porter Clinic).

Biographies: CurBio, 1943; J. Kasanin, *J. Nerv. Ment. Dis.,* 1943, *97,* 501–3; *NYT,* Jan. 8, 1943, 20.

Shakow, David. American psychologist (b. New York City, January 2, 1901, d. Bethesda, Maryland, February 26, 1981). Shakow's Ph.D. was in psychology from Harvard University (1946). From 1928 to 1946 he had been chief psychologist at the Worcester State Hospital. Shakow was at the University of Illinois from 1946 to 1954 and at the University of Chicago from 1948 to 1954. During the remaining years, he was with the National Institutes of Mental Health. Shakow's work was in clinical psychology. He pioneered in the development of an experimental psychopathology of schizophrenia.

Biographies: Amer. Psychologist, 1976, *31,* 64–71; *APA Dir.,* 1975; N. Garmezy, *Amer. Psychologist,* 1984, *39,* 698–99.

KIESOW'S AREA. A small region of the inner cheek, opposite the second lower molar, that is insensitive to pain.

Kiesow, Federico. German-Italian psychologist (b. Brüel, near Schwerin, Mecklenburg, March 28, 1858, d. December 9, 1940). Kiesow received his Ph.D. from Wilhelm Wündt* at the University of Leipzig in 1894. He moved to the University of Turin in 1895, remaining there until 1933. At Turin, Kiesow established a psychological laboratory, bringing Wundtian experimental psychology to Turin. He studied sensation and perception, especially touch, producing numerous publications. For many years Kiesow was Italy's most prominent psychologist. He described the pain-insensitive area in 1894 (*Phil. Stud., 9,* 510–27).

Biographies: CE, 8; *HPA,* 1; H. Misiak & V. M. Staudt, *Catholics in Psychology,* 1954; M. Ponzo, *Psychol. Rev.,* 1941, *48,* 268–69; *PR,* 3.

KILNER SCREEN. Also referred to as Kilner goggles, it is a liquid or solid light filter containing decyanin, a coal tar dye, or other suitable dye. When an object, such as a person, is viewed through the screen, it appears to be surrounded by a faintly luminous, cloudy emanation. Before directing the gaze at the object, the viewer looks briefly at some bright surface, such as the sky on a sunny day or a bright electric bulb, and then immediately at the object. It is claimed that the luminous emanation represents the aura or the etheric body and that states of health, emotion, and other mental processes are reflected in the changing luminosity and colors of the aura.

Kilner, Walter John. English medical electrician (b. Bury St. Edmonds, Suffolk, May 23, 1847, d. London, June 23, 1920). Kilner studied at Cambridge University, medicine at St. Thomas Hospital in London, and in the process acquired the B.A. degree in 1870, MRCS, and LSA degrees in 1871 and the M.B. degree in 1872. He became employed by the St. Thomas Hospital in 1879, became a member of the Royal College of Physicians in 1883, and in the same year went into private practice while keeping his St. Thomas position. In 1911, Kilner came upon the method of viewing the human "aura," announcing it the same year in the book, *The Human Atmosphere*.
   Biographies: Shepard, 2.

KINNEY'S LAW. In cases of postnatally developing deafness, the length of time over which changes in speech develop is directly proportional to the length of time during which normal speech has been present.

Kinney, Richard. American educator and author (b. 1924, d. Evanston, Illinois, February 19, 1979). Kinney lost eyesight at seven and was totally deaf at twenty, yet he became widely known as educator, lecturer, chess expert, and world traveler. He graduated from Mount Union College, Alliance, Ohio, in 1947 and joined the faculty of the Hadley School for the Blind in 1950, becoming president of the school in 1975. He was the author of four books of poetry and a textbook on the deaf-blind.
   Biographies: Chic. Trib., Feb. 21, 1979, sec. 5, p. 11; ConAu, 85R.

KINSEY REPORTS. The results of 18,500 personal interviews concerning sexual behavior published by Alfred Kinsey in his two books, *Sexual Behavior of the Human Male* (1948) and *Sexual Behavior of the Human Female* (1953). These were the first large-scale empirical studies of sexual behavior ever conducted.

Kinsey, Alfred Charles. American biologist (b. Hoboken, New Jersey, June 23, 1894, d. Bloomington, Indiana, August 25, 1956). Kinsey's Ph.D. was in zoology (Harvard University, 1920). He was at Indiana University from 1920 to 1956, first as a zoology professor and then, beginning in 1947, director of the Institute for Sex Research. Kinsey's interest and research on human sexual behavior, which started in 1938, led to the establishment of the institute. Kinsey's reports presented quantified descriptions of sexual behavior, showed an unexpected range of variation in such behavior, corrected misconceptions, and upset many established opinions concerning human sexual behavior.
   Biographies: C. V. Christensen, *Kinsey, a Biography*, 1971; *DAB*, Suppl. 6; *IESS*, 8; *NCAB*, H; W. B. Pomroy, *Dr. Kinsey and the Institute for Sex Research*, 1972; L. Rosenzweig & S. Rosenzweig, *J. Hist. Behav. Sci.*, 1969, 5, 173–91.

KIRLIAN PHOTOGRAPHY. A method of lensless photography in which the image of the corona discharge of an object is obtained by placing the object in contact with photographic film and sandwiching them between two insulated metal plates that are connected to a source of high-voltage (16 to 32 kilovolts), high-frequency (75 kilohertz and up) electricity. The claim is made that the photograph is that of the "aura" of the object and that its shape, details, or color in the photograph vary with its mental or health state, if it is living matter, or registers the effect of external influences, such as handling, healing, or emotions.

Kirlian, Semyon Davidovich. Russian electrician (b. Ekaterinburg [now Krasnodar], 1897). With no more than a fourth-grade education, Kirlian became an extremely skillful mechanic who could repair any type of device or machinery. While repairing an electrotherapy device in his home town in 1939, Kirlian observed sparks jumping from the electrodes of the equipment to a person lying nearby. Interposing a photographic plate between the spark and the person's hand, Kirlian obtained an outline of the hand surrounded by a luminance. Kirlian did not know that Nicolas Tesla had already obtained photographs of such sparks. Working with his wife, Kirlian developed a technique for obtaining clear, still pictures of objects surrounded by luminous discharges, as well as images of objects in motion. His work led to widespread recognition in the 1940s. He now holds a research position with the Agricultural Research Institute near Krasnodar and has been awarded the title of meritorious inventor.

Biographies: H. Gris & W. Dick, *The New Soviet Psychic Discoveries,* 1978.

Kirlian, Valentina Khrisafovna. Russian schoolteacher (b. n.a., d. Krasnodar, December 1971). Valentina Kirlian, Semyon Kirlian's wife, collaborated with her husband in developing their photographic technique. She not only lent credibility to her husband's work because of the education she had received in a teachers' college, but she also appears to have been the main subject in the numerous tests and tryouts of their equipment. It is alleged that she died as a direct result of overexposure to the type of electricity used in Kirlian photography.

Biographies: H. Gris & W. Dick, *The New Soviet Psychic Discoveries,* 1978.

KIRSCHMANN'S LAW OF CONTRAST. The saturation of the induced color in simultaneous color contrast is directly proportional to the logarithm of the saturation of the inducing color.

Kirschmann, August. German psychologist (b. Oberstein a/d Nahe, July 21, 1860, d. Leipzig, October 24, 1932). Kirschmann's Ph.D. was in psychology, which he obtained in 1890 working under Wilhelm Wundt.* He was at the University of Toronto from 1893 to 1915 and at the University of Leipzig from 1915 to 1932. He presented the law of contrast in 1891 (*Phil. Stud., 6,* 417–92).

Biographies: J. C. Poggendorff (ed.), *Biographisch-Literarisches Handwörterbuch für Mathematik etc.,* vol. 5, 1863–1904; *PR, 3.*

KJERSTAD-ROBINSON LAW. A generalization concerning human verbal learning according to which the amount of material learned during equal portions of the learning time is the same for different lengths of the material to be learned.

Kjerstad, Conrad Lund. American psychologist (b. Dakota Territory [Charles Mix County, South Dakota], July 11, 1883, d. Canton, South Dakota, December 23, 1967). Kjerstad worked as a teacher before obtaining his Ph.D. in psychology from the University of Chicago in 1917. He occupied various academic and administrative positions in North Dakota and was professor of philosophy and education at the University of North Dakota from 1936 to 1954. His fields of interest were the psychology of learning, personality and character, and the philosophy of education. The Kjerstad-Robinson law is based on the results reported by Kjerstadt in 1919 (*Psychol. Monog., 26,* No. 5) and two papers by Robinson.
Biographies: APA Dir., 1965; WhAm, 6.

Robinson, Edward Stevens. American psychologist (b. Lebanon, Ohio, April 18, 1893, d. New Haven, Connecticut, February 27, 1937). After he received his Ph.D. in psychology from the University of Chicago (1920), Robinson went to Yale University but returned to Chicago a year later. In 1927, he went back to Yale. Robinson was a Chicago functionalist. His initial work was on learning, particularly retroactive inhibition. The relationship expressed in the Kjerstad-Robinson law was described by Robinson in two papers (*J. Exp. Psychol.,* 1922, *5,* 428–48, with T. Heron; *Amer. J. Psychol.,* 1924, *35,* 235–43, with C. W. Darrow). Later Robinson turned to social psychology, believing that the functionalist approach could be applied here also. He lectured on law and psychology at the Yale Law School. Five books and sixty-seven papers completed Robinson's bibliography when he died in an accident.
Biographies: J. R. Angell, *Psychol. Bull.,* 1937, *34,* 801–5; R. P. Angier, *Psychol. Rev.,* 1937, *44,* 267–73; H. A. Carr, *Amer. J. Psychol.,* 1937, *49,* 488–89; *DAB,* 22; *NCAB,* 28; *PR,* 3; *WhAm,* 1.

KLEINE-LEVIN SYNDROME. Excessive sleepiness and sleepiness that attacks the victim, usually a teenager, periodically. This is often accompanied by inability to remember portions of the attacks and by irritability and confusion.

Kleine, Willi. German neuropsychiatrist (b. n.a., d. n.a.). Kleine described the syndrome in 1925 (*Mschr. Psychiat. Neurol. 57,* 285–320).
Biographies: Unavailable.

Levin, Max. American neurologist (b. Krustpils, Latvia, 1901). Levin received an M.D. from Johns Hopkins University (1924). He worked at several clinics and hospitals between 1924 and 1939, was a military psychiatrist from 1943 to 1946, and then went into private practice in New York City. Levin's contribution to the understanding of the Kleine-Levin syndrome appeared in 1936 (*Brain, 59,* 494–504).
Biographies: Dir. Med. Spec., 1985–1986.

KLINEFELTER'S SYNDROME. An endocrinological disorder in males that results in abnormally small testicles, enlarged mammary glands, and sterility. It is genetically transmitted and is associated with the presence of an extra X chromosome in a sex grouping: XXY. There is a statistically significant association between Klinefelter's syndrome and childhood schizophrenia. The syndrome affects one of every five hundred males.

Klinefelter, Harry Fitch. American physician (b. Baltimore, Maryland, March 20, 1912). Klinefelter, who received his M.D. from Johns Hopkins University (1937), was first at Harvard University (1941–1942) and then, after 1943, at the Johns Hopkins Medical School. Klinefelter's field is clinical medicine: rheumatology, endocrinology, and alcoholism. He described the syndrome with E. C. Reifenstein, Jr., and F. Albright in 1942 (*Clin. Endocrin.*, 2, 615–27).
   Biographies: AM&WS, 1982P; *Dir. Med. Spec.,* 1985–1986.

KLOPFER SYSTEM. A system for interpreting protocols of the Rorschach test* that uses a phenomenological approach.

Klopfer, Bruno. German-American psychologist (b. Augsburg, Bavaria, October 1, 1900). Klopfer graduated from the University of Munich with a Ph.D. in 1922. He served with various social welfare and educational agencies in Frankfurt and Berlin from 1922 to 1933. In the United States since 1934, Klopfer has held positions with Columbia University (1934–1945), City College of New York (1945–1947), and the University of California at Los Angeles (1946–1963). He had been also in private practice since 1936, doing Jungian analysis. Klopfer's first contact with the Rorschach test was in 1933. He wrote a series of articles on it, including one on a scoring system (*Rorschach. Res. Exch.,* 1936, *1,* 19–22, with S. Sender). He described the Klopfer system in his book, *The Rorschach Technique* (1942), which he wrote with D. Kelley.
   Biographies: AM&WS, 1962S; *APA Dir.,* 1968.

KLUVER-BUCY SYNDROME. A syndrome of psychic blindness (inability to recognize objects), aggressiveness, and hypersexuality that follows the ablation of regions in the anterior portion of the temporal lobe in the monkey.

Klüver, Heinrich. German-American psychologist (b. Schleswig-Holstein, Germany, May 25, 1897, d. Oak Lawn, Illinois, February 8, 1979). After he received his Ph.D. in psychology (Stanford University, 1924), Klüver taught at the University of Minnesota and did research at several other institutions until 1946. His last position was at the University of Chicago (1936–1962). Klüver first conducted some classic studies on the phenomenology of eidetic imagery (first ones in the English language) and the effects of mescal (first scientific investigation of this substance); then he devoted the rest of his life to work on neuroanatomical and psychological relationships, using monkeys of different species. Klüver and Bucy described the syndrome that bears their names in 1938 (*Arch. Neurol. Psychiat.,* *42,* 979–1000).

Biographies: AM&WS, 1976P; *Amer. Psychologist,* 1965, *20,* 1089–90; W. A. Hunt, *Amer. J. Psychol.,* 1980, *93,* 159–61; S. Schulman, *Amer. Psychologist,* 1980, *35,* 380–382; *WhAm,* 7.

Bucy, Paul Clancy. American neurosurgeon (b. Hubbard, Iowa, November 13, 1904). Bucy's M.D. was from the University of Iowa (1927). He taught at the University of Chicago (1928–1933), University of Illinois (1941–1954), Northwestern University (1954–1973), and the Bowman Gray Medical School (since 1974). Bucy has done research on spinal cord injury, involuntary movements, brain tumors, and other topics.

Biographies: AM&WS, 1982P; *WhoAm,* 1984–1985.

KNAUBER ART ABILITY TEST. A test of artistic ability for individuals in junior high school and above. It consists of seventeen subtests or artistic problems.

Knauber, Alma Jordan. American educator (b. Cincinnati, Ohio, August 24, 1893, d. Cincinnati, Ohio, February 23, 1975). With an M.A. from Ohio State University (1928), Knauber did graduate work at the Taos School of Art in 1950. She taught in the Cincinnati public schools (1916–1919), Ohio State University (1919–1927), and the University of Cincinnati (since 1927). The test was published in 1935 (*Education,* 56, 165–70; *Knauber Art Ability Test: Examiner's Manual.* Cincinnati: Author, 1935).

Biographies: WhoAmArt, 1961; *WhoAmWom,* 1961.

KNOX CUBE TEST. A nonlanguage performance test in which the testee must reproduce patterns of taps executed by the examiner with four cubes, touched by a fifth. It was originally used to test immigrants to the United States.

Knox, Howard Andrew. American psychiatrist (b. 1885). Knox published the test in 1914 (*J. Amer. Med. Ass.,* *62,* 741–47).

Biographies: Unavailable.

KOHLER-RESTORFF PHENOMENON. See VON RESTORFF PHENOMENON.

Köhler, Wolfgang. German-American psychologist (b. Revel [now Tallin], Estonia, January 21, 1887, d. Enfield, New Hampshire, June 11, 1967). A year after Köhler had obtained his Ph.D. from the University of Berlin in 1909, he, while at the University of Frankfurt, served as subject in a crucial experiment conducted by Max Wertheimer. Wertheimer, Köhler, and Kurt Koffka, another subject in the same experiment, became the founders of the Gestalt school of psychology. The years 1913 through 1920 Köhler spent at the Anthropoid Station in Tenerife, where he made a major contribution to Gestalt theory and to the study of learning. A second major contribution of Köhler was the postulation of the principle of isomorphism in 1920. After his return from Tenerife in 1921, Köhler joined the faculty at the University of Göttingen, only to leave it for Berlin a year later. Köhler left Germany in 1935, joining the faculty of Swarthmore College. He remained there until his retirement in 1955, having become a U.S. citizen in 1946. Köhler wrote *Gestalt Psychology* in 1929 and several other books on the Gestalt theory in subsequent years. The phenomenon was described by Von Restorff* in a 1933 paper and then in a joint paper, with Köhler as the senior author (*Psychol. Forsch.*, 1935, *21*, 56–112).

Biographies: *Amer. Psychologist*, 1957, *12*, 131–33; S. E. Asch, *Amer. J. Psychol.*, 1968, *81*, 110–19; *Asimov;* C. W. Crannell, *J. Hist. Behav. Sci.*, 1970, 6, 267–68; *EB*, 13; *EP*, 4; M. Henle, *Amer. Psychologist*, 1978, *33*, 939–44; *IESS*, 8; C. C. Pratt, in W. Köhler, *The Task of Gestalt Psychology*, 1969, pp. 3–29; *Yearb. Amer. Philos. Soc.*, 1968.

KOENIG BARS. A set of bars for assessing visual acuity. This measure defines normal visual acuity as the ability to discriminate two bars, each subtending a visual angle of three minutes, separated by a gap subtending a visual angle of one minute.

KOENIG CYLINDERS. A set of steel cylinders that, when struck with a metal hammer, emit very high frequency tones amid the clangor produced by the hammer. They were used to study the upper limits of pitch perception.

KOENIG'S COLOR TRIANGLE. A color diagram for predicting mixtures of colors from the three primaries of red, green, and blue.

Koenig, Arthur. German physicist (b. Krefeld, North Rhine-Westphalia, September 13, 1856, d. Berlin, October 26, 1901). Koenig's Ph.D. in physics was from the University of Berlin (1882), and he spent the rest of his life on the faculty of this university. In the 1880s and 1890s Koenig studied vision, especially color vision, making many original observations and discoveries. The color triangle appears in an article written by Koenig and C. Dieterici (*Z. Psychol. Physiol. Sinnesorg.*, 1892, *4*, 241–347). After Helmholtz's* death, Koenig published the second edition of Helmholtz's *Handbook of Physiological Optics*, adding to it a 7,833-item bibliography.

Biographies: *DSB*, 7.

KOHNSTAMM TEST. A procedure for preparing a subject for hypnosis. The subject is asked to press an extended arm against the wall as hard as possible for about two minutes. Afterward, the arm will rise automatically, whether a suggestion to that effect is given or not.

Kohnstamm, Oskar. German physician (b. Pfungstädt near Darmstadt, April 13, 1871, d. Königstein im Taunus, November 6, 1917). Kohnstamm was an

M.D., a psychiatrist, a local health official, and the owner and operator of an insane asylum in Königstein im Taunus. He was also a patron of the arts.
Biographies: Deutsches Biographisches Jahrbuch 1917–1920, 1928.

KOHS' BLOCK DESIGN TEST. A subtest in the Arthur Point Scale of Performance Tests,* consisting of a set of blocks, the sides of which are painted in different colors. The subject is shown seventeen colored designs and asked to reproduce them by assembling the blocks.

Kohs, Samuel Calmin. American psychologist (b. New York City, June 2, 1890, d. San Francisco, January 23, 1984). Kohs received a Ph.D. in educational psychology from Stanford University in 1919. He held a large number of positions, most of them clinical, institutional, and Jewish social work positions. He taught at Reed College from 1918 to 1923 and held brief lecturing appointments at other universities. His main areas of interest were psychology applied to social work and intelligence testing. Kohs published two books and a number of papers. The blocks test was published in 1923 (*Intelligence Measurement: A Psychological and Statistical Study Based upon the Block-Design Test.* Macmillan).
Biographies: AM&WS, 1973S; APA Dir., 1981; ConAu, 111.

KOLMOGOROV-SMIRNOV TEST. A nonparametric test of whether two independent samples have been drawn from the same population. The test is sensitive to any kind of difference in the distributions from which the two samples have been drawn: central tendency, scedasticity, or skewness. The data need to be on the ordinal scale.

Kolmogorov, Andreï Nikolaevich. Russian mathematician (b. Tambov, April 25, 1903). Kolmogorov graduated from Moscow University in 1925 and remained at that institution until 1957, the last four years as the dean of the faculty of mechanics and mathematics. From 1939 to 1959 he was also head of the department of probability theory and mathematical statistics of the Institute of Mathematics. Kolmogorov is the author of several books on statistics and mathematics. He presented the test in 1941 (*Ann. Math. Stat., 12,* 461–63).
Biographies: InternWho, 1985–1986; Soviet, 12.

Smirnov, Nikolaï Vasil'evich. Russian mathematician (b. Moscow, October 17, 1900, d. Moscow, June 2, 1966). Smirnov graduated from Moscow University in 1926. He became a researcher at the Institute of Mathematics in Moscow in 1938, heading its department of mathematical statistics beginning in 1957. His contributions lie in the areas of mathematical statistics and nonparametric statistics. Smirnov presented his contribution to the test in 1948 (*Ann. Math. Stat., 19,* 279–81).
Biographies: Soviet, 23.

KOPFERMANN CUBES. Two-dimensional projections of a stick cube, representing various perspectives of it. Depending on the perspective and the resulting complexity of the pattern, these projections may be seen as polygons or as representations of a three-dimensional object.

Kopfermann, Hans. German physicist (b. Breckenheim b. Wiesbaden, April 26, 1895, d. Heidelberg, January 28, 1963). Kopfermann's Ph.D. in physics was from the University of Göttingen (1924). He was at the Kaiser Wilhelm Institute for Physical Chemistry and Electrochemistry in Berlin from 1924 to 1932 and held positions at the University of Berlin (1932–1934), Berlin Technical University (1934–1937), University of Kiel (1937–1942), University of Göttingen (1942–1953), and the University of Heidelberg (1953–1963). Kopfermann's main field was nuclear physics. The cubes were presented in 1930 (*Psychol. Forsch., 13,* 293–364).
    Biographies: Nature, 1963, *200,* 403–4; *Physics Today,* March 1963, *16,* 90.

KORSAKOV'S PSYCHOSIS. Also known as Korsakov's syndrome, it is a mental disorder associated with alcoholism and other cases of vitamin B deficiency. It is characterized by neural irritation, memory loss, disorientation, and confabulation.

Korsakov, Sergei Sergeevich. Russian psychiatrist (b. Gus estate, Vladimir Province, January 22, 1854, d. Moscow, May 1, 1900). Korsakov began practicing medicine at the Preobrazhensk Hospital after graduating from the University of Moscow in 1875. In 1887, he presented a thesis on ''alcoholic paralysis'' that earned him a doctorate in medicine and, later, eponymity (*Ob al'kogol'nom paralichie,* 1887). It was Friedrich Jolly who named the syndrome after Korsakov in 1897 (*Charité Annalen,* Berlin, *22,* 580–612). Beginning in 1888, Korsakov was at the University of Moscow. Among Korsakov's other accomplishments are the introduction of the concept of paranoia, the writing of a textbook of psychiatry that rivaled the best for a generation, and the furtherance of humane treatment of psychiatric patients.
    Biographies: Haymaker; Soviet, 13; *Talbot;* S. Tarachow, *Amer. J. Psychiat.,* 1939, *95,* 887–99.

KORTE'S LAWS. Three statements of the conditions that govern the optimum perception of apparent movement produced by two stimuli appearing in rapid succession.

Korte, Adolf. German psychologist (b. n.a., d. n.a.). Korte presented the laws in a 1915 article (*Z. Psychol., 72,* 194–296).
    Biographies: Unavailable.

KRABBE'S DISEASE. Single recessive gene disorder that begins at the age of about one and is accompanied by rapid mental deterioration. The brain shows widespread demyelination and other abnormalities. Also known as early infantile diffuse sclerosis.

Krabbe, Knud H. Danish neurologist (b. March 3, 1885, d. Copenhagen, 1961). Krabbe's M.D. was from the University of Copenhagen, and he held positions there from 1915 to 1927 and 1929 to 1938. From 1933 on, Krabbe was chief physician at the Kommune Hospital, Copenhagen. He described the disease in 1916 (*Brain, 39,* 74–114).
  Biographies: WoWhoSci, 1968.

KRAEPELIN ERGOGRAPH. A form of ergograph, or device for measuring and recording muscular effort, in which the subject lifts a weight continually.

KRAEPELIN'S CLASSIFICATION. A systematic and extensive classification of mental disorders. It introduced such terms as *manic-depressive psychosis* and *paranoia* in their present meaning and led to an interest in the accurate description and classification of psychopathological categories.

Kraepelin, Emil. German psychiatrist (b. Neustrelitz, Mecklenburg, February 15, 1856, d. Munich, October 7, 1926). After receiving an M.D. from the University of Leipzig in 1878, Kraepelin held academic appointments at the universities of Munich (1879–1882, 1904–1926), Leipzig (1882–1886), Tartu (1886–1890), and Heidelberg (1890–1904). Kraepelin's work in psychiatry was influenced by Wilhelm Wundt.* Kraepelin extended the use of the Wundtian association experiment to psychiatric problems. At Tartu, he continued the work that he had begun in 1883 in Wundt's laboratory on psychopharmacology. For this work Kraepelin may be called the Father of Psychopharmacology. Concerning the etiology of mental disorders, Kraepelin was instrumental in establishing the organic viewpoint in psychiatry. It was first presented in his *Compendium der Psychiatrie* (1883), a major contribution to the development of psychiatry that underlies the present-day classificatory system of mental disorders. Kraepelin is therefore also known as the Father of Modern Psychiatry. His ergograph was described in 1903 (*Arch. ges. Psychol., 1,* 9–30).
  Biographies: F. J. Braceland, *Amer. J. Psychiat.,* 1957, *113,* 871–76; L. Brink & E. Jeliffe, *J. Nerv. Ment. Dis.,* 1933, *77,* 134–52, 274–82; *EB,* 13; E. Harms, in E. Kraepelin, *Dementia precox and Paraphrenia,* 1971, pp. vii–xviii; L. L. Havens, *J. Nerv. Ment. Dis.,* 1965, *141,* 16–28; *IESS,* 8; E. Kahn, *Amer. J. Psychiat.,* 1956, *113,* 289–94; E. Mapother, *J. Ment. Sci.,* 1927, *73,* 509–15; A. Meyer, *Amer. J. Psychiat.,* 1926–1927, *83,* 749–55; *Talbot.*

KRAUSE END BULBS. A type of nerve ending in skin areas that are transitional zones between glabrous and mucous skin. They may be the sensory end organs for the reception of cold.

Krause, Wilhelm. German anatomist (b. Hannover, July 12, 1833, d. Charlottenburg, February 2, 1910). Krause received his medical degree from the University of Zurich in 1854. He was at the universities of Göttingen from 1860 to 1892 and Berlin from 1892 to 1910. Krause wrote hundreds of articles and many books on anatomy. The end bulbs are described in his monograph, *Die terminalen Körperchen der einfach sensiblen Nerven* (1860).

Biographies: Pagel, *Biog. Lex.;* Hirsch, *Biog. Lex.*

KREBS CYCLE. Also known as the tricarboxylic acid cycle, the Krebs cycle describes the series of catalytic reactions whereby foodstuffs are converted to carbon dioxide and water, with accompanying release of energy that serves to keep the organism alive.

Krebs, Sir Hans Adolph. British biochemist (b. Hildsheim, Germany, August 25, 1900, d. Oxford, England, November 22, 1981). Krebs' M.D. was from the University of Hamburg (1925). From 1926 to 1933 he was at the Kaiser Wilhelm Institute and the universities of Hamburg and Freiburg. Krebs went to England in 1933, became naturalized in 1938, and served on the faculties of Cambridge (1933–1935), Sheffield (1935–1945), and Oxford (1945–1967). He described the tricarboxylic acid cycle in 1950 (*Harvey Lectures*) and received the Nobel Prize for it in 1953.

Biographies: Asimov; CurBio, 1954; *InternWho,* 1982; *McGMSE,* 2; *Who,* 1982.

KRUSKAL-SHEPARD SCALING. A method of nonmetric multidimensional scaling developed independently by J. B. Kruskal and R. N. Shepard.

Kruskal, Joseph Bernard. American mathematician (b. New York City, January 29, 1928). With a 1954 Ph.D. in mathematics from Princeton, Kruskal taught at Princeton, Wisconsin, and Michigan universities from 1955 to 1958 and then joined the Bell Telephone Laboratories in 1959. His research has been in the areas of statistics, psychometrics, and statistical linguistics. The scaling method was described in 1964 (*Psychometrika, 29,* 1–27, 115–29).

Biographies: AM&WS, 1982P.

Shepard, Roger Newland. American psychologist (b. Palo Alto, California, January 30, 1929). Shepard's Ph.D. in experimental psychology was from Yale University (1955). He was at the Bell Telephone Laboratories from 1958 to 1966 and Harvard University from 1966 to 1968 and has been at Stanford University since 1968. Shepard's research has been on cognitive processes and mathematical models. His multidimensional scaling model appeared in 1962 (*Psychometrika, 27,* 125–40, 219–46).

Biographies: AM&WS, 1978S; *Amer. Psychologist,* 1977, *32,* 62–67; *APA Dir.,* 1985; *WhoAm,* 1984–1985.

KRUSKAL-WALLIS *H* TEST. A test of statistical significance performed in one-way analysis of variance of ranked data to test the null hypothesis that the observed samples all come from the same population.

Kruskal, William Henry. American statistician (b. New York City, October 10, 1919). Kruskal took the Ph.D. in mathematical statistics at Columbia University in 1935. He has spent most of his professional career at the University of Chicago, first as instructor and professor, then as chairman of his department, and finally as the incumbent of an endowed chair and dean of the Division of Social Sciences. He has also held numerous concurrent positions. Kruskal's research has been on theoretical statistics, especially nonparametric statistics. The *H* test was published in 1952 (W. H. Kruskal, *Ann. Math. Stat.*, *23*, 525–40; W. H. Kruskal & W. A. Wallis, *J. Amer. Stat. Ass.*, *47*, 583–621).

Biographies: AM&WS, 1982P; *WhoAm*, 1984–1985.

Wallis, Wilson Allen. American economist and statistician (b. Philadelphia, Pennsylvania, November 5, 1912). Wallis had an A.B. from the University of Minnesota (1932) and did postgraduate work at the University of Chicago and Columbia University. Between 1935 and 1946 Wallis held a number of government and academic positions. He was at the University of Chicago from 1946 to 1962, becoming dean of the Graduate Business School in 1956. He was president and trustee of the University of Rochester from 1962 to 1978, then served as under secretary for economic affairs of the U.S. Department of State, as well as on numerous other governmental bodies, boards, and committees. Wallis is the author of a number of books and papers on statistics and economics.

Biographies: WhoAm, 1984–1985.

KUDER PREFERENCE RECORD—VOCATIONAL. A vocational interest inventory consisting of items in which the testee marks, among the three alternatives offered, the most and the least preferred activity. A profile of ten broad vocational areas is obtained.

KUDER-RICHARDSON COEFFICIENTS OF EQUIVALENCE. Formulas for estimating interitem consistency and therefore the degree of correlation between different forms of a test from a single administration of the test.

Kuder, G. Frederic. American psychologist (b. Holly, Michigan, June 23, 1903). Kuder's Ph.D. was in psychology (Ohio State University, 1937). Until 1948, Kuder held a variety of governmental positions. He taught at Duke University from 1948 to 1963 and was concurrently president of Personnel Psychology, Inc. His main fields of interest have been psychological measurement, vocational preferences, and aptitude testing. In addition to the Vocational Preference Record, Kuder published also the Kuder Preference Record—Occupational (1956) and the Kuder General Interest Inventory (1934). Of these, it is the Vocational Preference Record that is the eponymous "Kuder." It was first presented in 1939 (*J. Soc. Psychol.*, *19*, 47–50). The Kuder-Richardson formulas were given by the two authors in 1937 (*Psychometrika*, *2*, 151–60).

Biographies: AM&WS, 1978S; *APA Dir.*, 1985.

Richardson, Marion Webster. American psychologist (b. August 20, 1896). With the exception of the years 1932 to 1940, when Richardson taught at the University of Chicago (and received his Ph.D. there in 1936), he has held various government and private positions as psychometrician from 1931 onward, the last position being that of director of research with Richardson, Bellows, Henry & Co. (since 1946). Richardson concentrated on psychometric theory, aptitude testing, and personnel research.

Biographies: APA Dir., 1948.

KUFS' DISEASE. A type of amaurotic familial idiocy occurring in teenagers.

Kufs, H. German psychiatrist (b. 1871, d. 1955). Kufs' description of the disease appeared in 1925 (*Z. ges. Neurol. Psychiat., 95,* 169–88).

Biographies: Unavailable.

KUHLMANN-ANDERSON TEST. A group intelligence test for individuals in kindergarten through twelfth grade. The items are arranged in several overlapping test batteries, one for each age level. The scores are converted to mental age, and deviation IQs are obtained from the total score.

KUHLMANN-BINET TEST. While Henry Goddard produced the first translation of the Binet-Simon scale* into English, Kuhlmann's was the first revision in that it extended the scale downward to the age level of three months.

Kuhlmann, Frederick. American psychologist (b. Davenport, Iowa, March 20, 1876, d. St. Paul, Minnesota, April 19, 1941). After receiving his Ph.D. from Clark University in 1903, Kuhlmann remained there until 1907 when he went to the University of Illinois. In 1910, he became director of the Research Bureau of the Minnesota School for the Feebleminded in Faribault and, in 1921, director of the Division of Research of the Minnesota State Department of Public Institutions. Intelligence and mental deficiency were Kuhlmann's chief interests (*A Handbook of Mental Tests,* 1922; *Outline of Mental Deficiency,* 1924; *Tests of Mental Development,* 1939). He also wrote significant articles on mental imagery and memory and numerous other articles and reports. The Kuhlmann-Anderson Test was published in 1927 by Personnel Press, the Kuhlmann-Binet revision in 1912 (*J. Psycho-Asthen. Monog. Suppl.,* No. 1).

Biographies: CurBio, 41; K. M. Dallenbach, *Amer. J. Psychol.,* 1941, *54,* 446–47; N. A. Dayton, *Amer. J. Ment. Def.,* 1940–1941, *45,* 3–7; F. N. Maxfield, *Amer. J. Ment. Def.,* 1941, *46,* 17–18; *PR,* 3.

Anderson, Rose Gustava. American psychologist (b. Gothenburg, Nebraska, June 23, 1893, d. Hightstown, New Jersey, September 7, 1978). Anderson received her Ph.D. from Columbia University in 1925. She held a number of clinical and research positions with governmental bodies and private institutions. She was with the Psychological Service Center in New York from 1932 to 1978. Anderson did research in child clinical psychology and test construction.

Biographies: APA Dir., 1976; *WhAm,* 7.

Binet, Alfred. See BINET-SIMON SCALE.

KUNDT DUST METHOD. A method for measuring the length of sound waves. When fine powder is placed inside a Kundt tube, it will congregate at the nodes of a stationary sound wave, the distance between adjacent nodes being one-half the wavelength.

KUNDT'S RULE. The rule refers to two phenomena that pertain to the perception of divided linear extents. 1. Of two line segments, one divided into equal distances by marks and the other not, the distance filled with dividing marks will appear longer. 2. In bisecting a line segment while using one eye only, there will be the tendency to place the halfway mark closer to the nasal side of the open eye.

KUNDT TUBE. A device for determining the length of a sound wave. It consists of a tube with an inside air column of adjustable length. When properly adjusted, the air column will resonate with the sound wave. The length of the sound wave may be measured by measuring the distance between two adjacent nodes that form in any fine powder placed inside the tube.

Kundt, August Adolph. German physicist (b. Schwerin, Mecklenburg, November 18, 1839, d. Israelsdorf, near Lübeck, May 21, 1894). Kundt graduated with a Ph.D. in physics from the University of Berlin in 1864. He held several brief academic appointments and was at the University of Strasbourg from 1872 to 1888 and the Berlin Physical Institute after 1888. Kundt described the resonating tube in 1865 (*Ann. Phys. Chem.*, *126*, 513–27), the dust method in 1866 (*Ann. Phys. Chem.*, *127*, 497–23), and the rule pertaining to the perception of visual extent in 1863 (*Pogg. Ann. Phys. Chem.*, *120*, 118–58).
   Biographies: Asimov; DSB, 7; EB, 13.

KWALWASSER-DYKEMA MUSIC TEST. A battery of ten musical tests that measure such functions as tonal memory, pitch and loudness discrimination, and melodic taste.

Kwalwasser, Jacob. American educator (b. New York City, February 27, 1894, d. Pittsburgh, Pennsylvania, August 7, 1977). Kwalwasser received the Ph.D. degree from the State University of Iowa in 1925. He was visiting professor of musical education at various schools and universities and research professor of musical education at Syracuse University from 1926 to 1954. Kwalwasser was a pioneer in research on musical education in the United States. He wrote several books, a number of articles, and prepared several tests in the area. The Music Test was first published in 1930.
   Biographies: WhAm, 7.

Dykema, Peter William. American music educator (b. Grand Rapids, Michigan, November 25, 1873, d. Hastings-on-Hudson, New York, May 13, 1951). After obtaining the M.L. degree from the University of Michigan, Dykema studied voice and music theory in the United States and abroad. He was professor of music at the University of Wisconsin from 1913 to 1924 and at Teachers College, Columbia University, from 1924 to 1940. Dykema wrote music, and books and pamphlets on music and musical education.

Biographies: J. W. Beattie, *Mus. Ed. J.*, June 1951, *37*, 11–12; *NCAB,* 40; *NYT,* May 15, 1951, 31; *School & Soc.*, 1951, *73,* 334; *WhAm,* 3.

L

LADD-FRANKLIN THEORY OF COLOR VISION. According to this theory, the most primitive color vision is achromatic, black-white. The white process separated into yellow and blue during the course of evolution, and then yellow separated into green and red. There is only one photochemical substance in the retina, but it decomposes, selectively stimulating the nerves in terms of the black-white, yellow-blue, and red-green pairs.

Ladd-Franklin, Christine. American mathematician (b. Windsor, Connecticut, December 1, 1847, d. New York City, March 5, 1930). Christine Ladd graduated from Vassar College in 1869. She had studied astronomy and physics. She did graduate work in mathematics at Johns Hopkins University, where she married a mathematics professor, Fabian Franklin, and she published in the field of mathematics. Her interest in mathematics and physics led her to study color vision. Her work between 1891 and 1892 in Georg Müller's* laboratory at Göttingen and in Helmholtz's* laboratory in Berlin led her to develop her own theory of color vision, for which she is best known (*Z. Psychol. Physiol. Sinnesorg.*, 1892, *4*, 211–21). A year before her death, Ladd-Franklin published a book on color vision (*Colour and Colour Theories*, 1929).

Biographies: *DAB*, 10; *NCAB*, 26; *Notable American Women, 1607–1950*, vol. 2, 1971; *WhAm*, 1; R. S. Woodworth, *Science*, 1930, *71*, 307.

LAMARCKIAN TRANSMISSION. Also referred to as Lamarckism or Lamarckianism, this is the theory that changes that originate in individuals in their lifetime due to the use or lack of use of organs can be transmitted to subsequent generations genetically.

Lamarck, Jean Baptiste Pierre Antoine de Monet. French biologist (b. Bazentin, Somme, August 1, 1744; d. Paris, December 18, 1829). Lamarck studied medicine, meteorology, and botany at the University of Paris. He held various appointments in botany and beginning in 1793 taught invertebrate zoology at the University of Paris. In addition to his significant contributions to the development of taxonomy of the vertebrates, Lamarck was the first biologist of prominence to adopt the evolutionary point of view, though his doctrine of the genetic transmission of acquired characteristics was soon proved to be wrong after he first proposed it in his *Philosophie zoologique* (1809).

   Biographies: M. Barthélemy-Madaule, *Lamarck the Mythical Precursor,* 1982; *DSB,* 7; *EB,* 13.

LAMAZE METHOD. A method of pain control in birthing women that involves concentration, controlled breathing, and muscular relaxation and is drug free.

Lamaze, Fernand. French obstetrician (b. June 20, 1891, d. 1957). Lamaze had an M.D. from the University of Paris. Having observed Pavlovian conditioning* in the USSR, Lamaze began teaching patients behavioral methods in pain control in 1951. He called it psychoprophylaxis. His *Painless Childbirth* was published in 1956 and translated into English in 1958.

   Biographies: EA, 16.

LAMBERT. A photometric unit of surface brightness. A perfectly diffusing surface that emits or reflects one lumen per square centimeter has a brightness of one lambert.

LAMBERT'S LAW. The illumination of a surface or the brightness of a luminous surface varies directly with the cosine of the angle between the reflected or emitted rays and the perpendicular to the surface. It is also referred to as Lambert's cosine law.

LAMBERT'S METHOD. A method of mixing colors in which a piece of clear glass is placed at 45 degrees to two color patches, one horizontal and the other vertical. Mixing of colors occurs as the partially reflected color of the vertical patch is superimposed on the color of the horizontal patch, seen directly.

Lambert, Johann Heinrich. German mathematician (b. Mulhouse, Alsace, August 26, 1728, d. Berlin, September 25, 1777). Lambert was poor, self-taught, and earned a living as a tutor. It was only during the last ten years of his life that he lived in reasonable comfort, thanks to the financial support he received from Frederick II of Prussia who had recognized his talent. In addition to his work in mathematics, physics, and cosmology, Lambert also studied light, publishing a book on this subject in 1760, *Photometria sive de mensura et gradibus luminis, colorum et umbrae.* The cosine law and the color mixing method are described in this book. The term *albedo* is Lambert's, and he also devised methods for the accurate measurement of light intensities. Other areas in which Lambert made contributions are magnetism, map making, and meteorology.

Biographies: Asimov; DSB, 7; S. L. Jaki, *Physics Today,* Sept. 1977, *30,* 25–30.

LAND EFFECT. The perception of color in black-and-white photographs of natural scenes. Two black-and-white photographs are taken of the same natural scene, one through a long-wave filter and the other through a short-wave filter. The two positive slides are then projected on a screen in exact register. If a long-wave filter is now made to intercept the beam of the projector with the "long" slide, the objects in the projected image will appear in nearly their original colors, although desaturated.

Land, Edwin Herbert. American inventor (b. Bridgeport, Connecticut, May 7, 1909). While attending Harvard University as an undergraduate, Land invented the method for polarizing light by means of tiny, aligned crystals embedded in a sheet of plastic. The material was named Polaroid. Land organized the Polaroid Corporation for the manufacture and sale of polarizing materials in 1937 and dropped out of college. He made other inventions, the most successful of which was the Polaroid Land camera that took instant pictures, the first such camera to be built. The article in which Land described the effect and presented a new theory of color vision was published in 1959 (*Proc. Nat. Acad. Sci., 45,* 115–29, 636–44).

Biographies: AM&WS, 1982P; *Asimov; CurBio,* 1981; *McGMSE,* 1980; *WhoAm,* 1984–1985.

LANDOLT CIRCLES. Circles with gaps used in eye charts to determine visual acuity. Also known as Landolt's rings or Landolt's Cs, the circles in a chart are arranged from small to large, with the gap in each oriented in a different direction. The size of the gap whose direction is identified correctly by the person tested is taken as a measure of that person's visual acuity.

Landolt, Edmund. French ophthalmologist (b. Aaran, Switzerland, May 17, 1846, d. Paris, July 1926). Landolt obtained his M.D. from the University of Zurich in 1869 and then specialized in ophthalmology. From 1874 on he and Louis Javal headed a private eye clinic that became popular. Landolt wrote many works on ophthalmology and was the inventor of many pieces of research and measuring apparatus. Landolt presented the broken circles in 1889 (*Soc. franç. d'ophthalm., 1,* 385).

Biographies: Fischer, Biog. Lex.; Pagel, *Biog. Lex.*

LANGE'S SYNDROME. See CORNELIA DE LANGE SYNDROME.

LASHLEY'S JUMPING STAND. An animal training apparatus in which the animal (rat) is forced to make a discrete, positive response to one of two stimuli by jumping at it. The animal is placed on a small platform, with a gap between it and the target. If the rat jumps against the correct target, it yields, allowing the animal access to food. If the jump is made against the incorrect target, the rat falls into a net and is placed back on the platform.

LASHLEY-WADE HYPOTHESIS. In learning, stimulus generalization will not occur unless the animal is given differential training in which several values of the stimulus dimensions are presented.

Lashley, Karl Spencer. American neuropsychologist (b. Davis, West Virginia, June 7, 1890, d. Poitiers, France, August 7, 1958). Lashley's Ph.D. was in genetics (Johns Hopkins University, 1914). He held a variety of teaching and research positions, those at the University of Chicago (1929–1935), Harvard University (1935–1955), and the Yerkes Laboratory of Primate Biology (1942–1955) being the longest. Lashley's contribution was his studies of the cerebral localization of functions using learning and discrimination as the behavioral measures of the effect of ablation. In 1929, he published a book summarizing the results of his work (*Brain Mechanisms and Intelligence*). Some of the findings were revolutionary in view of the then-current conception of the brain. Lashley published more than one hundred major papers. He described the jumping stand in 1930 (*J. Genet. Psychol., 37*, 453–60) and the stimulus generalization hypothesis in a joint paper with Marjorie Wade in 1946 (*Psychol. Rev., 53*, 72–87).
   Biographies: F. C. Bartlett, *Biog. Mem. Fellows Roy. Soc.*, 1959, *5*, 107–18; L. Carmichael, *Science*, 1959, *129*, 1410–12; *DSB*, 8; *EB*, 13; D. O. Hebb, *Amer. J. Psychol.*, 1959, 72, 142–50; *IESS*, 9; *NCAB*, 44.

Wade, Marjorie. American psychologist (b. February 8, 1911). Wade's B.S. was from Wayne University (1944). She served as research assistant to Lashley at the Yerkes Laboratory of Primate Biology from 1944 to 1946 and at the Harvard Psychological Laboratory from 1947 onward.
   Biographies: APA Dir., 1948.

LEHMANN'S ACOUMETER. An older form of the audiometer, a device employed for measuring sound intensity thresholds, in which the intensity of the sound was varied by varying the height from which a pellet dropped into a sound-producing surface.

Lehmann, Alfred Georg Ludwig. Danish psychologist (b. Copenhagen, December 29, 1858, d. Copenhagen, September 26, 1921). Lehmann's Ph.D. was in psychology (University of Copenhagen, 1884). After obtaining his doctorate, Lehmann worked for a year in Wilhelm Wundt's* laboratory in Leipzig. There he studied brightness contrast and then worked out pulse and breathing curves and correlated them with psychological processes. This work was published in 1892, causing considerable stir because of its supposed accurate demonstration of the relationship between physiological and psychological processes. Upon his return to Copenhagen (where he held positions from 1886 to 1921), Lehmann started the first Danish psychological laboratory. *Die Hauptgesetze des menschlichen Gefühlslebens* (1892) was his best-known book, but he wrote several additional ones, in both Danish and German.

Biographies: A. Aal, *Scand. Sci. Rev.*, 1922, *1*, 7–13; *EUI*, 29; R. H. Pederson, *Arch. ges. Psychol.*, 1921–1922, *42*, 283–94.

LEIPZIG SCHOOL OF GESTALT PSYCHOLOGY. A branch of the Gestalt school associated with the name of Felix Krüger, its founder. It is also known as holistic psychology (*Ganzeheitspsychologie*). Krüger was influenced by the Graz, or Austrian school of psychology.* Although he accepted the Gestalt idea of wholes, or Gestalten, as basic, he criticized the Berlin Gestalt school of Wertheimer and Köhler for not including all psychological phenomena in its purview, such as emotions, feelings, and cultural and social phenomena. Krüger's goal was to study the totality of the person, which he named structure. It included not only the phenomenology of experience but also all dispositional and determining tendencies that underlie mental events. In Germany, holistic psychology became the leading school of psychology in the mid-twentieth century.

Leipzig, University of. Krüger was at the University of Leipzig when he founded his school, and he spent most of his career there (1901–1905, 1909–1910, 1917–1935). The university played an extremely important role in the development of scientific psychology because of the importance of the names of Ernst Heinrich Weber,* Gustav Theodor Fechner,* and Wilhelm Wundt* that were associated with it for so long.

LEITER INTERNATIONAL PERFORMANCE SCALE. A nonverbal performance intelligence scale for young children who are handicapped, retarded, or do not speak English. The points scored are converted to mental age scores, from which an IQ may be calculated.

Leiter, Russel Graydon. American psychologist (b. July 16, 1901). With a Ph.D. in clinical psychology from the University of Southern California (1938), Leiter occupied a succession of positions with governmental agencies, hospitals, institutions, and private agencies. After 1959, he was also an instructor at Ohio University at Portsmouth. Leiter worked in the areas of mental disorders, psychodiagnosis, and intelligence. The performance scale appeared in 1936 (*Univ. Hawaii Bull.*, *15*, No. 7).

Biographies: APA Dir., 1975.

LEONARDO'S PARADOX. Da Vinci's observation that, when an object is viewed binocularly, it is as if it were transparent because each eye separately sees the background behind the object that is not visible to the other eye, and thus, together, the two eyes see the entire background behind the opaque object. For this reason, it is impossible to reproduce in a painting that which is seen with the two eyes.

Leonardo da Vinci. Italian artist and scientist (b. Vinci, near Florence, April 15, 1452, d. Cloux, near Amboise, France, May 2, 1519). Leonardo da Vinci, the most brilliant figure of the Italian Renaissance, made his observation concerning binocular vision and painting in his notebooks sometime between 1497 and 1516. It may be found in J. P. Richter (comp.), *The Notebooks of Leonardo da Vinci,* vol. 1, New York: Dover (originally published 1883).
   Biographies: DSB, 8; *EB,* 13.

LESBIANISM. Female homosexuality.

Lesbos. Island in the Aegean Sea, home of Sappho, the Greek poetess (early sixth century B.C.), leader of a group of women among whom strong homosexual attraction prevailed.

LICHTHEIM'S TEST. A test for the presence of inner speech in aphasic patients. The patient is asked to state the number of syllables in a word he or she cannot say.

Lichtheim, Ludwig. German physician (b. Breslau [now Wroclaw], Silesia, December 7, 1845, d. Bern, Switzerland, June 13, 1928). Lichtheim's M.D. was from Berlin (1867). He held academic positions both at Königsberg and Bern Universities. A pioneer in modern neurology, Lichtheim wrote three books on the subject.
   Biographies: WoWhoSi.

LIEBMANN EFFECT. As the luminosity of a colored figure increases, the contrast between the figure and the ground on which it lies begins to diminish, and, if the figure is complex, it becomes simpler. When the luminosities of figure and ground are equal, the figure cannot be distinguished from ground.

Liebmann, Susanne Elisabeth. German psychologist (b. Berlin, January 29, 1897). Liebmann described the effect in her 1927 doctoral dissertation at the University of Berlin (*Psychol. Forsch., 9,* 300–53).
   Biographies: PR, 3.

LIKERT SCALE (LIKERT PROCEDURE). A method for measuring the strength and directionality of attitudes toward a topic. A list of statements is drawn up that reflect both positive and negative attitudes toward a topic. The statements are given to a large number of people who respond to them on a five-point scale. The items that correlate most highly with the total score are selected for inclusion in the final version of the scale.

Likert, Rensis. American psychologist (b. Cheyenne, Wyoming, August 5, 1903, d. Ann Arbor, Michigan, September 3, 1981). Likert obtained the Ph.D. degree from Columbia University in 1932. From 1935 through 1970, he headed a succession of research teams engaged in survey studies, including the Institute for Social Research at the University of Michigan, which Likert headed from 1948 to 1970. He was chairman of the board of Rensis Likert Associates after 1971. Likert's contributions were in the areas of social psychology and industrial organization. His scaling procedure has been used in countless studies after Likert introduced it in his dissertation work in 1932. He may be considered one of the chief creators of modern population survey methods. Likert's theory of organization was instrumental in creating the new field of organizational psychology. He wrote several books on survey techniques and industrial organization, contributed numerous chapters to edited books, and wrote more than sixty journal articles.

Biographies: AM&WS, 1978S; ConAu, 93; IESS, 18; L. Kish, Amer. Statistician, 1982, 36, 124–25; S. E. Seashore & D. Katz, Amer. Psychologist, 1982, 37, 851–53; WhoAm, 1974.

LILLIPUTIAN HALLUCINATION. Also known as microptic hallucination, it is the hallucination that objects are extremely small. It occurs in toxic psychoses and fever states.

Lilliput. An imaginary country in Jonathan Swift's *Gulliver's Travels* (1726) whose inhabitants were six inches tall.

LINCOLN-OSERETSKY MOTOR DEVELOPMENT SCALE. A diagnostic sensorimotor test battery for children aged six to fourteen. Thirty-six items assess the child's general motor ability.

Lincoln. The *Lincoln Adaptation of the Oseretsky Tests of Motor Proficiency* (1948) was constructed by William Sloan, who at the time was at the Lincoln State School and Colony at Lincoln, Illinois.

Oseretsky, N. I. Russian psychologist (fl. 1926–1931). Oseretsky's original work, *Oseretsky Tests of Motor Proficiency* (in Russian), written in 1923, was translated into Portuguese and then from Portuguese into English in 1946. Sloan used this translation to construct his adaptation of the test.

Biographies: Unavailable.

LINK INSTRUMENT TRAINER (LINK TRAINER). A device used in pilot training and human engineering research in which the conditions of piloting an airplane are closely simulated without leaving the ground.

Link, Edwin Albert. American inventor, industrialist, and marine engineer (b. Huntington, Indiana, July 26, 1904, d. Binghamton, New York, September 7, 1981). Link went to public schools in Binghamton, New York, and attended the Lindsley Institute. He learned to fly and obtained his commercial pilot's license in 1927. In 1929, Link and his brother George built the training cockpit. There were few customers until 1934 when the U.S. Air Corps began using it. In 1935, Link established the Link Aviation company, of which he was president for eighteen years. During these years more than 2 million military and commercial pilots were trained in Link trainers. In 1958, Link installed the first trainer that simulated the cockpit of a DC–8 jet airliner. A long-time skindiver, Link began to recover treasures from sunken ships in the 1950s. In the 1960s, he devised apparatus and vessels for locating and retrieving such treasures and for exploring the riches of the ocean floor in general. Ocean Systems, Inc. was founded by Link, General Precision, and Union Carbide to develop underseas mineral and petroleum resources.

Biographies: AM&WS, 1979P; *CurBio,* 1974; *NYT,* Sep. 9, 1981, B–7; *WhoAm,* 1980–1981.

LIPPS ILLUSION. A figure consisting of a circle, with the apexes of short-sided right angles tangent to it at the 12, 3, 6, and 9 o'clock points. At these points, the circle appears somewhat flattened.

Lipps, Theodor. German psychologist (b. Wallhalben, Rhineland-Palatinate, July 28, 1851, d. Munich, October 17, 1914). Lipps had a Ph.D. in philosophy from the University of Bonn (1874). He taught at Bonn (1877–1890), Breslau (1890–1894), and Munich (1894–1914) universities. Lipps is best known for his empathy theory and aesthetics (*Raumaesthetik und geometrisch-optische Täuschungen,* 1897). According to the theory, the perceiver perceives the nature of an object when he or she feels like that object or projects himself or herself into the object. Lipps applied this theory to both aesthetics and the geometric illusions. The Lipps illusion was presented in *Helmholtz-Festschrift* (1891, p. 217). Lipps produced several other books (including *Grundtatsachen des Seelenlebens,* 1883) and many articles and monographs.

Biographies: Amer. J. Psychol., 1915, *26,* 160; *EB,* 14; *EP,* 4.

LISSAJOUS FIGURES. The closed curves produced by the interaction of two wave fronts, such as those emanating from two tuning forks. If the forks are set at right angles to each other and a narrow beam of light is reflected successively from small mirrors attached to the forks, a stationary Lissajou figure will result if both forks vibrate at exactly the same rate. This method was used by nineteenth-century investigators of hearing to calibrate tuning forks.

Lissajous, Jules Antoine. French physicist (b. Versailles, March 4, 1822, d. Plombières, Côte d'Or, June 24, 1880). Lissajous had the *agrégé* degree from the Ecole normale supérieure (1847). He taught at the Lycée Saint-Louis from 1847 to 1874, when he became the rector of the academy at Chambéry and, a year later, at Besançon. Lissajou's work was mostly on vibrations. He described the optical method for demonstrating acoustical vibrations in 1855 (*C. r. hebd. séances Acad. sci., 41,* 93–95, 814–17).

Biographies: DSB, 8.

LISSAUER TRACT. An ascending nerve tract in the spinal cord that carries nerve fibers for pain.

Lissauer, H. German neurologist (b. Neidenburg, East Prussia, September 12, 1861, d. Hallstatt, Austria, September 21, 1891). Lissauer's M.D. was from the University of Leipzig (1886). He worked at the Psychiatric Clinic of the Univer-

sity of Breslau and was concerned with the pharmacology, anatomy, and pathology of the central nervous system. He described the tract in 1885 (*Neurol. Zbl.,* *4*, 245–46).
   Biographies: Fischer, *Biog. Lex.*

LISTING'S LAW. When the eye moves from the primary position (its position when one is looking straight ahead horizontally) to any other position, it rotates without torsion, that is, about an axis that is perpendicular to the initial and final lines of regard at the point where they intersect.

Listing, Johann Benedikt. German physicist and physiologist (b. Frankfurt-am-Main, July 25, 1808, d. Göttingen, December 24, 1882). Listing taught at the University of Göttingen from 1839 to 1882. He published *Monograph on Physiological Optics* in 1845 and a few papers on vision, optics, and optical apparatus. Listing never published the law himself. It was C. G. T. Reute who named it after Listing in a book of his published in 1853.
   Biographies: Amer. J. Physics, 1958, *26*, 108; *Nature*, 1882–1883, *27*, 316.

LLOYD MORGAN'S CANON. A form of the principle of parsimony, applied to the interpretation of animal behavior: "In no case may we interpret an action as the outcome of the exercise of a higher psychical faculty, if it can be interpreted as the outcome of the exercise of one which stands lower in the psychological scale." The canon serves as a guideline to avoid the anthropomorphization of animal behavior when it can be explained in terms of instincts or simple learned habits.

Morgan, C. Lloyd. English psychologist and biologist (b. London, February 6, 1852, d. Hastings, Sussex, March 6, 1936). Morgan received a D.Sc. from the University of Bristol in 1910 upon becoming professor emeritus. Before that, he had held a lectureship in South Africa (1878–1883) and professorships at the University College, Bristol, in zoology and geology from 1884 to 1901 and in psychology and education from 1901 to 1909. From 1919 to 1936, Morgan was a lecturer at Clark and Harvard universities. Morgan was one of the pioneers in comparative psychology. He performed the first psychological experiments on animals outside a laboratory and reported them in his early books, such as *Introduction to Comparative Psychology* (1894) and *Animal Behavior* (1900). His best-known book is *Introduction*, which contains a statement of the principle that bears his name. Between 1905 and 1933 Morgan published seven additional books on comparative psychology.
   Biographies: DNB, Suppl. 5; G. C. Grindley, *Brit. J. Psychol.*, 1936, *27*, 103; *HPA*, 2; *IESS*, 10; *Obit. Not.*, 2; *PR*, 3.

LORD'S PARADOX. When analysis of covariance is used to equate groups statistically that are unequal on the covariate, an erroneous conclusion is reached. The situation is paradoxical because this conclusion is just the opposite of the conclusion that may be reached using common sense.

Lord, Frederic Mather. American psychometrician (b. Hanover, New Hampshire, November 12, 1912). With an M.A. from the University of Minnesota (1943), Lord held several positions as a psychometrician between 1941 and 1949. He obtained a Ph.D. in psychology from Princeton University in 1951 and was with that university from 1959 to 1971. He has been with the Educational Testing Service since 1949. Lord has over one hundred publications on mental test theory and the application of mathematical statistics to psychological problems. He presented the paradox in 1967 (*Psychol. Bull., 68,* 304–5).

Biographies: AM&WS, 1978S; *APA Dir.,* 1985.

LORGE-THORNDIKE INTELLIGENCE TESTS. A group intelligence test for individuals in kindergarten through high school. The test has five age levels and a verbal and a nonverbal battery at each level from ages three to five. The raw score is translated into an IQ equivalent.

Lorge, Irving Daniel. American psychologist (b. New York City, April 19, 1905, d. New York City, January 23, 1961). Lorge was an educational psychologist (Ph.D., Columbia University, 1930), known for his contributions to the measurement of intelligence. Lorge was at the Teachers College, Columbia University, from 1927 to 1946 when he became the executive officer of the Institute of Psychological Research. Lorge's primary contribution was in the area of readability, however. He developed a readability scale, improved army training of illiterates, and, with E. L. Thorndike,* established the frequency of occurrence of words in the general literature (*The Teacher's Word Book of 30,000 Words,* 1944; *Semantic Count of the 570 Commonest English Words,* 1949). These counts have been used extensively by researchers.

Biographies: EJ, 11; *NYT,* Jan. 24, 1961, 29; *PR,* 3; *WhAm,* 4.

Thorndike, Edward Lee. See under eponyms that begin with THORNDIKE.

LOWENFELD MOSAIC TEST. A projective test consisting of 456 small, differently shaped cardboard pieces, each shape in six different colors, that the testee is instructed to "do something with." Interpretations of personality, neurotic or psychotic tendencies, brain damage, aptitude, and other characteristics are made on the basis of the shape and colors used and patterns produced.

Lowenfeld, Margaret Frances Jane. English psychiatrist (b. London, February 4, 1890, d. London, February 2, 1973). Lowenfeld studied at the London School of Medicine for Women, obtaining intermediate M.B., B.S. in 1914, and a Licentiate of the Royal College of Physicians in 1918. She occupied various medical positions from 1919 to 1925. In 1928, she founded the Institute of Child Psychology. The test (*The Lowenfeld Mosaic Test*) was published in 1954.

Biographies: Wh, 1971–1980.

LUESCHER COLOR TEST. A personality test used to infer personality traits from the testee's performance on a forced-choice color preference task.

Luescher, Max. Swiss psychoanalyst (b. Basel, September 9, 1923). Luescher obtained his Ph.D. from the University of Basel in 1945. He was a psychoanalyst and lecturer at the universities of Basel, Zurich, and Paris from 1949 to 1957. He taught at the University of Amsterdam from 1957 to 1960 and has been a lecturer at the University of Linz since 1978. The test appeared in 1949 under the title *Psychologie der Farben: Textband zum Luescher-Test.* It was translated into English in 1969. Luescher has written four other books on personality.
   Biographies: ConAu, 101.

LUMMER-BRODHUN CUBE. A cube that is silvered along the sides of its diagonal plane but is clear in the middle. Mounted in an illuminometer, such as the Macbeth illuminometer,* it allows the direct visual comparison of the brightness of a standard light source, built into the illuminometer and reflected in the annular mirror, with that of the light source that is being measured, seen directly as the enclosed circle.

Lummer, Otto Richard. German physicist (b. Gera, Thuringia, July 17, 1860, d. Breslau [now Wroclaw], Silesia, July 5, 1925). After receiving the Ph.D. degree from the University of Berlin, Lummer remained there as assistant to Helmholtz* until 1887. He was at the Physikalisch-Technische Reichsanstalt from 1887 to 1901 and the University of Berlin from 1901 to 1904, and he spent the rest of his life at the University of Breslau. His work was mostly in optics. Lummer and Brodhun described the new photometeric device in 1889 (*Z. Instrumentenk.*, *9*, 41–50).
   Biographies: DSB, 8.

Brodhun, Eugen. German physicist (b. 1860, d. n.a.).
   Biographies: Webster's Biographical Dictionary.

LUNEBURG'S THEORY OF VISUAL SPACE. A geometric theory that binocular visual space, in contrast to physical space, is best described as a Riemannian space of constant Gaussian curvature.*

Luneburg, Rudolph Karl. German-American mathematician (b. Volkersheim, Germany, 1903, d. Great Falls, Montana, August 19, 1949). Between 1930 and 1934, Luneburg was at the universities of Göttingen and Leyden, New York University between 1935 and 1938, and held a position with the Spencer Lens Company of Buffalo, New York, where, after 1939, he made fundamental advances in miscroscopy. His last position was with the University of Southern California. Luneburg's theory was presented in his book, *Mathematical Analysis of Binocular Vision* (1947).
   Biographies: NYT, Aug. 20, 1949, 11; Science, 1949, 110, 266.

LURIA-NEBRASKA NEUROPSYCHOLOGICAL BATTERY. A battery of tests used to diagnose cerebral dysfunction and to determine lateralization and localization. The battery includes tests of motor, tactile, and visual functions, speech, writing, reading, arithmetic, memory, and intellectual processes. It is based on the neuropsychological theorizing of A. R. Luria and represents a standardization of Luria's Neuropsychological Investigation* by C. J. Golden and others (1980).

LURIA'S NEUROPSYCHOLOGICAL INVESTIGATION. A neuropsychological assessment procedure, the first English-language version of A. R. Luria's test battery, consisting of eleven investigations broken down into thirty subtests. The test manual was published by A. L. Christensen in 1975.

Luria, Aleksandr Romanovich. Russian neuropsychologist (b. Kazan', July 16, 1902, d. Moscow, August 15, 1977). Luria received a doctorate in psychology from Moscow University in 1936 and a doctorate in medical sciences from the same university in 1943. He held a variety of academic, clinical, and research positions, notably those in the Laboratory of Neuropsychology of the Institute of Neurosurgery (1936–1953) and the Department of Neuropsychology, Moscow University (1945–1977). Luria's earliest research was a series of studies on the evolution of psychological processes and on mental retardation. He next began the study of changes in mental functioning that occur in aphasia and continued to work on brain organization, brain processes and speech functions, and the restoration of brain functions during and after World War II. The last work produced international fame for him. In the 1950s, Luria made several important findings in the development and pathology of speech and in the 1960s and 1970s published a considerable number of papers and books that established a new branch of science, neuropsychology. His scientific works number more than 300.

　　Biographies: Amer. J. Psychol., 1978, *91*, 349–52; M. Cole, *Amer. Psychologist*, 1977, *32*, 969–71; *ConAu*, 25; *HPA*, 6; *IESS*, 18; *Prominent Personalities in the USSR*, 1968; *Psychol. Today*, March 1971, 79–89; *WhoWo*, 2.

Nebraska, University of. The second part of the Luria-Nebraska Neuropsychological Battery eponym comes from the University of Nebraska, the institution at which the principal one of the three developers of the test battery, Charles J. Golden, was working at the time the battery was published.

M

MACBETH ILLUMINOMETER. An instrument for the precise measurement of luminance. The unknown source is compared with the output of a known light source built into the instrument. The two sources form two concentric fields in the Lummer-Brodhun cube,* which may be visually compared. By adjusting the distance of the standard lamp from the cube and by utilizing the inverse square law of illuminance, the luminance of the unknown source may be determined.

Macbeth, Norman. American entrepreneur (b. Alberta, Canada, 1874, d. Plattsburgh, New York, 1936). After his father died, Macbeth left school after the tenth grade in order to support his family. He first worked for a gas company. In 1915, he started his own business, the Macbeth Artificial Daylighting Company, which made lighting products containing a filter that made incandescent light appeal more like daylight. In 1917, Macbeth published *The Lighting of Offices, Streets, and Shop Windows* and a year later took out a patent for his illuminometer. At Macbeth's death, the business was taken over by his son, Norman Macbeth, who became an illumination engineer. The Leeds & Northrup Co. continued selling the illuminometer into the late 1940s, when it was discontinued.
Biographies: Unavailable.

MACH BANDS. At the border of a sharp transition from one luminance level to another, the enhancement of the darker of the two areas and the lightening of the lighter area in a narrow band along the border.

MACH-BREUER-BROWN THEORY OF LABYRINTHINE FUNCTIONING. The theory that information about rotary acceleration and deceleration is conveyed to the brain by the sensory cells located in the crista, the enclosing cupula being moved by the movements of the endolymph in the ampulla and the semicircular canals.

MACH CARD. A drawing of a folded card or an actual card under suitable viewing conditions presents ambiguous information concerning its orientation in space, so that perspective reversals will occur spontaneously.

MACH-DVORAK STEREOILLUSION. Depth shifts associated with alternating glimpses of a moving target by the left and right eyes.

MACHIAN POSITIVISM. Ernst Mach's position that immediate experience provides all the basic data of science. Experience is the observational ultimate because even in reading instruments, scales, or dials, we still have to rely on sense organs.

Mach, Ernst. Austrian physicist (b. Chirlitz-Turas, Moravia, February 18, 1838, d. Vatterstetten, near Haar, Bavaria, February 19, 1916). Mach studied physics at the University of Vienna and received a Ph.D. in that field in 1860. He worked first at the University of Graz (1864–1867), then at the University of Prague (1867–1895), and finally at the University of Vienna (1895–1901). Mach's contributions to psychology stem from his work as a philosopher of science, as well as his purely psychological work. The latter included research on visual space perception, time perception, and the perception of rotation. His book, *Lehre von den Bewegungsempfindungen* (1875), presented his theory of labyrinthine functioning and described the rotation frame used in its study. Mach's first paper on labyrinthine functioning had appeared two years earlier, however (*Sitzber. Akad. Wiss. Wien., math.-naturwiss. Kl., 68*, 124–40). Mach's description of the bands that bear his name appears in a four-part paper published over several years (*Sitzber. Akad. Wiss. Wien, math.-naturwiss. Kl.,* 1865, 52–2, 303–22; 1866, *54–2,* 131–44, 393–409; 1868, *57–2,* 11–19). The Mach card appeared in the 1866 installment of this paper. Mach's most important work was *The Analysis of Sensations* (1886, English translation 1897), in which he set forth the principles of a positivist philosophy of science.

Biographies: J. T. Blackmore, *Ernst Mach: His Life, Work, and Influence*, 1972; *DSB,* 8; *EB,* 14; *EP,* 5; H. W. Pittenger, *Science,* 1965, *150,* 1120–22; F. Ratliff, *Mach Bands,* 1965, pp. 7–36.

Breuer, Josef. Austrian psychoanalyst (b. Vienna, January 15, 1842, d. Vienna, June 20, 1925). Breuer received his medical degree from the University of Vienna in 1867; he remained at the university for four years and then went into private practice. He is known both as the discoverer, independently of Mach, of the function of the semicircular canals (*Allg. Wien. med. Z.,* 1873, *18,* 598, 606; *Wien. med. Jb.,* 1874, *4,* 72–124; 1875, *5,* 87–156) and as Sigmund Freud's* intimate friend and father figure, more as the latter. It was Breuer's famous patient, Anna O., who set Freud's thinking along lines that later became the foundation of psychoanalysis. The book by Breuer and Freud, *Studies in Hysteria* (1895), is held to mark the beginning of psychoanalysis.

Biographies: S. Bernfeld, *Psychoanal. Quart.*, 1944, *13*, 341–62; *DSB*, 2; *EB*, 4; *EJ*, 4; *Jewish*, 2; A. Kleyn, *Acta Otolaryng.*, 1926, *10*, 167–71; M. Schlessinger et al., *J. Amer. Psychoanal. Ass.*, 1967, *15*, 404–22; W. A. Stewart, *Psychoanalysis: The First Ten Years, 1888–1898*, 1967.

Brown, Alexander Crum. English chemist and physiologist (b. Edinburgh, March 26, 1838, d. Edinburgh, October 28, 1922). Brown received the M.D. degree from the University of Edinburgh in 1861 and the D.Sc. degree from the University of London in 1862. He was at the former university from 1863 to 1908. In structural chemistry, Brown introduced the graphic formulas that are still used today. In physiology, his main interest was in the effects of rotation. Brown came across the earlier papers of Mach and Breuer after he had formulated a theory of labyrinthine functioning and had built a mechanical model but before he had published his own paper in 1874 (*J. Anat. Physiol.*, 8, 327-31).

Biographies: DSB, 2; *J. Chem. Soc.*, 1923, *123*, 3422–31; J. E. Mackenzie, *Chem. Ind.*, July 2, 1949, No. 27, 461–63.

Dvořák, Vinko. Czech physicist (b. 1848, d. 1922). Dvořák was Mach's assistant, and some of the experiments Dvořák described he conducted on Mach's instigation. Mach presented Dvořák's work on the stereoillusion in 1872 (*Sitzber. kön. böhm. Ges. Wiss. Prag, math.-naturwiss. Cl.*, March 8, 1872, 65–74).

Biographies: Unavailable.

MACHIAVELLIANISM SCALE. A psychological scale designed to assess the level of machiavellianism in a person. High scorers are generally less trusting, more willing to use amoral interpersonal strategies for personal advantage, and more successful in optimizing for themselves outcomes of interpersonal interactions.

Machiavelli, Niccolò. Italian court adviser, writer, and thinker (b. Florence, May 3, 1469, d. Florence, June 21, 1527). Born into a noble but impoverished family, Machiavelli was largely self-educated. He entered the Florentinian political scene in 1498 when the Borgias were in power and during the course of his career made observations of the political scene that were to become part of his famous analysis of statesmanship and power, *The Prince*. He wrote it when, in 1512, he had fallen out of favor due to political upheaval. This treatise on how to gain and maintain political control was published in 1513. Machiavelli wrote other political works, as well as literature. In 1520, he was restored to state duty with the Medicis and wrote a history of Florence and other historical works. His second fall from political favor came with the end of the tenure of the Medicis in Florence in 1527, the year Machiavelli died. The Machiavellianism scale was constructed by the American psychologist Richard Christie (R. Christie & F. Geis, *Studies in Machiavellianism*, 1970).

Biographies: EB, 14; R. Ridolfi, *Life of Niccolo Machiavelli*, 1963.

MACH NUMBER. A number that indicates multiples of the speed of sound at sea level at 15 degrees Celsius (340 meters per second), which is Mach 1.

Mach, Ernst. See under eponyms that begin with MACH BANDS.

MACHOVER DRAW-A-PERSON TEST. Also called the Machover Figure Drawing Test, this is a projective test requiring the drawing of a person, followed by the telling of a story about the person.

Machover, Karen Alper. American psychologist (b. September 2, 1902). Machover studied clinical psychology at New York University (M.A., 1929), worked as psychologist at the Bellevue and Kings County Hospital, New York City, beginning in 1931, and entered private practice in 1946. She also taught at Brooklyn College (1949–1952) and New School for Social Research (1950–1953) and was a clinical assistant professor at the Downstate Medical Center of the State University of New York from 1950 to 1984. Machover's test was published in 1949 (*Personality Projection in the Drawing of the Human Figure: A Method of Personality Investigation*).
   Biographies: APA Dir., 1985.

MACH ROTATION FRAME. Two frames, one within the other, the larger frame rotating about a vertical axis and the smaller frame about a horizontal axis, with a pivoted chair in the middle, used in the study of bodily movement.

Mach, Ernst. See under eponyms beginning with MACH BANDS.

MACKWORTH CLOCK TEST. A vigilance task in which the subject watches the sweeps of the single hand of a clock against a plain background. Each sweep takes one second to complete, except that the clock is programmed to make the sweeps twice as long on occasion. The subject's task is to press a key when this happens.

Mackworth, Norman Humphrey. English-American psychologist (b. Bareilley, United Provinces, India, December 2, 1917). Mackworth received the Ph.D. degree in experimental psychology from Cambridge University in 1947. He held positions with the Medical Research Council at Cambridge from 1948 to 1958, the government and private firms between 1958 and 1963, and was research fellow at Harvard and Stanford Universities from 1963 to 1976. He lectured on psychology at Stanford after 1971. Mackworth's specialty was thinking processes, attention, expectancy and set, vigilance, and eye movements. The clock test was presented in 1950 (Researches on the measurement of human performance. *Special Reports Series, Medical Research Council*, London, 1950, No. 268).
   Biographies: AM&WS, 1973S; APA Dir., 1981.

MACLEAN'S THEORY OF EMOTION. See PAPEZ-MACLEAN THEORY OF EMOTION.

MACQUARRIE TEST FOR MECHANICAL ABILITY. A test of mechanical ability that emphasizes eye-hand coordination and spatial relations in its seven subtests: tracing, tapping, dotting, copying, location, blocks, and pursuit.

Macquarrie, Thomas William. American psychologist (b. n.a., d. n.a.). Macquarrie was at the University of Southern California in 1927 when he published his test (*J. Personnel Res., 5,* 329–37).
   Biographies: Unavailable.

MADDOX ROD TEST. A test for ocular muscle imbalance (strabismus) in which the subject looks through colored glass rods that make a point source of light appear as a streak, interfering with binocular fusion.

Maddox, Ernest Edmund. English ophthalmic surgeon (b. 1860, d. November 10, 1933). From 1884 on, Maddox was on the staff of the Edinburgh Royal Infirmary. He published *Tests and Studies of the Ocular Muscles* (1898), which contains the description of the rod test.
   Biographies: WoWhoSci.

MAERZ AND PAUL COLOR DICTIONARY. A system for classifying colors. It contains 7,000 color samples and 4,000 color names.

Maerz, Aloys John. (b. 1885, d. n.a.). At the time Maerz and Paul published *A Dictionary of Color* (1930), Maerz was the director of American Color Research Laboratory.
   Biographies: Unavailable.

Paul, Morris Rea. (b. 1885, d. n.a.), Paul, coauthor of *A Dictionary of Color,* was consulting colorist with research laboratories of the National Lead Company.
   Biographies: Unavailable.

MAHALANOBIS'S D^2. In two-group linear discriminant analysis, the Euclidean or generalized distance between two centroids in p-dimensional space.

Mahalanobis, Prasanta Chandra. Indian statistician (b. Calcutta, June 29, 1893, d. Calcutta, June 28, 1972). Mahalanobis obtained the bachelor's degree in physics from Presidency College, Calcutta, and he graduated from Cambridge University in science in 1915. He taught physics at the Presidency College from 1915 until the 1950s. Mahalanobis' work was on sample surveys and multivariate analysis. He also worked out an economic theory that became India's economic strategy for two decades. Mahalanobis founded the Indian Statistical Institute in 1931. The D^2 statistic was presented in 1936 (*Proc. Nat. Inst. Sci. India, 12,* 49–55).
   Biographies: W. E. Deming, *Amer. Statistician,* 1972, 26(4), 49–50; *IESS,* 18; C. R. Rao, *Biog. Mem. Fellows Roy. Soc.,* 1973, 455–92; H. Sanyal, *Sankhyā,* 1973, *35* (suppl.), 3–11.

MAIN SYNDROME. A personality disorder in which the individual, by assuming the role of one who is helpless, misunderstood, or maltreated, manipulates those around him or her by causing dissension among them over his or her management.

Main, Thomas Forrest. English psychiatrist (fl. 1937–1972). Main's M.D. was from the University of Durham (1937). He was medical director of Cassel Hospital, Ham Common, Richmond, Surrey, and editor of *British Journal of Medical Psychology*. Main described the syndrome in 1957.

Biographies: The Medical Directory. London: Churchill, Livingstone, 1970.

MALTHUSIAN THEORY. The theory that while population increases on a geometric scale, food production increases on an arithmetic scale, and that for this reason humanity is destined to live in hunger and poverty.

Malthus, Thomas Robert. English economist and demographer (b. Dorking, Surrey, February 14, 1766, d. St. Catherine's, near Bath, Somersetshire, December 23, 1834). Graduating from Cambridge with an M.A. in 1791, Malthus took holy orders in 1797; he then served as professor of history and political economy at East India Company's Haileybury College from 1805 to 1834. Malthus published his theory in 1798 (*An Essay on the Principle of Population*). The theory implied a struggle for survival, and Charles Darwin,* Herbert Spencer, and Alfred Russel Wallace, having read Malthus' essay, were stimulated to begin thinking along the lines of natural selection. In addition to the *Essay*, Malthus wrote works on political economy, anticipating some of the discoveries that were made in the 1930s by John Maynard Keynes.

Biographies: J. Bonar, *Malthus and His Work*, 1924; *DNB*, 12; *EB*, 14; *EP*, 5; *IESS*, 9; J. M. Keynes, *Essays in Biography*, 1951.

MANN-WHITNEY *U* TEST. A nonparametric statistical test of whether two independent samples have been drawn from the same population. The data must be at least on the ordinal scale of measurement. It is the most powerful nonparametric alternative to the parametric *t* test.

Mann, Henry Berthold. American mathematician (b. Vienna, Austria, October 27, 1905). Mann's Ph.D. in mathematics was from the University of Vienna (1935). He held positions at the University of Colorado, Bard College, Ohio State University (1946–1964), University of Wisconsin (1964–1970), and the University of Arizona (1970 to his retirement). Mann worked in the areas of number theory, group theory, and mathematical statistics. The *U* test appeared in 1947 (H. B. Mann & D. R. Whitney, *Ann. Math. Stat.*, *18*, 50–60).

Biographies: AM&WS, 1979P.

Whitney, Donald Ransom. American statistician (b. Cleveland Heights, Ohio, November 27, 1915). Whitney obtain a Ph.D. in mathematics from Ohio State University in 1948. He remained at that institution and has occupied the chair of the statistics department since 1970. Whitney has published two books and more than twenty papers in the area of statistics and mathematical statistics.

Biographies: AM&WS, 1982P.

MARBE'S LAW. In word association tests, the more common words have the shorter latencies as compared with less common words.

Marbe, Karl. German psychologist (b. Paris, France, August 31, 1869, d. Würzburg, Germany, January 2, 1953). Marbe, who received the Ph.D. from the University of Bonn in 1893, taught at the University of Würzburg (1895–1903, 1909–1934) and the Academy of Social and Commercial Sciences at Frankfurt (1905–1909). Marbe worked on some classical problems in psychophysics and perception, but at Würzburg he made important contributions to the imageless thought school of Oswald Külpe. Later Marbe turned to applied psychology. He wrote eighteen books and more than one hundred articles on psychological topics. His law appears in a book, *Experimentelle Untersuchungen über die psychologische Grundlage der sprachlichen Analogiebildung* (1901), written with A. Thumb.

Biographies: *HPA*, 3; K. Marbe, *Selbstbiographie*, 1945; W. Peters, *Amer. J. Psychol.*, 1953, *66*, 645–47.

MARBURG SCHOOL. A group of psychologists and psychiatrists at the University of Marburg, who, following the lead of its main figure, Erich Rudolf Jaensch (on the Marburg faculty from 1913 to 1940), adopted the classification of human types by the strength of eidetic imagery. The B-type was characterized by good eidetic ability that was under voluntary control and was caused by a hyperactive thyroid gland; the T-type was characterized by afterimages that were not under voluntary control and were caused by the hypoactivity of the parathyroid. The descriptions of each type were later adjusted by Jaensch to suit the National-Socialist ideology, and the concept lost its value to science.

Marburg. German university town, Marburg an der Lahn, in the state of Hesse. It received official recognition as a town in 1211. The university, Philipps-Universität, was founded in 1527. It was the first Protestant university in Europe.

MARCHIAFAVA-BIGNAMI DISEASE. A rare toxic disease in which the pathology is the progressive degeneration of the corpus callosum. The individual is confused to the point of being psychotic. There are no hallucinations, but there is progressive mental deterioration, loss of attention, apathy, and seizures.

Marchiafava, Ettore. Italian physician (b. Rome, January 3, 1847, d. Rome, October 23, 1935). Marchiafava obtained his medical degree from the University of Rome in 1869 and worked at that institution from 1872 until his retirement in 1922. Marchiafava did research on malaria and the nervous system. In an intensive, eleven-year study, he established the life cycle of Plasmodium falciparum and discovered that the disease is transmitted through blood. He also practiced internal medicine as the personal physician to three popes and the royal

house. The paper in which the eponymous disease was described, written with Bignami, appeared in 1903 (*Riv. pat. nerv. ment., 8*, 544–49).
   Biographies: DSB, 9.

Bignami, Amico. Italian pathologist (b. Bologna, April 15, 1862, d. Rome, September 8, 1929). Bignami's M.D. was from the University of Rome (1882). His career was spent at the University of Rome in work on brain pathology and malaria. On the latter subject, he and Marchiafava were coauthors of a book.
   Biographies: Fischer, Biog. Lex.; EI, 6.

MAREY TAMBOUR. A device for recording physiological processes, such as the pulse or breathing. It consists of a small, shallow pan covered with a membrane to which is attached the short arm of a lever. The long arm is equipped with a stylus for recording on a kymograph. The membrane of the tambour moves up and down when activated by air pressure changes within the tambour. These are produced by a similar tambour, fitted to and attached to the appropriate bodily part and connected to the recording tambour with a rubber hose.

Marey, Etienne Jules. French physiologist and inventor (b. Beaune, Côte d'Or, March 5, 1830, d. Paris, May 16, 1904). Marey received his M.D. from the University of Paris in 1859. From 1867 on he occupied the chair of natural history at the Collège de France. Marey invented the sphygmograph and the cardiograph. As part of the sphygmograph, the tambour was described in *Recherches sur le puols au moyen d'un nouvel appareil enregistreur—le sphygmographe* (1860). Marey also pioneered in the development of motion pictures and studied animal movement (*Animal Mechanism,* 1873). His first scientific studies of bird flight inspired the early pioneers of aeronautics, including the Wright brothers.
   Biographies: EB, 14.

MARIANNE FROSTIG DEVELOPMENTAL TEST OF VISUAL PERCEPTION. A diagnostic test intended to uncover deficiencies in visual perception that might affect the learning of various school tasks that emphasize visual perception. It consists of an eye-motor coordination subtest, a figure-ground test, a form constancy subtest, a position in space subtest, and a spatial relations subtest.

Frostig, Marianne B. Austrian-American psychologist (b. Vienna, Austria, March 31, 1906, d. June 20, 1985). From 1932 to 1937 Frostig was chief of rehabilitation therapy at the Zofiowka Research Hospital, Otwock, Poland. She received her Ph.D. in educational psychology from the University of Southern California in 1955. Frostig was the founder of the Marianne Frostig Center of Educational Therapy in Los Angeles and its executive director after 1947. She held concurrent positions as school psychologist for Los Angeles county (1949–1955) and lecturer and professor at Los Angeles State College, San Fernando Valley State College, Mt. St. Mary's College, and the University of Southern California. In addition to her test, which appeared in 1961, Frostig was

the author or coauthor of several books on the interaction of aptitude and treatment in the classroom and over fifty other publications.
Biographies: AM&WS, 1978S; APA Dir., 1985.

MARIOTTE'S SPOT. An older name for the blind spot.

Mariotte, Edme. French physicist (b. probably Chazeuil, Burgundy, c. 1620, d. Paris, May 12, 1684). Although self-taught, Mariotte was prior of the St. Martin-sous-Beaune monastery near Dijon who became one of the founders of experimental physics in France and an independent discoverer of Boyle's law. Virtually nothing else is known about his life. In 1668, Mariotte discovered the blind spot in the retina (*Nouvelle discouverte touchant la veüe*) and showed how it can be located. He described the macula and other parts of the eye. Mariotte also performed experiments on light, color, and vision (*De la nature des couleurs,* 1681) and was interested in a great variety of physical subjects. He spent most of his time in Paris doing research instead of attending to his duties as a prior.
Biographies: L. Darmstaedter, J. Chem. Educ., 1927, 4, 320–22; DSB, 9; EB, 14.

MARKOV CHAIN. A sequence of mutually dependent states in which the probability of any particular state is independent of all other states in that sequence except the immediately preceding state is called a Markov process.* If, in a Markov process, the probability of a state following a particular sequence is independent of the trial numbers on which that sequence occurs, the process is called stationary. A process that is both Markovian and stationary is called a Markov chain.

MARKOV PROCESS (MARKOVIAN PROCESS). A sequence of mutually dependent states in which the probability of any particular state is independent of all other states in that sequence except the immediately preceding state.

Markov, Andreï Andreevich. Russian mathematician (b. Ryazan', June 14, 1856, d. Petrograd, July 20, 1922). Markov graduated from the University of St. Petersburg (Ph.D., 1878) and served on its faculty from 1880 to his retirement in 1905. Markov first worked on number theory and then, from about 1900, on probability theory. He was the first to give a complete proof of the central limits theorem. His work on mutually dependent variables is one of the sources from which the modern theory of stochastic processes was developed. The idea of the Markov chain* was first described in a 1906 article (generalization of the law of large numbers to mutually dependent variables), followed by a series of others that developed the concept.
Biographies: DSB, 9; EB, 14; Soviet, 15.

MARSTON DECEPTION TEST. A method of lie detection based on the measurement of systolic blood pressure.

Marston, William Moulton. American psychologist (b. Saugus, Massachusetts, May 9, 1893, d. Rye, New York, May 2, 1947). In 1915, Marston discovered a relationship between systolic blood pressure and lying. He published the first paper on the subject in 1917 (*J. Exp. Psychol.*, *2*, 117–63). It was followed by a number of additional papers and, in 1938, a book, *The Lie Detection Test*. In 1918, Marston obtained an LL.B. from Harvard Law School, was admitted to the bar, and practiced law briefly. In 1921, he obtained a Ph.D. in psychology from Harvard and went to Washington, D.C., to conduct research on lie detection and the psychology of evidence, becoming the first professor of legal psychology in the United States at the American University, Washington, D.C., in 1922. After 1925, Marson held a variety of teaching positions and worked as consulting psychologist to motion picture and advertising companies. In the early 1930s, he became increasingly engaged in popular psychological writing and lecturing. In December 1941, the first Wonder Woman comic strip issue appeared. It was a creation of Marston, who, under the pseudonym of Charles Moulton, continued to originate the story line and dialog until his death. Marston produced a large number of books and articles, both scientific and popular.

Biographies: A Dictionary of North American Authors, 1951; *Encyclopedia of American Biography*, 1974; *NCAB*, E, 35; *NYT*, May 3, 1947; *Obituaries on File*, 1979; *PR*, 3; *WhNAA; WhAm*, 2; M. Horne (ed.), *The World Encyclopedia of Comics*, 1976.

MARTIUS DISK. A method for determining the value of a shade of gray. The disk consists of a central, concentric circular area of variable grays, ranging from black to white, an identical peripheral annulus, and an intermediate annular space between them, into which is inserted an annulus of the shade of gray whose value is to be determined. The peripheral and central grays are varied until they are neither darkened nor lightened by the comparison gray. The gray of the variable standards then gives the value of the comparison gray.

Martius, Götz. German psychologist (b. 1853, d. Kiel, May 27, 1927). Martius studied under Wundt* at Leipzig and was on the faculty of the University of Bonn. He described the disk in an 1896 article (*Beitr. Psychol. Philos.*, *1*, 95–119).

Biographies: Unavailable.

MASHBURN COMPLEX COORDINATOR (MASHBURN APPARATUS). An apparatus for measuring eye-hand and eye-foot coordination. The object is to align sets of green and red lights by means of control levers within a given amount of time. It was used as a basic psychomotor test for pilot selection.

Mashburn, Neely Cornelius. American surgeon (b. Bolivar, Tennessee, June 17, 1886, d. June 22, 1974). Mashburn received an M.D. from the University of Vanderbilt. He was in the armed services from 1917 to 1948 when he retired with the rank of colonel. Mashburn served as station or base surgeon and staff medical officer at various U.S. Army Air Force and U.S. Air Force bases around the country. He was also instructor at the Aviation School of Medicine, at Brooks Field (1926–1931), and at Randolph Field (1934–1940). Mashburn was recalled to active duty in 1948 and served until 1955. The Mashburn apparatus was second in a series of five versions undergone by the School of Aviation Medicine Complex Coordination Test, receiving the specific appellation of Mashburn Auto

matic Serial Action Apparatus (*J. Avi. Med.*, 1934, *5*, 155–60). It was superseded by the Constable Reaction Apparatus, Models A1 and A2, designed by Major Asa F. Constable in 1932 and patented in 1934.
   Biographies: Unavailable.

MASOCHISM. A disorder in which the individual obtains pleasure from receiving pain, inflicted by oneself or others or, more generally, the enjoyment of suffering and the seeking of painful experiences, physical or psychological, often in connection with sexual relations.

Sacher-Masoch, Leopold Ritter von. Austrian novelist (b. Lemberg, Austria, January 1, 1836, d. Lindheim, Hesse, March 3, 1895). Sacher-Masoch's fictional characters associated sexual pleasure with pain. He was a prime example of a masochist, with early childhood antecedents perceptible in his continuous exposure to violent, gruesome tales by his wet nurse and his father, a police chief. Sacher-Masoch studied law, received his juris doctor at the age of nineteen, and was already acting out machochistic fantasies in his life, becoming a ''slave'' to several mistresses. His novel published in the 1890s, *Venus in Furs,* is a full statement of the masochistic relationship. This and other novels made Sacher-Masoch a leading literary figure of his time. The complementary sadistic impulse was also manifest in him: he made several attempts to kill his second wife, who was forced to commit him to an asylum before he was fifty. He died in the asylum ten years later. The term *masochism* was first used by Richard Krafft-Ebing (in *Arbeiten aus dem Gesamtgebiet der Psychiatrie und Neuropathologie,* 1897–1899, vol. 4, pp. 127–31).
   Biographies: J. Cleugh, *The First Masochist,* 1967; J. Cleugh, *Marquis and the Chevalier,* 1952; *DE;* G. Deleuze, *Sacher-Masoch: An Interpretation,* 1971; *EA,* 24; S. J. Kunitz & V. Colby (eds.), *European Authors, 1000–1900,* 1967.

MASSON DISK. A disk with black rectangles arranged on one of the radii. When rotated, the rectangles produce gray annuli whose lightness increases from the center of the disk to its periphery. The ring whose lightness is at the observer's sensory threshold appears to merge with the background and then reemerge. Measuring the ratio of black to white in this annulus enables calculation of the observer's difference threshold. In the original version, the Masson disk had a single rectangle, and the testing for thresholds was done utilizing a series of such disks with varying rectangle-to-disk area ratios.

Masson, Antoine-Philibert. French physicist (b. Auxonne, Côte-d'Or, August 22, 1806, d. Paris, December 1, 1860). Masson taught at the Lycée Louis-le-Grand and the Ecole centrale in Paris. He invented an electric telegraph and in 1841 conducted discharges from a induction coil through rarified gases before Heinrich Geissler. He also studied the production of sounds, vision, and other phenomena. The disk was described in 1845 (*Ann. chim. phys., 14,* 150).
   Biographies: Pagel, *Biog. Lex.; Larousse,* 7.

MAUDSLEY PERSONALITY INVENTORY. A forty-eight-item personality inventory that yielded a neuroticism and an extroversion score. It was superseded by the Eysenck Personality Inventory* in 1963.

Maudsley Hospital. The inventory was named after Maudsley Hospital where H. J. Eysenck,* the author of the inventory, once worked as a research psychologist. The hospital, formerly the London University Psychiatric Hospital, is named after Henry Maudsley (1835–1918), the famous English psychiatrist who conceived the idea of building the hospital and advanced some money toward its construction.

MAXWELL DISKS. Disks cut from colored paper and slit along a radius so that two or more may be mounted together superimposed on each other on a color wheel. Different color mixtures may be obtained by exposing different amounts of each color and rotating the wheel at a rate at which the separate colors blend.

MAXWELLIAN VIEW. A means of eliminating fluctuations in the amount of light entering the eye due to fluctuations in pupil size. All light coming from an object is concentrated by means of a spherical lens that focuses it in the plane of the pupil. Because all light enters the eye through its center without touching the rim of the pupil, changes in the size of the pupil have no effect on the brightness of the image.

MAXWELL'S SPOT. A dark ring surrounding the fixation point to an extent of two to three degrees is seen when a brightly illuminated white surface is looked at alternately through a blue and a yellow filter. The ring appears during the first few seconds when looking through the blue filter. In addition, most observers see a smaller dark spot at the fixation point itself. Green, orange, red, gray, and even an opaque screen may be used instead of the yellow filter, but the spot is best seen when both the blue and the contrasting light are of about the same brightness.

MAXWELL TRIANGLE. J. Clerk Maxwell stated the equations for color mixing in a quantitatively exact form. He then represented the mixtures within a triangle that was placed on the color circle. The color triangle gave recognition to the fact that in a color mixture, intensity must also be taken into account; hence all properties of all colors must be represented as a three-dimensional solid rather than a two-dimensional plane figure.

Maxwell, James Clerk. Scottish mathematician and physicist (b. Edinburgh, November 13, 1831, d. Cambridge, November 5, 1879). After receiving a Ph.D. in natural philosophy from Cambridge University, Maxwell held positions at Mariscal College, Aberdeen (1856–1860), King's College, London (1860–1865), and Cambridge University (1871–1879). Maxwell, famous for his work in physics and electricity (kinetic theory of gases, equations connecting electricity and magnetism, the concept of the electromagnetic spectrum of energies), contributed to psychology during his two postgraduate years at Trinity College, Cambridge. Here he worked out the quantitative laws of color mixture, invented the color disks (*Trans. Roy. Soc. Edin.*, 1855, *21*[2], 275–298), and originated the idea of the color triangle (*Phil. Trans. Roy. Soc.*, 1860, *150*, 57–84). Maxwell invented the fish-eye lens, making the Maxwellian view possible (W. D. Niven [ed.], *The Scientific Papers of J. Clerk Maxwell*, 2 vols., 1890 (reprinted 1952), vol. 1, p. 79). The report on Maxwell's spot appeared in the *Reports of the British Association*, 1856, p. 12.

Biographies: Asimov; L. Campbell & W. Garnett, *The Life of James Clerk Maxwell,* 1970; *DNB,* 13; *DSB,* 9; *EB,* 15; D. K. C. MacDonald, *Faraday, Maxwell, and Kelvin,* 1964; J. R. Newman, *Sci. Amer.,* 1955, *192*(6), 58–71; W. D. Niven, in *The Scientific Papers of J. Clerk Maxwell,* vol. 1, 1890 pp. ix–xxix.

MCADORY ART TEST. One of the first tests to measure artistic appreciation. It became useless because of the dated nature of the materials.

McAdory, Margaret. American educator (b. 1890, d. n.a.) McAdory obtained a Ph.D. from Teachers College, Columbia University, in 1929. Her test was based on her dissertation and appeared in the same year (*Teachers College, Columbia University, Contributions to Education,* 1929, No. 383; *The McAdory Art Test: Manual,* Teachers College, Columbia University, Bureua of Publications, 1929).

Biographies: Unavailable.

MCCALLIE'S AUDIOMETER. A device for measuring sound intensity thresholds, similar to Politzer's acoumeter, in which sound was produced by a hammer striking a sound-producing surface and the intensity of the sound was varied by varying the size of an opening in the box in which the hammer mechanism was enclosed.

McCallie, Joseph Madison. American psychologist (b. Knoxville, Tennessee, February 18, 1863, d. 1942). McCallie's Ph.D. was from the University of Pennsylvania (1912). From 1890 to 1903 he was superintendent of schools in Tennessee, Illinois, and New Jersey. He was principal of the Franklin School, Trenton, New Jersey from 1903 to 1919 and worked in the New Jersey public school system from 1919 to 1936. McCallie did research on the acuteness of hearing and vision and on educational statistics.

Biographies: AMS, 1938.

MCCARTHY SCALES OF CHILDREN'S ABILITIES. A psychological instrument for the assessment of the abilities of children aged two and a half to eight and a half. It consists of eighteen tests that yield six scores: verbal, perceptual-performance, quantitative, general cognitive, memory, and motor.

McCarthy, Dorothea Agnes. American psychologist (b. Minneapolis, Minnesota, March 4, 1906, d. Bronxville, New York, September 22, 1974). McCarthy received the Ph.D. degree in psychology from the University of Minnesota in 1928. She worked for child welfare institutions until 1930, taught for two years at the University of Georgia, and then went to Fordham University in 1932, where she remained until she retired as professor emeritus in 1971. McCarthy's main area of interest was child development, particularly language development and language disorders. The scales were published in 1970.
   Biographies: AM&WS, 1973S; APA Dir., 1968; NYT, Sep. 23, 1974, p. 38.

MCCARTHY'S REFLEX. Contraction of the eyelid muscle by a tap over the supraorbital foramen. It is also known as the supraorbital reflex.

McCarthy, Daniel Joseph. American neurologist (b. Philadelphia, Pennsylvania, June 22, 1874, d. Ventnor, New Jersey, October 9, 1958). McCarthy, who received his Ph.D. from the University of Pennsylvania in 1895, also obtained a certificate in medical jurisprudence in 1896 and taught this subject at the University of Pennsylvania Medical School from 1904 to 1940, as well as at its law school (1926–1932). McCarthy was also in private practice and established three foundations for furthering medical research. He established his reputation in 1917 when he published *The Prisoner of War in Germany*. McCarthy described the reflex in 1901 and 1902 (*Neurol. Zbl., 20,* 800; *21,* 843).
   Biographies: AMA J., 1958, 168, 2037–38; DAB, Suppl. 6.

MCCOLLOUGH EFFECT. A vertical grating of black lines on an orange background is alternated every few seconds with a horizontal grating on a blue background. After the subject is exposed to these stimuli for two to four minutes, achromatic gratings are presented. The vertical grating now appears tinged with blue and the horizontal grating with orange. The phenomenon is also known as the color-contingent aftereffect.

McCollough, Celeste Faye. American psychologist (b. Boulder, Colorado, September 12, 1926). McCollough obtained her Ph.D. degree from Columbia University in 1955. She was assistant professor at Olivet College from 1954 to 1956 and then taught at Oberlin College. Her research is in perception and in thinking and brain functions. She described the color-contingent aftereffect in 1965 (*Science, 149,* 1115–16).
   Biographies: APA Dir., 1965; WhoAmW, 1972–1973.

MCNAGHTEN **RULES.** A principle for establishing criminal responsibility. The gist of the rules is that in order to establish a defense on the ground of insanity, it must be demonstrated that at the time the crime was committed, the defendant, either because of mental disorder or because of temporary insanity, did not know what he or she was doing, or, if he or she knew, did not know that it was wrong.

McNaghten, Daniel. (b. 1813, d. May 3, 1865). On January 20, 1843, McNaghten, suffering from the delusion that he was being persecuted by Sir Robert Peel, the British prime minister, shot and killed his secretary, Edward Drummond, whom he mistook for Peel. Although he was charged with murder, he was acquitted by reason of insanity. Because of the public outcry against the verdict, the House of Lords posed certain questions to the judges, which were answered by the chief justice. The justice's answers to these questions constitute the *McNaghten* rules. McNaghten spent the rest of his days in the Bethlehem Hospital and the Broadmoor Criminal Lunatic Asylum. He died of general physical deterioration at the latter institution. The proper spelling of the principal's name is probably *McNaughton,* but it has been spelled in at least ten different ways. *McNaghten* or *M'Naghten* is the preferred American spelling.

Biographies: D. West & A. Walk, *Daniel McNaughton: His Trial and the Aftermath,* 1977.

MCNEMAR TEST. A nonparametric statistical test for the significance of change when repeated measurements are used and the measurements are on the nominal or ordinal scale, such as in a before-and-after design.

McNemar, Quinn. American psychologist (b. Greenland Gap, West Virginia, February 20, 1900, d. July 3, 1986). McNemar received a Ph.D. in psychometrics from Stanford University in 1932 and spent most of his career at that institution working in the fields of psychometrics, statistics, test theory, and the measurement of individual differences. He became emeritus in 1965, went to the University of Texas, and retired in 1975. He was the author of a revision of the Stanford-Binet Intelligence Scale* (1942) and *Psychological Statistics* (1949, revised editions in 1955, 1962, and 1969). The test was published in 1947 (*Psychometrika, 12,* 153–57).

Biographies: AM&WS, 1973S; *APA Dir.,* 1985; *HPA,* 7; *WhoAm,* 1976–1977.

MEDEA COMPLEX. A mother's wish of death toward her children as a means of taking revenge on her husband.

Medea. An enchantress who appears in the Greek legend of the Argonauts. She helped Jason to obtain the Golden Fleece, but when Jason left her, she killed their two children, Mermerus and Pheres. The term was coined by Edward S. Stern (*J. Ment. Sci.,* 1948, *94,* 321–31).

MEIER AESTHETIC PERCEPTION TEST. See MEIER ART TESTS.

MEIER ART JUDGMENT TEST. See MEIER ART TESTS.

MEIER ART TESTS. Of the two Meier art tests, the Meier Art Judgment Test and the Meier Aesthetic Perception Test, the latter was published in 1963, the former in 1929 and revised in 1942, when it replaced the Meier-Seashore Art

Judgment Test, published in 1930. The Meier-Seashore and the Meier Art Judgment Test have been the most widely used tests of artistic appreciation. They consist of pairs of reproductions of timeless artwork, an original and a version altered in some respect so as to be aesthetically less adequate.

Meier, Norman Charles. American psychologist (b. February 23, 1893, d. Iowa City, November 2, 1967). Meier received the Ph.D. degree from the University of Iowa in 1926 and remained there for the rest of his career except for visiting professorships at several other universities. He was the director of the Bureau for Audience Research after 1946, and his main research interests were public opinion measurement and aesthetics. Meier published several books in these areas.
   Biographies: APA Dir., 1965; *NCAB*, 54; *NYT*, Nov. 4, 1967, 33; *WhAm*, 4.

MEIER-SEASHORE ART JUDGMENT TEST. See MEIER ART TESTS.

Seashore, Carl Emil. See under eponyms that begin with SEASHORE.

MEISSNER CORPUSCLES. Oval nerve endings found in the hairless skin of the palms and feet. They are probably involved in the sensing of pressure or touch.

Meissner, Georg. German physiologist (b. Hannover, November 19, 1829, d. Göttingen, March 30, 1905). After short stays at the universities of Basle (1855–1857) and Freiburg (1857–1860), Meissner returned to Göttingen, where he had obtained his M.D. in 1852, and remained there to the end of his life. Meissner became known for his histological studies of the skin and the pressure receptors, achieving instant fame when he discovered the corpuscles that now bear his name (*Beiträge zur Anatomie und Physiologie der Haut*, 1853). In his *Beiträge zur Physiologie des Sehorgans* (1854), Meissner reported on his work in physiological optics. He continued to publish until 1872, when severe criticism of his work by other physiologists stopped him from going into print under his own name.
   Biographies: DSB, 9; *Rothschuh.*

MENDELIAN RATIO. The ratio of individuals in a given generation in whom a trait, inherited from a biparental mating, will and will not manifest itself. The best-known Mendelian ratio is three-to-one, observed in the offspring of purebred lines of parents in one of whom the trait is dominant and in the other recessive: for every three individuals who will manifest the trait, one will not.

MENDELISM. A theory, now modified after Mendel's original formulation, of genetic transmission based on the Mendelian principles that there exist genetic units that represent unitary characteristics, that these may be dominant or recessive, and that the genetic material is segregated from somatic material and therefore not affected by experience.

MENDEL'S LAW. A principle of genetic transmission that postulates the transmission of parental characteristics to offspring in units without change, the manifestation of some of these characteristics in the first generation and of others in later generations, and of a specified ratio of individuals in each generation in whom a characteristic will or will not be manifest.

Mendel, Gregor Johann. Austrian geneticist (b. Heizendorf, Austria [now Hyncice, Czechoslovakia], July 22, 1822, d. Brünn [now Brno, Czechoslovakia], January 6, 1884). Mendel studied philosophy at the University of Olmütz and physics and natural science at the University of Vienna. He entered a monastery in 1843, became abbot in 1868, and taught high school at Brünn from 1849 to 1868. In 1856, Mendel began his experiments with pea hybrids and in 1865 published the first paper describing the experiments and stating his theory of factorial inheritance (*Verh. naturforsch. Ver. Brünn, 4,* 3–47; 1869, *8,* 26–31). Although Mendel's papers started the science of genetics, they did not receive much attention at first, were forgotten, and had to be rediscovered thirty-four years later.
  Biographies: Asimov; CE, 9; *DSB,* 9; *EB,* 15; H. Iltis, *Life of Mendel,* 1932 (reprinted 1966); C. Zirkle, *Isis,* 1951, *42,* 97–104.

MENIERE'S DISEASE. A disease affecting the labyrinth characterized by violent bouts of disturbance in its functioning: falling, severe vertigo, extreme nausea, and violent nystagmic movements.

Ménière, Prosper M. French otologist (b. Angers, Maine-et-Loire, 1799, d. Paris, February 7, 1862). Ménière obtained his medical doctorate in 1828, after which he held various hospital appointments. In 1938 he became head of the Institute for Deaf-Mutes in Paris. Ménière described the disease in 1861 (*Gaz. méd. Paris,* 3e série, *16,* 597–601). In addition to his medical work, Ménière produced studies of Roman classics that were of enduring value.
  Biographies: Talbot.

MERKEL CORPUSCLES. Tiny knobs or expansions at the ends of nerve fibers in the skin, particularly hairless skin. They are thought to be receptors for pressure.

MERKEL'S LAW. The generalization that to equal differences between stimuli at above-threshold strength there correspond equal differences in sensation.

Merkel, Friedrich Sigmund. German anatomist (b. Nuremberg, April 5, 1845, d. Göttingen, May 28, 1919). Merkel's doctorate in medicine was from the University of Erlangen (1869). From 1869 to 1885 he was at the universities of Erlangen, Rostock, and Königsberg and from 1885 onward at Göttingen. Merkel's work was in macroscopic and microscopic anatomy, histology, fine anatomy of the sense organs, and microscopic techniques. He described the corpuscles in 1875 (*Arch. mikrosk. Anat., 11,* 636).
  Biographies: Fischer, Biog. Lex.

MERRILL-PALMER SCALE OF MENTAL TESTS. Formerly one of the best-known intelligence scales for preschool children (twenty-four to thirty-six months). Most of the thirty-eight tests are performance items, and the others are language items. The test is administered as an age scale but scored as a point scale.

Merrill-Palmer School. The Merrill-Palmer Scale was developed by Rachel Stutsman at the Merrill-Palmer School, Detroit, Michigan, in 1931. The Merrill-Palmer School was founded in 1930 as a result of a testamentary endowment by Elizabeth Pitts Merrill Palmer, wife of one-time U.S. senator and ambassador to Spain Thomas Witherell Palmer. Now the Merrill-Palmer Institute, it is affiliated with Wayne State University.

MESMERISM. An early name given to the phenomenon of hypnotism.

Mesmer, Franz Anton. Austrian physician (b. Iznang, Baden-Württemberg, Germany, May 23, 1734, d. Meersburg, Baden-Württemberg, March 5, 1815). Mesmer, at first a physician in Vienna (M.D., University of Vienna, 1766), came under the influence of the occult teachings of Paracelsus, believing that magnetism emanating from the stars affected human lives. His experiments on the effects of magnets on the human body led to the discovery that his passes made some people go into a trance. They also led him to believe that the magnetism of iron and of celestial bodies was similar to that possessed by living organisms. Mesmer therefore began to use the term *animal magnetism,* although the term had been used by others before him. In 1766, he published a work on the postulated relationships (*De planetarium influxu*) and in 1779 an account of what later came to be called mesmerism (*Mémoire sur la découverte du magnétisme animal*). Although Mesmer thought that animal magnetism was a natural force, he was repeatedly accused of magic and charlatanism and was forced to change residence several times. In 1778, Mesmer moved to Paris. His seances around a tub filled with chemicals and iron protrusions that his patients held on to became famous in Paris, and Mesmer achieved many hypnotic cures. Eventually he fell into disrepute because he maintained his belief in animal magnetism but could not explain it satisfactorily to the scientists who investigated him.

Biographies: Asimov; R. Darnton, *Mesmerism and the End of the Enlightenment in France,* 1968; *DSB,* 9; *EB,* 15; *IESS,* 10; D. M. Walmsley, *Anton Mesmer,* 1967; B. Winters, *J. Gen. Psychol.,* 1950, *43,* 63–75.

MEYER'S EXPERIMENT. A way of demonstrating simultaneous color contrast. A small patch of gray paper is placed on a large area of the inducing color, and both are covered with tissue paper. A color complementary to that of the background is induced in the gray patch. The experiment is also referred to as Meyer's contrast experiment and Meyer's contrast pattern.

Meyer, H. German physicist and physiologist (b. n.a., d. n.a.). Meyer described the experiment in an 1855 article (*Ann. Phys. Chem., 171,* 170–71).

Biographies: Unavailable.

MIDAS SYNDROME. Increase in the libido of the female with a corresponding decrease in sexual desire and performance in her male partner.

Midas. Midas was the name of a king of Phrygia who flourished around 700 B.C., but, since even then it was an ancient name with legends attached to it, it is by no means certain that the golden touch legend pertains to him. The golden touch legend speaks of the foolish King Midas who wished that everything he touched should turn into gold and who, granted that wish by Dionysius, almost starved to death. He was rescued also by Dionysius who had him bathe in a certain stream to wash away the gold-producing power or the Midas touch. The term was introduced by G. W. Bruyn and U. J. DeJong (*Amer. Imago*, 1959, *16*, 251–62).

MIGNON DELUSION. The delusion that one is not the real child of one's parents but the child of a distinguished family.

Mignon. Mignon is a mysterious child in Johann Wolfgang von Goethe's novel, *Wilhelm Meister's Apprenticeship* (1795–1796). Wilhelm buys her from a troupe of rope dancers who mistreat her.

MILLER ANALOGIES TEST. A widely used test for the selection of candidates for graduate school. It consists of one hundred verbal analogy items of the type "A is to B as C is to ??," where the testee supplies the appropriate term in the blank space.

Miller, Wilford Stanton. American psychologist (b. January 6, 1883, d. n.a.). Miller received his Ph.D. from the University of Illinois. He was active as teacher and school administrator before his doctorate. He continued to teach educational psychology afterward, for the most part at the University of Minnesota.
  Biographies: APA Dir., 1948.

MILL HILL VOCABULARY SCALE. A test to measure the ability to recall information and to state it verbally. The subject supplies synonyms for stimulus words and provides definitions for them.

Mill Hill. The Mill Hill Emergency Hospital, Hertsfordshire, England, was the location where the author of the scale, English psychologist John C. Raven,* worked during World War II (1938–1943). The scale was published in 1943.

MILLILAMBERT. One one-thousandth of a lambert,* a common measure of luminance or surface brightness.

Lambert, Johann Heinrich. See under eponyms that begin with LAMBERT.

MILLON CLINICAL MULTIAXIAL INVENTORY. A 175-item true-false inventory for the diagnosis of emotional disturbance, similar to the Minnesota Multiphasic Personality Inventory.*

Millon, Theodore. American psychologist (b. New York City, August 18, 1929). Millon, a clinical psychologist, has been concerned with psychopathology and clinical assessment. He is the author of several books in these areas. Millon obtained his Ph.D. from the University of Connecticut in 1954 and has held faculty positions at Lehigh University (1954–1970), and the University of Illinois Medical Center (1970–1977). He has been at the University of Miami since 1977.

   Biographies: AM&WS, 1978S; *APA Dir.*, 1985; *ConAu*, 57.

MILL'S CANONS. Principles that govern inductive reasoning about cause-effect relationships, hence a statement of the logic of scientific inquiry. 1. The law of agreement: if a large number of instances of a phenomenon all have a common factor, that factor is the probable cause of the phenomenon. 2. The law of differences: differences found among effects that are otherwise similar are due to their antecedents. 3. The law of joint agreement and disagreement: if A always leads to B and non-A always leads to non-B, then A is a cause or partial cause of B. This law underlies the use of control groups in psychological experiments. 4. The law of residues: if there is an unexplained remainder in an effect, it is owing to an unexplained remainder in the antecedent condition. 5. The law of concomitant variation: variables that vary together are connected as cause and effect or have a single common cause.

Mill, John Stuart. English philosopher and economist (b. Pentonville [London], May 20, 1806, d. Avignon, France, May 8, 1873). Taught by his father and himself, John Stuart Mill was a lesser figure of a psychologist than his father, James Mill, but he exercised a far greater influence as a philosopher, logician, and economist. Mill's psychological views as well as his canons may be found in *A System of Logic* (1843). Additional psychological writings are his *Examination of Sir William Hamilton's Philosophy* (1865) and the notes written for the 1869 edition of his father's *Analysis of the Phenomena of the Human Mind*.

   Biographies: DNB, 13; *DSB*, 9; *EB*, 15; *EP*, 5; *IESS*, 10; J. S. Mill, *Autobiography*, 1979; H. McCloskey, *John Stuart Mill: A Critical Study*, 1971; A. Ryan, *John Stuart Mill*, 1970.

MINNESOTA MULTIPHASIC PERSONALITY INVENTORY. The MMPI, as it is usually referred to, is a checklist of 550 simple statements that describe universal, everyday experiences. The respondent marks them true, false, or "cannot say." The responses are evaluated on fourteen scales, nine of them clinical. The MMPI is the most widely used personality inventory. Of the scores of psychological instruments that are Minnesota eponyms, this is the most famous.

Minnesota, University of. The MMPI was developed in the 1930s. It appeared in 1940, and the official manual appeared in 1943. The developers were a physiological psychologist, Starke R. Hathaway, and a psychiatrist, J. Charnley McKinley, both at the University of Minnesota.

MOLYNEUX'S QUESTION. A famous question, addressed by William Molyneux to John Locke: "Suppose a man born blind, and now adult, and taught by his touch to distinguish between a cube and a sphere. . . . Suppose then the cube and sphere placed on a table and the blind man made to see; query, Whether by his sight, before he touched them, he could now distinguish and tell which is the globe, which the cube?''

Molyneux, William. Irish astronomer and mathematician (b. Dublin, April 17, 1656, d. Dublin, October 11, 1698). Molyneux received the B.A. degree from Trinity College, Dublin (1675) and taught there briefly (1695–1698). In *Dioptrica nova: A Tratise of Dioptricks* (1692), the first English work on optics, Molyneux discussed the problem of how we see the world right-side up when the retinal image is upside down. It was in this context that Molyneux addressed his question to Locke in a letter dated about 1688 (and quoted by Locke in *An Essay Concerning Human Understanding,* 1690). Molyneux himself supplied the answer, and Locke confirmed it by saying that a newly sighted person indeed would not be able to identify objects by sight alone. Molyneux was thus one of the first thinkers to suggest that meaning accrues to perception through experience.

Biographies: DNB, 13; *The New Century Encyclopedia of Names,* vol. 2, 1954.

MONTE CARLO METHOD. Any procedure in which the generation of data, selection of variables, selection of subjects, determination of the order of events, and so on is made by a process governed by a set of probabilistic rules. Specifically, the term is applied to the use of such procedures in computer simulation of actual experiments in order to derive the consequences of particular theoretical models of behavior. The electronic subjects are sometimes referred to as stat-rats or stat-subjects.

Monte Carlo. The name of the method comes from the principality of Monaco that derives its main income from tourists who go there to gamble in its casinos, the generation of ''data'' in gambling being determined by the laws of chance.

MONTESSORI METHOD. The main features of the method are attracting the child's attention to a task by using certain specified educational materials, allowing the child freedom of movement, and gearing the task to be learned to the developmental level of the child. The Montessori school is a prepared environment in which teachers keep themselves in the background, providing only minimum guidance and discipline, and the children are entrusted with keeping things in their places. They acquire concepts through sensory-motor exercises and activities with Montessori's educational materials. From her observations, Montessori derived certain generalizations concerning education and development: children go through certain sensitive periods during which they are particularly apt to learn certain things; they prefer to work with creative materials rather than toys; they are capable of extreme concentration if the situation is properly structured; they love orderliness; and under the conditions of a Montessori school no punishment is necessary to maintain discipline.

Montessori, Maria. Italian educator (b. Chiaravalle, near Ancona, August 31, 1870, d. Noordwijk, Netherlands, May 6, 1952). Montessori was the first woman in Italy to receive a medical degree (University of Rome, 1894). She held medical positions until 1901, taught briefly at a women's teachers college in Rome and the University of Rome, and dedicated the rest of her life to the Case dei Bambini, the Montessori schools. She described her work, begun with defective children in 1899, in the book, *Metodo della pedagogica scientifica applicata all' educazione infantile nelle case dei bambini* (1909; English translation, *The Montessori Method,* 1912). Montessori wrote several additional books on the education of young children.
   Biographies: EB, 15; *IESS,* 10; E. M. Standing, *Maria Montessori: Her Life and Work,* 1962.

MOONEY PROBLEM CHECKLIST. Designed for use with high school and college students in guidance and counseling, the checklist is a means of communication between the counselor and the student, not a measuring instrument.

Mooney, Ross Lawler. American psychologist (b. n.a., d. n.a.). Mooney received a Ph.D. from Yale University (1935). He was with the Bureau of Education Research and, in the 1940s and 1950s, at Ohio State University. The checklist was published in 1941.
   Biographies: Unavailable.

MORGAN'S CANON. See LLOYD MORGAN'S CANON.

MORO REFLEX. A reflex, observed in infants up to four months of age, that is elicited by some of the same stimuli that produce the startle response in an older individual. When the individual suddenly loses support or is exposed to a sudden, loud noise, there is flexion of the legs, throwing up of the arms, and turning of the head. As the cortex matures and takes over control over motor behavior from subcortical structures, the reflex changes its pattern and becomes the startle response, partially under voluntary control. Absence of the Moro reflex when it should be present indicates diffuse central nervous system damage. Presence of the reflex after the sixth month of age indicates disturbance in cortical functioning.

Moro, Ernst. Austrian pediatrician (b. Laibach, Austria, December 8, 1874, d. 1951). In addition to the reflex, Moro was known for his work on digestive disorders in children. He received his M.D. from the University of Graz (1899). He was assistant at a children's clinic in Graz (1899–1902), an assistant at the University of Vienna (1902–1904), and held positions at the universities of Munich (1906–1911) and Heidelberg (after 1911). He described the reflex in 1918 (*Münch. med. Wschr., 65,* 1149).
   Biographies: Fischer, *Biog. Lex.*

MOSSO BALANCE. A device for comparing the amounts of blood supply in the upper and lower parts of the body. It consists of a tilting board on which the subject lies. A flow of blood toward the head or toward the feet registers in the tilting of the balance, which in turn produces a record on a kymograph.

MOSSO ERGOGRAPH. An instrument for measuring muscular contractions and the changes that take place in them during prolonged exertion.

Mosso, Angelo. Italian physiologist (b. Turin, May 30, 1846, d. Turin, November 24, 1910). Mosso (M.D., University of Turin, 1870), who taught physiology at the University of Turin from 1875 to 1910, is best known for the invention of various pieces of apparatus, among them the plethysmograph, that became important in psychological research. He was also known for his work on movement, respiration, circulation, and blood composition, especially the work on physiological changes taking place at high altitudes. Turin became the center of physiological studies in Italy. A laboratory he founded on the southern slope of Monte Rosa bears the name Instituto Angelo Mosso. In 1904, Mosso developed locomotor ataxia and turned to archaeology. He became as well known in this field as in physiology. The balance was described in 1886 (*Arch. Anat. Physiol.*, Suppl. d. phys. Abt.) and the ergograph in 1883 (*Rendic. Accad. med. Torino*, *31*, 667).

Biographies: DSB, 9.

MULLER-LYER ILLUSION. Two-line segment of the same length appear to be unequal if inward-pointing, slanted lines (''arrowheads'') are attached to both ends of one line and similar but outward-pointing lines (''feathers'') to the ends of the other. It is the best-known and most researched of all geometric illusions.

MULLER-LYER RECTANGLES. Two identical rectangles, one flanked by two squares, the other by two rectangles of the same length as the squares, do not appear to be of equal size.

Müller-Lyer, Franz Carl. German psychiatrist (b. Baden-Baden, February 5, 1857, d. Munich, October 29, 1916). After obtaining his M.D. from the University of Strasbourg in 1880, Müller-Lyer remained at its psychiatric clinic as assistant director from 1881 to 1883. From 1884 to 1888 he studied psychology and sociology, and he is best known for his sociological writings, though he was also in private practice in Munich after 1888. Müller-Lyer established a sociological and cultural philosophical system based on an analysis of the social causes of suffering. It had many adherents. In psychology, Müller-Lyer wrote two monographs on psychophysics, but his name is firmly associated with a simple geometric illusion rather than psychophysics or psychiatry. The illusion was presented in 1889 (*Arch. Anat. Physiol.*, Physiol. Abt. (Suppl.), *2*, 263–70).

Biographies: R. H. Day & H. Knuth, *Perception*, 1981, *10*, 126–46; G. Solomon, *Encycl. Soc. Sci.*, 1933, *11*, 83–84.

MULLER-SCHUMANN LAW. A principle in human learning that states that once an association has been formed between two items, it becomes more difficult to establish an association between either one of these items and a third one.

Müller, Georg Elias. German psychologist (b. Grimma, Saxony, July 20, 1850, d. Göttingen, December 23, 1934). Although Müller's degree was in philosophy (Ph.D., University of Göttingen, 1873), he became one of the pioneers in experimental psychology. He spent all of his professional life at Göttingen (1876–1880, 1881–1921). After Fechner's* death, Müller became the leading psychophysicist. The psychophysics of vision and the study of learning and memory were the two areas in which Müller continued to work for the rest of his life. *Zur Analyse der Unterschiedsempfindlichkeit* (1899, with L. J. Martin) is a classic in psychophysics. Müller's experimental work on memory is brought together in the three installments of a monograph published in 1911, 1913, and 1917. The Müller-Schumann law appears in a joint paper published in 1893 (*Z. Psychol. Physiol. Sinnesorg.*, *6*, 81–190, 257–339).

Biographies: E. G. Boring, *Amer. J. Psychol.*, 1935, *47*, 344–48; *IESS*, 10; D. Katz, *Psychol. Bull.*, 1935, *32*, 377–80; *PR*, 3.

Schumann, Friedrich. German psychologist (b. Hildsheim, Lower Saxony, June 16, 1863, d. Frankfurt-am-Main, January 10, 1940). Schumann's Ph.D. was in physics (University of Göttingen, 1885), but he also studied psychology under G. E. Müller at Göttingen. While at Göttingen (1885–1894), Schumann conducted experiments and published with Müller studies on psychophysics, memory, sensory psychology, and perception, and, in general, influence Müller to become a real experimenter. At the University of Berlin (1894–1905), Schumann conducted a large number of experiments that make him the direct precursor of the founders of the Gestalt school of psychology. After Berlin, Schumann went to Zurich (1905–1910) and then to the University of Frankfurt (1910–1928).

Biographies: EUI, 54; W. Metzger, *Z. Psychol.*, 1940, *148*, 1–18; *PR*, 3.

MULLER'S CIRCLE. See VIETH-MULLER CIRCLE.

MULLER-URBAN METHOD. A method in psychophysics for treating data collected by the method of constant stimuli. It hinges on the assumption that the best estimate of the difference threshold is the median of the ogive that best fits the distribution of the threshold measurements obtained.

MULLER-URBAN WEIGHTS. Weights used in fitting the data to the ogive by the Müller-Urban method* to determine the best value of *h*, a measure of precision with which the data have been fitted.

Müller, Georg Elias. See MULLER-SCHUMANN LAW.

Urban, Frederick Mary. Austrian psychologist (b. Brünn [now Born, Czechoslovakia], Moravia, December 18, 1878, d. Maisons-Lafitte, near Paris, France, May 4, 1964). Urban first obtained a Ph.D. in philosophy from the University of

Vienna in 1902 and then a Ph.D. in psychology from the University of Leipzig (1903?). He was on the faculty of Harvard University (1904–1905) and the University of Pennsylvania (1905–1914). From 1914 to 1917 Urban was at the Kungliga Vetenskapliga Akademien in Stockholm. Urban was a psychophysicist who contributed a book (*The Application of Statistical Methods to the Problem of Psychophysics,* 1908) and some fifteen papers to the area. He introduced a correction in the table of weights furnished by G. E. Müller* in 1903 for fitting the psychometric function (*Arch. ges. Psychol.,* 1909, *15,* 261–55; *16,* 168–227) and also contributed the concept of the psychometric function, the phi-gamma function. When circumstances forced Urban to remain in his home town between 1917 and 1948, unable to be active in psychology, he used his statistical knowledge in insurance work. He published a text on probability calculus and the theory of observation errors in 1923.

Biographies: J. E. Ertle, R. C. Bushong, & W. A. Hillix, *J. Hist. Behav. Sci.,* 1977, *13,* 379–83; M. M. Sokal, *J. Hist. Behav. Sci.,* 1978, *14,* 170–72.

MUNCHAUSEN SYNDROME. A personality disorder in which the individual derives pleasure from describing or simulating dramatic but false symptoms of illness, undergoing examinations, treatment, and hospitalization. Upon being told the real nature of his or her case, the patient will often leave the facility and move to another.

Münchausen, Baron. German traveler and soldier (b. 1720, d. 1797). The reputed source of incredibly tall tales about travel adventures, Karl Friedrich Hieronymus, Freiherr von Münchausen hunted in peacetime and served in war with the Russians against the Turks. At age forty, he retired to his estate, becoming a legendary source of tall tales about his experiences as a traveler, soldier, and sportsman. The first collection of his tales appeared in 1781, but even then some of them were not original with him. The tales grew in number as they passed from one edition to the next, with the editors also changing. The tales were translated into English, then back into German again, with more tales added.

Biographies: Allibone, 2; EB, 15.

MUNSELL COLOR SYSTEM. A system for specifying hues, brightnesses, and saturations of color in an atlas form. For each shade, there is a color chip with a code stating the values of the three dimensions of color, which in the Munsell system are called hue, value, and chroma. The distances between adjacent color chips are perceptually equal.

Munsell, Albert Henry. American artist (b. Boston, Massachusetts, January 6, 1858, d. Chestnut Hill, Massachusetts, June 28, 1918). Munsell obtained the A.M. degree from the Massachusetts Normal Art School in 1881. He remained as an instructor at that institution until 1885, when he went to Paris to study at the Ecole des beaux arts (until 1888). In addition to his art work, which was exhibited in salons in Paris and the United States, Munsell invented a new easel, patented a color sphere, and introduced a new photometer. He developed the idea of a color notation in 1905 (*A Color Notation*) and published the *Atlas of the Munsell Color System* in 1910. After publishing a second edition of the *Atlas* in 1915, Munsell formed the Munsell Color Company in 1918. After his death, the company issued the *Munsell Color Book* in 1929. In it, the value scale was closer to psychological brightness than it had been in the 1915 atlas edition, and the book remains the basis of the present-day system.

Biographies: NCAB, 12, 36; *Physics Today,* 1958, 26, 111–12; *WhAm,* 1.

MYERS-BRIGGS TYPE INDICATOR. A personality inventory for nonpsychiatric populations, consisting of forced-choice items that assess personality in terms of Jungian psychology. It yields four scores: extroversion-introversion, sensation-intuition, thinking-feeling, and judgment-perception.

Myers, Isabel Briggs. American personologist (b. Washington, D.C., October 18, 1897, d. Swarthmore, Pennsylvania, May 5, 1980). Isabel Briggs married Clarence Myers in 1918, graduating a year later from Swarthmore College. Until World War II she was a mother and a homemaker and published two successful mystery novels. The war served as an impetus for her to develop some method that would help people understand each other. She had been influenced by and had accepted her mother's admiration of the Jungian types of personality and proceeded to develop an item pool and test it on anyone available. Eventually she obtained data from more than 15,000 individuals. She had had no formal courses in psychology, and she learned statistics through self-study and personal apprenticeship. Recognition of the value of the test came late. Even when it became successful, Myers continued to work on it until her final illness. Her work is continued by the Center for Applications of Psychological Type, Gainesville, Florida.

Biographies: J. D. Black, in I. B. Myers & P. B. Myers, *Gifts Differing,* 1980, pp. ix–xii.

Briggs, Katharine Cook. (b. East Lansing, Michigan, January 3, 1875, d. Swarthmore, Pennsylvania, July 10, 1968). Isabel Briggs Myers was the daughter of Katharine Cook and Lyman Briggs, a well-known scientist and director of the National Bureau of Standards. From her studies of biography, Katharine Briggs developed a typology of human personality that was similar to that of Jung.* When she learned of the latter's work, she accepted it and elaborated it further, influencing her daughter's thinking along these lines. Her name appears on the Myers-Briggs Type Indicator* as one of the coauthors.

Biographies: J. D. Black, in I. B. Myers & P. B. Myers, *Gifts Differing,* 1980, pp. ix–xii.

N

NAGEL'S ANOMALOSCOPE. A screening device for color blindness based on measurements of the Rayleigh equation.* It uses the spectroscope to generate light stimuli of the appropriate wavelength.

Nagel, Wilibald. German physiologist (b. Tübingen, Baden-Württemberg, June 19, 1870, d. Rostock, Mecklenburg, January 14, 1911). Nagel had both the Ph.D. (1892) and M.D. (1893) degrees. He served on the faculties of the universities of Freiburg (1894–1902), Berlin (1902–1908), and Rostock (1908–1911). Nagel was primarily interested in vision, but he also worked on the chemical senses and on touch. He published many papers and monographs in these areas. He was the editor of *Handbuch der Physiologie* (1905–1910) and one of the editors and a contributor to the third edition of Helmholtz's* *Handbook of Physiological Optics*. Nagel described the anomaloscope in 1898 (*Arch. Augenheilk.*, *38*, 31–66).

Biographies: Fischer, *Biog. Lex.*; *EI*, 24; *EUI*, 37.

NANCY SCHOOL. The teaching about the nature of hypnotism and the associated use of hypnotism in psychotherapy originated with the neurologist Hippolyte Bernheim* at Nancy, France. In 1882, Bernheim became impressed by the hypnotic cures achieved by the country doctor Ambroise-Auguste Liébeault and became his pupil. Together they established a clinic at Nancy in which the method of treatment was that of hypnotic suggestion. Liébeault and Bernheim held that hypnosis was not essentially different from natural sleep, that anyone could be hypnotized, and that cures could be achieved during induced sleep via suggestion. This position differed from that of the famous neurologist Jean-Martin Charcot* and the La Salpêtrière school,* the main rival of the Nancy school. Developments in the area of hypnosis have tended to support the views of the Nancy school.

Nancy. A city of about 1250,000 in the northeastern portion of France, department of Meurthe-et-Moselle. Bernheim went there from Strasbourg in 1872, taught at its university for ten years, went into private practice, and in 1919, died in Nancy.

NARCISM (NARCISSISM). Self-love, or excessive concern with oneself. In psychoanalysis, the extreme concern for oneself and unconcern for others that characterizes an early stage in the child's development but may persist into adulthood.

Narcissus. The beautiful youth of a Greek legend who falls in love with his own reflection in a pool of water.

NECKER CUBE. A two-dimensional representation of a three-dimensional skeletal cube. It is subject to both spontaneous and deliberate perspective reversals because it corresponds to two equally likely alternatives in perspective, the same that are present in the retinal projection of an actual skeletal cube.

Necker, Louis-Albert. Swiss mineralogist and geologist (b. Geneva, April 10, 1786, d. Portree, Skye, Scotland, November 20, 1861). Necker studied mineralogy and geology at the University of Edinburgh, after which (1810–1830s) he taught at the Academy in Geneva. In the 1830s, Necker moved from place to place. He finally settled in Portree, remaining a recluse. Necker was concerned with the classification of minerals, emphasizing their use rather than their chemical composition as the basis for classification. He noticed the reversible perspective in examining the cubical crystals of salt and described his observation in 1832 (*Phil. Mag.*, 3 ser., *1*, 329–37, esp. 336ff.).
   Biographies: DSB, 10; V. A. Eyles, *Trans. Edinb. Geol. Soc.*, 1952, *14*, 93–127.

NEWMAN-KEULS TEST. A statistical test of the significance of differences between means in a set of means obtained in the analysis of variance.

Newman, D. English statistician (b. n.a., d. n.a.). At the time Newman described the test in 1939 (*Biometrika, 31,* 20–30), he was on the faculty of University College, London.
   Biographies: Unavailable.

Keuls, M. Dutch statistician. Keuls published his contribution to the test in 1952 (*Euphytica, 1,* 112–22), when he was at the Institute of Horticultural Plant Breeding, Wageningen, the Netherlands.
   Biographies: Unavailable.

NEWTON'S COLOR CIRCLE. The first version of the modern color circle. Newton arranged the spectral colors in a circle so that colors that were complementaries of each other lay on the ends of a diameter. White was at the center of the circle. The circle explained color mixtures: colors that are close together on the circle produce intermediate mixtures, while complementaries yield gray or white. There was no extraspectral gap between red and indigo in Newton's circle.

NEWTON'S LAW OF COLOR MIXTURE. If two color mixtures give rise to the same color sensation, then the mixture of these two mixtures will also give rise to the same color sensation.

Newton, Sir Isaac. English scientist and mathematician (b. Woolsthorpe, Lincolnshire, December 25, 1642, d. London, March 20, 1727). One of the greatest scientists of all time, Newton received the B.A. degree from Cambridge University in 1665, held an appointment at that university from 1667 to 1703, and was president of the Royal Society from 1703 to 1727. In his principal work, *Philosophiae naturalis principia mathematica* (1687), he outlined the laws of the material universe that were to be accepted by the scientific world for the next two hundred years. He formulated the laws governing motion, planetary motion in particular, and universal gravitation, invented (independently of Leibniz) the calculus, invented the reflecting telescope, and discovered the spectral composition of white light. The Newtonian view of the physical world had a direct effect on the thinking of the British associationists, the first, informal school of psychological thought. All of Newton's work on light and color was published in *Opticks* (1704).

Biographies: Asimov; D. Brewster, *Memoirs of the Life, Writings, and Discoveries of Sir Isaac Newton,* 1965; G. E. Christianson, *In the Presence of the Creator,* 1984; *DNB,* 14; *DSB,* 10; *EB,* 16; *EP,* 5; F. E. Manuel, *A Portrait of Isaac Newton,* 1968; L. T. Moore, *Isaac Newton: A Biography,* 1962; J. D. North, *Isaac Newton,* 1967.

NIEMANN-PICK DISEASE. A single recessive gene disorder, almost identical to the Tay-Sachs disease,* except that the lipid that infiltrates the nervous system is sphingolipid rather than ganglioside, and it invades the liver and spleen as well. The disease leads to progressive mental deterioration.

Niemann, A. German pediatrician (b. Berlin, February 23, 1880, d. Berlin, March 22, 1921). Niemann's M.D. was from the University of Strasbourg (1903). He held positions in various clinics and institutions in Berlin from 1903 to 1914 and was on the faculty of the University of Berlin from 1914 to 1921. Niemann's main work was on infant digestion. He described the disease in 1914 (*Jb. Kinderheilk.,* 79, 1–10).

Biographies: Fischer, *Biog. Lex.*

Pick, Ludwig. German pediatrician (b. Landsberg a. d. Warthe, Pomerania, August 31, 1868, d. Berlin, 1935). Pick, who received the M.D. from the University of Leipzig in 1893, worked at the Landau Women's Clinic in Berlin (1893–1906) and the Municipal Hospital at Friedrichshain in Berlin (1906–1935), and he also taught at the University of Berlin (1899–1935). He

wrote many works on pathology, especially that of the female sex organs. His contribution to the eponymous disease appeared in 1926 (*Ergeb. inn. Med. Kinderheilk., 29*, 519–627).
   Biographies: Fischer, Biog. Lex.; Pagel, *Biog. Lex.*

NISSL BODIES. Granules of a chromatin-like material that stains blue with certain dyes and permits the identification of the cell bodies of neurons and glial cells because it is not contained in the axons or dendrites of a cell.

Nissl, Franz. German neuropathologist and psychiatrist (b. Frankenthal, Palatinate, September 9, 1860, d. Munich, August 11, 1919). Nissl obtained his medical degree from the University of Munich in 1885. He held various hospital appointments in Munich, Frankfurt, and Heidelberg from 1885 to 1918 and taught at the University of Heidelberg from 1896 to 1918. He was at the German Research Institute in Munich from 1918 to 1919. Nissl's work was on the histology of cerebral neurons and brain pathology. He developed the technique of staining nerve cells with aniline dyes and discovered the substance in the cytoplasm of neuron bodies that bears his name (*Neurol. Zbl.,* 1894, *13,* 676–85, 781–89, 810–14). Nissl wrote *Die Neuronenlehre und ihre Anhänger* (1903).
   Biographies: DSB, 10; *Talbot.*

NON-EUCLIDEAN. With reference to spatial relations, physical or psychological, not conforming to the propositions of Euclidean geometry, such as the binocular perception of space and the relationships among objects in psychological space, which may be thought of as curved or containing more than three dimensions.

Euclid. Greek mathematician (fl. 300 B.C.). Of Euclid's life little is known. He taught at Alexandria, where he also founded a school. His greatest work was the thirteen books of his *Elements.* This textbook of geometry continued in use almost unchanged for more than two thousand years.
   Biographies: DSB, 4; *EB,* 8.

O

OCCAM'S RAZOR. A form of the more general principle of parsimony. In its original form it states that "entities should not be multiplied beyond necessity," the "entities" referring to demons, spirits, and other ideal objects of the universalists that would be invoked to explain phenomena. The term is now used mostly as a synonym for the principle of parsimony in the formulation of explanations, namely that explanations consistent with the smallest number of assumptions are to be preferred.

Occam, William of. English schoolman (b. Occam, near London, c. 1285, d. Munich, Germany, 1349). Occam became a Franciscan friar at an early age. He obtained the degree of inceptor in theology from Oxford University in 1319 and became one of the most influential scholastic philosophers. Occam initiated nominalism. He rejected Plato's* universals as a metaphysical idea, proposing instead that universal concepts should be made identical with the names given to classes of objects whose common features have been learned through experience with concrete, individual members of such classes. In addition to proposing the use of the principle of parsimony, Occam furthered the separate consideration of matters of experience by drawing an even sharper distinction between reason and faith than had been done by Thomas Aquinas.
   Biographies: Asimov; DNB, 41; *DSB,* 10; *EB,* 16.

O'CONNOR WIGGLY BLOCK. A test of spatial ability that uses as its material a wooden block cut into nine sections along wavy lines. The block is disassembled before the person being tested. The score is the time taken to reassemble the block.

O'Connor, Johnson. American psychometrician (b. Chicago, January 22, 1891, d. Boston, July 1, 1973). With an A.M. degree from Harvard University (1914), O'Connor did astronomical, mathematical, metallurgical, and electrical engineering research at various locations from 1911 to 1922. Between 1928 and 1934 he lectured on psychology at the Stevens Institute of Technology and MIT. In 1930, he organized Human Engineering Laboratory, Inc. It became the Johnson O'Connor Research Foundation in 1942, with branches in several cities. O'Connor wrote several books on aptitudes. The Wiggly block test was published in 1928.

Biographies: AM&WS, 1973S; *WhAm,* 6.

OEDIPUS COMPLEX. In Freudian theory,* the boy's sexual longing for his mother and consequent rivalry with his father (Oedipus conflict) that appears and is enacted during the phallic stage (two and a half to five years) of development. The resulting anxiety over the father's retaliation (castration anxiety) leads to the boy's identification with his father and the development of a superego. The term is now used to apply equally to children of either sex.

Oedipus. A figure in Sophocles' plays *Oedipus* and *Oedipus at Colonus.* Son of the king of Thebes, Laius, and Jocasta, Oedipus unwittingly murders his father and marries his mother. Upon learning the truth, Oedipus puts out his own eyes, banishes himself from Thebes, and is led by his daughter Antigone* to Colonus, where the earth opens and receives him. Freud introduced the term *Oedipus complex* in his *Three Essays on the Theory of Sexuality* (1905).

OHIO METRIC FIGURES. Figures generated by a method that produced representative samples of measurable visual forms from a population of forms whose parameters had been previously specified. The method consists of filling in cells in a square matrix according to rules. The appearance of the basic figure is that of a histogram. The figures were the first attempt to achieve stimulus representativeness in work on visual form perception.

Ohio State University. The Ohio metric figures were originated in the Laboratory of Aviation Psychology at the Ohio State University during the 1950s by a group of psychologists under the direction of Paul M. Fitts.*

OHM'S ACOUSTIC LAW. In audition, the principle that the ear breaks down complex sounds into simple harmonic components that are the same as the sine wave components obtained in Fourier* analysis of complex sounds.

Ohm, Georg Simon. German physicist (b. Erlangen, Bavaria, March 16, 1787, d. Munich, July 7, 1854). Ohm, who received his Ph.D. in mathematics from the University of Erlangen in 1811, was a high school teacher with aspirations to become a university professor. Reasoning by analogy from Fourier's* discoveries concerning the flow of heat, Ohm demonstrated experimentally that in a conductor, the strength of electric current is directly proportional to the difference in potentials applied to it and inversely proportional to its resistance. Later Fourier was also inspiration for Ohm to formulate the acoustic principle (*Ann. Phys. Chem.*, 1843, *135*, 497–565). Discovery of the electrical law, however, led to such opposition and criticism that Ohm lost his high school job. Recognition came to Ohm from abroad first, some fourteen years after the discovery. He was finally appointed professor at the University of Munich in 1849. The unit of electrical resistance was named after him only after his death.

Biographies: Asimov; DSB, 10; *EB,* 16.

ONANISM. Coitus interruptus, or the withdrawal of the male partner prior to ejaculation. The subsidiary meaning of masturbation is the primary one in languages such as German.

Onan. A biblical character (Genesis 38:9) who practiced coitus interruptus.

OPPEL ILLUSION. The illusion that a filled space is longer than an unfilled space, both spaces being physically of the same length. The original illusion consisted of a number of parallel upright line segments continuous with an empty space of the same length whose end was marked by a single upright segment.

Oppel, Johann Joseph. German physicist (b. 1815, d. 1894). Oppel, who had a doctorate in physics, presented the illusion and also coined the term *geometric-optical illusion* in 1854 (*Jber. phys. Ver. Frankf.,* 1854–1855, 37–47).

Biographies: Unavailable.

OPPEL-KUNDT ILLUSION. See OPPEL ILLUSION.

Kundt, August Adolph. See under eponyms that begin with KUNDT.

OPPENHEIM'S REFLEX. Flexion of the big toe in response to the downward stroking of the medial side of the tibia. It is seen in corticospinal lesions.

Oppenheim, Hermann. German neurologist (b. Berlin, January 1, 1858, d. Berlin, May 22, 1919). Author of *Lehrbuch der Nervenkrankheiten* (1894), Oppenheim was a professor at the University of Berlin. He described the reflex in 1903 (*Mschr. Psychiat. Neurol., 14*, 241–46).

Biographies: WoWhoSci.

ORBISON ILLUSION. This illusion takes two forms. In one, a small circle is inscribed in a larger circle so that it passes through the center of the larger circle. If the larger circle is filled with equally spaced radii, the segment of the smaller circle that is near the center of the larger circle appears to flatten out. In the other form, a square is superimposed upon a series of equally spaced concentric circles so that its center coincides with the center of the circles. Here the sides of the square appear to be concave.

Orbison, William Dillard. American psychologist (b. January 11, 1912, d. South Coventry, Connecticut, February 14, 1952). Orbison received his Ph.D. from Yale University in 1945; he taught at Connecticut College and later at the University of Connecticut. The paper in which he described the illusion (*Amer. J. Psychol.*, 1939, *52*, 31–45) was published just after Orbison had obtained his master's degree from the University of Kansas (1938).

Biographies: *APA Dir.*, 1948; *NYT*, Feb. 16, 1952, 6.

ORESTES COMPLEX. In psychoanalysis, the repressed desire of the son to kill his mother, held to be the outcome of the Oedipus conflict.

Orestes. In Sophocles' play, *Electra,* Orestes is Electra's brother. With her aid he kills their mother, Clytemnestra,* to avenge the death of their father, Agamemnon, who was put to death by Clytemnestra and her lover, Aegisthus.

ORGAN OF CORTI. A structure, located on the basilar membrane in the cochlea, that contains the epithelial hair cells that are the receptor cells for hearing.

Corti, Alfonso Giacomo Gaspare. See under CORTI'S TEETH.

OSTWALD COLOR ATLAS. A system of color specification, based on the color spindle, in which gradations of lightness and saturation are obtained by adding, in fixed proportion, equally spaced neutral colors, from black to white, to each of the twenty-four hues that lie on the color circle.

Ostwald, Friedrich Wilheim. German chemist (b. Riga, Latvia, September 2, 1853, d. Grossbothen, near Leipzig, April 4, 1932). Ostwald studied at Tartu University, obtaining a Ph.D. in chemistry in 1878. He taught at the University of Riga from 1881 to 1887 and then left for the University of Leipzig, where he remained for the rest of his career. Ostwald was one of the founders of physical chemistry. His most important work was in the field of catalysts, for which he received the Nobel Prize in 1909. In later life he became interested in the philosophy of science and also originated his color classification scheme (*Die Farbenlehre,* 4 vols., 1918–1940).

Biographies: *Asimov; DSB,* 10; *EB,* 16.

OTHELLO SYNDROME. Overwhelming jealousy and delusion that one's spouse is unfaithful.

Othello. The title character in Shakespeare's 1604 tragedy, "a noble Moor in the service of the Venetian state," who in blind jealousy kills his wife, Desdemona.

OTIS QUICK-SCORING MENTAL ABILITY TESTS. A series of group intelligence tests, this is the most widely used Otis test, designed for grades one through four (the Alpha test), four through nine, and nine through sixteen.

Otis, Arthur Skinton. American psychologist (b. Denver, Colorado, July 28, 1886, d. St. Petersburg, Florida, December 31, 1963). Otis received his Ph.D. from Stanford University in 1920. He developed a group intelligence test as part of his dissertation. When Lewis Terman,* under whom Otis studied, and other psychologists were called upon during World War I to develop an intelligence test for screening army recruits, Otis' test served as the model for what became known as the Army Alpha and Beta tests, subsequently used on millions of drafted men. For twenty-five years, Otis was the editor of tests and mathematics for the World Book Company. He wrote many books, a number of them outside psychology, and also musical comedy, and he developed half a dozen other tests that bear his name. The Quick-Scoring Tests were published in 1936 and 1937.

Biographies: NYT, Jan. 2, 1964, 27; *WhAm,* 4.

OTTOSON POTENTIAL. The electro-olfatogram, the olfactory equivalent of the electroretinogram and of the cochlear response. It is the negative deflection that can be recorded from an electrode in contact with the olfactory epithelium when an odorant flows over the latter.

Ottoson, David. Swedish physiologist (b. Chalgan, China, August 18, 1926). Ottoson obtained his doctorate in medicine from the University of Stockholm in 1956. He was professor of physiology at the Karolinska Institute from 1956 to 1966 and again after 1974 and taught at the Royal Veterinary School in Stockholm from 1966 to 1974. He described the electro-olfatogram in 1956 (*Acta physiol. scand., 35,* suppl. 122, 1–83).

Biographies: Vem ar det? Svensk biografisk handbok, 1985.

P

PACINIAN CORPUSCLES (PACINI CORPUSCLES, VATER-PACINI CORPUSCLES). Largest of the specialized nerve endings, visible to the naked eye, that are found in subcutaneous tissue, as well as in joints and ligaments. They are thought to mediate pressure sensations and kinesthesis.

Pacini, Filippo. Italian anatomist (b. Pistoia, May 25, 1812, d. Florence, July 9, 1883). Pacini began his studies of anatomy at Pistoia's school for surgeons in 1830. He continued at the University of Pisa in 1840 and graduated in medicine in the same year. He remained at Pisa until 1847 when he went to Florence, becoming professor of topographical anatomy and histology at the medical school in Florence. Pacini did important research and made many discoveries in the microscopic anatomy of the retina and the skin. Pacini discovered the touch corpuscles in fingers in 1835 and made a presentation of his finding before a medicophysical society in Florence, but he failed to receive recognition. The finding was published in 1840 (*Nuovi organi scoperti nel corpo umano*).
  Biographies: DSB, 10.

PANUM PHENOMENON. A phenomenon observed in the stereoscopic image produced by three equal, parallel lines, two of them close together and presented to one eye, the third line presented to the other eye. If the single line is made to overlap one of the other two lines, the combined line will appear to be closer to the viewer than the other line in the pair.

Panum, Peter Ludwig. Danish physiologist (b. Rönne, Bornholm, Denmark, October 19, 1820, d. Copenhagen, May 2, 1885). Panum studied medicine at the University of Copenhagen. Even before graduation, he conducted important studies on the epidemiology of measles. His training was interrupted by war and government assignments to study epidemics, but he graduated with an M.D. in 1851. After two years of postgraduate work, Panum accepted a teaching position at the University of Kiel (1853–1864) and then returned to the University of Copenhagen to organize the first Danish laboratory of physiology. Panum became the founder of Danish physiology. He wrote the first Danish text in physiology and made important contributions to the development of public health. Panum published on a variety of medical subjects, as well as on vision. The Panum phenomenon is described in his *Physiologische Untersuchungen über das Sehen mit zwei Augen* (1858).

   Biographies: W. M. Gafafer, *Bull. Inst. Hist. Med.,* 1934, *2,* 258–80; V. Meissen, *Prominent Danish Scientists,* 1932, pp. 134–37.

PAPEZ-MACLEAN THEORY OF EMOTION. A theory that postulates the limbic system as the central system in emotion. It stresses the roles of the hippocampus and the amygdala, in addition to that of the hypothalamus, and of the more primitive portions of the brain in the integration of information during emotional arousal.

Papez, James Wenceslas. American neuroanatomist (b. Glencoe, Minnesota, 1883, d. Columbus, Ohio, August 13, 1958). Papez received an M.D. from the University of Minnesota (1911). He taught anatomical sciences at the Atlanta College of Physicians and Surgeons from 1911 to 1920 and for the next thirty-one years at Cornell University. After retirement in 1951, Papez went to Columbus, Ohio, to be director of biological research at the state hospital. He proposed a mechanism of emotion in a paper published in 1937 (*Arch. Neurol. Psychiat., 38,* 725–43), but it was ignored for a number of years. Papez's main contribution was his teaching. He wrote *Comparative Neurology* in 1929, and his lectures were attended by both American and foreign scientists.

   Biographies: Haymaker; NYT, April 14, 1958, 25; *NCAB,* 48; *WhAm,* 3.

MacLean, Paul Donald. American neurophysiologist (b. Phelps, New York, May 1, 1913). McLean, who received his M.D. from Yale University in 1940, was assistant, research assistant, and research fellow at various medical schools and hospitals from 1940 to 1949. He taught at Yale from 1949 to 1956 and served at the National Institutes of Health from 1957 to 1971 and the National Institutes of Mental Health after 1971. His research has been on forebrain mechanisms of species-typical and emotional behavior. MacLean developed Papez's theory in two papers (*Psychosom. Med.,* 1949, *11,* 338–53; *J. Nerv. Ment. Dis.,* 1958, *127,* 1–11).

   Biographies: AM&WS, 1982P; *WhoAm,* 1984–1985.

PARKINSONISM (PARKINSON'S DISEASE). A type of degenerative disorder in which motor incoordination and constant tremor, particularly of the hands, are present ("shaking palsy"). The tremors spread from one arm to the leg, then to the face, and from there to the other arm and leg. The face may be immobilized and speech slurred. The gait is characterized by short, mincing steps, with the body leaning forward. Mental functions are usually not impaired, but withdrawal may be the afflicted person's reaction to the physical symptoms.

Parkinson, James. English physician (b. Shoreditch, London, 1755, d. Shoreditch, London, 1824). Parkinson was a modest medical practitioner who lived and worked all his life in a London suburb. His classical description of six cases of the disease that bears his name appeared in *An Essay on the Shaking Palsy* in 1817, but almost half a century passed before he received proper recognition. In 1861 and 1862, Jean-Martin Charcot* referred to the disease as Parkinson's (*Gaz. hebd. méd. chir.*, 1861, *8,* 765; 1862, *9,* 54). One reason for the neglect that Parkinson suffered was his sympathies for the underprivileged and the French Revolution. He wrote numerous pamphlets on political and social subjects. He also engaged in paleontological research.
   Biographies: DNB, 43; Haymaker; Talbot.

PASCAL'S TRIANGLE. A triangular matrix that may be used to obtain the values of binomial coefficients for a binomial expansion without actually calculating them.

Pascal, Blaise. French philosopher (b. Clermont-Ferrand, Puy-de-Dôme, June 19, 1623, d. Paris, August 19, 1662). Pascal was educated by his father. Through 1654, Pascal did scientific research and published a variety of scientific and mathematical treatises. In response to the queries of a gentleman gambler, Pascal and Pierre de Fermat worked out the answers as to why he was losing money in games of dice (*De alea geometriae,* 1654). This work included a fragment on the famous Pascal triangle, *Traité du triangle arithmétique.* Pascal's work on chance was the beginning of probability calculus, of immense importance to science. In his last years, Pascal distinguished himself as a religious thinker (*Pensées; Les provinciales*).
   Biographies: DSB, 10; EB, 17; EP, 6.

PAVLOVIAN CONDITIONING. Associative learning in which the simultaneous pairing of a stimulus (the unconditioned stimulus) that normally elicits a reflex (the unconditioned response) with a neutral stimulus leads to the elicitation of the reflex response (the conditioned reflex) by the neutral stimulus (the conditioned stimulus) alone.

PAVLOVIANISM. The experimental procedures of conditioning introduced by Pavlov and the point of view held by him that mental processes and physiological processes (''higher nervous activity'') are identical and that the former are to be studied by means of the latter. Pavlov visualized both the unconditioned and the conditioned reflexes as effecting a connection between the organism and its environment. The nervous activity involved in forming the temporal (conditioned) connections he called higher nervous activity, to distinguish it from lower nervous system activity, which served to integrate the organism in Charles Sherrington's sense. Environmental stimuli significant to the organism's survival constituted the first signal system. A second signal system had developed in humans, Pavlov held, as a result of their practical experience. This system does not represent reality directly but through its data in the nervous system, which are then called thought or, in their physical manifestation, language.

PAVLOVIAN SESSIONS. The six sessions of 1950 and 1951 of the Scientific Council on Problems of the Physiological Theory of Academician I. P. Pavlov, established by the joint assemblage of the USSR Academy of Sciences and the USSR Academy of Medical Sciences, in which physiologists were reprimanded for deviating from Pavlov's original teachings and psychologists taken to task for failing to incorporate Pavlov's ideas in their work. As a result, psychology became "pavlovianized."

PAVLOVIAN WEDNESDAYS. Seminars held since 1924 by I. P. Pavlov for his coworkers on Wednesday of each week to discuss current work.

Pavlov, Ivan Petrovich. Russian physiologist (b. Ryazan', September 26, 1849, d. Leningrad, February 27, 1936). Pavlov received his doctorate in medicine from the University of St. Petersburg in 1883. He taught at the Military Medical Academy in St. Petersburg from 1890 to 1924 and was then director of the Physiological Institute of the Russian Academy of Science. Pavlov, the most important of the Russian physiologists, was fifty-five when he received the Nobel Prize for his work on the physiology of digestion. Before 1900, he had made the observation that dogs salivated not only when food was given to them but also to other stimuli that accompanied feeding. By 1901, he had named this type of response *conditioned reflexes*. Pavlov spent the next three decades studying conditioning. He opened up the way for the experimental study of neuroses and for the classification of nervous systems by type. The conditioned response became the cornerstone of American behaviorism before World War I. Pavlov himself, however, considered his work to be physiology, not psychology.
   Biographies: E. A. Asratyan, *I. P. Pavlov: His Life and Work,* 1953; B. P. Babkin, *Pavlov, a Biography,* 1949; H. Cuny, *Ivan Pavlov: The Man ahd His Theories,* 1965; *DSB,* 10; *EB,* 17; *IESS,* 11; *Obit. Not.,* 2; *Soviet,* 19; H. K. Wells, *Ivan P. Pavlov: Toward a Scientific Psychology and Psychiatry,* 2 vols., 1956, 1960.

PEARSON'S r (PEARSON CORRELATION, PEARSONIAN CORRE-LATION) A product-moment correlation coefficient, or a statistical measure of the degree to which two variables vary together. Its values range from 0 to $+1.00$ (perfect direct correlation) and -1.00 (perfect inverse correlation).

Pearson, Karl. English mathematician (b. London, March 27, 1857, d. London, April 27, 1936). Pearson graduated from King's College, Cambridge, in 1879. He was at the University College, London, from 1884 to 1933. In 1911 he became the director of the Department of Applied Statistics and Sir Francis Galton Professor of Eugenics. Pearson was one of the fathers of modern statistics. Around 1890 he acquired an interest in heredity, eugenics, and biological problems in general and in the application of statistics to such problems. He developed a number of statistical treatments of biological data that are among the most widely used ones today, such as the chi-square and the correlation coefficient. The idea for the latter was conceived by Sir Francis Galton.* Pearson, his student and biographer, developed his idea and made it computationally simpler. The correlation coefficient was presented in a series of eighteen papers published between 1893 and 1912 under the title "Mathematical Contributions to the Theory of Evolution."

Biographies: B. H. Camp, J. Amer. Stat. Ass., 1933, 28, 395–491; DNB, Suppl. 5; DSB, 10; EB, 17; J. B. S. Haldane, Biometrika, 1957, 44, 303–13; IESS, 11; Obit. Not., 2; R. Pearl, J. Amer. Stat. Ass., 1936, 31, 653–64; E. S. Pearson, Karl Pearson: An Appreciation of Some Aspects of His Life and Work, 1938; B. Semmel, Brit. J. Sociol., 1958, 9, 111–25; S. S. Wilks, Sci. Mon., 1941, 53, 249–53.

PERKY EFFECT. Subjective impression of imagery with the objective presence of a physical stimulus. When a person is asked to form a mental image of an object and a very faint image of the object is then presented on a screen, the projected image may be taken to be the mental image.

Perky, Cheves West. American psychologist (b. n.a., d. n.a.). Perky received his Ph.D. from Cornell University in 1910. He described the effect in 1910 (Amer. J. Psychol., 21, 422–25).

Biographies: Unavailable.

PETERSON AND PETERSON TECHNIQUE. A technique for testing short-term memory storage. The subject is given the task of recalling three-letter clusters after delays of varying length but is prevented from rehearsing by having him or her count backward by threes from a three-digit number during the delay.

Peterson, Lloyd Richard. American psychologist (b. Minneapolis, Minnesota, October 1, 1922). Since receiving a Ph.D. in experimental psychology from the University of Minnesota in 1954, Peterson has held positions at Indiana University. He specializes in verbal learning and memory and is the author of Learning (1975). He described the technique in a joint paper with Margaret Peterson in 1959 (J. Exp. Psychol., 58, 193–98).

Biographies: AM&WS, 1978S; APA Dir., 1985; ConAu, 107.

Intons-Peterson, Margaret Jean Lowther. American psychologist (b. Minneapolis, Minnesota, October 3, 1930). Intons-Peterson obtained her Ph.D. in experimental psychology from the University of Minnesota in 1955. She taught at Indiana University from 1956 to 1972 and then became associate dean of the College of Arts and Sciences there. Her field is human learning and memory.

Biographies: AM&WS, 1978S; APA Dir., 1985; WhoAmW, 1970.

PHAEDRA COMPLEX. A mother's sexual love for her son.

Phaedra. In the Greek legend, Phaedra was the wife of Theseus. She developed a desire for her stepson Hippolytus and tried to seduce him. Hippolytus rejected her, and she hung herself, leaving a note that accused him of having attacked her. The enraged Theseus asked Poseidon for revenge. It took the form of Poseidon's having a sea monster startle Hippolytus' horse. Hippolytus died under the wheels of his own chariot.

PHINEAS GAGE SYNDROME. Personality changes produced by frontal lobotomy or equivalent frontal lobe damage, such as a shift from good social adjustment, ambition, high motivation, foresight, and consideration of others to a lack of drive, unconcern with the consequences of one's actions, diminished initiative, and a general unconcern with one's language, the feelings of others, and ethical and moral considerations.

Gage, Phineas P. American construction worker (b. 1823, d. 1861). Gage was the foreman of a railroad construction gang. On September 13, 1848, near Cavendish, Vermont, the four-foot iron rod that he had used to tamp down some gunpowder preparatory to blasting struck a spark and ignited the gunpowder. The explosion drove the rod through Gage's head. It entered Gage's head through his left cheek and exited through the top of his head. It was the world's first unpremediated frontal lobotomy. Gage recovered from the infection caused by the rod but found himself unable to hold his former job. Although he had been a considerate husband and father, he now abandoned his family, began to use coarse language, and in general showed complete unconcern for the future and the future consequences of any of his actions. He took up with the Barnum circus and began to exhibit himself and the rod. He died twelve years later in a barroom brawl in San Francisco. It was then that an autopsy showed that the accident had severely damaged Gage's left frontal lobe. Gage's skull and the tamping iron are in the Harvard Medical School Museum. The case was described by Dr. J. M. Harlow (*Publications of the Massachusetts Medical Society*, 1868, 2, 327; *Recovery from the Passage of an Iron Bar Through the Head*, 1869).

   Biographies: J. M. Harlow, *Publ. Mass. Med. Soc.*, 1868, 2, 327; J. M. Harlow, *Recovery from the Passage of an Iron Bar Through the Head*. Boston: Clapp, 1869.

PIAGETIAN TASKS. Simple physical problems given children to assess the level of development of certain basic concepts, such as the conservation concepts. The tasks include the estimation of numerosity of bunched and spread-out items, the prediction of water levels in a container upon the immersion of solid objects, the estimation of the volume of liquid in one as compared with several containers, the estimation of the length of straight and zigzag paths, the comparison of the weights and volumes of plastic materials that are balled up or spread out, and others.

Piaget, Jean. Swiss psychologist (b. Neuchâtel, August 9, 1896, d. Geneva, September 16, 1980). Piaget received a Ph.D. in biology from the university of his home town in 1918. He studied psychology at the Sorbonne for two years and then took a position with the Institut J. J. Rousseau in Geneva (1921–1933). He was professor of child psychology at the University of Geneva from 1929 to 1971. The founding and direction of the International Center of Genetic Epistemology (1955–1980) reflected Piaget's interest in the philosophical implications of developmental issues. Piaget was the most influential developmental theorist of the twentieth century. At his death he had produced some thirty books and more than three hundred other items on cognitive development. Many of the books appeared in several editions and were translated into many languages.

Biographies: Amer. Psychologist, 1970, *25,* 65–79; *ConAu,* 101; *CurBio,* 1958; *EB,* 17; D. Elkind, *Amer. Psychologist,* 1981, *36,* 911–13; *HPA,* 4; *IESS,* 18; *McGMSE,* 3; *Psychology Today,* May 1970; *Time,* Dec. 12, 1969, Sept. 29, 1980; *WhAm,* 7.

PICK'S DISEASE. A progressive, degenerative disease of the brain in which circumscribed cerebral atrophy occurs, accompanied by mental deterioration (loss of motivation, dulled affect, stereotypy, and impaired moral judgment). It sets in generally between ages forty-five and fifty and occurs more often in women than in men. Pick's disease is also another name for Niemann-Pick disease and for a disease named after Friedel Pick, a German physician (1867–1926).

Pick, Arnold. Czechoslovak physician (b. Velke Mezirici, Moravia, July 20, 1851, d. Prague, April 4, 1924). Pick studied medicine at the University of Vienna (M.D., 1875). He worked at some mental hospitals at first and then, from 1886 to 1921, was professor of psychiatry at the German University of Prague. Pick contributed some 350 items to the medical literature. He first described the disease that bears his name in 1892 (*Prag. med. Wschr., 17,* 163–67).

Biographies: Haymaker.

PIDERIT DRAWINGS. Line drawings of the profile of a male face in which the brow, eye, nose, and mouth regions are movable so as to create different emotional expressions and to observe the effect of single features on the overall emotional expression.

Piderit, Theodor. German anatomist (b. 1826, d. 1912). Piderit lived for many years in Chile. Hoping to make anatomy useful to artists, he developed a theory of expressive movements, especially facial expressions. To illustrate it, he presented drawings of faces, both frontal and profile, showing how the combination of changing features in the mouth, nose, eye, and brow regions yielded changing emotional expressions. He wrote on the subject in 1859 in *Grundzüge der Mimik und Physiognomik* and then his main work, *Wissenschaftliches System der Mimik und Physiognomik,* which appeared in several editions, beginning in 1867. In 1923, E. G. Boring and E. B. Titchener* wrote an article (*Amer. J. Psychol., 34,*

471–85) describing models for the demonstration of emotional expression using Piderit's drawings.

Biographies: Unavailable.

PILLAI-BARTLETT TRACE. A criterion for hypothesis testing in multivariate analysis of variance, based on all eigenvalues.

Pillai, Krishna Chennakkadu Sreedharan. Indian-American statistician (b. Veliyanadu, Kerala, India, February 24, 1920, d. Lafayette, Indiana, June 5, 1985). Pillai obtained the M.Sc. degree from the University of Kerala in 1945, and he taught at that university from 1941 to 1951. His Ph.D. was from the University of North Carolina (1954). Pillai worked for the United Nations Organization in New York City from 1954 to 1955 and again from 1960 to 1962. He was at the University of the Philippines from 1956 to 1959, became a U.S. citizen in 1966, and taught at Purdue University from 1962 to 1985. Pillai wrote two books and many papers on topics in statistics. Pillai presented the trace concept in his *Statistical Tables for Tests of Multivariate Hypotheses* (1960).

Biographies: AM&WS, 1982P; *WhoAm,* 1984–1985.

Bartlett, Maurice Stevenson. See BARTLETT'S TEST.

PILLARS OF CORTI. See RODS OF CORTI.

PILTZ'S REFLEX. Change in the size of the pupil upon the sudden fixation of attention. The reflex is mediated by emotional arousal, positive arousal resulting in an enlarged pupil and negative arousal in its contraction.

Piltz, Jan. Polish neurologist and psychiatrist (b. Alexandrow, near Warsaw, January 15, 1870, d. Cracow, December 1930). Piltz studied at Zurich, specializing in psychiatry at several other universities. He obtained the Dr. med. degree in 1894. From 1895 to 1902, Piltz held positions at the University of Zurich and various clinics and asylums in Geneva, Zurich, and Lausanne. He was at the Municipal Hospital, Cracow, from 1902 to 1905 and at the University of Cracow and the Neuropsychiatric Clinic, Cracow, after 1905. Piltz's research was on the cortical control of the pupils and the symptomology of nervous disorders, especially pupillary symptoms. He described the reflex in 1899 (*Neurol. Zbl., 18,* 14).

Biographies: Fischer, *Biog. Lex.; PR,* 3.

PINTNER-PATERSON SCALE OF PERFORMANCE TESTS. This scale was the first major attempt to develop a standardized scale of performance tests. The scale was intended for the deaf, the handicapped, and those whose native language was not English. It consisted of fifteen tests, scorable in terms of completion time, errors, and quality. The scores were converted to mental age equivalents, and these to IQ. The scale as a whole is no longer in use, but some of the individual tests have been incorporated in other tests.

Pintner, Rudolf. American psychologist (b. Lytham, Lancashire, England, November 16, 1884, d. New York City, November 7, 1942). Pintner went for his Ph.D. to the University of Leipzig, obtaining it in 1913. He taught at Ohio State University from 1913 to 1921 and at Teachers College, Columbia University, from 1921 to 1942. Pintner's scientific interests lay in the field of mental measurement. His work promoted the study of individual differences in the United States. The *Scale of Performance Tests* was published in 1917. Pintner constructed several other tests, including the *Pintner-Durost Elementary Test* (1941) and the *Pintner Non-Language Test* (1945).

Biographies: S. Arsenian, *In Memoriam: Rudolf Pintner,* 1953; H. L. Hollingworth, *Amer. J. Psychol.,* 1943, *56,* 303–5; D. G. Paterson, *J. Consult. Psychol.,* 1943, *7,* 50–52; P. M. Symonds, *Teach. Coll. Rec.,* 1942, *44,* 204–11; *PR,* 3; *WhAm,* 2.

Paterson, Donald Gildersleeve. American psychologist (b. Columbus, Ohio, January 18, 1892, d. St. Paul, Minnesota, October 4, 1961). Paterson was Rudolf Pintner's student, under whom he received his M.A. in psychology at Ohio State University in 1916. Between 1916 and 1921, Paterson was at the University of Kansas, in the U.S. Army, and with the Scott Company. From 1921 to 1960 he held positions with the University of Minnesota. Paterson was an applied psychologist who developed vocational guidance techniques and became a leader in the field of student counseling (*Men, Women, and Jobs,* 1936, with J. Darley; *Student Guidance Techniques,* 1938, with G. Schneidler amd E. Williamson). Paterson also worked extensively in the field of intelligence and ability measurement. Paterson and his collaborators constructed such tests as the *Minnesota Mechanical Ability Test* (1930) and other mechanical ability tests. He also worked on the legibility of type (*How to Make Type Readable,* 1940, with M. Tinker). A bibliography of Paterson's publications contains more than three-hundred items.

Biographies: IESS, 11; *J. Appl. Psychol.,* 1961, *45,* 352; *NCAB,* 53; *PR,* 3; *WhAm,* 4; E. Williamson, *Personnel Guid. J.,* 1961, *40,* 235.

PIOTROWSKI SYSTEM. An approach to the interpretation of the Rorschach test,* lying somewhere between the approaches introduced by Samuel Beck* and Bruno Klopfer.* It differs considerably from that of Rorschach* himself as well as from the approaches of other interpreters of the test.

Piotrowski, Zygmunt A. Polish-American psychologist (b. Poznan, Poland, April 18, 1904). Piotrowski's Ph.D. was in psychology, which he received from the University of Poznan in 1927. He became a naturalized U.S. citizen, teaching at the Columbia University College of Physicians and Surgeons from 1931 to 1954. He worked for New Jersey state agencies from 1954 to 1957 and then taught at the Jefferson Medical College from 1957 to 1970. In 1970, Piotrowski became director of personality research with Edward N. Hay & Associates. He also holds part-time teaching positions at Temple University and Hahnemann Medical College. Piotrowski described his system in 1957 (*Perceptomalysis*).

Biographies: AM&WS, 1973S; *APA Dir.,* 1985.

PIPER'S LAW. A relationship between threshold luminance and area of the retina illuminated for retinal areas of intermediate size and located several degrees out from the fovea. Here threshold luminance is inversely proportionate to the square root of the area.

Piper, Hans. German physiologist (b. Altona [Hamburg], January 8, 1877, d. Eastern Front, August 20, 1915). Piper received an M.D. from the University of Freiburg (1902). He worked at the Physiological Institute in Berlin (1903, 1908–1915) and the University of Kiel (1904–1908) conducting physiological studies. Piper formulated the luminance law in 1903 (*Z. Psychol. Physiol. Sinnesorg., 32*, 98–112).
    Biographies: Fischer, Biog. Lex.

PLACIDO'S DISK. A disk with concentric black rings and a sight hole in the middle used for viewing the reflections of the rings on the cornea. Distortions in the shape of the rings indicate irregularities in the surface of the cornea.

Plácido da Costa, Antonio. Portuguese ophthalmologist (b. Covilha, 1848, d. 1916). Plácido, whose M.D. was from the Escola Médico-Cirúrgica do Pôrto (1879), was professor of ophthalmology at that school. He described his invention in 1880 (*Periódico de ophthalmologia pratica*, Lisbon, 2[2], 27; [5–6], 44).
    Biographies: WoWhoSci.

PLATEAU'S SPIRAL. An arithmetic (equally spaced arms) spiral that, when rotated slowly, produces the following phenomena: colored rings, if the spiral is white on black background; seeming expansion or contraction of the spiral, depending on the direction of rotation, and the contrary apparent movement when the spiral is stopped. The contrary expansion or contraction is transferred to any stationary object one happens to be looking at.

Plateau, Joseph Antoine Ferdinand. Belgian physicist (b. Brussels, October 12, 1801, d. Ghent, September 13, 1883). After receiving a doctorate in physics and mathematics from the University of Liége in 1829, Plateau spent most of his professional life at the University of Ghent (1835–1872). He became blind in 1843 but continued his research with the help of his son and his son-in-law. Plateau introduced the psychophysical method of bisection, was the first to propose the power form of the psychophysical law, wrote a history of visual sensation, and invented the stroboscope. In 1850, Plateau described the color sensations and the movement aftereffect obtained by looking at a rotating spiral (*Bull. Acad. sci. belge, 16*[2], 254–60). Plateau used a narrow white spiral on black background. The spiral is sometimes attributed to Ernst Mach,* who used a black and somewhat wider spiral on white background.
    Biographies: DSB, 11.

PLATONIC LOVE (PLATONIC RELATIONSHIP). Love or relationship between a man and a woman that does not have the sexual element. It is a term of common speech rather than a technical term in psychology. From the Renaissance through the nineteenth century, the term also meant homosexual love.

Plato. Greek philosopher (b. Athens, 428 or 427 B.C., d. Athens, 348 or 347 B.C.). Plato, a student of Socrates and the founder of the Academy at Athens, is one of the great philosophers of all times. His philosophical views are to be found in the Socratic dialogues, such as *Timaeus, Phaedo, Crito, Meno, Ion, The Republic, Laws,* and *Symposium.* The idea of Platonic love is presented in the last dialogue.
  Biographies: Asimov; DSB, 11; *EB,* 18; *EP,* 6; *IESS,* 12.

POGGENDORFF ILLUSION. The two portions of an oblique line appear to be offset with respect to each other when the line is interrupted by an elongated vertical rectangle.

Poggendorff, Johann Christian. German physicist (b. Hamburg, December 29, 1796, d. Berlin, January 24, 1877). Poggendorff studied science at the University of Berlin. He invented a galvanoscope in 1820 and later did other research in physics. In 1823, he was commissioned by the Berlin Academy to make meteorological observations. In 1824, Poggendorff took over the editorship of the *Annalen der Physik und Chemie.* He continued in that position for fifty-two years, bringing out 160 volumes. The journal became known simply as "the Poggendorff." In 1834, he became full professor at the University of Berlin. Poggendorff was also interested in the history of science. He started publishing the *Biographisch-literarisches Handwörterbuch zur Geschichte der exakten Wissenschaften* in 1863, a publication that saw the appearance of its eighteenth volume in 1974. Poggendorff first told only F. Zöllner* about the the illusion, which Zöllner then described in 1860 (*Ann. Phys. Chem., 186,* 500–25). E. Burmester named the illusion after Poggendorff in an 1896 paper (*Z. Psychol., 12,* 355–394).
  Biographies: DSB, 11.

POISSON DISTRIBUTION. Binomial distribution for an event when the probability for one of the outcomes is very small. When the terms of the equation for the distribution are written out, it is called the Poisson series.

Poisson, Simeon-Denis. French mathematician and physicist (b. Pithiviers, Loiret, June 21, 1781, d. Paris, April 25, 1840). Poisson began the study of mathematics at the Ecole polytechnique in Paris in 1798 and was made deputy professor there as early as 1802. In 1806, he succeeded Fourier* in the latter's chair as full professor. In 1808, Poisson was appointed astronomer at the Bureau de longitudes and professor of pure mechanics at the Faculté de sciences in 1809. He made important contributions to the application of mathematics to physics and to the field of pure mathematics. He presented the binomial distribution in 1837 (*Recherches sur la probabilité des jugements en metière criminelle et en metière civile*).
  Biographies: DSB, 15; *EB,* 18.

POLITZER'S ACOUMETER. An older form of an audiometer, a device employed for the measurement of sound intensity thresholds. The sound was produced by a hammer falling on a sound-producing surface. Its intensity was varied by varying the distance of the device from the ear.

Politzer, Adam. Austrian otologist (b. Alberti, Hungary, October 1, 1835, d. Vienna, August 10, 1920). Politzer earned the M.D. degree from the University of Vienna in 1859. From 1861 to 1907, Politzer taught at the University of Vienna, being the first professor of otology at that institution. He also worked in the ear clinic of the Vienna General Hospital and was its director from 1898. He wrote many articles on hearing and on the anatomy and physiology of the ear.
Biographies: Talbot.

POLLYANNA MECHANISM. An ego defense mechanism characterized by blind optimism—the belief that all is well even when it is not.

Pollyanna. A character in Eleanor Porter's novels, *Pollyanna* (1913) and *Pollyanna Grows Up* (1914), who has been brought up to believe that there is some good in any situation. Her playing the "glad game" makes people whom she comes in contact with happier and kinder.
Biographies: Dictionary of Literary Biography, v. 9, pt. 2, 1981.

POLYCRATISM. The superstitious fear that God will mete out correspondingly heavier punishment if things go too well with one.

Polycrates. Greek ruler (fl. 535–522 B.C.). Polycrates was the tyrant of Samos, all of whose enterprises succeeded exceedingly well. He had power, riches, and respect. To avert the envy of the gods, he deliberately lost a valuable ring while on a boat trip. When a few days later a fisherman brought him a very large fish, his ring was found inside the fish, which was taken by Polycrates as a sign that the gods would not be appeased. He was put to death by the Persian governor of Sardis.
Biographies: EB, 18.

POMPADOUR FANTASY. The fantasy of being the mistress of a king.

Pompadour, Jeanne-Antoinette Poisson, marquise de. (b. Paris, December 29, 1721 d. Versailles, April 15, 1764). Of middle-class origin, Jeanne-Antoinette Poisson was an attractive woman. She married C. G. Le Normant d'Etioles at the age of twenty. She soon began to attract attention because of her accomplishments as a hostess and her artistic and intellectual abilities. She also attracted the attention of King Louis XV, who in 1745 created her marquise of Pompadour and made her his official mistress. The marquise had excellent taste and a keen intellect, and she was influential both in politics and in fostering the intellectual and artistic life of France. Her physical relationship with the king ended in 1751, but she remained on friendly terms with him and continued to advise him until her death.

Biographies: EB, 18; N. Mitford, *Madame de Pompadour,* 1954.

PONZO ILLUSION. Two objects, such as line segments or circles, of identical size and placed between a pair of converging lines do not appear to be of the same size, the one closer to the point of convergence of the lines appearing larger than the other.

Ponzo, Mario. Italian psychologist (b. Milan, June 23, 1882, d. Rome, January 9, 1960). Ponzo obtained the M.D. from the University of Turin in 1911, but he also studied psychology under F. Kiesow* at the same time. He was at the University of Turin from 1905 to 1931 and at the University of Rome from 1931 to 1958. Ponzo did research on the psychophysics of touch and taste but turned to applied psychology after 1940 and pioneered in introducing applied psychology in Italy. He made contributions to aptitude testing and professional selection. Ponzo's bibliography numbers some 280 items, most of them on the chemical senses, touch, temperature sensations, geometric illusions, and breathing as a function of mental activity. The Ponzo illusion was described in 1912 (*Arch. ital. biol., 58,* 327–29).

Biographies: L. Canestrelli, *Amer. J. Psychol.,* 1960, *73,* 645–47; H. Misiak & V. M. Staudt, *Psychol. Bull.,* 1953, *50,* 347–61.

PORTEUS MAZE TEST. An individual performance test of intelligence consisting of a series of scaled pencil-and-paper mazes where the subject plans the course before actually running it, making the measurement of foresight possible.

Porteus, Stanley David. Australian-American psychologist (b. Box Hill, Victoria, Australia, April 24, 1883, d. Honolulu, Hawaii, October 21, 1972). Porteus studied at the University of Melbourne and was employed by the Education Department in Melbourne from 1912 to 1915 and the University of Melbourne from 1915 to 1919. He spent the years 1919 to 1928 at the Vineland Training School in New Jersey and was also associated with the University of Hawaii from 1922 to 1948. Porteus was the first practicing psychologist in Australia. His main interest was the effect of the environment on mental and cultural evolution. He studied the Australian aborigines and African natives and published four books on the general subject. He published several other books and some one hundred articles and papers. Porteus presented the first version of the test in 1913.

Biographies: ConAu, 1R; S. D. Porteus, *A Psychologist of Sorts,* 1969; *WhAm,* 7.

POTZL PHENOMENON. After single tachistoscopic exposures (1/100 second) of scenes, the subject's dreams the next night reflect with the greatest clarity those portions of the scene the subject fails to report immediately after exposure or does not remember seeing.

POTZL SYNDROME. Symbol agnosia for written materials and impaired color vision. It is the result of lesions in the medullar layer of the lingual gyrus of the dominant hemisphere and in the corpus callosum.

Pötzl, Otto. Austrian psychiatrist (b. Vienna, October 29, 1877, d. n.a.). Pötzl obtained his M.D. from the University of Vienna in 1901. From 1901 to 1911 he was at various clinics and hospitals in Vienna and from 1911 to 1922 and again after 1928 at the University of Vienna. He was at the German University in Prague from 1922 to 1928. Pötzl worked on aphasia, hysteria, brain disorders, and sleep and dream disorders. He described the recall phenomenon in 1917 (*Z. ges. Neurol. Psychiat., 37,* 278–349) and the syndrome in 1928 (*Die Aphasielehre vom Standpunkt der klinischen Psychiatrie: die optisch-agnostischen Störungen*).
Biographies: Fischer, *Biog. Lex.*

PRAY'S LETTERS. A set of capital letters in which the strokes go in different directions for each letter. They are used as a test of astigmatism. The derivation of this eponym is undetermined.

PREMACK'S RULE. Activities vary in their intrinsic value to the actor. A given activity can be used to reinforce those that have a lower value but not those of a higher value.

Premack, David. American psychologist (b. Aberdeen, South Dakota, October 26, 1925). Premack's Ph.D. was in experimental psychology (University of Minnesota, 1955). He was at the University of Missouri, Columbia, from 1956 to 1965 and has been at the University of California at Santa Barbara since 1965. Premack's areas of interest are quantitative behavior theory and comparative psychology.
Biographies: AM&WS, 1978S.

P. T. BARNUM EFFECT. The acceptance as accurate for oneself of almost any set of generalized and flattering self-descriptions alleged to have been derived systematically. It is the principle of personalized generality, used by fortune-tellers, astrologers, and mind readers.

Barnum, Phineas Taylor. American showman (b. Bethel, Connecticut, July 5, 1810, d. Bridgeport, Connecticut, April 7, 1891). After failing in operating lotteries and business as a young man, Barnum began exhibiting a black woman, Aunt Joice Heth, in 1835, falsely claiming that she was the 162-year-old nurse of George Washington. Many came and paid to see her, starting the pattern that was to characterize Barnum's subsequent career as the archetypal showman. The saying "There's a sucker born every minute" is attributed to him. The exhibition of freaks, fake monsters, and other items calculated to attract sensation seekers for a price highlighted Barnum's career. He started a circus in 1871 and toured the world with it, labeling it "the greatest show on earth." The Ringling Brothers

Barnum and Bailey Circus still bears his name. In spite of the ballyhoo and false pretenses, Barnum became popular, to the point of being elected mayor of Bridgeport, Connecticut, being sent to the state legislature, and having half a dozen towns named after him. The term *P. T. Barnum effect* was introduced by the psychologist Paul Meehl (see C. R. Snyder & R. J. Schenkel, *Psychology Today*, March 1975, pp. 52–54).

Biographies: DAB, 1; *NCAB,* 3; *WhAm,* HS.

PULFRICH EFFECT. If the bob of a pendulum, swinging in the same plane, is observed with the two eyes, one of which is covered with a dark filter, the bob appears to describe an ellipse (that is, to move also in depth). The stereoscopic effect is produced by the retarded arrival in the brain of signals from the filter-covered eye.

Pulfrich, Carl P. German physicist (b. Strässchen near Burscheid, Solingen, September 24, 1858, d. Baltic Sea near Timmerdorferstrand, August 12, 1927). Pulfrich's P.D. in physics was from the University of Bonn (1882). He was assistant at that university from 1883 to 1889 and then joined the Zeiss Company in 1890, working for it for many years. Pulfrich did research on photometry and refractometry. He invented many new instruments and was the father of stereo photogrammetry. He described the stereo effect in 1922 (*Naturwiss., 10,* 533–64, 569–601, 714–22, 735–43, 751–61).

Biographies: DSB, 11; *Physics Today,* 1958, *26,* 116–17.

PURDUE PEGBOARD. A test of the activity of arms and hands and of finger dexterity. Pins, collars, and washers are inserted and assembled in each hole of a pegboard, with the right hand, with the left hand, and with both hands.

Purdue University. The test was designed under the direction of Joseph Tiffin, an industrial psychologist at Purdue University. The name of the university derives from that of John Purdue, a Lafayette, Indiana, businessman whose gift of land made the establishment of this land-grant university possible. Many other commercially available tests bear the name Purdue. The Purdue Pègboard was first published in 1941.

PURKINJE AFTERIMAGE. An afterimage obtained when a black-and-white sectored disk is rotated at a certain speed and under certain conditions of illumination. The afterimage is a shadowy white that follows the edge of a black sector. It is the second positive phase of an afterimage, having a latency of 0.2 second and the same duration. *Bidwell's ghost* is a synonym.

PURKINJE FIGURES. The entoptical image of retinal capillaries that are the shadows cast directly by them on the immediately adjacent retinal receptor cells. The figures are invisible under steady illumination because they are stabilized with respect to the retina. They become visible in intermittent light, as when a pinhole admitting bright light is moved rapidly back and forth in front of the eye.

PURKINJE-SANSON IMAGES. The reflections of an object in the cornea and the front and rear surfaces of the lens of the eye.

PURKINJE SHIFT. The shift in relative brightness of colors that occurs in dimming light. Although all colors become less bright, the red end of the spectrum loses brightness faster than does the blue end when darkness increases. Thus the dark-adapted eye will continue to see blue when red already appears black. The mechanism of the shift is the switch from the photopic (cone) visual system to the scotopic (rod) visual system.

Purkinje, Jan Evangelista. Czech physiologist (b. Libochovice, Bohemia, December 17, 1787, d. Prague, July 28, 1869). Purkinje, who had an M.D. from the University of Prague (1818), pioneered in several areas: experimental physiology, microtechnique, neuroanatomy, histology, embryology, pharmacology, and vision. He held positions at the universities of Prague and Breslau between 1818 and 1869. In 1839 at the University of Breslau, he established the first physiological institute in the world. In physiology and anatomy, several structures, such as Purkinje's cells, Purkinje's fibers, and others, are named after him. Purkinje is also one of the great figures in the phenomenological approach to sensation and perception. His main contributions in this area are to be found in his *Beiträge zur Kenntnis des Sehens in subjektiver Hinsicht* (1818–1819), which contains a description of the Purkinje figures, and *Neue Beiträge zur Kenntnis des Sehens in subjektiver Hinsicht* (1825), which describes the Purkinje shift and Purkinje afterimage. The Purkinje-Sanson images are described in *De examine physiologico organi visus et systematis cutanei* (1823). In addition, Purkinje described the phenomenology of a variety of other organismic states: vertigo, nystagmus, disturbances in the sense organs, hearing, touch, sleep, and the effect of drugs.

    Biographies: Asimov; DSB, 11; *EB*, 18; *Haymaker;* O. Hykes, *Osiris*, 1936, *2*, 464–71; V. J. Kruta, *J. E. Purkinje (1787–1869), Physiologist*, 1969; V. Robinson, *Sci. Mon.*, 1929, *29*, 217–29.

Sanson, Louis Joseph. French physician (b. Nogent-sur-Seine, Aube, January 24, 1790, d. Paris, August 2, 1841). Sanson, who in 1817 received his Dr. méd. from the University of Paris, worked as a hospital surgeon until 1830 and then taught at the University of Paris. He became the director of the eye clinic at the Hôtel-Dieu hospital in 1836. He published works on surgical procedures, especially those concerning the bladder and kidney stones. He described the images in his *Leçons sur les maladies des yeux* (1837–1838).

    Biographies: WoWhoSci.

PYGMALION EFFECT. The hypothesis that the expectations of the teacher affect the performance of the students.

Pygmalion. In Ovid's recounting of a Greek tale, Pygmalion was a king of Cyprus and a famous sculptor who became a misogynist. Although he decided never to marry, he made a beautiful sculpture of a woman and fell in love with her.

He prayed to the goddess of love, who instilled life in the sculpture. Pygmalion named her Galatea, married her, and had a daughter, Paphos, by her. The term *Pygmalion effect* was introduced by R. Rosenthal and L. Jacobson in their book, *Pygmalion in the Classroom* (1968).

Q

QUASIMODO COMPLEX. Socially maladaptive behavior and emotional and personality problems that are a reaction to one's deformity or disfigurement.

Quasimodo. The ugly hunchback and bell ringer of the Notre Dame cathedral in Victor Hugo's novel, *Notre Dame de Paris* (1831), often titled *The Hunchback of Notre Dame* in English translations.

QUINCKE TUBES. A series of small glass tubes that produce high-frequency sounds when air is blown across their tops. They were formerly used to study auditory difference thresholds.

Quincke, Georg Hermann. German physicist (b. Frankfurt-an-der-Oder, November 19, 1834, d. Heidelberg, January 13, 1924). Quincke's Ph.D. was in physics (University of Berlin, 1858). From 1859 to 1865 he taught at the Berliner Gewerbeakademie, from 1865 to 1872 at the University of Berlin, from 1872 to 1875 at the University of Würzburg, and from 1875 to 1909 at the University of Heidelberg. Quincke was most interested in making measurements. Most of his work was on the measurement of properties and constants of materials. The tubes developed from his interest in capillarity, the subject of his doctoral dissertation.
  Biographies: DSB, 11.

R

RABKIN TEST. A set of plates of the isochromatic variety for testing for color blindness.

Rabkin, E. B. Soviet ophthalmologist (b. n.a., d. n.a.). Docent Dr. Rabkin prepared the plates while at the color vision laboratory of the Girshman Ophthalmic Institute. At the time he was also at the Second Ophthalmic Clinic of the University of Khar'kov. The plates were first published in 1936 in both Russian and English (*Polychromatic Plates for Color Sense Examination*). The second edition, published in 1939, was retitled *Polychromatic Plates for Studying Color Deficiency*. The work saw several additional editions.
   Biographies: Unavailable.

RAGONA-SCINA EXPERIMENT (RAGONA SCINA METHOD OF IN-DUCING COLOR CONTRAST). A method similar to Lambert's method* of color mixing. Vertically and horizontally placed black and white color patches are combined optically by means of a piece of tinted glass placed at forty-five degrees to both patches. The method produces very vivid induced color, complementary to the color of the glass.

Ragona-Scinà, Domenico. Italian scientist (b. n.a., d. n.a.). Ragona-Scinà taught at the University of Palermo. He described the method of producing induced color in a paper published in 1847 (*Racc. fis.-chim. ital.*, 2, 207–10).
   Biographies: Unavailable.

RAMAN SHIFT. Many liquids, when scattering Monochromatic light, change the frequency of the incident light waves. The difference between the incident and transmitted frequencies is called the Raman shift. There is evidence that odorous liquids produce a Raman shift within certain specified limits, but the relationship is yet to be established as a general principle.

Raman, Sir Chandrasekhara Venkata. Indian physicist (b. Tiruchirappalli, Madras, November 7, 1888, d. Bangalore, November 21, 1970). Raman obtained the master's degree in science from Presidency College, Madras, in 1907. Because scientific opportunities were virtually nonexistent in India at the time, Raman took a civil service job and worked at science in his spare time. His ability was recognized by the University of Calcutta, which offered him a professorship in physics in 1917. His work was mostly on acoustics and optics, especially the scattering of light. Raman discovered the spectral shift in scattered light in 1928 and reported on it at the Science Congress at Bangalore in March 1928. It proved to be an extremely valuable tool in determining the molecular structure of substances. Raman was awarded the Nobel Prize for his discovery in 1930, having been knighted the year before. In 1947, he became the director of the Raman Research Institute in Bangalore.

Biographies: Asimov; S. Bhagavantam, *Biog. Mem. Fellows Roy. Soc.,* 1971, 565–92; *CurBio,* 1948; *DSB,* 11; *EB,* 18.

RANKIAN PSYCHOANALYSIS. A form of psychoanalysis that is based on Otto Rank's major theme, the trauma of birth as a source of anxiety. Other Freudian concepts are also reinterpreted. Rank saw weaning as anxiety-provoking beause of the implied separation from mother rather than because it frustrated the oral drive and possibly cathected the libido in the oral region. The male sexual urge was interpreted as an urge to return to the mother's womb. Rankian therapy consists of helping the client to reexperience the birth trauma. This approach reduces the length of analysis to only weeks or months at most. Rankian psychoanalysis is also sometimes called will therapy, after the title of the last book Rank wrote.

Rank, Otto. Austrian psychoanalyst (b. Vienna, April 22, 1884, d. New York City, October 31, 1939). Rank joined the psychoanalytic movement in the 1900s. He showed ability in applying Freudian concepts to the interpretation of mythology, art, dreams, and literary works and was encouraged by Freud* to take a nonmedical degree. Thus Rank obtained a Ph.D. in German philology from the University of Vienna in 1912. Rank became a private practitioner of psychoanalysis and wrote several books in which psychoanalysis was applied to art, artists, and myths. Rank published his own original contribution to psychoanalysis, *The Trauma of Birth,* in 1923. Although Freud tried to reconcile his views with Rank's, a break occurred, Rank leaving Vienna in 1924. He came to the United States in 1936 and founded the Pennsylvania School of Social Work, where his method of therapy was used.

Biographies: F. H. Allen, *Amer. J. Orthopsychiat.,* 1940, *10,* 186–87; *EB,* 18; *EJ,* 13; *IESS,* 13; *Jewish,* 9; E. Jones, *Intern. J. Psycho-Anal.,* 1940, *21,* 112–13; J. Jones,

Commentary, Sept. 1960, 219–29; A. Nin, *J. Otto Rank Ass.*, 1967, *2*, 101–25; J. Taft, *Otto Rank*, 1958; *WhAm*, 4.

RANSCHBURG INHIBITION. Mutual interference among like elements presented for recognition. In Ranschburg's experiments, when numbers were presented tachistoscopically, more of them were recognized when they were all different than when some of them were the same.

Ranschburg, Paul. Hungarian psychiatrist (b. Gyor, January 3, 1870, d. Budapest, January 18, 1945). Ranschburg received his M.D. from the University of Budapest in 1894 and taught at that university beginning in 1910. Ranschburg contributed equally to the psychiatric and the psychological literature. Most of his approximately thirty papers in psychology are on memory and the pathology of memory. His most important contribution was the experimental demonstration of retroactive inhibition in 1905 (*Jb. Psychiat. Neurol., 5,* 560–78).
  Biographies: PR, 3; P. H. Schiller, *Amer. J. Psychol.,* 1947, *60,* 444–46.

RAVEN PROGRESSIVE MATRICES TEST. An intelligence test that uses abstract designs to measure Spearman's* *g* factor of intelligence. It consists of sixty designs (matrices). A part of each design has been removed. The respondent selects the missing part from several alternatives.

Raven, John C. English psychologist (b. 1902, d. 1970). Raven, a clinical psychologist, obtained the M.Sc. degree and worked at the Mill Hill Emergency Hospital from 1938 to 1943 and the Chrichton Royal at Dumfries from 1943 to 1964. He introduced the Progressive Matrices in 1938 (*Brit. J. Med. Psychol.,* 1941, *19,* 137–50) and revised and extended them, upward and downward, several times over the following decades.
  Biographies: J. H. Court, *Bull. Brit. Psychol. Soc.,* 1971 (Jan.), *24(82),* 47–48.

RAYLEIGH DISK. A very light plate that will orient itself at right angles to the direction of sound waves if suspended in a sound field. It is used to calibrate microphones.

RAYLEIGH EQUATION. The amounts of spectral green and spectral red required to match a given yellow. Amounts deviating from normal indicate that the person making the match is an anomalous trichromat.

RAYLEIGH TEST. A test for red-green color blindness involving the use of the Rayleigh equation.*

Rayleigh, John William Strutt, third baron. English physicist (b. Maldon, Essex, November 12, 1842, d. Witham, Essex, June 30, 1919). Rayleigh graduated from Trinity College, Cambridge, in 1865, headed the Cavendish Laboratory at Cambridge from 1879 to 1884, was professor of natural philosophy at the Royal Institution of Great Britain from 1887 to 1905, and became the president of the Royal Society, a post he held until 1908. Rayleigh worked in almost every area of physics. In the process, he produced some work of importance to psychology. He worked out the equation for color mixture and a method of testing for color blindness in 1881 (*Nature*, 25, 64–66). He also studied auditory localization and established the factors (binaural ratio of intensities, beats) that determine it. He described the disk method of determining the direction of sound in 1872 (*Proc. London Math. Soc.*, *4*, 253–83). For his discovery of argon, Rayleigh received the Nobel Prize in 1904.

  Biographies: DNB, 1912–1921, DSB, 13; EB, 18; R. J. Strutt, Life of John William Strutt, Third Baron Rayleigh, 1968.

RECKLINGHAUSEN'S DISEASE. Also known as nuerofibromatosis, this disease is due to a dominant gene with varying expressivity and low penetrance. Its symptoms include skin lesions and small tumors in the retina. In about one-third of the cases, there is mental defect.

Recklinghausen, Friedrich Daniel von. German pathologist (b. Gütersloh, Westphalia, December 2, 1833, d. Strasbourg, August 26, 1910). Recklinghausen received his M.D. degree from the University of Berlin in 1855. He remained there until 1864, when he went to the universities of Königsberg, Würzburg (in 1866), and Strasbourg (in 1872), where he remained until 1906. In addition to neurofibromatosis, described in 1882 (Uber die multiplen Fibrome der Haut und ihre Beziehung zu den Neuromen, in *Festschrift . . . Rudolf Virchow dargebietet*), Recklinghausen's name is also attached to a bone disease and the smallest lymph channels in connective tissue.

  Biographies: EB, 19; Talbot.

REICHENBACH PHENOMENON. A force or emanation (the od, odic, or odylic force) that a ''sensitive'' person could allegedly see issuing from all matter. This, along with such mysterious emanations as the N-rays and auras, proved to be another case of self-deception.

Reichenbach, Baron Karl Ludwig von. German chemist (b. Stuttgart, February 12, 1788, d. Leipzig, January 19, 1869). With a Ph.D. in chemistry from the University of Tübingen, Reichenbach first worked as a civil servant. Although he became financially independent through marriage, he engaged himself in the design of factories and had some of his own. He discovered such substances as paraffin and kerosene and wrote a long series of papers on meteorites. In 1839, Reichenbach disposed of his industrial properties and went to live in his castle at Reisenberg, devoting his life to science. His research into the odic force began about 1844 and continued for about two decades. Reichenbach published his first experiments in 1849 in Liebig's *Annalen der Chemie* (''Untersuchungen über Dynamide'') and, later, a larger work, *The Sensitive and His Relationship to the*

Odic Force (1854–1855). Eventually Reichenbach lost much of his former wealth and became a recluse and an eccentric. He died in Leipzig while on a visit there to convince Gustav Fechner* that the odic force was real.

Biographies: DSB, 11; M. Kohn, *J. Chem. Educ.,* 1955, *32,* 188–89; *Shepard,* 3.

REICHER-WHEELER EFFECT. When letters are briefly presented for recognition, they are recognized more easily when presented in the context of a word than when presented singly. It is also known as the word-superiority effect.

Reicher, Gerald Melvin. American psychologist (b. Los Angeles, California, May 30, 1939). Reicher obtained his Ph.D. from the University of Michigan in 1968. He was with the University of Oregon from 1967 to 1979 and has been with the Managerial Communications Systems, Eugene, Oregon, since 1979. The original report on the effect, later confirmed by Wheeler, was published by Reicher in 1968 (Technical Report No. 7, University of Michigan, Human Performance Center).

Biographies: Unavailable.

Wheeler, Daniel D. American psychologist (b. August 28, 1942). Wheeler received a Ph.D. in experimental psychology from the University of Michigan in 1969, specializing in thinking and computer applications. He was at the University of Texas from 1969 to 1971 and has been at the University of Cincinnati since 1971. Wheeler published a more elaborate experiment that confirmed Reicher's original finding in 1970 (*Cogn. Psychol., 1,* 59–85).

Biographies: APA Dir., 1985.

REICHIAN ANALYSIS. Centers on the idea of character as an ego defense mechanism and stresses the libidinal factor in personality and psychopathology. Character is profound and long-lasting changes in personality that serve as armor (character armor) against experiences considered dangerous, especially those arising from strong libidinal motives. It manifests itself as resistance to insight during therapy. To break down this resistance, Reich advocated a therapy more active than Freud's,* one that involves the physical touching of the client so that the client's posture and expressive movements that are the muscular counterpart of attitude might be changed and the attitude (armor) with it. Reich also held that sexual energy builds up in the body and requires release through orgasm that involves the whole body, pent-up sex energy leading to neurosis.

Reich, Wilhelm. Austrian psychoanalyst (b. Dobrzcynica, Galicia, March 24, 1897, d. Lewisburg, Pennsylvania, November 3, 1957). Reich, who received his M.D. from the University of Vienna in 1922, was at first a close associate of Sigmund Freud, but later differences led Freud to reject Reich and expel him from the International Psychoanalytic Association in 1934. Reich had been in private practice in Vienna and Berlin and, because he was a Jew, had already left Berlin in 1933. Between 1933 and 1939 Reich lived in several countries and then came to the United States. He came to equate sex energy with life energy and named it *orgone*. Beginning with a 1923 paper on genitality, Reich's ideas developed through a series of papers and books, among them *The Function of the Orgasm* (German original in 1927) and *Character Analysis* (German original in 1933). His experiments with orgone accumulators, radiation, and cancer cures led to problems with the U.S. Food and Drug Administration. Criticism and rejection of his theories accentuated his own personality problems, leading to a persecution complex and some outlandish developments of the orgone theory. Reich's refusal to obey a court injunction against the use of orgone accumulators led to his imprisonment.

Biographies: M. Cattier, *The Life and Work of Wilhelm Reich*, 1971; P. Marin, *Psychol. Today*, Sept. 1982, 56–65; I. Ollendorff Reich, *Wilhelm Reich*, 1969; *Shepard*, 3.

RENSHAW CELL. A small interneuron, in conjunction with a recurrent collateral from a spinal motor neuron, acts to inhibit the discharges in the motor neuron if the latter fires too rapidly, thus serving as a damper of neural activity. The inhibition produced is called Renshaw inhibition.

Renshaw, Birdsey. American neurophysiologist (b. Middletown, Connecticut, October 10, 1911). Renshaw's Ph.D. was from Harvard University (1938). He was with the Rockefeller Institute from 1938 to 1941 and then joined the faculty of Oberlin College. He described the inhibitory neuron in 1940 (*J. Neurophysiol.*, 3, 373–87).

Biographies: AMS, 1944.

RIBOT'S LAW. The principle that, in amnesia, the retrograde memory loss is such that events that occurred closer in time to the onset of amnesia are remembered less well than those that occurred further back in time.

Ribot, Theodule Armand. French psychologist (b. Guingamp, Côtes du Nord, December 18, 1839, d. Paris, December 8, 1916). Ribot received the *agrégé* degree in philosophy from the Ecole normale supérieure in 1865. He taught at various high schools until 1872 and then did clinical studies of mental abnormalities for the city of Paris. Ribot taught experimental psychology at the Sorbonne from 1885 to 1889 and then, until 1896, at the Collége de France. Ribot had an interest in a wide variety of fields in psychology. He wrote a large number of books that introduced French psychologists to the idea of evolution, the works of the German experimental psychologists, the thinking of the British associationists, and dynamic psychology. Ribot's pattern of interests resembled that of the French psychiatrist or physiologist who stressed medical psychology. His books on behavior disorders reflect this orientation. *Les maladies de la mémoire* (1885), one of these books, contains the principle governing retrograde memory loss. Ribot was one of the first French psychologists to relate pathology to problem areas in general psychology. He thereby helped to fix the character of French psychology along these lines.

Biographies: J. W. Baird, *Amer. J. Psychol.*, 1917, *28*, 312–13; *CE*, 12; *EP*, 7; *NYT*, Dec. 10, 1916, 21.

RICCO'S LAW. A statement of the relationship between luminance and retinal area as it determines the absolute threshold for brightness. For very small areas of the retina, subtending angles of less than ten minutes, the relationship is one of a trade-off, the product of area and luminance being a constant.

Riccò, Annibale. Italian astronomer (b. Modena, September 15, 1844, d. Rome, September 23, 1919). Riccò graduated in natural sciences from the University of Modena and in engineering from the Milan Polytechnic. He was an assistant at the observatories of Modena and Palermo. In 1865, he founded the observatory in Catania and in 1890 became professor of astrophysics at the University of Catania, the first such academic position in Italy. Riccò produced numerous publications in astrophysics. His law was stated in 1877 (*Mem. Regia Acc. sci. let. art., 17,* 47–160).
Biographies: DSB, 11.

RIDGWAY COLORS. An obsolete color classification system consisting of 1,115 colors varying in hue, saturation, and brightness.

Ridgway, Robert. American ornithologist (b. Mt. Carmel, Illinois, July 2, 1850, d. Olney, Illinois, March 25, 1939). In 1867, Ridgway was employed as a zoologist by the U.S. Geological Survey. Upon his return, Ridgway became curator of birds at the Smithsonian Institute, a position he held until his retirement. He was a descriptive taxonomist and the leading professional ornithologist in the United States. Ridgway described many new species and genera of birds, leaving a 500-item bibliography. His color scheme, described in *Color Standards and Color Nomenclature* (1912), developed as a result of his effort to specify the color of bird plumage exactly. It was also used by florists and paint, chemical, and wallpaper manufacturers. Ridgway's system was the best available until the advent of the Munsell color system.*
Biographies: Biog. Mem. NAS, 1932, 15, 57–101; *DAB,* 15; *DSB,* 11; H. Harris, *Condor,* 1928, *30,* 5–118; *NCAB,* 8; *WhAm,* 1.

RODS OF CORTI. Structures in the organ of Corti whose base rests on the basilar membrane and whose upper ends are between the inner and outer hair cells, the receptors for hearing. The upper ends of the rods fuse to form the arches of Corti. The rods are larger at the apex of the basilar membrane and smaller at its base. The rods of Corti are also known as pillars of Corti.

Corti, Alfonso. See CORTI'S TEETH.

ROGERIAN THERAPY. Technically known as client-centered therapy, it is a type of nondirective therapy. The emphasis is on the client rather than the therapist. The therapist's main role is to be a sympathetic listener who lets the client know that he or she understands and empathizes with the client's feelings by occasionally restating the client's statements and clarifying them by emphasizing some point. The therapist abstains from interpretations, adhering to a role as a provider of a warm and permissive atmosphere in which the client can feel free to talk and act as his or her own therapist. Self-understanding that removes the effects of distorted experience and the realization of one's own worth are the essence of Rogerian therapy.

Rogers, Carl Ransom. American psychologist (b. Oak Park, Illinois, January 8, 1902), d. La Jolla, California, February 4, 1987). Rogers was a leader of the humanistic psychology movement and often thought of as an antithesis to B. F. Skinner.*Rogers received his Ph.D. in clinical psychology from Teachers College, Columbia University, in 1931. He worked first at the Rochester Guidance Center, directing it for nine years, before taking an academic position at Ohio State University in 1940. In 1945, Rogers moved to Chicago, where he developed the client-centered approach to therapy. His most important work, *Client-Centered Therapy,* was published in 1951. In 1957 Rogers moved again, this time to the University of Wisconsin. In 1964, he joined the staff of the Western Behavioral Sciences Institute, La Jolla, California; in 1968 he became resident fellow of the Center for Studies of the Person, which he helped to found. Rogers published a dozen books and some sixty papers.

Biographies: APA Dir., 1985; *ConAu,* 1R; *CurBio,* 1962; *HPA,* 5; *IESS,* 18; *WhoAm,* 1984–1985.

ROKEACH VALUE SURVEY. Used for value therapy and value clarification, the survey compares the respondent's rankings of thirty-six value statements with those of a reference group.

Rokeach, Milton. American psychologist (b. Poland, December 27, 1918). Rokeach received his Ph.D. in social psychology from the University of California (1947). He was at Michigan State University from 1947 to 1972 and then at Washington State University. He has researched thinking, attitudes, values, and beliefs in the social-psychological context and has published several books in the area, the best known being *The Three Christs of Ypsilanti* (1964). The Value Survey was first published in 1967.

Biographies: AM&WS, 1978S; *APA Dir.,* 1985; *ConAu,* 3R, 5NR.

ROLANDIC FISSURE. Also known as central fissure, it is one of the two most conspicuous fissures on each side of the brain. It begins above the lateral fissure and ends at the median fissure, separating the frontal lobe from the parietal lobe. The immediately adjacent frontal lobe gyrus, the central gyrus, is the motor cortex; the gyrus posterior to it, the postcentral gyrus, is the body sensory area.

Rolando, Luigi. Italian anatomist (b. Turin, July 20, 1773, d. Turin, April 20, 1831). Rolando's M.D. was from the University of Turin (1793). He served as personal physician to the king of Savoy in Turin. From 1807 to 1814 he taught at the University of Sassari and from 1814 to 1831 at the University of Turin. Rolando studied the anatomy and pathology of the brain. He steered away from phrenology, did actual experiments on the brain, which included electrical stimulation of brain tissue, and used postmortem examinations. Rolando localized the higher mental functions in the cerebral hemispheres. He described the central fissure in 1831 (*Mem. Regia accad. sci. Torino, 35,* 103–45), and it was named after him by Leuret.

Biographies: *DSB,* 11; *Haymaker.*

ROLFING. A method of very deep massage to return the body to its proper structural and postural position. It is based on the work of Wilhelm Reich* and Moshe Feldenkrais,* both of whom postulated that the way we respond to the world and other people is reflected in our bodies. Restoring the proper physical balance, especially with respect to the force of gravity, leads to concomitant mental adjustment.

Rolf, Ida P. American biochemist and physical therapist (b. New York City, 1896, d. New York City, March 19, 1979). Rolf earned a Ph.D. in biological chemistry from the College of Physicians and Surgeons, Columbia University, in the 1920s. She held positions with the Rockefeller Institute from 1916 to 1935. Rolfing was developed in the 1930s, but it did not become widely known until the 1960s when it became an ingredient in the human potential movement that centered on the Esalen Institute, Big Sur, California. The Rolf Institute was established at Boulder, Colorado, in 1975.

Biographies: *Newsweek,* April 2, 1979, *93,* 70; *NYT,* March 21, 1979, D–21; *Time,* April 2, 1979, *113,* 8.

ROMBERG SIGN. An individual swaying or falling when standing with eyes closed and feet together, indicative of locomotor ataxia, or tabes dorsalis, that involves the posterior columns of the spinal cord.

Romberg, Moritz Heinrich von. German neurologist (b. Meiningen, Thuringia, November 11, 1795, d. Berlin, June 16, 1873). Romberg studied medicine at the University of Berlin (M.D., 1817). During his tenure at that university (1830–1873), he published the first systematic textbook of neurology (*Lehrbuch der Nervenkrankheiten des Menschen,* 1840–1846). It appeared first in parts and saw two more editions before 1857. It contains a classical description of tabes dorsalis and the Romberg sign (1846, p. 795).

Biographies: *Haymaker; Talbot;* H. R. Viets, *Bull. NY Acad. Med.,* 1948, *24,* 772–82.

ROMEO AND JULIET EFFECT. Increase in interpersonal attraction in two people attributable to the efforts of their parents to keep them apart.

Romeo and Juliet. The lovers in William Shakespeare's play of same name, published in 1597, members of two feuding families, the Montagues (Romeo's) and the Capulets (Juliet's). Romeo and Juliet were also actual people who lived in Verona, Italy, both dying for each other in 1303. They were models for several literary works even before Shakespeare wrote his play.

RORSCHACH CATEGORY. Any of the classificatory descriptions of the content of a testee's response to a Rorschach inkblot.

RORSCHACH DETERMINANT. A physical characteristic of a Rorschach inkblot that a testee responds to, such as form, detail, color, or shading.

RORSCHACH RANKING TEST. A variant of the Rorschach test* in which the respondent ranks a set of nine responses to a Rorschach card from "best," or most descriptive, to "worst."

RORSCHACH TEST (RORSCHACH METHOD, RORSCHACH INK BLOT TEST, RORSCHACH PSYCHODIAGNOSTIC, THE ROR-SCHACH) A projective personality test consisting of ten plates with symmetrical, black-on-white inkblots, some with other colors added. The respondent is instructed to describe what the blot reminds him or her of. The rationale behind the test is that, given an unstructured stimulus, the respondent is more likely to reveal concealed, problematic, or unconscious contents of the mind in its description than when asked direct questions about such matters.

Rorschach, Hermann. Swiss psychiatrist (b. Zurich, November 8, 1884, d. Herisau, Appenzell-Ausser Rhoden, April 2, 1922). After obtaining his M.D. from the University of Zurich in 1912, Rorschach held positions at several mental hospitals in Switzerland. His life and work are completely overshadowed by the test he invented. Rorschach used the inkblot test beginning in 1911 but did not publish the ten inkblots and a manual until 1921 (*Psychodiagnostics,* English translation, 1942). Although its validity is seriously doubted, it has been in constant use since its inception, and it boasts a literature of several thousand items. The methods of interpretation of the Rorschach protocols currently in use, however, were developed by others.
   Biographies: Asimov; EB, 19; H. Ellenberger, *Bull. Menninger Clin.,* 1954, *18,* 173–219; *IESS,* 13; E. Oberholzer, *J. Project. Techn.,* 1968, *32,* 502–8.

ROSANOFF ASSOCIATION TEST. See KENT-ROSANOFF FREE ASSOCIATION TEST.

ROSCOE-BUNSEN LAW. See BUNSEN-ROSCOE LAW.

ROSENTHAL EFFECT. The effect of the researcher's attitudes, expectations, beliefs, or biases on the phenomenon being researched and on the outcome of the research.

Rosenthal, Robert. American psychologist (b. Giessen, Germany, March 2, 1933). Rosenthal received all of his academic degrees from the University of California in Los Angeles (Ph.D. in clinical psychology, 1956). He was at the University of North Dakota from 1958 to 1962 and has been at Harvard University since 1962. The eponymous effect, which Rosenthal himself calls the *experimenter effect*, was coined after Rosenthal published his *Experimenter Effect in Behavioral Research* in 1966, although the effect had been known for some time in the physical, biological, and behavioral sciences as the observer effect.

Biographies: AM&WS, 1978S; *APA Dir.,* 1985; *WhoAm,* 1984–1985.

ROSENZWEIG PICTURE FRUSTRATION STUDY. A projective personality test that measures a person's response to frustrating situations. The situations are depicted in twenty-four drawings that show two characters, one in some common, mildly frustrating situation and the other saying something frustrating or commenting on the frustrating situation. The respondent, who is assumed to identify with the first character, supplies the text of what this character would say under the circumstances. The responses are scored in terms of the type and direction of aggression.

Rosenzweig, Saul. American psychologist (b. Boston, Massachusetts, February 7, 1907). Rosenzweig' received his Ph.D. in clinical psychology from Harvard University (1932). He has held positions at Harvard (1929–1934), Worcester State Hospital (1934–1943), Western State Psychiatric Institute and Clinic in Pittsburgh (1943–1948), and Washington University (1949–1975). His fields are personality theory, creativity, and the history of psychology.

Biographies: AM&WS, 1978S; *APA Dir.,* 1985; *WhoAm,* 1984–1985.

ROSSOLIMO METHOD. An early intelligence test and the first attempt to develop a profile test of intelligence. Ten test items were constructed for each of eleven mental abilities, the strength of each being measured on a ten-point scale, that is, the number of items passed. The scale points were connected to form a psychological profile of the individual.

ROSSOLIMO REFLEX. Tapping of the plantar surface of the toes produces the reflexive flexion of the second and fifth toes. The reflex is stronger in cases of pyramidal tract lesions.

Rossolimo, Grigorii Ivanovich. Russian neurologist (b. Odessa, December 17, 1860, d. Moscow, September 29, 1928). Rossolimo graduated from medical school in Moscow in 1884. In 1890, he became head of the department of nervous diseases in A. A. Ostroumov's Clinic of Internal Disorders. Rossolimo also became intensely interested in child development and in 1911 founded the Institute for Child Psychology and Neurology. After 1917, Rossolimo was at the First State University of Moscow. The intelligence test is described in Rossolimo's book, *Psikhologicheskie profili* (1910).

Biographies: Soviet, 22.

ROTTER BOARD. A device for the study of level of aspiration. Neither skill nor motivation affects performance on the perceptual motor task given because it is the experimenter who controls the subject's success.

ROTTER INCOMPLETE SENTENCE BLANK. A verbal projective test consisting of forty incomplete sentences or "stems" that the respondent is directed to complete expressing his or her true feelings. Although used primarily in clinical settings, the format has been used to study attitudes.

ROTTER'S INTERNAL-EXTERNAL CONTROL SCALE. A scale that measures the extent to which individuals feel they control their own lives (internal locus of control) or the extent to which they feel their lives are being controlled by fate, chance, or powerful others (external locus of control).

Rotter, Julian Bernard. American psychologist (b. New York City, October 22, 1916). A clinical psychologist (Ph.D., Indiana University, 1941), Rotter was in the U.S. Air Force from 1942 to 1946 and then taught and was director of clinical training at Ohio State University from 1946 to 1963. He was professor and director of clinical training program at the University of Connecticut after 1963. Rotters specialties are personality theory and personality measurement. He described the board in 1942 (*J. Exp. Psychol., 31,* 410–22). The Incomplete Sentence Blank was constructed by Rotter and Janet E. Rafferty in 1950, and the Internal-External Scale was presented in 1966 (*Psychol. Monog., 80* [1, Whole No. 609]).
  Biographies: AM&WS, 1973S; *APA Dir.,* 1985; *ConAu,* 33R.

ROY'S LARGEST ROOT. A criterion for testing hypotheses in multivariate analysis, considering only the largest eigenvalue.

Roy, Samarendra Nath. Indian mathematician (b. Calcutta, December 11, 1906, d. Chapel Hill, North Carolina, July 23, 1964). From 1934 to 1964, after obtaining his master's degree in mathematics from the University of Calcutta in 1931, Roy held positions at both the Indian Statistical Institute and the University of Calcutta. He held a concurrent position at the University of North Carolina from 1950 to 1964. The largest root criterion was presented in Roy's book, *Some Aspects of Multivariate Analysis* (1957).
  Biographies: R. C. Bose, *Amer. Statistician,* 1964, *18*(5), 26–27; R. C. Bose et al. (eds.), *Essays in Probability and Statistics,* 1970, pp. xi–xiv.

RUBIN'S FIGURE (RUBIN'S VASE-FACE FIGURE, RUBIN'S GOBLET-PROFILE FIGURE). A reversible figure-ground that can be seen as a goblet (or vase) or as two facial profiles. It is used to illustrate the factors that make for the perception of a configuration as either figure or ground.

Rubin, Edgar John. Danish psychologist (b. Copenhagen, September 6, 1886, d. Copenhagen, May 3, 1951). During his lifetime, Rubin was Denmark's most distinguished psychologist. His doctorate was from the University of Copenhagen (1915), where he remained for the rest of his career. Rubin made a direct contribution to the raw material of which Gestalt psychology was made. It was the analysis of visual perception in terms of its two basic components, figure and ground. Rubin began research on this phenomenon in 1912. A first report of it was published in German in the proceedings of the Sixth Congress of Experimental Psychology, then in Danish (*Synslopevede figurer,* 1915), and finally, again in German, but in a monograph form (*Visuell wahrgenommene Figuren,* 1921). The figure-ground concept is now part of general psychology.

Biographies: D. Katz, *Psychol. Rev.,* 1951, *58,* 387–88; *PR,* 3; W. C. H. Prentice, *Amer. J. Psychol.,* 1951, *64,* 608–9.

RUBINSTEIN-TAYBI SYNDROME. A form of mental retardation characterized by physical malformation, such as broad thumbs and toes and facial deformities.

Rubinstein, Jack Herbert. American pediatrician and radiologist (b. New York City, August 4, 1925). Rubinstein obtained his M.D. from Harvard University in 1952. Since 1956 he has held various hospital appointments in pediatrics and has been teaching at the University of Cincinnati. Rubinstein and Taybi described the syndrome in 1963 (*Amer. J. Dis. Child.,* *105,* 588–608).

Biographies: Dir. Med. Spec., 1974–1975; *WhoMW,* 1978.

Taybi, Hooshang. Iranian-American pediatrician and radiologist (b. Malayer, Iran, October 22, 1919). Taybi's medical degree was from the University of Teheran (1944). He interned in New York, was resident in Akron, Ohio, and then held hospital appointments in New York and Ohio until 1959. After teaching periods at Oklahoma and Indiana universities, Taybi held hospital appointments in California from 1964 to 1967. He has been at the University of California in San Francisco since 1967.

Biographies: AM&WS, 1979P; *WhoAm,* 1980.

RUDOLPH POSES. Photographs of a male actor expressing various emotions, used by psychologists in research on emotions.

Rudolph, Heinrich. German painter (b. n.a., d. n.a.). Rudolph, who studied art at the art academy in Breslau, theorized that all emotional expressions are just variants of a few basic ones, primarily approach and avoidance. He took hundreds of photographs to be used as artists' aids, although they were retouched and idealized in the process. The photographs were published in Rudolph's book, *Der Ausdruck der Gemütsbewegungen des Menschen* (1903).

Biographies: Unavailable.

RUD'S SYNDROME. A syndrome of hyperkeratosic skin lesions and mental caused by a dominant gene. It is also known as xerodermatic mental deficiency the Sjögren-Larsson syndrome.

Rud, Einar. Danish physician (b. Engum, February 7, 1892, d. n.a.). Rud a physician in 1917, obtained the M.D. degree from the University of Copenin 1925, held hospital appointments from 1918 to 1931, and taught at the Univerof Copenhagen from 1925 to 1931. He has been chief physician of the Montebello in Helsingør since 1931. Rud described the eponymous syndrome in 1927 (*Hospitalstidende, 70*, 525–38).

Biographies: Kraks Blaa Bog: 6066 Nulevende Danske Maend og Kvinders Kraks Legat, 1949.

RUFFINI CYLINDERS (RUFFINI CORPUSCLES). A type of nerve ending in the skin, thought to mediate the sensation of warm.

RUFFINI PAPILLARY ENDINGS (RUFFINI ENDING, RUFFINI END RUFFINI PLUME). Any of the nerve endings found in the papillary layer of the skin, thought by some to mediate pressure sensations.

Ruffini, Angelo. Italian anatomist (b. Pretare, near Arquata del Tronto July 17, 1864, d. Baragazza, near Castiglione dei Pepoli, September 7, 1929). received his M.D. from the University of Bologna in 1890. He was on the of the universities of Florence (1894–1897), Sienna (1897–1912), and Bologna (1912–1929). His work on the structure of dermal receptors, as well as on brought him recognition in the form of eponymous terms and in having the of Histology and General Embryology at the University of Bologna named after him. Ruffini described the cylinders in 1893 (*Atti Accad. naz. Lincei*, 4 ser., vol. 7) and the papillary endings in 1898 (*Sulla presenza di nuove forme di terminazione nervose nello strato papillare e subpapillare della cute dell'uomo*).

Biographies: DSB, 11.

RULON TEST (RULON RELIABILITY FORMULA). A formula for estithe reliability of a test, used especially with test-scoring computers.

Rulon, Phillip Justin. American educational psychologist (b. Keokuk, Iowa, 11, 1900, d. Cambridge, Massachusetts, August 1968). Rulon had a Ph.D. from the University of Minnesota (1932). From 1930 to 1948, he was at Harvard the last five years as acting dean of the Graduate School of Education. He was research associate at Tufts College from 1942 to 1946, special consultant to the secretary of war from 1940 to 1948, and an officer of the Educational Corporation from 1938 to 1968. Rulon wrote four books and many papers on psychology. The reliability formula was presented in 1939 (*Harvard Educ. Rev., 9*, 99–103).

Biographies: AM&WS, 1962S; *WhAm,* 5.

RUNGE'S COLOR PYRAMID. The forerunner of the modern representation of all colors as a color spindle. Runge placed the major six colors on an oval and them to white above the plane of the oval and to black below it.

Runge, Philipp Otto. German painter (b. Wolgast, Mecklenburg, July 23, 1777, d. Hamburg, December 2, 1810). Influenced by seventeenth-century German Runge was a romantic painter who belonged to the Dresden circle of painters, by Ludwig Tieck and Caspar David Friedrich. His paintings were characterized esoteric nature symbolism. Runge studied in Copenhagen from 1799 to 1801 and in Dresden from 1801 to 1804. He had lived in Hamburg since 1804. He described the color pyramid in 1810 (*Farbenkugel*).

Biographies: R. M. Bisanz, *German Romanticism and Philipp Otto Runge, McGDcArt,* 5.

S

SADISM. The deriving of sexual pleasure from the infliction of pain upon others.

Sade, Donatien-Alphonse-François, comte de. French author (b. Paris, June 2, 1740, d. Charenton, near Paris, December 2, 1814). Marquis de Sade, as he is usually referred to, took up a military career in 1754 but abandoned it in 1763. Being the governor-general and lord of several places, de Sade led a life of leisure and dissipation. He was repeatedly accused, convicted, reprieved, arrested, and jailed for a variety of offenses that included the infliction of pain on sexual partners. He spent twenty-seven years of his life in prison, where he also wrote most of his works, such as *Justine, 120 Days of Sodom,* and *Philosophy in the Boudoir.* He was last arrested in 1801 as the author of an obscene book, *Justine,* and was committed to the Charenton lunatic asylum in 1803.

    Biographies: DE; EA, 24; *EB,* 19; G. Lely, *The Life of Marquis de Sade,* 1961.

SAINT VITUS' DANCE. A form of psychic epidemic that broke out repeatedly between the eleventh and fifteenth centuries in Europe, especially the German and Flemish countries. People gathered near churches, dancing and singing for days on end. Some would lose consciousness; some would have convulsions. A similar epidemic that occurred in the south of Italy in the fifteenth century was named *tarantism* or *tarantulism* because of the belief that the excited behavior was due to the bite of the tarantula. It is now recognized that both the St. Vitus' dance and tarantism were cases of emotional contagion that centered on a core of individuals suffering from a form of acute chorea, now known as Sydenham's chorea.*

Saint Vitus. Saint Vitus was a third- or fourth-century Christian martyr, protector of epileptics, and patron of dancers and actors. The name *St. Vitus' dance* comes from the association of the dancers with chapels dedicated to Saint Vitus. They were either treated in such a chapel in Saverne, Alsace-Lorraine, or gathered around them in the belief that this particular saint had the power to cure them. Since nothing factual is known about the life of St. Vitus, it cannot be established whether his association with dance and epilepsy came first and was the reason why the St. Vitus dancers flocked to the chapels dedicated to him or whether his reputation was established after cures had occurred at these chapels.

SALPETRIERE SCHOOL. The teachings concerning psychopathology and hypnosis, associated with the name of Jean-Martin Charcot.* He propounded them in his neurological clinic at the La Salpêtrière psychiatric hospital beginning in the late 1870s. Charcot believed that only individuals suffering from hysteria were susceptible to hypnosis and that hypnotic phenomena themselves were the result of hysteria. He distinguished three progressively deeper states of hypnosis: lethargy, catalepsy, and somnambulism. A competing view was offered by the Nancy school.* Subsequent research showed that the latter was the more correct view of the nature of hypnosis.

La Salpêtrière. A very large Parisian hospital, dating from 1656. The name derives from saltpeter (potassium nitrate), one of the three ingredients of gunpowder. On the present site of the hospital there stood, until 1634, a gunpowder factory, a *salpêtrière*. Louis XIV made the hospital into an asylum for beggars, prostitutes, and the insane. At times it housed up to 8,000 persons. Philippe Pinel instituted his reforms in the treatment of the insane there, but it was relatively unknown until Charcot's physical and administrative changes converted it into a palace of science and a mecca for visiting practitioners and researchers from France and abroad.

SANDER'S PARALLELOGRAM. From a point about one-third the length of the longer side of the parallelogram, three lines are drawn: two lines to the vertices of the two angles opposite and one line parallel to the shorter sides. The first two lines, although physically of equal length, appear unequal, the one drawn to the farther corner appearing to be considerably longer than the one drawn to the nearer corner.

Sander, Friedrich. German psychologist (b. Greiz, Thuringia, November 19, 1889, d. Bonn, November 29, 1971). Sander received his Ph.D. under Wilhelm Wundt* at Leipzig (1913). He was Wundt's last assistant. Sander and Felix Krüger were cofounders of the ''second Leipzig school'' or holistic psychology (*Ganzheitspsychologie*). Sander was the originator of the concept of microgenesis, the development, in time, of full-fledged Gestalten from a more elementary, diffuse germ of a Gestalt. During the Third Reich, Sander placed psychology in the service of Nazi ideology. Although the illusion is sometimes called the Heiss-Sander illusion, credit for it is usually given to Sander (*Neue psychol. Stud.*, 1925, *1*, 159–67). There are, however, earlier representations of it.
Biographies: Bonin; PR, 3.

SANFORD ENVELOPES. A series of weighted envelopes used to measure the difference threshold for lifted weights.

Sanford, Edmund Clark. American psychologist (b. Oakland, California, November 10, 1859, d. Boston, Massachusetts, November 22, 1924). After receiving a Ph.D. in psychology from Johns Hopkins University in 1888, Sanford was on the faculty of Clark University (1889–1909). His most important contribution was the publication of a laboratory manual, which first came out in installments in the *American Journal of Psychology* beginning in 1891 and then in book form in 1898 (*Course in Experimental Psychology*). Sanford's only book served as the standard laboratory manual for a long time. He published about thirty papers on a variety of subjects in psychology.
  Biographies: W. H. Burnham, *J. Genet. Psychol.*, 1925, *32*, 2–7; *DAB*, 16; *NCAB*, 12; E. B. Titchener, *Amer. J. Psychol.*, 1925, *36*, 157–70; *WhAm*, 1.

SANSON'S IMAGES. See PURKINJE-SANSON IMAGES.

SAVART'S WHEEL. A device for generating high-frequency sounds. A large, hand-turned wheel turned a smaller toothed wheel on the same axle. At 33 revolutions per second the 720 teeth of the wheel could produce 24,000 vibrations in a card or a thin wedge of wood held against it. Savart held this figure to be the lowest value of the upper limit of hearing.

Savart, Félix. French physicist (b. Mézières, Seine-et-Oise, June 30, 1791, d. Paris, March 16, 1841). Although Savart had a medical degree from the University of Strasbourg (1816), he was always interested in vibrations, building his first experimental violins in 1817 and presenting the results in 1819 to the Paris Academy of Science. After 1820, Savart was professor of experimental physics at the Collège de France. Savart performed numerous experiments on vibrations and acoustics. He described the wheel in 1830 (*Ann. chim. phys.*, 2 ser., *44*, 337–52).
  Biographies: DSB, 12.

SCHAFHAUTL PHONOMETER. An old form of an audiometer, or a device for measuring intensity thresholds for sound, in which variation in the intensity of the sound produced could be made by varying the height of drop of a pellet unto a sound-producing surface.

Schafhäutl, Karl Franz Emil von. German acoustician (b. Ingolstadt, Bavaria, February 16, 1803, d. Munich, February 25, 1890). A student of acoustics, Schafhäutl was also a professor of mining (University of Munich, 1843–1849) and custodian (after 1849) of the geological collection of the state of Bavaria in Munich. He obtained both his Ph.D. (1833) and Dr. med. (1838) in England. Schafhäutl produced a number of papers on acoustics, including one on tone color in which he disagreed with Helmholtz.* He described the phonometer in 1854 (*Abh. Kön. bayr. Akad. Wiss.*, II Kl., Bd. VII, Abt. II).
  Biographies: N. Slonimsky, *Baker's Biographical Dictionary of Musicians*, 1984.

SCHEFFE TEST. In single-factor ANOVAs, a test for homogenity of variance that is relatively insensitive to violations of the assumption of a normal distribution in the variable studied.

SCHEFFE'S *S* METHOD. A method to make all possible a posteriori comparisons in ANOVA if the overall *F* is significant.

Scheffé, Henry A. American mathematician and statistician (b. New York City, April 11, 1907, d. Berkeley, California, July 5, 1977). With a Ph.D. in mathematics (University of Wisconsin, 1935), Scheffé held positions at eight universities during the years 1935–1953. He was at the University of California at Berkeley from 1953 to 1975 and at Indiana University from 1975 to 1977. Scheffé's test appeared in 1959 (*The Analysis of Variance*) and the *S* method in 1953 (*Biometrika, 40,* 87–104).
   Biographies: AM&WS, 1979P; *IESS,* 18.

SCHEINER'S EXPERIMENT. A demonstration of ocular accommodation by means of two pinholes punched in a card. If the distance between the pinholes is smaller than the size of the pupil, looking through them with one eye, the other closed, makes all objects that are not in the focal plane appear double.

Scheiner, Cristoph. German astronomer (b. Wald, near Mindelheim, Swabia, July 25, 1573, d. Neisse [now Nysa], Silesia, June 18, 1650). Having joined the Jesuit order, Scheiner was sent to Ingolstadt to study philosophy and mathematics. He was a teacher trainee from 1603 to 1605 and during that time invented the pantograph. Scheiner returned to Ingolstadt to study theology; he was then appointed professor of Hebrew and mathematics in that city in 1610. In 1611, Seheiner built a telescope and observed sun spots, although Galileo claimed priority for that discovery. From 1616 to 1620, Scheiner was at Maximilian's court at Innsbruck. Here he performed experiments on vision and published them in *Oculus, hoc est: fundamentum opticum* (1619). The ocular accommodation experiment is described in this work (book 3, p. 163). From 1620 to 1624, Scheiner was at various schools and universities; he spent the years 1624 to 1633 in Rome, where he was detained on a journey to Spain. Scheiner lived the remaining years of his life in Vienna (1633–1639) and Neisse (1639–1650).
   Biographies: Asimov; DSB, 12.

SCHRODER STAIRCASE. A reversible perspective drawing of staircase steps. It can be seen either as a view from above or as the underside of the staircase.

Schröder, Heinrich Georg Friedrich. German bacteriologist (b. 1810, d. Karlsruhe, 1885). Schröder was school director in Mannheim for some time. He conducted research on the prevention of spoiling of fluids by reducing air-fluid contact. He presented the staircase in 1858 (*Ann. Phys. Chem., 181,* 298–311).
   Biographies: W. Bulloch, *The History of Bacteriology,* 1938, p. 396.

SEASHORE MEASURES OF MUSICAL TALENTS. Seashore's is the oldest of the musical aptitude tests. A phonograph record contains the stimuli used to measure the ability to discriminate small differences in pitch, loudness, rhythm, time, and timbre and to remember tonal patterns.

SEASHORE'S AUDIOMETER. A device employed in the measurement of sound intensity thresholds. A buzzer or electrically activated tuning fork produces the sound that is conducted to a microphone-telephone system. Its intensity is varied by means of a potentiometer.

Seashore, Carl Emil. American psychologist (b. Mörlunda, Sweden, January 28, 1866, d. Lewiston, Idaho, October 16, 1949). Seashore's Ph.D. in psychology was from Yale University (1895), and he spent his professional life at the University of Iowa (1897–1938), where he established a psychological laboratory and the second psychological clinic in the United States. He was also instrumental in promoting the Iowa Child Welfare Research Station and was its general supervisor until his death. During his time, the station issued some 1,000 publications. Seashore wrote a number of texts in psychology, contributed in the areas of the psychology of speech and phonetics, and produced a classic treatise on the psychology of music, *Psychology of Music* (1938), his lifelong interest. Seashore developed the audiometer soon after coming to Iowa. The musical talents test was first published in 1919 (*The Psychology of Musical Talent*).
   Biographies: Biog. Mem. NAS, 29; *DAB,* Suppl. 4; *HPA,* 1; *IESS,* 14; M. Metfessel, *Science, 1950, 111,* 713–17; *NCAB,* A; D. Starch, *J. Educ. Psychol.,* 1950, *41,* 217–18; G. D. Stoddard, *Amer. J. Psychol.,* 1950, *63,* 456–62; *WhAm,* 2.

SEGLAS TYPE. Psychomotor type of paranoia.

Séglas, Jules. French physician (b. 1856, d. 1939). Séglas (M.D., 1881) served at the la Salpêtrière hospital* (1881–1898, 1907–?) and the Bicêtre (1898–1907). He wrote *Leçons cliniques sur les maladies mentales et nerveuses* (1895) and about twenty-five other publications. His first paper on psychomotor hallucinations appeared in 1891 and was followed by others during the same decade.
   Biographies: La Presse médicale, Paris, Feb. 7–10, 1940, *48,* 173–74.

SEGUIN FORM BOARD. A form board, one of the earliest performance tests developed for the training of the mentally defective. It consists of a number of geometric figures, cut from wood, that must be inserted in holes of the same shape cut in a board. The Seguin form board has been made part of a number of performance tests of intelligence, such as the Grace Arthur Point Scale.*

Seguin, Edouard. French-American psychiatrist (b. Clamecy, Nièvre, France, January 20, 1812, d. Mt. Vernon, New York, October 28, 1880). Seguin was a pioneer in the study of mental retardation. At the time when Jean Itard was trying to improve the behavior of the famous wild boy of Aveyron, Seguin was his assistant. He continued Itard's efforts with mentally defective individuals. In 1839, Seguin opened the first school for the feebleminded in the world, and from 1846 to 1848 he headed the Institution for the Training of the Feebleminded, Paris. Seguin came to the United States in 1848. He was one of the organizers of the School for Defectives at Randall's Island, New York, and for two decades worked to improve training methods for mentally retarded children. He stated the main points of the training of the mentally defective in his *Traitement moral, hygiène et éducation des idiots* (1846), and in 1866 published his second major work, *Idiocy and Its Treatment by the Physiological Method*. Seguin, who had no university education, was given an honorary M.D. by the University of the City of New York in 1861.

Biographies: C. L. Dana, *Ann. Med. Hist.*, 1924, *6*, 475–79; S. P. Davies, *Encycl. Soc. Sci.*, 1934, *13*, 647; H. Holman, *Seguin and His Physiological Method of Education*, 1914; L. Kanner, *Amer. J. Ment. Def.*, 1960, *65*, 2–10; *NCAB*, 15; M. E. Talbot, *Amer. J. Ment. Def.*, 1967–1968, *72*, 184–89; *WhAm*, HS.

SELYE'S SYNDROME. The stages that an organism goes through in adapting to stress: the alarm reaction, or the mobilization of resources to cope with stress; the adaptation or resistance stage, in which the recruitment of coping resources plateaus; and the exhaustion stage, which occurs if stress persists and is characterized by the depletion of resources and the progressive lowering of performance.

Selye, Hans. Austrian-Canadian physiologist (b. Vienna, January 26, 1907, d. Montreal, October 16, 1982). From the German University of Prague, Selye received an M.D. in 1929 and a Ph.D. in chemistry in 1931 and from McGill University a D.Sc. in 1942. Selye worked at Johns Hopkins University (1931–1932) and McGill University (1932–1944) and was professor and director of the Institute of Experimental Medicine and Surgery at the University of Montreal from 1945 to 1976. For his research on stress and the endocrine system, Selye became one of medicine's most honored individuals. He introduced the term *stress* from physics to describe the body's response to physical and emotional stressors. He first presented the concept of stress and the general adaptation .syndrome (his term) in 1936 (*Nature*, *138*, July 4, p. 32). It was followed by a very large number of articles and many books, resulting in the most original contribution to psychosomatic medicine since its inception.

Biographies: AM&WS, 1982P; *ConAu*, 5R, 2NR; *CurBio*, 1953, 1981; R. B. Malmo, *Amer. Psychologist*, 1986, *41*, 92–93; *Psychology Today*, March 1978; *WhAm*, 8.

SHANNON-WIENER MEASURE OF INFORMATION. The quantity $H = - \sum_i p_i \log p_i$ where p_i is the probability of an alternative in which an event can occur, i the number of such alternatives, and H the average amount of information, in bits, contained in the event.

Shannon, Claude Elwood. American mathematician (b. Gaylord, Michigan, April 30, 1916). After obtaining a Ph.D. in mathematics (Massachusetts Institute of Technology, 1940), Shannon joined the staff of Bell Telephone Laboratories in 1941 to work on the problem of how to transmit information most efficiently. To do so, he had to specify what information was. In 1948, Shannon published a paper (*Bell Syst. Tech. J., 27,* 379–423, 623–56) showing how information could be measured. A full-fledged work, *The Mathematical Theory of Communication* (1949, with W. Weaver), was the beginning of information theory. From 1958 to 1980, Shannon taught electrical engineering at the MIT. His research has been on Boolean algebra* and switching circuits, communications theory, computers, and cryptography.

Biographies: AM&WS, 1982P; *Asimov; McGMSE,* 3.

Wiener, Norbert. American mathematician (b. Columbia, Missouri, November 26, 1894, d. Stockholm, Sweden, March 18, 1964). Wiener's Ph.D. was in philosophy (Harvard University, 1913). From 1919 to 1960, he held positions at the Massachusetts Institute of Technology. The idea of a new discipline, cybernetics, grew out of Wiener's work in devising a system for the rapid direction of antiaircraft gunfire. The discipline was launched when Wiener published his book, *Cybernetics,* in 1948. In a chapter of *Cybernetics,* Wiener proposed essentially the same method for measuring information as had Shannon. Both had arrived at the idea independently.

Biographies: Asimov; ConAu, 107; *CurBio,* 1950, 1964; *DSB,* 14; *IESS,* 16; *WhAm,* 4; N. Wiener, *Ex-prodigy: My Childhood and Youth,* 1953; N. Wiener, *I Am a Mathematician: The Later Life of a Prodigy,* 1968.

SHEPPARD'S CORRECTION. A correction of the standard deviation that has been computed from grouped data, with the number of class intervals smaller than twelve.

Sheppard, William Fleetwood. English mathematical statistician (b. Sydney, Australia, 1863, d. London, October 12, 1936). Sheppard was educated at Cambridge (A.B. 1884, fellow of Trinity College 1887, A.M. 1888, LL.M. 1889, Sc.D. 1908). He was assistant secretary of the London Board of Education from 1914 to 1921. Sheppard wrote on the method of finite differences, the normal curve, other subjects in mathematical statistics, and, later, pure mathematics (*From Determinant to Tensor,* 1923). The correction appeared in 1907 (*Biometrika, 5,* 404–6).

Biographies: A. C. Aitken & E. T. Whittaker, *Proc. Roy. Soc. Edinb.,* 1937, *56,* 270–82; R. C. Archibald, *Scripta Math.,* 1945, 11, 242–43; C. M. Neale, *The Senior Wranglers of the University of Cambridge,* 1907, p. 49; *The Times,* London, Oct. 14, 1936, 1c, 19d; Oct. 17, 14b; Oct. 22, 11a; G. U. Yule, *Nature,* 1938, *138,* 872–873.

SHIPLEY-INSTITUTE FOR LIVING SCALE FOR MEASURING INTEL-LECTUAL IMPAIRMENT. A scale designed to diagnose pathological deterioration in mental functioning. The difference in scores obtained on a forty-item vocabulary test and a twenty-item series-completion test yields a conceptual quotient. A score far below 100 is taken as an indication of pathological deterioration.

Shipley, Walter Cleveland. American psychologist (b. St. Louis, Missouri, December 29, 1903, d. Norton, Massachusetts, June 5, 1966). Shipley received a Ph.D. from Yale University in 1933. He held positions at the Delaware Mental Hygiene Clinic (1933–1935), University of Idaho, Southern Branch (1935–1938), the Hartford Retreat (1938–1941), Wesleyan University (1938–1941), and Wheaton College (1941–1966). Shipley's work was on test contruction, memory, and judgment. The scale was developed while Shipley was research associate at the Neuro-Psychiatric Institute of the Hartford Retreat and was initially published as the Shipley-Hartford Retreat Scale for Measuring Intellectual Impairment (1940). The Retreat was later renamed the Institute for Living, and the new name became part of the scale (1946).
Biographies: APA Dir., 1966; NCAB, 54; NYT, June 6, 1966, 41.

SIDMAN AVOIDANCE. Avoidance training in which the animal is shocked briefly but regularly if it fails to make the appropriate response. An appropriate response between shocks postpones them, and continued response leads to continued postponement. The procedure results in a relatively high and even rate of responding over long periods of time.

Sidman, Murray. American psychologist (b. Boston, Massachusetts, April 29, 1923). After receiving his Ph.D. from Columbia University in 1952, Sidman was with the Walter Reed Army Institute of Research (1952–1961) and the Massachusetts General Hospital's Department of Neurology in Boston (from 1961). Sidman's most significant work, *Tactics of Scientific Research,* appeared in 1960. He described the avoidance training technique in 1953 (*J. Comp. Physiol. Psychol., 46,* 253–61).
Biographies: AMS, 1962S.

SILVA MIND CONTROL. A system of relaxation, meditation, and imagery to improve memory, control pain, further healing, stimulate creativity, control habits, enhance extrasensory perception, and the like. It can be learned individually or during a four-day group course. The system is based on the hypothesized enhanced utilization of cognitive abilities that becomes possible upon entering the mental state characterized by increased alpha component of the electroencephalogram.

Silva, José. American electronics technician and educator (b. Laredo, Texas, August 11, 1914). With no formal education, Silva learned radio repair by correspondence and became owner of a thriving radio repair business. The business was interrupted by his service in the Signal Corps during World War II, but he resumed it afterward. Silva taught electronics at Laredo Junior College and began to study hypnosis and do hypnotic experiments. He first used hypnosis to improve the school grades of his own children and then abandoned this method for one in which the subject controlled his or her own mind. Silva taught this method to other children in the community, perfecting it by about 1969. Silva Mind Control courses are now taught throughout the United States and in many foreign countries.

Biographies: J. Silva & P. Miele, *The Silva Mind Control Method,* 1977.

SINSTEDEN'S WINDMILL. A reversible perspective figure, depicting what Sinsteden saw when looking at the silhouette of a windmill against the light evening sky, with the vanes rotating. Since Sinsteden could not decide whether he was looking at the windmill from the front or the back, the direction of rotation of the windmill's vanes seemingly kept changing direction depending on which perspective view Sinsteden assumed he had at the moment.

Sinsteden, Wilhelm Josef. German physician (b. Kleve, Westphalia, May 6, 1803, d. Xanten am Rhein, Westphalia, 1871?). Although Sinsteden worked as a surgeon (M.D., Friedrich-Wilhelm Institute, Berlin, 1828), his writings were primarily on vision and electricity. He was at the Friedrich-Wilhelm Institute from 1832 to 1839 and then, until 1871, in Pasewalk, serving as regimental surgeon. He presented the windmill in 1860 (*Ann. Phys. Chem., 187,* 336–39).

Biographies: ADB, 34; Hirsch, *Biog. Lex.*

SISYPHUS DREAM. Frustration dream.

Sisyphus. Sisyphus was a king of Corinth who had drawn the wrath of Zeus upon himself for telling the river god Asopus that he had seen Zeus, in the form of an eagle, carry off Asopus' daughter. In Hades, Sisyphus was condemned to roll a large stone up a hill, a stone that would foreover roll down on him.

SJOGREN-LARSSON SYNDROME. Hereditary mental retardation, with spastic paralysis and ichthyosis. A synonym is Rud's syndrome.*

Sjögren, Torsten. Swedish psychiatrist (b. Södertälje, January 30, 1896). Sjögren obtained the Med. lic. degree from the University of Stockholm in 1925 and the Med. dr. degree from the University of Lund in 1931. He held various hospital and other medical appointments from 1925 to 1945 and was at the Karolinska Institute, Stockholm, from 1945 to 1961, when he retired. Sjögren and Larsson published a joint paper on the syndrome in 1957 (*Acta psychiat. neurol. scand.,* Suppl. 113, 1–112).

Biographies: Vem ar Det? Svensk biografisk Handbok. Norstedt, 1973.

Larsson, Tage Konrad Leopold. Swedish statistician (b. Köpinge, Malmö, November 11, 1905). Larsson received the master's degree in 1927 and the lic. fil. degree in 1933 from the University of Lund. He was awarded an honorary

M.D. degree by the University of Stockholm in 1951. From 1929 to 1934 Larsson was assistant in statistics at the University of Lund and then held life insurance positions in Skandia and Thule from 1934 to 1970. Larsson's writings are on statistics, insurance, taxation, and human genetics.

Biographies: Vem ar Det? Svensk biografisk Handbok. Norstedt, 1973.

SKAGGS-ROBINSON HYPOTHESIS. A statement of the expected relationship between the efficiency of recall and the degree of similarity between materials learned originally and interpolated activity. Maximum similarity leads to maximum recall. Recall decreases with decreasing similarity, but maximum dissimilarity increases recall again.

Skaggs, Ernest Burton. American psychologist (b. Gatesville, Florida, July 7, 1893). Skaggs' Ph.D. was from the University of Michigan (1923). After 1924, he was on the faculty of the College of the City of Detroit. Skaggs' research was on learning. In 1925, he wrote a monograph on retroactive inhibition (*Psychol. Monog., 34,* No. 161). Robinson formulated the hypothesis using Skaggs' work and his own (*Amer. J. Psychol.,* 1927, *39,* 297–312), and the psychologist John McGeoch later named it after the two researchers.

Biographies: APA Dir., 1947; *PR,* 3.

Robinson, Edward Stevens. See KJERSTAD-ROBINSON LAW.

SKINNER BOX. A boxlike enclosure for keeping an animal whose learning behavior is being studied in the vicinity of a device that, when properly activated, delivers a reward to the animal. Depending on the animal species used, the device may be a bar, lever, key, or window connected to a food magazine. The frequency of the presentation of the reward is under the control of the experimenter, while the bar pressing or key pecking is produced by the animal, and its acquisition is shaped by the schedule of reinforced trials.

SKINNERIAN CONDITIONING. A term sometimes used for operant conditioning, or learning that occurs when the spontaneous emission of a behavior is followed by a reinforcer, so that the probability of the repeated occurrence of the behavior is increased.

Skinner, Burrhus Frederick. American psychologist (b. Susquehanna, Pennsylvania, March 20, 1904). Skinner is the most eminent living psychologist. His ideas have stimulated countless experimental analyses of behavior, prompted a wide repertoire of practical applications, from teaching machines to behavior modification to the founding of utopian communities, and stimulated a passionate debate concerning the control of human behavior. Having decided that he was not cut out to be a writer, Skinner turned to psychology, obtaining his Ph.D. from Harvard University in 1931. Before and after graduation, Skinner was a research fellow at Harvard. He went to the University of Minnesota in 1936 and from there to Indiana in 1945. He returned to Harvard in 1948, remaining there until the present. Skinner's major works are *Behavior of Organisms* (1938), *Walden Two* (1948), and *Beyond Freedom and Dignity* (1971). Skinner developed the animal training box during 1930 and 1931.

Biographies: AM&WS, 1978S; *Amer. Psychologist,* 1972, 27, 71–72; *ConAu,* 9R; *HPA,* 5; *IESS,* 18; *McGMSE,* 3; B. F. Skinner, *Particulars of My Life,* 1976; B. F. Skinner, *The Shaping of a Behaviorist,* 1979; B. F. Skinner, *A Matter of Consequences,* 1983; *Time,* Sept. 20, 1971; *WhoAm,* 1984–1985.

SLOSSON INTELLIGENCE TEST. An oral intelligence test of 195 items arranged on a chronological scale from fifteen days to twenty-seven years. It yields an estimate of mental age and IQ.

Slosson, Richard Lawrence, Jr. American psychologist (b. July 18, 1910). From 1932 to 1941 Slosson worked for the *Buffalo Evening News* and from 1941 to 1948 was a psychologist in the U.S. Army. From 1948 to 1963 he was a child psychologist at the Erie County Health Department, Buffalo. He obtained the M.A. degree from the University of Buffalo in 1954. Beginning in 1963, Slosson was a rehabilitation psychologist with the Division of Vocational Rehabilitation, New York State, and director of Slosson Educational Publications, Inc. The test was published in 1961.

Biographies: APA Dir., 1968.

SNELLEN CHART (SNELLEN LETTERS). A chart containing specially designed letters of different sizes, used to test visual acuity. Each letter fits a square area, the height of a letter being five times the width of the stroke. The row of the smallest letter at the bottom of the chart subtends a visual angle of one minute and can be seen by a person with normal vision from a distance of twenty feet (20/20 vision).

Snellen, Hermann. Dutch ophthalmologist (b. Zeist [Utrecht], February 19, 1834, d. Utrecht, January 18, 1908). After graduating with an M.D. from the University of Utrecht in 1857, Snellen practiced privately as an ophthalmologist until 1862. From 1862 until 1899, Snellen taught at the Netherlands Hospital for Eye Disease and was its director until 1903. From 1877 to 1889 he was also professor at the University of Utrecht. Snellen published numerous articles in ophthalmology and other medical topics. The letters were presented in his monograph, *Optotipi, ad visum determinandum* (1862), which was translated in many languages and saw many editions in each.

Biographies: EI, 31; Hirsch, *Biog. Lex.;* Pagel, *Biog. Lex.*

SODOMY. Anal intercourse between males, sexual intercourse with animals, or, more generally, any other illicit or unnatural sexual act. The verb *to sodomize* and the noun *sodomite* are additional derivatives.

Sodom. Ancient city at the southern end of the Dead Sea, which, according to the Bible, was destroyed by brimstone and fire that God rained upon it from heaven because its men engaged in homosexuality (Gen. 19). In sixteenth-century England, the name of Sodom's twin city Gomorrah was attached to lesbians, called gomorrheans.

SOMMER TRIDIMENSIONAL MOVEMENT ANALYZER. An instrument for the recording in a single plane, such as the kymograph tape, the three spatial components of the free movements of the arm and two fingers. It was used to record involuntary responses to such stimuli as odors.

Sommer, Robert. German psychiatrist (b. Grottkau, Silesia, December 19, 1864, d. Giessen, February 2, 1937). Sommer had both the Ph.D. (Berlin, 1887) and M.D. degrees (University of Würzburg, 1891). He worked in a psychiatric clinic in Würzburg from 1890 to 1895 and was on the faculty of the University of Würzburg (1892–1895). From 1895 to 1933 he directed the psychiatric clinic at Giessen. Sommer stood for a psychophysiologically oriented medicine. Influenced by Wilhelm Wundt,* with whom he had worked in 1888 and 1889, Sommer sought to apply the methods of experimental psychology to psychiatry. He invented a number of pieces of apparatus for psychophysiological research, including the movement analyzer to record expressive movements, which he first reported in a congress of internal medicine (E. Leyden & E. Pfeiffer [eds.], *Verhandlungen des Congresses für innere Medicin*, Wiesbaden, 1896, pp. 573–76). A more complete description, with drawings, appeared in 1898 (*Z. Psychol. Physiol. Sinnesorg.*, *16*, 278–97). Sommer produced many other works in psychiatry, psychology, and neuropathology.
    Biographies: Fischer, *Biog. Lex.*; *EUI*, 57; *PR*, 3; M. Meyer zum Wischen, *Gesch. Psychol.*, 1986, *3* (no. 7), 8–10.

SPEARMAN-BROWN PROPHECY FORMULA. A formula for predicting, from the original correlation, the reliability of a test that has been lengthened or shortened.

SPEARMAN RANK-ORDER CORRELATION COEFFICIENT. A product-moment correlation coefficient for ranked data, symbolized by the Greek letter rho.

Spearman, Charles Edward. English psychologist (b. London, September 10, 1863, d. London, September 17, 1945). Spearman received his Ph.D. from the University of Leipzig in 1904. He spent several years in postdoctoral study with Oswald Külpe and Georg Müller.* From 1906 to 1931 he was at University College, London. Spearman's most important contributions lie in the areas of the structure of intelligence and of statistics. He proposed the two-factor theory of intelligence (one general factor, several specific factors) and contributed to the development of factor analysis, the extension of the use of correlation measures to infer structures and processes, and several specific statistical procedures. Spearman proposed the prophecy formula in 1910 (*Brit. J. Psychol.*, *3*, 271–95).

He presented the rank-order correlation coefficient in 1904 (*Amer. J. Psychol., 15,* 72–101).

Biographies: C. Burt & C. S. Myers, *Psychol. Rev.,* 1946, *53,* 67–71; R. B. Cattell, *J. Pers.,* 1945–1946, *14,* 85–92; *CurBio,* 1945; J. C. Flugel, *Brit. J. Psychol.,* 1946, *37,* 1–6; *HPA,* 1; *IESS,* 15; E. L. Thorndike, *Amer. J. Psychol.,* 1945, *58,* 558–60.

Brown, William. English psychologist (b. Slinfold, Sussex, December 5, 1881, d. Oxford, May 17, 1952). Brown received a D.Sc. in mathematics from the University of London (1910) and a D.M. from Oxford University (1918). He was a reader in psychology at the University of London from 1914 to 1921 and held the Wilde Readership in Mental Philosophy at Oxford from 1921 to 1947. He also directed the Institute of Experimental Psychology at Oxford from 1936 to 1945 and acted as a psychotherapist at King's College Hospital from 1925 to 1931. In his most important work, *Essentials of Mental Measurement* (1911, revised editions with G. H. Thompson in 1921 and 1925), Brown attempted to give a joint treatment to psychophysical methods and psychological statistics. Later in his career, Brown devoted increasingly more time to abnormal psychology and psychiatry, publishing half a dozen books in the area. He published the prophecy formula simultaneously with Spearman (*Brit. J. Psychol.,* 1910, *3,* 296–322).

Biographies: Brit. Med. J., 1952, No. 4768, 1136; *Lancet,* 1952, *262,* 1073, 1119; *Nature,* 1952, *170,* 911; J. D. Sutherland, *Brit. J. Med. Psychol.,* 1953, *26,* 1.

SPIELMEYER-VOGT DISEASE. Amaurotic familial idiocy that begins between the ages of six and twelve and results in death in two years. It is characterized by cerebroretinal degeneration and represents a variety of Tay-Sachs disease.*

Spielmeyer, Walther. German neurologist (b. Dessau, 1879, d. 1935). Spielmeyer's M.D. was from the University of Halle. He was at the universities of Freiburg (1906–1911) and Munich (1911–1928) and from 1928 to 1935 at the Kaiser-Wilhelm Institut. His work was on the histopathology of the nervous system (*Histopathologie des Nervensystems,* 1922). His description of the disease was published in 1908 in *Nissle Beiträge zu Nerven- und Geisteskrankheiten,* Berlin).

Biographies: Haymaker.

Vogt, Oskar. German neurologist (b. Husum, Prussia, April 6, 1870, d. Freiburg, Baden, August 3, 1959). Until 1937, Vogt was the director of the Brain Research Institute at Berlin-Buch. He worked in various military hospitals during World War II. With his wife, Martha Vogt, a physiologist, he studied the structure of the human brain, availing himself of the largest collection of brains in the world. He was the neurologist who examined Lenin's brain after Lenin died. Vogt's description of the disease appeared in 1905 (*Mschr. Psychiat. Neurol., 18,* 161–71, 310–57).

Biographies: Amer. Med. Ass. J., 1959, *171,* 231; *WoWhoSci; NYT,* Aug. 11, 1959, 27.

SPILLMAN-REDIES EFFECT. If the Ehrenstein illusion* is placed on a background of random dots, instead of brightness enhancement in the illusory areas, apparent change in the texture of the background is observed within these areas. The dots appear to be less densely packed, and the seemingly circular illusory areas appear to lie in front of the background. If the random-dot background is moved with respect to the stationary Ehrenstein illusion, the illusory patches seem to move in the same direction.

SPILLMAN'S ILLUSION. A variant of the Hermann grid,* expanded to include both white squares and dark alleys and black squares and light allays. In addition, there is a gradient of lightness in the alleys from top to bottom of the grid and from left to right. As a result, light regions are seen in the intersections of dark alleys on light background and dark regions at the intersections of light alleys on dark background when the alleys subtend a visual angle of six to eighteen minutes at the observer's eye.

Spillman, Lothar A. D. German psychologist (b. Münsterberg, Silesia, April 11, 1938). Spillman obtained his Ph.D. from the University of Freiburg in 1964. He was research associate at MIT from 1964 to 1966 and the Retina Foundation, Boston, from 1966 to 1970. From 1967 to 1971, Spillman was assistant in ophthalmic optics at the Massachusetts Eye and Ear Infirmary, Boston. He has been head of the Psychophysics Laboratory of the Neurological Clinic at the University of Freiburg and professor of visual psychophysics and perception since 1971. Spillman and Redies presented the effect in a joint paper in 1981 (*Perception, 10,* 411–15). It was named after them by D. M. McKay (*Perception, 1981, 10,* 417–20). The illusion was published by Spillman and J. Levine in 1971 (*Exp. Brain Res., 13,* 547–59).
Biographies: Unavailable.

Redies, Christoph. German biophysicist (b. Krefeld, North Rhine-Westphalia, July 19, 1958). Redies obtained the M.D. degree from the University of Gottingen in 1984. He did psychophysical and biophysical research at the universities of Freiburg (1979–1982) and Göttingen (1982–1984) and is now at the Montreal Neurological Institute of McGill University.
Biographies: Unavailable.

STANFORD ACHIEVEMENT TEST. A standard achievement test battery for grades one through nine. One of the earliest standard achievement tests, it has been revised several times to reflect changes in educational programs. The norms are based on hundreds of thousands of students from hundreds of communities throughout the United States.

STANFORD-BINET INTELLIGENCE SCALE. The adaptation to American conditions of the Binet-Simon Scale.* It is an individually administered test, the current version of which measures intelligence of individuals aged two through adulthood. The test items are grouped into age levels, each level containing six items. Each item presents a task, such as verbal memory or the recognition of absurdities. For passing an item, a credit of two months of mental age is given. Items are administered beginning with the age level at which all are answered correctly and ending with the level where all are failed.

Stanford University. The achievement test battery was developed by Truman L. Kelley,* Richard Madden, Eric F. Gardner, and Herbert C. Rudman and published in 1923. At that time (1920–1931), Kelley was at Stanford University, hence the name. Although Henry Goddard had prepared the first adaptation of the Binet-Simon Scale in the English language in 1910, it was Lewis M. Terman's* version that prevailed. Terman published his version in 1916 and, again, with Maude A. Merrill* in 1937. A further revision occurred in 1960. The Stanford-Binet Intelligence Scale was named after Stanford University because Terman was on its faculty when he adapted Binet's scale (1910–1943).

STATUE OF CONDILLAC. In arguing that all of our mental life could be derived from sensation alone, neither reflection nor innate ideas being necessary, Etienne de Condillac imagined a statue, endowed with nothing but a single sense, that from that one sense alone would quite naturally develop attention, memory, judgment, discrimination, and other abstract qualities.

Condillac, Etienne Bonnot de. French philosopher (b. Grenoble, Isère, September 30, 1715, d. Beaugency, Loiret, August 3, 1780). Condillac studied theology at Saint Suplice, Sorbonne, and was ordained in 1740. He held various appointments as priest and tutor. Condillac, a philosophical empiricist and sensationalist, introduced John Locke's philosophy to France. He presented Locke's ideas in his *Essai sur l'origine des connaissances* (1746), but his best-known work is the *Traiteé des sensations* (1754). It includes the famous statue analogy.
  Biographies: DSB, 3; EB, 6; EP, 2; IESS, 3.

STERNBERG TASK. A task for the experimental study of human memory. The subject is presented with a set of four or five items to memorize. Then a single item is presented, and the subject must state as quickly as possible whether the item was part of the set.

Sternberg, Saul. American psychologist (b. New York City, August 30, 1933). Sternberg has a Ph.D. in social psychology from Harvard University (1960). He was at the University of Pennsylvania from 1960 to 1964 and has been with the Bell Telephone Laboratories since 1964. His main research areas have been human information processing and memory. He introduced the task in 1969 (*Amer. Scientist, 57,* 421–57).
  Biographies: AM&WS, 1978S; APA Dir., 1985.

STERN VARIATOR. A device by means of which pure tones of variable frequency may be produced by varying the length of a resonating air column. An attached scale gives readings of the frequency of vibrations.

Stern, (Louis) William. German psychologist (b. Berlin, April 29, 1871, d. Durham, North Carolina, March 27, 1938). Stern's Ph.D. in psychology was from the University of Berlin (1893). He held appointments at the universities of Breslau (1897–1916) and Hamburg (1916–1933) and Duke University (1933–1938). Stern was a versatile man. In a 1903 pamphlet he presented both the concept and the term *applied psychology,* as well as *psychotechnics.* In a three-volume work, *Person und Sache: System der philosophischen Weltanschauung* (1906), Stern presented a synthesis of laboratory psychology and "understanding psychology." In the area of developmental psychology, he published several books, introduced a developmental theory (the convergence theory), and introduced the concept of the mental quotient. His name is also associated with the concept of differential psychology. Stern's publications number 139. He introduced his variator in the book, *Psychologie der Veränderungsauffassung* (1898).
    Biographies: G. W. Allport, *Amer. J. Psychol.,* 1938, *51,* 770–74; *CE,* 13; *EJ,* 15; *EP,* 8; *IESS,* 15; *Jewish,* 10; R. B. McLeod, *Psychol. Rev.,* 1938, *45,* 347–53; *PR,* 3.

STEVENS' LAW. Also known as the power law, it was the second major law of psychophysics to appear after Fechner's* logarithmic law. According to this law, to equal stimulus ratios there correspond equal ratios in sensation, or sensation is directly proportional to a power of the stimulus.

Stevens, Stanley Smith. American psychologist (b. Ogden, Utah, November 4, 1906, d. Vail, Colorado, January 18, 1973). Stevens' Ph.D. was from Harvard University (1933), and he returned there in 1936 to remain as professor of psychophysics for the rest of his career. He became the most prominent psychophysicist of the twentieth century. His early work was on audition. Stevens constructed isophonic curves, introduced the mel and sone units, and showed that the perception of pitch and loudness was quantal rather than continuous (*Hearing,* 1938, with H. Davis). In his scaling work (*Theory of Scales,* 1941), Stevens developed the direct scaling methods. He found that when scaled by these methods, most physical continua obeyed the power law. He presented the power law in 1953 (*Science, 118,* 576). Stevens wrote more than 150 articles. He also edited the classic handbook, *The Handbook of Experimental Psychology* (1951), and was a coauthor of two books on somatotypes.
    Biographies: AM&WS, 1976P; *Amer. Psychologist,* 1960, *15,* 794–97; *Biog. Mem. NAS,* 47; *HPA,* 6; *McGMSE,* 3.

STILES-CRAWFORD EFFECT. Light beams that pass through the middle of the pupil are stronger than those that enter along the edges of the pupil.

Stiles, Walter Stanley. English physicist (b. June 15, 1901). Stiles was a scientific officer at the National Physical Laboratory from 1925 to 1961, when he retired. He obtained a Ph.D. from the University of London in 1929 and a D.Sc.

in 1939. Stiles is the author of *Color Science* (1967, with G. Wyszecki), *Mechanisms of Color Vision* (1978), and many papers on illumination engineering and physiological optics. Stiles and Crawford described the effect in a joint paper in 1933 (*Proc. Roy Soc., 112B*, 428–50).
Biographies: Who, 1986–1987.

Crawford, Brian Hewson. English physiologist. Crawford had the D.Sc. degree from the University of London (1948). He was with the Rodenside Laboratory of Ilford, Ltd., from 1926 to 1929 and then joined the National Physical Laboratory at Teddington. His work has been on color, lighting, and photometry.
Biographies: Directory of British Scientists, vol. 1. London: E. Benn, 1966–1967.

STILLING TEST. A test of color weakness consisting of charts made up of multicolor dots. Some of the dots of like color form numerals that are visible to the normal but not the color-weak eye.

Stilling, Jakob. German ophthalmologist (b. Kassel, September 22, 1842, d. Strasbourg, April 30, 1915). Stilling received his M.D. in 1865. He practiced ophthalmology in Kassel from 1867 to 1880 and then joined the faculty of the University of Strasbourg. Stilling's research was on myopia, color vision, and perimetry. He used his color vision test first in 1877 (*Die Prüfung des Farbensinnes beim Eisenbahn- und Marinepersonal*), publishing the plates in 1878 (*Pseudo-isochromatische Tafeln*). It was the first color-blindness test to use isochromatic plates and was later adapted and modfied by Shinobu Ishihara* in his own test.
Biographies: Fischer, Biog. Lex.; Pagel, Biog. Lex.

STRATTON'S EXPERIMENT. A classic experiment in which Stratton wore lenses that turned the world 180 degrees for eighty-seven hours, distributed over eight days. The experiment answered questions about perceptual and behavioral changes that take place during prolonged exposure to an inverted world.

Stratton, George Malcolm. American psychologist (b. Oakland, California, September 26, 1865, d. Berkeley, California, October 8, 1957).

Stratton obtained his Ph.D. in psychology under Wilhelm Wundt* in 1896. Stratton was at the University of California at Berkeley from 1896 to 1904 and again from 1908 to 1935, with the intervening years at Johns Hopkins University. He did research on sensations at the University of Leipzig and established a psychological laboratory at the University of California upon his arrival there. Stratton is remembered primarily for having performed the first of the very few experiments on the effects of prolonged distortion of the visual field (*Psychol. Rev.*, 1897, *4*, 341–60, 463–81).
Biographies: Biog. Mem. NAS, 35; O. Bridgman, *Amer. J. Psychol.*, 1958, *71*, 460–61; C. W. Brown, *Science*, 1958, *127*, 1432–33; *NCAB*, 13; *WhAm*, 3.

STRAUSS SYNDROME. A pattern of hyperactivity, perseveration, and perceptual disorders seen in certain children with learning disability. Also known as minimal brain dysfunction syndrome.

Strauss, Alfred Adolph. German-American psychiatrist (b. Karlsruhe, Germany, May 29, 1897, d. Chicago, Illinois, October 27, 1957). Strauss' M.D. (1922) was from the University of Heidelberg. After internship and residency in psychiatry and neurology (1922–1927), he went into private practice. He left Germany for Spain and was on the faculty of the University of Barcelona from 1933 to 1937. Strauss was at the Wayne County School in Northville, Michigan, from 1937 to 1949 and was president of Cove Schools in Racine, Michigan, which he also founded. Strauss' main field of interest was the diagnosis and education of brain-damaged children. His *Psychopathology and Education of the Brain Injured Child* (vol. 1, 1947, with L. E. Lethinen; vol. 2, 1955, with N. C. Kephart) served as guideline for school programs treating children with minimal brain damage. The syndrome was described in the first volume of this work.
    Biographies: R. A. Gardiner, *Excep. Child.*, 1958, *24*, 373–74; *J. Spec. Educ.*, 1973, 7(1), 2–3.

STREET FIGURES. Representations of objects made to look like incomplete mosaics. Although the figure may be difficult to see at first, it comes into view as soon as the total configuration is apprehended.

Street, Roy F. American psychologist (b. Englewood, Colorado, December 12, 1898). Street, who received his Ph.D. from Columbia University in 1931, held a position with the Kellogg Foundation from 1931 to 1938. He went into private practice as a consulting psychologist in 1941. Street specialized in speech and language development and pathology, as well as the development of clinical tests. The figures were published in 1931 (*Teach. Coll. Contr. Educ.*, No. 481).
    Biographies: APA Dir., 1948.

STRONG VOCATIONAL INTEREST BLANK FOR MEN. An interest inventory that provides scores for fifty-four occupations. The rationale is that if one's pattern of interests resembles that of people who are successful in a given occupation, the probability that one will succeed in this occupation is higher than for other occupations. There is also an SVIB for Women, now published under the name of Strong-Campbell Interest Inventory.

Strong, Edward Kellog, Jr. American psychologist (b. Syracuse, New York, August 18, 1884, d. Menlo Park, California, December 4, 1963). Strong obtained his Ph.D. in psychology from Columbia University in 1911. He subsequently served on the faculties of the George Peabody College of Teachers (1914–1917), Carnegie Institute of Technology (1919–1923), and Stanford University (1923–1949). Strong was an industrial psychologist prominent in vocational interest measurement (*Vocational Interests of Men and Women*, 1943; *Vocational*

Interests 18 Years After College, 1955). The Vocational Interest Blank was first published in 1927.

Biographies: J. G. Darley, *J. Appl. Psychol.*, 1964, *48*, 74–75; *NCAB*, 51; *WhAm*, 4.

STROOP EFFECT. The longer response time in naming colors than in reading names of colors, especially the interference in the naming task by the reading task and the even longer response time when the colors are presented in the form of words, the words spelling out color names different from the colors in which they are printed (for example, the word *green* printed in red ink).

Stroop, John Ridley. American psychologist (b. Murfreesboro, Tennessee, March 21, 1897). With a Ph.D. in psychology from Peabody College (1933), Stroop held a number of positions in the Tennessee educational system; he was professor of psychology and department head of Lipscomb College from 1936 to 1964 and professor of Bible from 1954 to 1967. He was dean and registrar of Ohio Valley College from 1967 to 1971. Stroop's main interest was in religion, and his publications are mainly in this area. He described the color effect in 1935 (*J. Exp. Psychol.*, *18*, 643–62).

Biographies: AM&WS, 1973S.

STUDENTIZED RANGE STATISTIC. A statistic used to test the hypothesis that there is no difference between the means of treatments in a single factor experiment. It is defined as the ratio of the difference between the largest and the smallest treatment means and the quantity mean-square experimental error over *n*.

STUDENT'S *t*. A statistic used to test the hypothesis of no difference between the means of two samples of elements when the sample size is twenty-five or smaller. It is the ratio of the difference between the means and the standard error of the difference between the means.

Student, pseud. Gosset, William Sealy. English statistician (b. Canterbury, Kent, June 13, 1876, d. London, October 16, 1937). Gosset studied chemistry and mathematics at Oxford University. He then entered the service of the brewers Guinness, Son & Co., first in Dublin (1899–1935) and later in London (1935–1937). He produced his statistical work while working as a brewer and later as a statistician but was prohibited by the company's rules from publishing his research on the variability in the brewing process. The rules were relaxed to allow Gosset to publish under a pseudonym, for which he chose "Student." The paper on the *t* statistic was published under that pseudonym (*Biometrika*, 1908–1909, *6*, 1–25).

Biographies: DNB, Suppl. 4; DSB, 5; R. A. Fisher, *Ann. Eugen.*, 1939, *9*, 1–9; L. McMullen, *Biometrika*, 1939, *30*, 205–210; *IESS*, 6; E. S. Pearson, *Biometrika*, 1939, *30*, 210–50.

STURGE-WEBER DISEASE. The disease encephalotrigeminal angiomatosis caused by a dominant gene and characterized by an angioma in the area innervated by the trigeminal nerve and ipsilateral calcification in the occipital cortex. Epilepsy, mental retardation, and hemiparesis are present in this disease.

Sturge, William Allen. English physician (b. Bristol, 1850, d. Mildenhall, Suffolk, March 27, 1919). Sturge, who received his M.D. from the University of London, practiced in London hospitals, as well as in Nice, France (1881–1907). He wrote papers on various medical subjects and was also known for his large private collection of ancient artifacts. His description of the disease appeared in 1879 (*Clin. Soc. London, Trans., 12,* 162).

  Biographies: G. H. Brown (comp.), *Lives of the Fellows of the Royal College of Physicians of London, 1826–1925,* 1955, pp. 352–53; *Wh,* 1916–1928.

Weber, Frederick Parkes. English physician (b. London, May 8, 1863, d. London, June 2, 1962). Weber's M.D. was from Cambridge University (1892). He practiced at several hospitals, as well as privately, and published many works on rare diseases, congenital abnormalities, balneology, and other topics. His contribution to the understanding of encephalotrigeminal angiomatosis was made in 1922 (*J. Neurol. Psychopath.,* London, *37,* 301–11).

  Biographies: Brit. Med. J., May 9, 1953, No. 4818, 1044; *Wh,* 1961–1970.

SWINDLE'S GHOST. A prolonged positive afterimage.

Swindle, Percy Ford. American psychologist (b. Newtonia, Missouri, 1889, d. n.a.). After receiving an A.M. from the University of Missouri in 1912, Swindle went to the University of Berlin for his Ph.D. (1915). He was at four different universities between 1916 and 1920 and then joined the faculty of Marquette University in 1920. Swindle's research was on physiological and comparative subjects. He described the prolonged afterimage in 1916 (*Amer. J. Psychol., 27,* 324–34).

  Biographies: APA Dir., 1930; *PR,* 3.

SYDENHAM'S CHOREA. A form of acute chorea, characterized by irritability, agitation, and sometimes delirium. The chorea was the basis of the medieval outbreaks of the so-called St. Vitus' dance.*

Sydenham, Thomas. English physician (b. Wynford Eagle, near Dorchester, 1624 [baptized September 10], d. London, December 29, 1689). The civil war interrupted Sydenham's medical studies, and he never did receive much training in medicine. He was "created" bachelor of medicine in 1648 and then participated actively in the war on the side of Oliver Cromwell. He began practicing medicine in 1655 and eventually revolutionized clinical medicine by refocusing it from theory- and speculation-based treatment to one that centered on the patient's actual condition and needs. After the Restoration, Sydenham studied the periodic epidemics in London and wrote a treatise on them in 1666. Others followed, *Observationes medicae* (1676) being the most important one. Various medical innovations were among his other accomplishments. In his last book, *Schedula* *monitoria de novae febris ingressu* (1785), Sydenham described the chorea that bears his name.

Biographies: K. Dewhurst, *Dr. Thomas Sydenham,* 1966; *DNB,* 55; *DSB,* 13.

University of North Dakota from 1958 to 1962 and has been at Harvard University Also known as the lateral fissure, it is one of the two most prominent fissures on the side of the cerebral cortex. It extends horizontally and separates the temporal lobe from the frontal and parietal lobes of the cortex.

Sylvius, Jacobus. French anatomist (b. Louisville, near Amiens, 1478, d. Paris, January 13, 1555). Jacobus Sylvius is the Latinized form of Jacques Dubois. Dubois was poor and could not finish the Collége at Tournay, turning to teaching anatomy. He then went to Montpellier and obtained an M.B. in 1529 and an M.D. in 1530. Upon returning to Paris, he resumed the teaching of anatomy at the Collége de Tréguier. Andreas Vesalius and Michael Servetus were among his students. He stressed the naming rather than numbering of muscles and blood vessels and introduced a series of terms by which to describe them. Of the six anatomical structures that bear his name, only the valve of the heart known as the Eustachian valve was first clearly described by him. The others, including the Sylvian fissure, had been identified and described prior to the publication of Sylvius' anatomical works. As a coincidence, the Sylvian fissure was first described by the Dutch physician Franciscus Sylvius, or François de la Boë (1614–1672).

Biographies: F. Baker, *Bull. Johns Hopkins Hosp.,* 1909, *20,* 329–339; *DSB,* 4; *Talbot.*

SYMONDS' PICTURE-STORY TEST. A projective personality test, patterned after the Thematic Apperception Test but intended for adolescents. It consists of twenty pictures depicting situations of interest to adolescents, about which the respondent tells a story. The responses are analyzed to establish the motivational dynamics that gave rise to them.

Symonds, Percival Mallon. American psychologist (b. Newtonville, Massachusetts, April 18, 1893, d. New York City, August 6, 1960). Symond's Ph.D. was in educational psychology (Columbia University, 1923). He held faculty appointments at the University of Hawaii from 1922 to 1924 and Teachers College, Columbia University, from 1924 to 1958. Symonds was the author of twenty-one books, more than two hundred articles, and many inventories and questionnaires in the areas of educational and psychological measurement, personality assessment, the psychology of adolescence, and the psychology of the teacher. The Picture-Story Test was published in 1948.

Biographies: *NCAB,* 46; *WhAm,* 4.

SZONDI TEST. A projective personality test that consists of forty-eight photographs of psychiatric patients. The respondent's expressed preferences and rejections are taken as indications of his or her own mental problems.

Szondi, Leopold. Hungarian psychoanalyst, (b. Nyitra, Hungary [now Czecho-slovakia], March 11, 1893). Szondi obtained the M.D. degree from the University of Budapest in 1919. He held positions at the Hochschule fur Heilpädagogik in Budapest from 1924 to 1941, was put in a concentration camp by the Germans in 1944, and then emigrated to Switzerland. Szondi's psychoanalysis attempts to combine Freudian analysis with hereditary notions in a *Schicksalsanalyse,* or "destiny analysis." Szondi began work on the test in 1937. The diagnostic pictures first appeared in 1947 in his *Experimentelle Triebdiagnostik.*

Biographies: Bonin; PR, 3.

T

TADOMA METHOD. A method of communication used by the deaf and deaf-blind in which their fingers are placed on the speaker's lips, cheeks, nose, and throat to pick up vibrations.

Tadoma. A combination of the names of Tad Chapman and Oma Simpson, the first two children instructed by this method by its originator, Sophia K. Alcorn. Alcorn, a graduate of Clarke School for the Deaf, Northampton, Massachusetts, and Wayne University, developed the method while at the Kentucky School for the Deaf, Danville, Kentucky. She subsequently taught at schools for the deaf in Sioux Falls, North Dakota; Cincinnati, Ohio; and Detroit, Michigan.
   Biographies: S. Alcorn, *J. Exc. Child.*, 1945, *11*, 117–19.

TALBOT. A unit (*Q*) of radiant light energy.

TALBOT BRIGHTNESS. The fused luminance of an intermittent light stimulus.

TALBOT-PLATEAU LAW. A statement of the relationship between the duration of the on phase of an intermittent light and its brightness. When a flickering light reaches a frequency at which it is perceived as steady, its brightness, in comparison to a steady light, is reduced by the ratio of the time the light is actually on and the total time (on time plus off time). The fused luminance is called Talbot brightness.*

Talbot, William Henry Fox. English inventor (b. Melbury House, Dorsetshire, February 11, 1800, d. Lacock Abbey, Wiltshire, September 17, 1877). Talbot graduated from Cambridge University in 1821 but did not hold any academic positions, being active as a gentleman-scholar. He became an eponym in the field of the study of light because of his interest in photography, a field he entered in 1833 after a brief attempt at a political career. Independently of Daguerre, he invented a photographic process, the calotype, patenting it in 1841. Talbotype used, for the first time, a negative from which any number of positive prints could be obtained. It led to the publication in 1844 of the first book illustrated with photographs. Further work by Talbot led to a drastic reduction in the exposure times required to produce a photograph. In his 1829 dissertation, Plateau introduced the initial version of the law. He wrote again (*Bull. Acad. roy. sci. lett.*, Bruxelles, 1835, 2, 52–59), discussing the principle and giving it specific formulation. The law came to be called the Talbot-Plateau law after Talbot had used it in photometric matches (*Phil. Trans. Roy. Soc.*, 1834, 3, 298).

   Biographies: Asimov; A. H. Booth, *William Henry Fox Talbot,* 1965; *DNB,* 55; *DSB,* 13; *EB,* 21; A. Jammes, *William H. Fox Talbot, Inventor of the Negative-Positive Process,* 1973.

Plateau, J. A. F. See PLATEAU'S SPIRAL.

TARCHANOFF PHENOMENON. A form of galvanic skin response* that is observed without applying electric current to the skin, that is, differences in potential that may be observed between any two points of the skin. These differences vary further as a function of the activity of the nervous system, especially arousal.

Tarchanoff (Tarkhanov), Ivan Ramazovich. Russian physiologist (b. Tblisi, Georgia, June 3, 1846, d. Krzeszowice, Galicia [or St. Petersburg], September 6, 1908). I. R. Tarkhanov, also known as I. R. Tarkhanishvili and I. R. Tarkhanov-Muravi, was a Russian prince who signed the papers he published in German as Johann Tarchanow. He studied medicine at the Medico-Surgical Academy and the University of St. Petersburg, graduating in 1869, and physiology at various physiological institutes abroad. He was professor of physiology at the Medico-Surgical Academy from 1875 to 1895 and at the University of St. Petersburg from 1895 to 1901. Tarkhanov studied central nervous system functions, sleep, hypnosis, and secretions. He was one of the first to note the effect of X-rays on living organisms. He described the eponymous effect in 1890 (*Pflügers Arch. ges. Physiol.,* 46, 46–55).

   Biographies: Soviet, 25.

TARTINI'S TONE. A difference tone, or a tone generated by two tones of different frequencies, with a frequency equal to the difference between the two generating frequencies.

Tartini, Giuseppe. Italian musician (b. Pirano, Istria, April 8, 1692, d. Padua, February 26, 1770). Tartini, a violinist and composer, first studied at Padua. While teaching himself violin at the monastery of Assisi he noticed that, when double-stopping, a third tone could be heard in addition to the tones produced by the two bowed strings. This was in 1714, but he did not describe the phenomenon in print until 1754 (*Trattato di musica secondo la vera scienza dell' armonia*). By that time, the phenomenon of difference tones had been rediscovered twice by others: G. A. Sorge in 1744 and J. B. Romieu in 1751. In 1716, Tartini went to Venice and then to Ancona, but he later returned to Padua. He wrote a large number of musical works, as well as several volumes on the theory of music.

   Biographies: EB, 21; S. Sadie (ed.), *The New Grove Dictionary of Music and Musicians*, v. 18, 1980.

TAYLORISM. The first formal system of scientific management, developed by F. W. Taylor. In a narrower sense, it is a system for improving industrial efficiency through the use of time-and-motion studies and wage incentives. In a broader sense, scientific management stresses the adoption of a scientific attitude and objective measures to work methods and workers' performance.

Taylor, Frederick Winslow. American engineer (b. Germantown, Pennsylvania, March 20, 1856, d. Philadelphia, Pennsylvania, March 21, 1915). Taylor graduated from the Phillips Exeter Academy. Eye problems forced him to abandon his early education plans and to take a job in a steel company. He worked his way up to become chief engineer in 1889. He had studied at night to obtain a degree in engineering from the Stevens Institute of Technology in 1883. Taylor made a number of useful inventions, but he is best known for applying the rational, engineering approach to the industrial worker. He did it first in 1881 at the plant where he was employed. Taylor spent the latter part of his life as an independent consultant in scientific management. He wrote *The Principles of Scientific Management* (1911) and four other books.

   Biographies: Asimov; F. B. Copley, *Frederick W. Taylor*, 1923; *DAB*, 13; *DSB*, 13; *EB*, 21; *NCAB*, 14, 23; Taylor Society, *Frederick Winslow Taylor, A Memorial Volume*, c. 1920; *Trans. Amer. Soc. Mech. Eng.*, 1915, *37*, 1459–96, 1527–1529; *WhAm*, 1.

TAYLOR MANIFEST ANXIETY SCALE. A research scale consisting of true-false statements, derived from the Minnesota Multiphasic Personality Inventory,* that yields a score indicating how anxious a respondent feels.

Spence, Janet Taylor. American psychologist (b. Toledo, Ohio, August 29, 1923). Janet Taylor received both her master's and doctor's degrees from the University of Iowa in 1949. She was at Northwestern University from 1949 to 1960, the Veterans Administration Hospital in Iowa City from 1960 to 1964, and at the University of Texas at Austin since 1964. Beginning in 1951, she published a large number of papers on anxiety, alone and with Kenneth Spence, whom she married. She has published about ten books and one hundred articles in the area of personality and social psychology. The manifest anxiety scale appeared in 1953 (*J. Abn. Soc. Psychol.*, 48, 285–90).

   Biographies: AM&WS, 1978S; *APA Dir.*, 1985; *WhoAm*, 1984–1985.

TAYLOR-RUSSELL TABLES. Tables for determining improvement, as compared to previous rate of success, in the selection of employees through the use of a test of known validity.

Taylor, Harold Claire. American psychologist (b. Barnes City, Iowa, December 21, 1905, d. Kalamazoo, Michigan, May 6, 1970). An industrial psychologist, Taylor obtained his Ph.D. from Yale University in 1934, holding a number of personnel management and research positions with private companies and institutes thereafter. He and Russell developed the tables when both were employed at the Hawthorne Works of Western Electric* (1936–1945). They presented the tables in a joint paper published in 1939 (*J. Appl. Psychol., 23,* 565–78). Taylor was the director of the W. E. Upjohn Institute for Employment Research from 1945 to 1970.
Biographies: APA Dir., 1968; NCAB, 55.

Russell, James Thomas. American psychologist (b. Beaver Falls, Pennsylvania, July 26, 1902, d. June 17, 1980). Russell obtained his doctorate in psychology from the University of Chicago in 1931. He held positions as psychologist and statistician at various private companies and government agencies. His work was on personnel selection, test theory, and test development.
Biographies: AM&WS, 1973S; APA Dir., 1968.

TAY-SACHS DISEASE. Also known as infantile amaurotic idiocy, the disease is a single recessive gene disorder, most frequently found in Jewish infants of Eastern European extraction. Beginning in the middle of the first year of life, it results in developmental retardation, visual failure, a variety of neurological problems, severe mental deterioration, and death in the second or third year.

Tay, Warren. English physician (b. 1843, d. West Croydon, May 15, 1927). Tay studied medicine at London Hospital and held positions at various hospitals in London. In describing infantile amaurotic idiocy, Tay mentioned primarily the ocular changes that occur during its course (*Trans. Ophthalm. Soc. UK,* 1880–1881, *1,* 55–57).
Biographies: Wh, 1916–1928.

Sachs, Bernard Parney. American neurologist (b. Baltimore, January 2, 1858, d. New York City, February 7, 1944). Sachs studied medicine at Harvard University and other universities in Europe, obtaining his M.D. from the University of Strasbourg in 1882. He began a private practice in New York City in 1884 but was also professor, consulting physician, and physician at various hospitals and clinics. Sachs published three books and many articles on neurology. He described the brain changes involved in the Tay-Sachs disease in four articles (*J. Nerv. Ment. Dis.,* 1887, *16,* 541–53; 1892, *19,* 603–7; *NY Med. J.,* 1896, *58,* 697–703; *J. Nerv. Ment. Dis.,* 1896, *21,* 475–79).
Biographies: NCAB, 34.

TERMAN-McNEMAR TEST OF MENTAL ABILITY. A group test of mental ability for high school students. Its seven subtests measure largely verbal comprehension. The test replaced the earlier Terman Group Test of Mental Ability.

TERMAN-MERRILL REVISION. Another name for the 1937 revision of the Stanford-Binet Scale* by Lewis Terman and Maude Merrill,* more often referred to as the Stanford-Binet.

Terman, Lewis Madison. American psychologist (b. Johnson County, Indiana, January 15, 1877, d. Palo Alto, California, December 21, 1956). Terman received the Ph.D. degree from Clark University in 1905. From 1906 to 1910 he was at the Los Angeles State Normal School and from 1910 to 1943 at Stanford University. Terman's major contribution to American psychology was his translation and adaptation to American circumstances of the Binet-Simon intelligence test in 1916 (*The Measurement of Intelligence*). One of Terman's changes was the introduction of William Stern's* mental quotient (Terman's intelligence quotient) measure of intelligence. During World War I, Terman with others participated in the construction of the first group intelligence test, the Army Alpha. Terman is also known for initiating a large-scale longitudinal study of the development of gifted children. The Terman-McNamar Test was first published in 1940, and the Terman-Merrill Revision was presented in *Measuring Intelligence* (1937), of which Terman and Maude Merrill were coauthors.
   Biographies: Biog. Mem. NAS, 33; *EB*, 21; E. R. Hilgard, *Amer. J. Psychol.*, 1957, *70*, 472–79; *HPA*, 2; *IESS*, 15; W. B. Lewis, *Brit. J. Stat. Psychol.*, 1957, *10*, 65–68; R. R. Sears, *Science*, 1957, *125*, 978–979; *WhAm*, 3.

Merrill, Maud A. American psychologist (b. Owatonna, Minnesota, April 30, 1888, d. Stanford, California, January 15, 1978). After receiving her Ph.D. in psychology from Stanford University in 1923, Merrill continued on the Stanford faculty until her retirement in 1954. She established a psychological clinic for children in the 1920s and became a consultant to the Juvenile Court in San Jose. Merrill began her collaboration with Lewis Terman on the revision of the Stanford-Binet Scale* in 1926. The amount of work was such that the revision was not published until eleven years later. The two forms of the revision, L and M, were initialed after the first names of the two authors.
   Biographies: APA Dir., 1975; R. R. Sears, *Amer. Psychologist*, 1979, *34*, 176.

McNemar, Quinn. See McNEMAR TEST.

THANATOS. In Freud's* psychoanalytic theory, the collective term for the instincts for aggression, destruction, and death, the opposite of Eros.*

Thanatos. The god of death of the ancient Greeks.

THERBLIG. A separate unit of a repeated work activity, such as grasp, transport, or search, isolated for observation or measurement in a time-motion study.

Gilbreth, Lilian Moller. American psychologist (b. Oakland, California, May 24, 1878, d. Montclair, New Jersey, January 2, 1972).

Gilbreth, Frank Bunker. American contractor (b. Fairfield, Maine, July 7, 1868, d. Montclair, New Jersey, June 14, 1924). Lilian Moller married Frank Gilbreth in 1904 and then proceeded to obtain a Ph.D. in psychology (Brown University, 1915) and in engineering (Rutgers College, 1929). At the time of their marriage, Frank Gilbreth was becoming known for his studies of motion in industrial workers. He and his wife became partners, establishing Gilbreth, Inc., an engineering consulting firm specializing in motion studies. The therblig unit, a reversal of *Gilbreth,* grew out of their motion study work during World War I. Lilian Gilbreth published the first book on the *Psychology of Management* in 1914. She and her husband later wrote three additional books on industrial efficiency as well as several papers. They also had twelve children, a fact Frank Gilbreth recorded in his book, *Cheaper by the Dozen,* later made into a movie. In 1984, Lilian Gilbreth became the first psychologist to be commemorated on a U.S. postage stamp.

Biographies (Lilian Gilbreth): J. Bales, *APA Monitor,* 1984, *15,* No. 2, 2; P. M. Bartle, *Hist. Psychol.,* 1984, *16*(4); *CurBio,* 1940, 1951; *Notable American Women—The Modern Period: A Biographical Dictionary,* 1980; *WhAm,* 5, 6; *WhoAmWom,* 1972.

Biographies (Frank Gilbreth): L. M. Gilbreth, *The Quest for the One Best Way: A Sketch of the Life of Frank Bunker Gilbreth,* 1973 (orig. publ. 1926); *NCAB,* 26; *WhAm,* 1.

THOMISTIC PSYCHOLOGY. Psychology based on the teachings of St. Thomas Aquinas, especially those presented in his *Treatise on Man,* which forms part of his *Summa Theologica.* In his psychology, Aquinas follows Aristotle,* although he disagrees with Aristotle on a number of points, elaborates and supplements his teachings, and interprets Aristotle so as to fit his ideas to Christian theology. Thomistic psychology is the present-day, official psychology of the Catholic church.

Aquinas, Saint Thomas. Italian theologian (b. Roccasecca, near Aquino, c. 1225, d. Rossanova Abbey, March 7, 1274). A member of the Dominican Order, Thomas studied liberal arts at the University of Naples and the Dominican House of Studies at the University of Paris. At Cologne, Thomas studied theology under Albert the Great. He taught at the University of Paris (1252–1259, 1268–1272), various places in Italy (1259–1268), and the University of Naples (1272–1273). Thomas' major work, the *Summa Theologica,* appeared from 1266 to 1273. The "divine doctor's" philosophy gained acceptance slowly and did not become the official philosophy of the Roman Catholic church until 1897.

Biographies: DSB, 1; *EB,* 2; *EP,* 8; *IESS,* 1.

THORNDIKE-LORGE LIST. First systematic word count in the English language. It is a tabulation of the frequencies of 30,000 words found in a variety of printed sources.

THORNDIKE PUZZLE BOX. A piece of laboratory equipment designed to study animal behavior. The earliest instance of such equipment, it consisted of a wooden crate with a door that the animal could learn to open from the inside. The incentive was food, placed outside the box, that the animal could see through the slats.

Thorndike, Edward Lee. American psychologist (b. Williamsburg, Massachusetts, August 31, 1874, d. Montrose, New York, August 9, 1949). Thorndike obtained his doctorate from Columbia University in 1898, and he remained on its faculty until 1940. He was the first psychologist to study animal behavior experimentally in a laboratory. His work led him to the formulation of the first general principles governing learning behavior, the law of effect, and the law of exercise. Later, Thorndike's interest turned to human learning, and he published classic papers and books on learning and education. Education led Thorndike to measurement, and he became one of the leaders in this field. He left a bibliography of over 450 articles and books. The word list appeared as *The Teacher's Word Book of 30,000 Words* (1944), of which Thorndike and Irving Lorge* were the coauthors. Thorndike described the puzzle box in 1898 (*Psychol. Rev. Monogr. Suppl.* 2, No. 8).

Biographies: *Biog. Mem. NAS*, 27; *EB*, 21; A. I. Gates, *Psychol. Rev.*, 1949, *56*, 241–43; F. L. Goodenough, *Amer. J. Psychol.*, 1950, *63*, 291–301; *HPA*, 3; G. Humphrey, *Brit. J. Psychol.*, 1949, *40*, 55–56; *IESS*, 16; G. M. Joncich, *The Sane Positivist: A Biography of Edward L. Thorndike*, 1969; *NCAB*, 15; W. F. Russell, *Teach. Coll. Rec.*, 1949, *51*, 26–28; *WhAm*, 2; R. S. Woodworth, *Science*, 1950, *111*, 250–51; *Yearb. Amer. Philos. Soc.*, 1949.

THOULESS RATIO. A modified version of the Brunswik ratio* in which the logarithmic transforms of the values of the stimulus S, albedo A, and response R are used. The degree of an observer's perceptual constancy with respect to lightness thus becomes

$$\frac{\log R - \log S}{\log A - \log S}.$$

Thouless, Robert Henry. English psychologist (b. Norwich, July 15, 1894, d. Cambridge, September 25, 1984). Thouless received his Ph.D. from Cambridge University in 1922. He was on the faculties of the universities of Manchester (1921–1926), Glasgow (1926–1938), and Cambridge (1938–1961). In addition to perception, Thouless' interests lay in the areas of psychology, religion, and parapsychology. He published twelve books and many articles. He presented the lightness constancy ratio in 1931 (*Brit. J. Psychol.*, *21*, 339–59; *22*, 1–30).

Biographies: *ConAu*, 5R, 77R; *Shepard*, 3; *Who*, 1983–1984.

THURSTONE SCALE. Thurstone's application of psychophysical methods to the construction of attitude scales. A large number of statements concerning the subject matter of an attitude is given to a large number of judges who classify them into eleven categories, according to the degree of favorableness expressed, from most favorable through neutral to least favorable. Other statements are placed in intermediate categories, so that the intervals between the categories all appear equal. A scale value is then computed for each statement.

THURSTONE TEMPERAMENT SCHEDULE. A scale consisting of 140 direct questions concerning one's temperament. It yields scores in the temperamental characteristics active, vigorous, impulsive, dominant, stable, sociable, and reflective.

Thurstone, Louis Leon. American psychologist (b. Chicago, Illinois, May 29, 1887, d. Chapel Hill, North Carolina, September 29, 1955). After obtaining the Ph.D. in psychology from the University of Chicago, Thurstone joined the faculty of the Carnegie Institute of Technology (1917–1923); he was at the University of Chicago from 1924 to 1952 and, after his retirement, at the University of North Carolina. Thurstone was the most eminent psychometrician of his time. In the United States, the development of the technique of factor analysis is connected mainly with his name (*Vectors of the Mind*, 1935; *Primary Mental Abilities*, 1938; *Factorial Studies of Intelligence*, 1941; *Multiple Factor Analysis*, 1947). In psychophysics, the law of comparative judgments was a contribution that Thurstone considered to be his best. Thurstone wrote twenty-three books and monographs, 165 articles, and 95 laboratory reports and constructed 47 tests. The Temperament Schedule was first published in 1949, and the scaling technique was presented in *The Measurement of Attitude* (1929, with E. J. Chave).

Biographies: D. C. Adkins, in N. Frederiksen & H. Gulliksen, *Contributions to Mathematical Psychology*, 1964, pp. 3–39; *Biog. Mem. NAS*, 30; *DAB*, Suppl. 5; *EB*, 21; J. P. Guilford, *Psychometrika*, 1955, 20, 263–65; P. Horst, *Science*, 1955, *122*, 1259–60; *HPA*, 4; *IESS*, 16; *WhAm*, 3; D. Wolfle, *Amer. J. Psychol.*, 1956, 20, 263–65; *Yearb. Amer. Philos. Soc.*, 1955.

TILTON'S *O*. A measure of overlap between two distributions of scores.

Tilton, John Warren. American psychologist (b. November 10, 1891, d. March 8, 1980). Tilton obtained his Ph.D. from Teachers College, Columbia University, in 1926. He was with Westinghouse Electric from 1925 to 1927 and Centro San Miguel in Puerto Rico from 1927 to 1932, and he worked in vocational education for the government of Puerto Rico from 1932 to 1945. After 1958, Tilton was associate professor emeritus at Yale University. Tilton's work was on learning and individual differences. He presented the overlap measure in 1937 (*J. Educ. Psychol.*, 28, 656–62).

Biographies: APA Dir., 1968.

TITCHENER CIRCLES. A visual illusion, also known as Ebbinghaus circles, it consists of two circles of identical size, one surrounded by a number of circles smaller than itself and the other surrounded by circles larger than itself. The first enclosed circle appears smaller than the second.

Titchener, Edward Bradford. English-American psychologist (b. Chichester, Sussex, January 11, 1867, d. Ithaca, New York, August 3, 1927). Titchener received his Ph.D. from Wilhelm Wundt* at Leipzig in 1892. He considered Wundt to be of utmost importance to psychology and spent his life expounding and systematizing the Wundtian point of view and producing laboratory research using Wundt's method of introspection. The school of structuralism was born at Cornell University, where Titchener spent all his career (1892–1927) and expounded by Titchener and the many doctoral students who studied under him. His most important book was *Experimental Psychology*. It appeared in four volumes between 1901 and 1905. The Titchener circles may be found in volume 1 (1901) of this work.

Biographies: E. G. Boring, *Amer. J. Psychol.*, 1927, *38*, 489–506; *DAB*, 18; *EB*, 22; R. B. Evans, *J. Hist. Behav. Sci.*, 1972, *8*, 168–80; *IESS*, 16; C. S. Myers, *Brit. J. Psychol.*, 1927–1928, *18*, 460–63; *NCAB*, 22; H. C. Warren, *Science*, 1927, *66*, 208–9; *WhAm*, 1.

TOMKINS-HORN PICTURE ARRANGEMENT TEST. A projective test to evaluate work attitudes of employees. It consists of twenty-five plates, each with three pictures, that can be arranged in six possible ways. The pictures represent people in various office and work situations.

Tomkins, Silvan Samuel. American psychologist (b. Philadelphia, Pennsylvania, June 4, 1911). Tomkins' Ph.D. was in philosophy (University of Pennsylvania, 1934), but by 1938 he had become research assistant in psychology at the Harvard Psychological Clinic (until 1943) and was instructor and lecturer at Harvard from 1943 to 1947. He then taught at Princeton University (1947–1964) and directed the Center for Research in Cognition and Affect of the City University of New York from 1964 to 1968. Tomkins was at Rutgers State University from 1969 to 1976. He specialized in personality psychology, personality measurement, and projective techniques. The Picture Arrangement Test was first published in 1942.

Biographies: AM&WS, 1973S; *APA Dir.*, 1985; *WhoAm*, 1978.

Horn, Daniel. American psychologist (b. Rochester, New York, May 28, 1916). After receiving a Ph.D. in personality psychology from Harvard University (1943), Horn held positions as research psychologist with the U.S. Navy and U.S. Air Force (until 1947) and the American Cancer Society (1947–1962). He simultaneously taught at Princeton (1949–1953) and Yale Universities (1953–1956). Horn took a research position with the U.S. Public Heath Service (USPHS) in 1962 and is now director of the National Clearinghouse for Smoking and Health, USPHS, in Atlanta. His main fields of interest are experimental design and psychological factors in health.

Biographies: AM&WS, 1973S; *APA Dir.*, 1985; *WhoAm*, 1978.

TORRANCE TEST OF CREATIVE THINKING. The test contains a verbal and a figural portion and assesses four characteristics of the respondent: fluency, flexibility, originality, and elaboration. It is based on the respondent's ability to visualize and transform words, meanings, and patterns.

Torrance, Ellis Paul. American psychologist (b. Milledgeville, Georgia, October 8, 1915). From 1936 to 1951, Torrance worked in public school education and counseling and college counseling. He received a Ph.D. in educational psychology from the University of Michigan in 1951 and was with the U.S. Air Force Personnel and Training Research Center from 1951 to 1957, the University of Minnesota from 1958 to 1966, and the University of Georgia from 1966 to 1984. Torrance did research on the measurement and development of creativity. He wrote several books on the subject, as well as over 500 other publications. The test was first published in 1966.

  Biographies: AM&WS, 1978S; *APA Dir.,* 1985; *ConAu,* 3R, NR3; *WhoAm,* 1984–1985.

TOURETTE'S SYNDROME. See GILES DE LA TOURETTE SYNDROME.

TOWER OF HANOI. A puzzle consisting of three pegs on one of which are stacked different-sized disks according to size, so that they form a tower or pyramid. The object is to transfer the pile, one disk at a time, to another peg without putting a larger disk on top of a smaller one. The puzzle is used in problem-solving experiments. It is also known as the Burmese pyramid.

Hanoi. The puzzle was invented in 1883 by the French mathematician Edouard Lucas and sold as a toy. Both names, *tower of Hanoi* and *Burmese pyramid,* refer to the resemblance of the stacked disks to the typical pagoda—round, tapering, and seemingly made of stacked disks—found in Southeast Asia.

TRAUBE-HERING WAVES. Slight, cyclic changes in arterial blood pressure, observable in plethysmographic recordings. The period of the cycle is somewhat variable, agreeing, by and large, with the cyclic fluctuation in attention.

Traube, Ludwig. German physician (b. Ratibor, Silesia, January 12, 1818, d. Berlin, April 11, 1876). Traube received his M.D. from the University of Berlin in 1840. He joined its faculty in 1848 and remained on it until his death. Traube introduced auscultation and percussion courses, as well as animal experimentation, in medical curricula in Germany. Traube published numerous papers on a variety of medical subjects. He described the waves in 1869 (*Sitzber. math.-wiss. Cl. Kais. Akad. Wiss.,* Jahrgang 1869, 1870, *60,* pt. 2, 820–56).

  Biographies: Talbot.

Hering, Ewald. See under eponyms beginning with HERING.

TROLAND. A unit of retinal illuminance, defined as the illuminance produced by viewing, through an artificial pupil of an area of one square millimeter and centered on the natural pupil, a surface that has a luminance of one candle per square meter.

Troland, Leonard Thompson. American psychologist (b. Norwich, Connecticut, April 26, 1889, d. Mount Wilson, California, May 27, 1932). Troland's Ph.D. in psychology was from Harvard University (1915), and he was on the Harvard faculty from 1916 to 1932. Troland was a versatile scientist who wrote several important papers on life and life processes, published a book on physics, was a coinventor of the Technicolor movie process, and wrote papers on philosophy and metaphysics. In psychology, his most notable contributions were in the field of vision. He presented his view of psychology in the three-volume *Principles of Psychophysiology* (1929–1932). The retinal illuminance unit was named after him posthumously.

Biographies: J. G. Beebe-Center, *Amer. J. Psychol.*, 1932, *44*, 817–20; *DAB*, 18; J. P. C. Southall, *J. Opt. Soc. Amer.*, 1932, *22*, 509–11; *WhAm*, 1.

TROXLER EFFECT. The fading of visual objects in the periphery of the visual field when a point in its center is steadily fixated. It may be observed when fixating, as rigidly as possible, such patterns as may be found in wallpapers, floor coverings, and fabrics. The effect is due to the organization of the peripheral retina, which requires larger eye movements than are needed in the fovea, to break the adaptation brought about by steady fixation.

Troxler, Ignaz Paul Vitalis. Swiss physician (b. Bern, August 17, 1780, d. Bern, March 6, 1866). After obtaining the M.D. degree from the University of Jena in 1803, Troxler immediately wrote several articles on physiological optics, among them one that described the fading of steadily fixated visual objects (*Ophthalm. Bibl.*, 1804, *2*, pt. 2, 1–53). Between 1806 and 1834, Troxler was in private practice in Luzern and other locations in Switzerland. He edited the *Archiv für Medizin und Chirurgie* from 1816 and was professor of philosophy at the University of Bern from 1834.

Biographies: Hirsch, *Biog. Lex.*

TUKEY TEST. In analysis of variance, an alternative procedure to the Newman-Keuls test* and Duncan's Multiple Range Test* for making a posteriori tests. Two variants of the test exist, one that is also called the honestly significant difference (hsd) procedure, and another that differs from the hsd procedure by the way in which the critical value is computed.

Tukey, John Wilder. American mathematician (b. New Bedford, Massachusetts, June 16, 1915). With a Ph.D. in mathematics from Princeton University (1939) that he had obtained in just two years with no previous training in mathematics, Tukey was appointed instructor in mathematics at Princeton in the same year. He became involved in statistical work during World War II, returning to teach in 1945 and also joining the staff of Bell Laboratories at Murray Hill. The test was first presented in 1953 (The Problem of Multiple Comparisons. Ditto, Princeton University, 396 pp.).

Biographies: AM&WS, 1982P; F. Mosteller, in Collected Works of John W. Tukey, vol. 1, xv–xvii, 1984; WhoAm, 1982–1983.

TURING MACHINE. A theoretical, universal computing machine. It consists of a magnetic tape and a reading head. The tape moves back and forth under the head, inserting and changing characters (0 and 1) and using information supplied from outside. The machine is "completely described" when every mark on the tape specifies the next character to be written, where it should be written, and whether the tape should move backward or forward. Any modern computer, no matter how complicated, is essentially a Turing machine; the brain itself may be represented as a Turing machine.

TURING TEST. A "test" to answer the question whether machines can think. If a computer is found to give answers to questions that cannot be distinguished from answers given by a person, it must be concluded that the computer can think.

Turing, Alan Mathison. English mathematician (b. London, June 23, 1912, d. Wilmslow, Cheshire, June 7, 1953). Turing graduated from Cambridge University in 1935. He was at Princeton University from 1936 to 1938 (receiving the Ph.D. degree there), at Cambridge in 1939, and the Communications Department of the Foreign Office from 1939 to 1948. From 1945 to 1948 he was also at the National Physical Laboratory at Teddington. Turing's last position was at the University of Manchester (1948–1953). In addition to mathematics, Turing was interested in machinery. He helped crack the German Enigma code and in the 1940s began building computers. He was a major influence on the development of computers in Great Britain. He and David Champernowne wrote the first chess-playing program for computers. Turing described the universal computing machine in 1937 (Proc. London Math. Soc., 42, 230–65). The term Turing machine was introduced by Alonzo Church in his 1937 review of Turing's paper in the Journal of Symbolic Logic. Turing offered the test of thinking in machines in 1950 (Mind, 59, 433–460).

Biographies: DSB, 13; A. Hodges, Alan Turing: The Enigma, 1983; Nature, 1954, 174, 535–36; M. H. A. Newman, Biog. Mem. Fellows Roy. Soc., 1955, 1, 253–63; S. Turing, Alan M. Turing, 1959.

TURNER'S SYNDROME. A syndrome that accompanies the absence of the Y chromosome in the male (the XO configuration of sex chromosomes). Morphologically, the individual resembles a sexually immature girl. He has short stature, possibly webbed fingers and toes, a small chin, and defects of the heart, kidneys, ureter, and hearing. The main cognitive deficit is in the perception of space—visualization, right-left distinction, and the ability to follow paths on a map without turning it.

Turner, Henry Hubert. American endocrinologist (b. Harrisburg, Illinois, August 28, 1892, d. Oklahoma City, Oklahoma, August 4, 1970). Turner received his M.D. from the University of Louisville (1921). He was an assistant in medicine at the university from 1921 to 1924, when he left for the University of Oklahoma. Turner became professor emeritus in 1969. He was also in private practice from 1925 to 1970. He described the syndrome in 1938 (*Endocrinology, 23,* 566–74).

Biographies: NCAB, 56; WhAm, 5.

U

URBAN'S CONSTANT PROCESS. See MULLER-URBAN METHOD.

URBAN'S TABLES. Tables of the Müller-Urban weights.*

URBAN'S WEIGHTS. See MULLER-URBAN WEIGHTS.

UZNADZE ILLUSION. In form, the Uznadze illusion is identical to the Delboeuf illusion*: two small, identical circles side by side, one of them enclosed by a concentric, larger circle. The difference is that in the Uznadze illusion, the two smaller circles are presented alternately with the larger circle instead of being viewed simultaneously with the larger circle. The enclosed circle appears smaller than the other small circle.

Uznadze, Dmitrii Nikolaevich. Georgian psychologist (b. Sakar, Georgia, January 1, 1887, d. Tblisi, Georgia, October 12, 1950). Uznadze obtained his Ph.D. from the University of Leipzig in 1909. He held positions at the University of Tblisi (1918–1930) and the Pedagogical Institute at Tblisi (1930–1950). Uznadze was the most prominent Georgian psychologist of his time. He was cofounder of the University of Tblisi and founder of its department of psychology and psychological laboratory as well as of the Georgian Institute of Psychology, now named after him. Uznadze studied thought, speech, and perception. His main contribution was his theory of set. The Georgian school of psychology is based on his theory.
Biographies: PR, 3; Soviet, 26.

V

VATER-PACINI CORPUSCLES. See PACINIAN CORPUSCLES.

Vater, Abraham. German anatomist (b. Wittenberg, December 9, 1684, d. Wittenberg, 1751). Vater received a Ph.D. (1706) and an M.D. (1710) from the University of Leipzig. From 1710 through 1712, he undertook a scientific journey through Europe, returned to Wittenberg, qualified to teach at the University of Wittenberg, and remained there until his death. Vater made many discoveries and wrote many papers on anatomy but also on other medical matters, as well as on botany, chemistry, and pharmacology. What are now called Pacinian corpuscles were discovered by Vater before 1741, but his discovery was forgotten until Filippo Pacini* rediscovered them. Vater apparently did not publish his finding, but J. G. Lehmann, in his *Dissertatio de consensu partium corporis humani* (1741), is said to have described Vater's discovery.
  Biographies: ADB, 39; *Brit. Med. J.*, 1951, No. 4741, 1214; Hirsch, *Biog. Lex.*

VERNIER ACUITY. Visual acuity determined by the ability to detect whether two colinear lines are continuous or offset with respect to each other. The degree of offset that the viewer cannot perceive is taken as a measure of visual acuity (two seconds of visual angle for normal vision).

Vernier, Pierre. French military engineer (b. Ornans, Doubs, August 19, 1580, d. Ornans, Doubs, September 14, 1638). Developing an early interest in measuring instruments, Vernier worked as a military engineer. Although the idea of juxtaposing two scales, one having one part fewer than the other, had already been advanced by Nuñez (Nonius), the fixed astrolab scales, where it was incorporated, were hard to use. Vernier's invention for measuring distance to the nearest tenth of the smallest division of the scale employed was an advance because it used mobile scales and thus solved the difficulty of engraving many fixed ones. Vernier presented his invention to the infanta of Spain and published a treatise on it in 1631 (*La construction, l'usage, et les propriétez du quadrant de mathematique*).

Biographies: DSB, 13.

VIENNA CIRCLE. A group of philosophers, the most prominent of whom were Moritz Schlick, Rudolf Carnap, Philipp Frank, Otto Neurath, Hans Reichenbach, Kurt Gödel,* Herbert Feigl, and Hans Hahn,* who, over the first thirty years of the twentieth century influenced the philosophy of science. They probed the meaning of scientific concepts, sentences, and symbols and, when possible, substituted mathematical symbols for them. Their position, logical positivism, was that the preinferential, basic data of science are the operations of scientific observation. Through Percy Bridgman, a Harvard University physicist, logical positivism, in the form of operational definitions that Bridgman proposed as a solution to the problem of how to define concepts, influenced psychological thinking after S. S. Stevens,* wrote a paper on operationism in 1935.

VIENNESE SCHOOL. Followers of Sigmund Freud* and of Freudian psychoanalysis.

Vienna. Capital of Austria-Hungary and, later, of Austria, where psychoanalysis was born. Freud lived and worked here from age four to age eighty-two, a year before his death.

VIERORDT'S LAW. The principle that the more mobile a bodily part is, the lower is the cutaneous two-point threshold.

Vierordt, Karl von. German physiologist. (b. Lahr, Württemberg, July 1, 1818, d. Tübingen, Württemberg, November 22, 1884). Vierordt received an M.D. from the University of Heidelberg in 1841, and he spent his career (1849–1884) at the University of Tübingen. Before Gustav Fechner* (in 1852), Vierordt used the method of constant stimuli to establish sensory thresholds. In 1868, he published a volume on the psychology of time. Vierordt conducted many additional researches on vision, hearing, and somesthesis. In 1869 and 1870 he measured the two-point threshold, formulating the law that bears his name (*Arch. ges. Physiol.*, 1869, *2*, 297–306; *Z. Biol.*, 1870, *6*, 53–72).

Biographies: R. H. Major, Ann. Med. Hist., 1938, 10, 463–473.

VIETH-MULLER CIRCLE. A circle passing through the fixation point and the optical centers of the lenses of the two eyes and lying in the plane of regard.

Vieth, Gerhard Ulrich Anton. German educator (b. Hooksiel, Oldenburg, January 8, 1763, d. Dessau, Saxony, January 12, 1836). Vieth worked in the city of Dessau, where he became headmaster in 1798 and member of the board of education in 1819. He furthered the introduction of physical education in the educational curriculum and developed a theory of physical exercise (*Versuch einer Encyclopädie der Leibesübung,* 1794–1795). Vieth conceptualized the circle in 1818 (*Ann. Phys.,* Leipzig, *58,* 233–55), but it was worked out by Johannes Müller in 1826 (*Zur vergleichenden Physiologie des Gesichtssinnes*), who also discovered it independently.

   Biographies: Brockhaus, 19.

Müller, Johannes Peter. German physiologist (b. Koblenz, Rhineland-Palatinate, July 14, 1801, d. Berlin, April 28, 1858). Müller obtained his Ph.D. in physiology from the University of Bonn in 1822. He was on the faculty of that university from 1824 to 1833 and of the University of Berlin from 1833 to 1858. Müller was the foremost physiologist of his day, sharing with Albrecht von Haller the appellation Father of Experimental Physiology. He wrote a compendium of physiological knowledge, the *Handbuch der Physiologie des Menschen* (1833–1840), which served as the primary reference text in physiology for some time. The fifth book of the *Handbuch* deals with the senses and contains the most important law of physiology of the early nineteenth century, the law of specific nerve energies.

   Biographies: B. Chance, *Arch. Ophthalm.,* 1944, *32,* 395–402; *DSB,* 9; *EB,* 15; *IESS,* 10.

VINCENT CURVE (VINCENT METHOD). A method for plotting learning curves so as to make data from individuals with different learning rates comparable. A given fraction of the total learning time required or of the total number of equally spaced trials for one individual is treated as equivalent to that of another. This makes the beginnings and ends of all learning curves coincide, but the amount learned during any portion of the curve differs for different individuals. The curve so transformed is said to be vincentized.

Vincent, Stella Burnham. American psychologist (b. May 3, 1862, d. Hampton, Illinois [or Pasadena, California], August 30, 1951). Before receiving her doctorate in 1912 (University of Chicago), Vincent taught psychology at the J. B. Stetson University (1902–1905) and Washington State Normal School (1907–1909). After 1914, she taught psychology at Chicago Normal School, retiring in 1930. She introduced her curve plotting method in 1912 (*Behav. Monog.,* No. 5).

   Biographies: AMS, 1944; *APA Dir.,* 1948.

VINELAND SOCIAL MATURITY SCALE. A developmental schedule that measures the individual's ability to cope with practical problems of life. The 117 items are grouped into age levels, from birth to age twenty-five. The information is obtained not from the subject but from an informant. The score is years and months of Social Age, which, when divided by chronological age and multiplied by 100, yields a Social Quotient.

Vineland, New Jersey. The scale is named after the Vineland Training School for the mentally retarded. The psychologist Edgar A. Doll, the author of the scale, was assistant psychologist at the school from 1913 to 1919 and its director of research from 1925 to 1949. The scale was first published in 1935.

VON BAER'S LAW. The embryos of different organisms are similar in the first stages of development but differ increasingly as development progresses. The embryos of species that are most dissimilar show diverging development first.

Von Baer, Karl Ernst. German-Russian embryologist (b. Pipe, near Jerwen, Estonia, February 29, 1792, d. Dorpat [now Tartu], Estonia, November 28, 1876). Von Baer, a Baltic German, received his M.D. degree from the University of Dorpat (Tartu) in 1814, but he never practiced medicine. Instead he turned to anatomy and comparative embryology, becoming a pioneer in the latter field. His *Embryologie der Thiere* (2 vols., 1828, 1837) may be considered the founding textbook of embryology. Von Baer secured an academic appointment at the University of Königsberg in 1817, where he remained until 1834. He made several important discoveries, such as that mammalian embryos develop from eggs and of the germ layers that give rise to the various tissue systems. In 1834, von Baer joined the Imperial Academy of Sciences in St. Petersburg but failed to develop his embryological work, turning instead to geography. The law that is named after him appears in his embryology text.

Biographies: Asimov; DSB, 1; EB, 2; Talbot.

VON FREY AESTHESIOMETER. A stiff bristle in a holder used to explore the skin surface in experiments on cutaneous sensitivity.

VON FREY HAIRS. Standard hairs, either human hairs or horse bristles, used in the von Frey aesthesiometer.*

VON FREY LIMEN GAUGE. An instrument for tactile stimulation of the skin at regular intervals. A pressure point is activated by a spring. The intensity and timing of the application of pressure is controlled by a lever acting on the spring. This lever is moved by a revolving drum.

Von Frey, Maximillian Ruppert. German physiologist (b. Salzburg, Austria, November 16, 1852, d. Würzburg, Bavaria, January 25, 1932). Von Frey (M.D., University of Leipzig, 1877) is known for his authoritative work on touch sensations performed while he was at the universities of Leipzig (1882–1892), Zurich (1892–1899), and Würzburg (1899–1932). Practically nothing was known about the physiology of the skin prior to von Frey's work. He wrote more than fifty papers on the haptic system. Much of this work was described in his *Lectures on Physiology* (1904). He described the aesthesiometer, hairs, and limen gauge in 1896 (*Abh. Sächs. Ges. Wiss., math.-phys. Cl.*, 1896, *23*, 175–266).

Biographies: E. G. Boring, Amer. J. Psychol., 1932, 44, 584–86.

VON KRIES THEORY OF VISION. Also known as the duplicity theory of vision, it explains visual phenomena in terms of two systems of retinal receptor cells: the rods, which function at low levels of illumination and are responsible for achromatic vision, and cones, which function at high levels of illumination and mediate color vision.

Von Kries, Johannes. German physiologist (b. Roggenhausen, West Prussia, October 6, 1853, d. Freiburg-im-Breisgau, Baden-Württemberg, December 30, 1928). Except for a few years at the University of Leipzig, von Kries spent most of his professional life at the University of Freiburg (1880–1924). He had graduated with an M.D. from the University of Leipzig in 1876. Von Kries' main contributions to psychology were in the physiology of vision, among the most notable of which was the duplicity theory of vision (*Ber. naturf. Ges. Freiburg i.B.*, 1894, *9*, 61–70). He also identified and named the main types of color blindness and color weakness.
  Biographies: Fischer, *Biog. Lex.;* Pagel, *Biog. Lex.;* E. v. Skramlik, *Z. Sinnesphysiol.*, 1929, *60*, 249–56.

VON RESTORFF PHENOMENON. In experiments with paired-associates learning, items are recalled better when a pair is presented for learning in isolation than when presented together with others in a series. It is also known as the Köhler-Restorff phenomenon.

Von Restorff, Hedwig. German psychologist and physician (b. 1903, d. n.a.). Von Restorff, who had a Ph.D. in psychology, was an assistant at the Psychological Institute, University of Berlin, under the direction of Wolfgang Köhler when she described the phenomenon that bears her name (*Psychol. Forsch.*, 1933, *18*, 299–342). A second paper on the phenomenon was written by Köhler and von Restorff in 1935 (*Psychol. Forsch.*, *21*, 56–112). On taking over the institute in 1933, the Nazis dismissed all Jews and others they considered undesirable, including von Restorff, who sought a career in medicine. She was at one time in Freiburg-im-Breisgau but died at a young age.
  Biographies: Unavailable.

VYGOTSKII BLOCKS. An early concept formation test consisting of wood blocks of different colors, shapes, and sizes that the person being tested groups according to their attributes. The blocks are now part of various mental ability tests.

Vygotskiĭ, Leon Semenovich. Russian psychologist (b. Orsha, Belorussia, November 5, 1896, d. Moscow, June 11, 1934). Vygotskiĭ whose name is variously spelled Vygotski, Vigotsky, and Wigotsky, graduated from the First State University of Moscow with a degree in law in 1917. He took psychology courses at the Shanyavskĭ People's University. He was on the faculty of the Teachers'

College in Gomel' from 1917 to 1924 and from 1924 to 1934 held positions at the Institute of Psychology, the Institute of Defectology, the Second State University, Krupskaya Academy of Communist Education, and the Gertsen Pedagogical Institute, all in Moscow. Vygoskiĭ dealt with the development of consciousness in the course of evolution and in ontogeny. He conducted some of the first studies on concept formation in children. In his best-known work, *Thought and Language* (1934, English translation 1962), Vygotskiĭ considered the determining factor of a child's psychological development to be social development, especially language development.

Biographies: A. N. Leont'ev, in L. S. Vygotskiĭ *The Psychology of Art,* 1917, pp. v–xi; A. R. Luria, *J. Genet. Psychol.,* 1935, 46, 224–25; *PR,* 3; *Soviet,* 5.

W

WADA TEST. A short-acting anaesthetic injected into the brain arteries in such a way that only one of the hemispheres is put to sleep. This makes it possible to establish with certainty which of the two hemispheres is dominant for language in an individual about to undergo brain surgery. If the anesthetic is injected in the nondominant hemisphere, understanding and production of speech are not interfered with; when the anesthetic acts on the dominant hemisphere, the individual is unable to respond to commands or to speak.

Wada, John A. Japanese-Canadian neurosurgeon (b. Tokyo, Japan, March 28, 1924). Wada obtained a doctorate in medical science from the Hokkaido Imperial University in 1951. He was at the hospital of that university until 1957, when he went to the University of British Columbia. He has been at its Health Science Center Hospital since 1970. A Canadian citizen, Wada has engaged in research on the neurological mechanisms of behavior, epilepsy, and electroencephalography. He introduced the test in 1949 (*Igaku to Seibutsugaku, 14*, 221–22).
   Biographies: AM&WS, 1982P.

WALD-WOLFOWITZ RUNS TEST. A nonparametric test of the null hypothesis that two independent samples have been drawn from the same population. The data must be at least on the ordinal scale, but the test examines any differences at all: central tendency, variability, skewness, or kurtosis.

Wald, Abraham. Rumanian mathematician (b. Cluj, Rumania, October 31, 1902, d. India, December 13, 1950). Wald studied mathematics at the universities of Cluj and Vienna (Ph.D., 1931). He came to the United States in 1938 and became naturalized in 1943 and was on the faculty of Columbia University from 1938 to 1950. Wald made many important contributions to mathematical statistics. His *Sequential Analysis* (1947) is based on his own work almost in its entirety. The runs test was presented in 1943 (*Ann. Math. Stat., 14*, 45–55).

Biographies: DSB, 14; WhAm, 3; J. Wolfowitz, Ann. Math. Stat., 1952, 23, 1–13.

Wolfowitz, Jacob. American mathematician (b. Warsaw, Poland, March 19, 1910, d. Tampa, Florida, July 16, 1981). Wolfowitz obtained his Ph.D. from New York University in 1942. He was on the faculties of Columbia University (1942–1951), the University of North Carolina (1945–1946), Cornell University (1951–1970), the University of Illinois at Urbana (1970–1978), and the University of South Florida (1978–1981). Wolfowitz made his contribution to the runs test in 1943 (*Ann. Math. Stat., 14*, 280–88).

Biographies: AM&WS, 1979P; NYT, July 23, 1981, B5; L. Weiss, Amer. Statistician, 1982, 36, 126–27; WhAm, 8.

WALLERIAN DEGENERATION. The breakdown of the myelin sheath of the axon that has been severed from the cell body. When the proper staining technique is applied, the course of the degeneration to the tip of the axon may be followed microscopically and nerve pathways thus established.

Waller, Augustus Wolney. English physician (b. Faversham, Kent, December 21, 1816, d. Geneva, Switzerland, September 18, 1870). Waller received his medical degree from the University of Paris in 1840, after which he practiced medicine in London for ten years. Whenever possible, Waller spent time at his microscope studying nerve degeneration. The paper in which the eponymous nerve degeneration was first described appeared in 1850 (*Philos. Trans. Roy. Soc., 140*, 423–29), followed a year later by a version in French (*C. r. hebd. séances Acad. Sci.*, 1851, 33, 370–74 et seq.). It was also in 1850 that Waller gave up his medical practice for full-time physiological research on neural structure and function and moved to Bonn. After his move to Paris in 1856, he became seriously ill and spent the remaining years in various places in Europe in search of health.

Biographies: DNB, 59; DSB, 14; Haymaker; Talbot.

WARTEGG DRAWING COMPLETION FORM. A projective test for children aged five and older. It consists of a sheet with eight two-inch boxes containing some lines or dots. Children connect the lines and dots to make pictures, title them, and then state which they like the most and which the least.

Wartegg, Ehrig. German psychologist (b. Dresden, July 7, 1897). Wartegg obtained his Ph.D. from the University of Leipzig in 1939. After World War II, he held positions at the Haus der Gesundheit in East Berlin. Wartegg's work has been in psychotherapy and psychodiagnostics. The Drawing Completion Form was first published in 1952.

Biographies: IDP.

WAT. Unit of reaction potential in Clark Hull's system, defined as "the mean standard deviation of the momentary reaction potential ($_sE_R$) of standard albino rats, ninety days of age, learning a simple manipulative act requiring a ten-gram pressure by twenty-four-hour distributed trials under twenty-three hours' hunger, water available, with reward in the form of a 2.5-gram pellet of the usual dry dog food, the mean being taken from all the reinforcement trials producing the habit strength from .75 to .85 habs inclusive.''

Watson, John Broadus. American psychologist (b. Greenville, South Carolina, January 9, 1878, d. New York City, September 25, 1958). The term *wat* was coined by Clark Hull (*Essentials of Behavior,* 1951, p. 100) to honor John B. Watson, the founder of behaviorism. Watson obtained his Ph.D. from the University of Chicago in 1903 and was on the faculty of that university until 1908 and on the Johns Hopkins University faculty from 1908 to 1920, when he was forced to resign because of a scandal. From 1921 to 1946 he held various positions with advertising firms. In a 1913 article, Watson presented a view of psychology that departed completely from all views of the past and started a new school of psychology, behaviorism. Watson's article and subsequent writings had such an impact on American psychology that it emerged as a new discipline, focusing on behavior, instead of mind, as the subject matter of psychology and emphasizing animal study (*Behavior: An Introduction to Comparative Psychology,* 1914) and the learning and conditioning processes (*Psychology from the Standpoint of a Behaviorist,* 1919). In 1918, Watson began experimentation with children, a pioneering effort, and later wrote *Psychological Care of the Infant and Child* (1928), becoming an instant authority on child care and rearing.
   Biographies: Asimov; EB, 23; *HPA,* 3; *IESS,* 16; *NCAB,* 48; *WhAm,* 2; R. S. Woodworth, *Amer. J. Psychol.,* 1959, 72, 301–10.

WATSON-GLASER CRITICAL THINKING APPRAISAL. A test of the ability to make inferences, recognize assumptions, make deductions, interpret, and evaluate arguments.

Watson, Goodwin Barbour. American psychologist (b. Whitewater, Wisconsin, July 9, 1899, d. Longboat Key, Florida, December 30, 1976). Watson received his Ph.D. in educational psychology from Teachers College, Columbia University, in 1925, remaining on its faculty until 1963, when he retired. He was professor at Newark State College from 1963 to 1970. Watson was both an ordained minister and an activist and innovator in education. He was an early critic of the validity of intelligence tests. At Teachers College, Watson developed the first overseas study course, including trips to the USSR, and was a cofounder of the University without Walls. Watson's psychological work was in personality, group psychotherapy, and management training and consultation. He was an associate of Edward Glaser Associates. The *Critical Thinking Appraisal* was first published in 1942.
   Biographies: AM&WS, 1973S; *APA Dir.,* 1975; T. M. Newcomb, *Amer. Psychologist,* 1979, *34,* 433–34; *NYT,* Jan. 5, 1977, B–18; *WhAm,* 7.

Glaser, Edward. American psychologist (b. New York City, April 8, 1911). Glaser is a clinical social psychologist who has conducted research in program evaluation, organizational research, knowledge transfer, and institutional change. He obtained his Ph.D. from Columbia University in 1940. After two years with the U.S. Public Health Service, Glaser took a position with management consultants Rohrer, Hibler & Replogle in 1947. In 1952, he became the managing associate of Edward Glaser & Associates and in 1971 president of Human Interaction Research Institute. Glaser was coauthor of the 1942 *Watson-Glaser Critical Thinking Appraisal* test.

   Biographies: AM&WS, 1978S; APA Dir., 1985.

WATSONIAN BEHAVIORISM. A school of psychology that John B. Watson initiated in 1913 with his article, "Psychology as the Behaviorist Views It." Watsonian psychology is an objective, experimental branch of natural science whose goal is to predict and control behavior. Introspection as a method is not part of it. Consciousness and mental states are not to be referred to. Conditioning as a research methodology and explanatory concept has a particularly prominent role to play. Central to Watson's view of psychology was his stimulus-response (S-R) formulation of behavior. The responses are muscular contractions or glandular discharges, and the S-R units are reflexes, innate or conditioned. There are no instincts in humans, nor do they possess any other abilities that are transmitted genetically. Most emotions are conditioned elaborations of three innate ones, language is learned through conditioning, thinking is conditioned responses in which the motor link is omitted, and personality a set of behavior habits established through conditioning.

Watson, John B. See WAT.

WEBER-FECHNER LAW. See FECHNER'S LAW.

WEBER'S LAW. In comparing physical stimuli, a perceiver responds not to the magnitude of the difference between them but to the ratio of the difference to the magnitude of the standard stimulus; or, for a given sensory continuum, the just noticeable difference that is added to or subtracted from a stimulus is a constant proportion of that stimulus.

Weber, Ernst Heinrich. German physiologist (b. Wittenberg, Saxony, June 24, 1795, d. Leipzig, January 26, 1878). Weber worked on the physiology of the internal organs (M.D., University of Wittenberg, 1815), but he is best known for his work on touch, on which subject he wrote a book, *De pulsu, resorptione, auditu et tactu: annotationes anatomicae et physiologicae* (1834). In this book (pp. 172–75) there appears a statement now known as Weber's law. Weber's discovery of the just noticeable difference in sensation passed almost unnoticed until its republication in Rudolph Wagner's *Handbook of Physiology* (1846) when Gustav Fechner,* at the time also at the University of Leipzig, made it into a cornerstone of psychophysics by introducing the response dimension into Weber's formulation. What is now called Fechner's law* was referred to by Fechner as Weber's law because he saw his own equation as simply a derivation of the more basic Weber's ratio.

Biographies: Asimov; P. M. Dawson, *Phi Beta Phi Quart.*, 1928, *25*, 86–116; *DSB*, 14; *EB*, 23; *IESS*, 16; *Talbot*.

WECHSLER ADULT INTELLIGENCE SCALE. A revision of Form 1 of the Wechsler-Bellevue Intelligence Scale,* this scale is intended for individuals aged sixteen and above. Based on factor analysis of intelligence tests, it consists of six verbal subtests and five performance subtests. Some of the subtests are diagnostic of brain damage. The scores are translated into deviation IQ scores.

WECHSLER-BELLEVUE INTELLIGENCE SCALE. Intended for individuals aged ten and above, this scale is the forerunner of both the Wechsler Adult Intelligence Scale* and the Wechsler Intelligence Scale for Children.* At first, it had two forms. Form 1, originally published in 1939, is no longer in print and was replaced by the Wechsler Adult Intelligence Scale. Form 2, first published in 1947, is essentially the same as the Wechsler Adult Intelligence Scale and was used as a retest form for the latter.

WECHSLER INTELLIGENCE SCALE FOR CHILDREN. A downward extension of Form 2 of the Wechsler-Bellevue Inteligence Scale (ages five to fifteen), this scale is based on the same rationale as the Wechsler Adult Intelligence Scale and has the same type of subtests.

Wechsler, David. American psychologist (b. Lespedi, Rumania, January 12, 1896, d. New York City, May 2, 1981). Wechsler's Ph.D. in psychology was from Columbia University (1925). He was with the Psychological Corporation from 1925 to 1927 and in private practice from 1927 to 1932. From 1932 to 1967, Wechsler was chief psychologist at the Bellevue Psychiatric Hospital, New York City, as well as clinical professor at the New York University Medical College (1933–1967). Beginning in the early 1930s, Wechsler dedicated most of his work to the development of intelligence tests, which became internationally known. The Bellevue scale was first published in 1939, the scale for children in 1949, and the adult scale in 1955.

Biographies: AM&WS, 1973S; *Amer. Psychologist*, 1974, *29*, 44–47; *ConAu*, 103; A. J. Edwards, *J. Hist. Behav. Sci.*, 1982, *18*, 78–79; *IESS*, 18; J. D. Matarazzo, *Amer. Psychologist*, 1981, 36, 1542–43; *WhAm*, 7.

Bellevue. The Bellevue Hospital, New York City, was established on its present site in 1794 for the treatment of infectious disease. Now the Bellevue Psychiatric Hospital, it is the institution at which Wechsler spent thirty-five years of his career and where he developed all of his tests.

WEDENSKY EFFECT. When a nerve-muscle preparation is stimulated at a certain rate, the preparation responds with a series of rapid contractions. If the rate of stimulation is increased beyond this point, the response becomes a single contraction, followed by relaxation. The theoretical inhibitory process underlying the effect is sometimes called Wedensky inhibition.

Wedensky (Vvedenskiĭ), Nikolaĭ Evgenevich. Russian physiologist (b. Kochkovo, Vologda Province, April 28, 1852, d. Petrograd, September 16, 1922). Vvedenskiĭ graduated from the Vologda Theological Seminary in 1872; he obtained a degree in natural sciences from the University of St. Petersburg in 1879 and the Dr. med. degree in 1886. In 1889, he became professor at the university. His main work is *Excitation, Inhibition, and Narcosis* (1901). He described the production of tetanus in his doctoral dissertation in 1886 (The interrelationship of Excitation and Stimulation in Tetanus).
    Biographies: I. A. Archavskiĭ, *N. E. Vvedenskiĭ: 1852–1922,* 1950; *Soviet,* 4; *WhUSSR.*

WEIGERT METHOD. A method of staining the myelin sheath of neurons with hematoxylin.

Weigert, Carl. German pathologist (b. Münsterberg, Silesia, March 19, 1845, d. Frankfurt-am-Main, August 4, 1904). Weigert's M.D. was from the University of Berlin (1866). He was on the faculty of that university from 1868 to 1878 and on the faculty of the University of Leipzig from 1878 to 1885. From 1885 to 1904 he served as director of the Senckenberg Foundation, Frankfurt. Weigert was the first person to stain bacteria (about 1871). He developed several stains to stain the nervous system, in the process discovering the glial cells in 1887. Weigert's method developed over a number of years. He finally applied it to myelin in 1882 (*Zbl. med. Wiss.,* 20, 753–57, 772–74). The stain made it possible to gain basic knowledge of the fine structure of the nervous system.
    Biographies: DSB, 14; *Talbot; WoWhoSci.*

WEIGL-GOLDSTEIN-SCHEERER COLOR FORM TEST. One of the five Goldstein-Scheerer Tests of Abstract and Concrete Thinking. It contains four squares, four circles, and four triangles, each in one of four colors. The subject sorts them according to one principle, such as color, and then again according to another, for instance, form.

Weigl, Egon. German psychologist (b. Hamburg, April 18, 1901, d. 1968?). Weigl received a Ph.D. from the University of Frankfurt in 1927. After a brief stay at that university, Weigl went to the University of Amsterdam (1927–1929). He was at the Zentralinstitut für Erziehung und Unterricht beginning in 1929.
    Biographies: Unavailable.

Goldstein, Kurt. See under eponyms beginning with GOLDSTEIN.

Scheerer, Martin. See under eponyms beginning with GOLDSTEIN.

WELSH FIGURE PREFERENCE TEST. A test consisting of 400 black-and-white geometric designs that the respondents report they either like or do not like. Ten basic and twenty additional scales are used to summarize the responses. The main scales are female response scale, origence scale (preference for the unstructured), intellectence (a dimension anchored in the literal and specific at one end and the abstract and symbolic at the other), two art scales, a neuropsychiatric scale, and two scales each for anxiety and repression.

Welsh, George Schlager. American psychologist (b. Kingston, Pennsylvania, September 24, 1918). After obtaining his Ph.D. in psychology from the University of Minnesota in 1948, Welsh held various teaching and mental health positions in the United States and abroad. He has been a consultant to the Veterans Administration since 1953 and professor of psychology at the University of North Carolina since 1961. Welch's main research interests have been personality theory, personality assessment, and aesthetics. The *Figure Preference Test* was first published in 1959. In addition to it, Welsh is the author of *An MMPI Handbook* (1960) and *Personality: A Behavioral Science* (1962).
   Biographies: AM&WS, 1973S; *APA Dir.,* 1985; *ConAu,* 17R.

WERNICKE-KORSAKOV SYNDROME. The occurrence of Wernicke's syndrome* and Korsakov's psychosis* in the same individual. Although both are related to severe alcoholism, they are distinct syndromes, each requiring separate treatment.

WERNICKE'S APHASIA. The loss of ability to understand the meaning of spoken language, while self-generated speech and the understanding of written language are preserved.

WERNICKE'S AREA. An area of the cerebral cortex that comprises parts of the first and second temporal gyri and the supramarginal angular gyrus. Wernicke identified it as the area responsible for the understanding of spoken language. Although it is so involved, the processing of speech is much more complicated than Wernicke envisioned.

WERNICKE'S SYNDROME. Also known as Wernicke's encephalopathy, this syndrome is observed in cases of acute alcoholic intoxication. It is a brain disorder involving eye movement disturbance, ataxia, confusion, and problems in orientation. Thiamine can sometimes prevent the following amnesia, but it is ineffective in the case of Korsakov's psychosis.

Wernicke, Carl. German neurologist (b. Tarnowitz [now Tarnowskie Gory], Upper Silesia, May 15, 1848, d. Dörreberg-im-Geratal, June 15, 1905). Wernicke received his medical education at the University of Breslau (M.D. 1870). He was an assistant at the universities of Breslau and Berlin and then practiced privately in Berlin from 1878 to 1885. Wernicke taught psychiatry at Breslau from 1885 to 1904. He moved to Halle and died a year later in a bicycle accident. Wernicke began his career with work on neuroanatomy, publishing the remarkable *Lehrbuch der Gehirnkrankheiten* (1881–1883), but it was his small book on aphasia, *Der aphasische Symptomenkomplex* (1874), that made him famous. Wernicke's aphasia and Wernicke's area are described in this book. The syndrome that bears Wernicke's name was described in vol. 2 of his *Lehrbuch* (pp. 229–42).
Biographies: DSB, 14; Haymaker.

WETZEL GRID. A device for plotting age, height, and weight of children aged five to eighteen. It yields developmental norms based on the interrelationship among these variables.

Wetzel, Georg. German anatomist (b. Wittenberge, Brandenburg, 1871, d. 1951). Specializing in developmental mechanics and child anatomy, Wetzel taught anatomy and development at the universities of Berlin (1901–1903), Breslau (beginning in 1903), Halle, and Greifswald. Wetzel introduced the grid in 1930 in a chapter of his *Handbuch der biologischen Arbeitsmethoden*.
Biographies: Fischer, Biog. Lex.

WEVER-BRAY EFFECT. Also known as aural microphonic, it is the electrical activity of the cochlea as it converts the mechanical energy of an auditory stimulus into nervous energy. While not identical with the nerve impulses that sound initiates in the auditory nerve, the aural microphonic corresponds closely to the properties of the auditory stimulus.

Wever, Ernest Glen. American psychologist (b. Benton, Illinois, October 16, 1902). After receiving a Ph.D. in 1926 from Harvard University and spending a year at the University of California at Berkeley, Wever obtained a position on the faculty of Princeton University, remaining there from 1927 to 1970. His main research interest has been the experimental psychology of hearing. He and Bray described the aural microphonic in four papers, all published in 1930 (main experiment in *J. Exp. Psychol., 13,* 373–87). Wever published four books and about two hundred papers on the psychology of hearing.
Biographies: APA Dir., 1965; IntWho, 1985–1986.

Bray II, Charles William. American psychologist (b. Pittsburgh, Pennsylvania, May 14, 1904, d. Vero Beach, Florida, December 4, 1982). A military psychologist, Bray obtained his Ph.D. in experimental psychology from Princeton University in 1928 and continued on its faculty until 1951. He held concurrent positions with the National Research Council and the Navy Department Research Center and continued his association with military research units after 1951. Bray became a consultant in Washington, D.C., in 1963. His collaboration with Wever during their years at Princeton resulted in thirty-six joint articles.

Biographies: APA Dir., 1981; G. Wever, *Amer. Psychologist*, 1985, *40*, 233.

WHEATSTONE'S CHRONOSCOPE. A chronoscope for measuring the velocity of cannon balls and later used to measure reaction time in psychological laboratories.

WHEATSTONE'S STEREOSCOPE. The first stereoscope ever constructed. The two pictures of the stereogram were fused by two mirrors placed side by side at an angle.

Wheatstone, Sir Charles. English physicist (b. Gloucester, Gloucestershire, February 1802, d. Paris, France, October 19, 1875). Wheatstone was an experimenter, inventor, and pioneer in acoustics, optics, and electricity. Although he had no university education, he became professor of experimental philosophy at King's College, London, and held that position between 1834 and 1840. He later received honorary degrees. Of Wheatstone's numerous discoveries and other achievements in physics, the inventions of the chronoscope and the stereoscope are of importance to psychology. The idea of the stereoscope occurred to Wheatstone in 1833, but he did not publish it until 1838 (*Phil. Trans. Roy. Soc.*, *128*, 371–94). He invented the chronoscope in 1840.

Biographies: Asimov; DNB, 20; *DSB*, 14; *EB*, 23.

WHERRY-DOOLITTLE METHOD. A method for selecting from a large number of tests a small number that will yield a predictor-criterion correlation coefficient that is only slightly lower than the correlation between criterion and the full set of tests.

Wherry, Sr., Robert James. American psychologist (b. Middletown, Ohio, May 16, 1904, d. Columbus, Ohio, December 13, 1981). Wherry received his Ph.D. from Ohio State University in 1929. He taught economics and psychology at Cumberland University from 1929 to 1937 and was associated with the University of North Carolina from 1937 to 1948, although during this time he also did statistical work for the government and the armed forces (1942–1947). Wherry was at Ohio State University from 1948 until his retirement in 1975. His main interest was the development of statistical models for prediction and factor analysis. He developed the test selection procedure while at Cumberland University, but he did not publish it until 1940 (W. H. Stead, C. L. Shartle et al., *Occupational Counseling Techniques*, pp. 245ff.). Other less well-known procedures also bear Wherry's name. In factor analysis, Wherry's most significant contribution was his hierarchical factor rotation prodcedure. He wrote more than one hundred articles and technical reports on quantitative methods and industrial psychology.

Biographies: P. D. Isaac & D. D. Wickens, *Amer. Psychologist*, 1983, *38*, 611–12; *WhAm*, 8.

Doolittle, M. H. American mathematician (b. n.a., d. n.a.). Doolittle was with the U.S. Coast and Geodetic Survey when he developed a method for computing multiple regression weights around 1857 (C. C. Peters & W. R. Van Voorhis, *Statistical Procedures and Their Mathematical Bases*, 1935).
   Biographies: Unavailable.

WHIPPLE TACHISTOSCOPE. A pendulum-activated rotary disk tachistoscope. It consists of a vertically mounted disk with an open sector and an attached weight. The disk is rotated so that the weight is in a raised position. The disk is held in place by a catch. As the catch is released, the pendulum action of the disk makes it swing downward. On its way down, the open sector briefly exposes the stimulus. Another catch prevents the disk from swinging back.

Whipple, Guy Montrose. American psychologist (b. Danvers, Massachusetts, June 12, 1876, d. Salem, Massachusetts, August 1, 1941). Whipple received the Ph.D. degree from Cornell University in 1900. He was at Cornell until 1914; then he went to the University of Illinois (1914–1917), Carnegie Institute of Technology (1917–1919), and the University of Michigan (1919–1925). From 1915 to 1941, Whipple was also the secretary-treasurer of the National Society for the Study of Education. Being mechanically minded and before he turned to educational psychology around 1909, Whipple designed and constructed several pieces of laboratory equipment. In 1910 he became a confounder of the *Journal of Educational Psychology,* and in 1915, at his instigation, the American Psychological Association expressed official disapproval of the use of psychological tests by unqualified individuals. Whipple produced about fifty publications in psychology, most of them on education and educational psychology. He described the tachistoscope in his *Manual of Mental and Physical Tests* (1910).
   Biographies: NCAB, 31; E. C. Ruckmick, *Amer. J. Psychol.,* 1942, *55,* 132–34; WhAm, 1.

WHORFIAN HYPOTHESIS. The hypothesis (linguistic relativity hypothesis) that language directly influences perception: what is perceived depends on the availability of appropriate linguistic categories.

Whorf, Benjamin Lee. American chemical engineer (b. Winthrop, Massachusetts, April 24, 1897, d. Wethersfield, Connecticut, July 26, 1941). Whorf studied chemical engineering at the Massachusetts Institute of Technology (B.S., 1918) and then worked as fire prevention engineer for the Hartford Fire Insurance Co. for the rest of his life. Linguistic theory was an avocational interest of Whorf, and it made him famous. He studied the Maya, Nahuatl, and Hopi languages and studied lingustics as a part-time graduate student at Yale University. On leave from Hartford, Whorf taught at Yale University in 1937 and 1938. He presented the linguistic relativity hypothesis in three essays, published in the *MIT Technology Review,* in 1940 and 1941. These and other essays were reprinted in 1956 in *Language, Thought, and Reality,* the usual reference for the Whorfian hypothesis.

Biographies: J. B. Benjamin, in T. A. Sebeok (ed.), *Portraits of Linguists,* vol. 2, 1966, pp. 563–85; J. B. Carroll, Introduction to J. B. Carroll (ed.), *Language, Thought, and Reality,* 1956; *DAB,* Suppl. 3; *NCAB,* 30.

WILCOXON MATCHED-PAIRS SIGNED-RANKS TEST. A nonparametric test for two related samples of ordinal data, useful to test the difference between sets of ranked data that come in pairs when both the direction and the magnitude of the differences in pairs of elements are known.

Wilcoxon, Frank. American chemist and statistician (b. Cork, Ireland, September 2, 1892, d. Tallahassee, Florida, November 18, 1965). Wilcoxon obtained a Ph.D. in chemistry from Cornell University in 1924. Between 1925 and 1950, he worked as a chemist for a number of chemical companies, including American Cyanamid Co., where he headed the team that developed the insecticide Malathion. His work was in colloid chemistry and the chemistry of insecticides and fungicides. Wilcoxon turned to statistics in 1950 and held positions as statistician with chemical companies, as well as professor of statistics at the Florida State University (1960–1965). He published the eponymous test in 1945 (*Biometr. Bull., 1,* 80–83).

Biographies: AMS, 1960; R. A. Bradley, *Amer. Statistician,* 1966, *20*(1), 32–33; *NYT,* Nov. 19, 1965, 39.

WILKS LAMBDA CRITERION. A criterion for linear hypothesis testing in multivariate analysis of variance that is based on all eigenvalues.

Wilks, Samuel Stanley. American mathematician (b. Little Elm, Texas, June 17, 1906, d. Princeton, New Jersey, March 7, 1964). Wilks' Ph.D. in mathematics was from the University of Iowa (1931). He was on the faculty of Princeton University from 1933 to 1964, during which time he made important contributions to multivariate analysis. He presented the lambda criterion in 1932 (*Biometrika, 24,* 471–494).

Biographies: T. W. Anderson, *Ann. Math. Stat.,* 1965, *36,* 1–23; W. G. Cochran, *Rev. Intern. Stat. Inst.,* 1964, *32,* 189–91; *DSB,* 14; *IESS,* 16; *J. Amer. Stat. Ass., 1965, 60,* 938–66; F. A. Mosteller, *Amer. Statistician,* 1964, *18*(2), 11–17; J. W. Tukey, *Yearb. Amer. Philos. Soc. for 1964,* 1965, 147–54; *WhAm,* 4.

WILSON-PATTERSON ATTITUDE INVENTORY. A social attitude scale that assesses conservatism-liberalism, realism-idealism, militarism (punitiveness), antihedonism, ethnocentrism (intolerance), and religion (puritanism). A high score reflects generalized aversion to uncertainty.

Wilson, Glenn Daniel. English psychologist (b. Christchurch, New Zealand, December 29, 1942). Wilson obtained his Ph.D. from the University of London in 1970, and he has been teaching there since that date. Wilson has done research on personality and the psychology of sex. He has published ten books, as well as book chapters and papers. The attitude scale was first published by Wilson and

Patterson in 1968 as a conservatism (C) scale (*Brit. J. Soc. Clin. Psychol.*, *7*, 264–69) and then was revised by Wilson in its present form in 1975 (*Manual for the Wilson-Patterson Attitude Inventory*. Windsor: NFER/Nelson).
Biographies: ConAu, 104R.

Patterson, John R. New Zealand psychologist (b. n.a., d. n.a.).
Biographies: Unavailable.

WILSON'S DISEASE. A single recessive gene disorder, hepatolenticular degeneration caused by defective synthesis of the protein ceruloplasmin. There is progressive choreo-athetosis, intellectual deterioration, and deterioration of emotional control.

Wilson, Samuel Alexander Kinnier. English neurologist (b. Cedarville, New Jersey, December 6, 1874, d. London, England, May 12, 1937). Wilson studied medicine at the universities of Edinburgh, Leipzig, and Paris and obtained the M.A. (1897), M.B. (1902), B.Sc. (1903), and M.D. (1912) degrees. He was house physician at the Edinburgh Royal Infirmary in 1903 and 1904, holding appointments at the National Hospital in London from 1904 to 1937, as well as at the Westminster Hospital Medical School (1912–1919) and King's College Hospital (1919–1937). He described the disease in 1912 (*Brain, 34*, 295–509).
Biographies: G. H. Brown (comp.), *Lives of the Fellows of the Royal College of Physicians of London, 1826–1925*, 1955; *DNB*, 1931–1940; *Talbot*.

WINSORIZATION. A statistical method for handling highly deviant data. The high and low extremes in data are replaced by the next to the highest and the next to the lowest extremes. The same can be done for the two or three highest and lowest extremes. In each case, the replacement is the next highest or lowest data point. The data are then processed in the same manner as the original data, using the special sampling distributions computed for winsorized data to perform the necessary statistical tests.

Winsor, Charles Paine. American biostatistician (b. Boston, Massachusetts, June 19, 1895, d. Baltimore, Maryland, April 4, 1951). Winsor's Ph.D. was in general physiology (Harvard University, 1935). Winsor was on the faculties of Johns Hopkins (1927–1932, 1946–1951), Iowa State (1938–1941), and Princeton Universities (1941–1945). He was concerned with the application of mathematics and statistics to biology.
Biographies: AMS, 1949; *NYT*, Aug. 7, 1951, 15; L. J. Reed, *Amer. Statistician 1953, 5*(3), 4; *School & Soc.*, 1951, *73*, 237.

WISCONSIN GENERAL TEST APPARATUS. An apparatus originally designed for testing discrimination of three-dimensional objects in monkeys and the formation of learning sets. The monkey passes from the transport cage into the test cage, facing the stimulus presentation chamber. The experimenter, concealed by a one-way vision screen, arranges the stimuli on a tray and pushes the tray forward to a point where the monkey can reach them. The correct stimulus covers a baited food well.

Wisconsin. The apparatus was named after the University of Wisconsin by Harry F. Harlow, who worked there from 1930 to 1974. Harlow founded and directed the University of Wisconsin primate laboratory in 1930, which in 1955 became the Regional Primate Research Center. He directed it until his retirement in 1974.

WISHART DISTRIBUTION. Multivariate analog of the chi-square distribution, or the joint distribution of variances and covariances in samples taken from a population characterized by several variables.

Wishart, John. Scottish statistician (b. Montrose, Scotland, November 28, 1898, d. Cambridge, England, July 14, 1956). Wishart obtained the M.A. degree in 1922 and the D.Sc. degree (University of London) in 1928. He was at the West Leeds High School (1922–1924), the University of London (1924–1927), the Rothamsted Experimental Station (1927–1931), and Cambridge University (1931–1956). Wishart wrote *Principles and Practice of Field Experimentation* (1935), *Field Trials* (1940), and other books and papers. The distribution that now bears his name was presented in 1928 (*Biometrika, 20A,* 32–52).
   Biographies: Wh, 1951–1960; *WhE&EA,* 3.

WISTAR RATS. The albino variety of the species Rattus norvegicus, at one time maintained at the Wistar Institute of Anatomy and Biology.

Wistar. The Wistar Institute of Anatomy and Biology in Philadelphia is the oldest independent biomedical research institute in the United States, famous for discoveries made relating to cancer, aging, multiple sclerosis, rabies, and degenerative diseases. Located on the campus of the University of Pennsylvania, it is named after Caspar Wistar (1761–1818), an anatomist whose large anatomical collection was presented to the university for a museum after his death. The museum received its present name in 1892, being endowed by a great-nephew of Wistar as an independent institution. The rat strain developed from a colony of H. H. Donaldson at the University of Chicago. He first used the albino rats in 1893 and then transferred them to the Wistar Institute in 1906. The Wistar Institute no longer supplies albino rats for research purposes.

WONDERLIC PERSONNEL TEST. Originally a shortened version of the Otis Self-Administering Test of Mental Ability, this is a brief test for screening of candidates for industrial employment. It is of the spiral-omnibus type of group intelligence tests.

Wonderlic, Eldon F. American psychologist (b. May 7, 1909, d. May 12, 1980). An industrial-organizational psychologist, Wonderlic obtained an M.A. from Northwestern University in 1934 and then worked as personnel director or president of several finance corporations. He was author and publisher, from 1938, of

the Wonderlic Personnel Test Co., and, after 1962, chairman of the board of E. F. Wonderlic & Associates.
  Biographies: APA Dir., 1975.

WOODWORTH PERSONAL DATA SHEET. This instrument was the prototype of the self-report personality inventories that were to follow. It consisted of 116 items indicative of neurotic or preneurotic symptoms, answerable by ''yes'' or ''no.'' Designed during World War I as a mass psychiatric interview instrument for the military, it was later adapted for civilian use. The Woodworth-Matthews Personal Data Sheet was designed for use with children and adolescents but is no longer employed in its original form.

Woodworth, Robert Sessions. American psychologist (b. Belchertown, Massachusetts, October 17, 1869, d. New York City, July 4, 1962). With a Ph.D. in psychology from Columbia University (1899), Woodworth joined the faculty of New York University but went to Columbia University in 1903, where he remained until his retirement in 1942. He continued as lecturer until 1958. Woodworth's contribution lay in taking a position on issues in dispute and clarifying them in such a way that his view became the accepted one in psychology. Woodworth called himself a dynamic psychologist who stressed the importance of the contribution of the experiencing individual to the stimulus-response relationship. He published some 220 papers and ten major books, among them a revision of G. T. Ladd's *Physiological Psychology* (1911), *Dynamic Psychology* (1918), *Psychology* (1921), *Contemporary Schools of Psychology* (1931), and *Experimental Psychology* (1938, revised in 1954 with H. Schlosberg). The Personal Data Sheet was published in 1918.
  Biographies: Biog. Mem. NAS, 39; *HPA,* 2; *IESS,* 16; G. Murphy, *Amer. Psychologist,* 1963, *18,* 131–33; *NCAB,* 48, A; A. T. Poffenberger, *Amer. J. Psychol.,* 1962, *75,* 677–89; *WhAm,* 4; *Yearb. Amer. Philos. Soc.,* 1962.

WUNDT GRAVITY PHONOMETER. A device for producing sounds of calibrated intensity in auditory threshold measurement work. Steel balls, held electromagnetically, are released from different heights to fall on a surface of hard wood. The sound they produce is approximately proportional to the product of the height of fall and the weight of the ball.

WUNDT ILLUSION. Two parallel lines, drawn on either side of the points where a sheaf of straight lines emanating from a single point meets its mirror image, appear not to be parallel but diverging from the middle of the figure outward.

WUNDT'S COLOR SPHERE. Wundt's proposal for representing hue, brightness, and saturation that in principle is like the color spindle except that the geometric solid on which the dimensions of color are arranged is not a spindle but a sphere.

WUNDT SOUND PENDULUM. Two pendulums, when at rest, barely touch either side of a wood block. When elevated and released, they produce a sound whose intensity may be varied by varying the height of release, which may be read on a semicircular scale. In a study of auditory difference thresholds, the two pendulums are released successively.

Wundt, Wilhelm Maximilian. German psychologist (b. Neckerau, Baden, August 16, 1832, d. Grossbathen, near Leipzig, Saxony, August 31, 1920). Wundt's fame is based principally on his having founded an experimental psychological science. He obtained a medical degree from the University of Heidelberg in 1856 but switched to physiology and taught it there until 1874. In his *Beiträge zur Theorie der Sinneswahrnehmungen* (1858–1862), Wundt made the point that psychology, before tackling metaphysical problems, should start by trying to understand the simplest experiences and that this should be done using the methods of physiology. In 1867, Wundt began teaching the first formal academic course in psychology and soon published his most important book, *Grundzüge der physiologischen Psychologie* (1873–1874). Upon his arrival at Leipzig in 1875, where he remained until 1917, Wundt established the first psychological laboratory in the world, and in 1881 he started the first journal of experimental Psychology, *Philosophische Studien*. He had close to 500 publications, with a total of some 54,000 pages. The color sphere was presented in his *Grundzüge,* the illusion in an 1898 paper (*Abh. Sächs. Ges. Wiss., math.-wiss. Cl., 24,* 53–178).

Biographies: Asimov; DSB, 14; *EB,* 23; *EP,* 8; G. Hicks, *Nature,* 1920, *106,* 83–85; G. Humphrey, in B. B. Wolman (ed.), *Historical Roots of Contemporary Psychology,* 1968, pp. 275–97; E. B. Titchener, *Amer. J. Psychol.,* 1921, *32,* 161–78; Various, *Psychol. Rev.,* 1921, *28,* 153–88.

WURZBURG SCHOOL. A term, applied during the first decade of the twentieth century, to the psychologists at the University of Würzburg and their ideas. The leader of this group was Oswald Külpe, but most of the experimental work and writing was done by such men as Narziss Ach, Karl Bühler, Karl Marbe,* Henry Jackson Watt, A. Mayer, and Johannes Orth, beginning with a paper by Mayer and Orth in 1901. Külpe distinguished between cognitive contents and cognitive acts. The cognitive acts were states of awareness of the existence of rules, relations, and intentions and could not be said to have a sensory content. It was imageless thought, hence the alternate name for the Würzburg school, the "imageless thought school." Wunelt, under whom Külpe studied, held that experiments on thinking were impossible. Külpe, however, did apply the method of "systematic experimental introspection" to thinking: subjects performed cognitive tasks under instructions and then analyzed their own thought processes used in the task. The lasting legacy of the school was the finding that the way a cognitive task is performed is not determined solely by the manifest content of the instructions but also by unconscious determinants—set, motivation, predisposition, and other imageless states of awareness.

Würzburg. Town in Bavaria and location of the University of Würzburg, in 1582. Külpe was at the university from 1894 to 1909, Marbe from 1895 to 1905 and from 1909 to 1934, and Bühler from 1907 to 1909. Ach obtained his doctorate in philosophy here in 1899 and Watt his Ph.D. in psychology under Külpe in 1904.

Y

YATES CORRECTION. A correction applied to the chi-square statistic when the expected frequencies are small (less than ten) and degrees of freedom equal one.

YATES NOTATION. Specialized notation for treatment combinations in factorial experimental designs.

Yates, Frank. English research scientist (b. 1902). After graduating from Cambridge University, Yates was with the Gold Coast Geodetic Survey from 1927 to 1931 and then held various positions at the Rothamsted Experimental Station until 1968. He was named honorary scientist in 1980. Yates' books include *Design and Analysis of Factorial Experiments* (1937), *Statistical Tables for Biological, Medical, and Agricultural Research* (1938, with R. A. Fisher), *Sampling Methods for Censuses and Surveys* (1949), and *Experimental Design: Selected Papers* (1970). Yates introduced the correction in 1934 (*J. Roy. Stat. Soc., 1*, 217–235) and the notation in 1937 (The design and analysis of factorial experiments. *Imperial Bureau of Soil Science Technical Communication* No. 35).
  Biographies: InternWho, 1985–1986; Who, 1986–1987

YERKES-BRIDGES POINT SCALE. An early American adaptation of the Binet-Simon Scale* by R. M. Yerkes, J. W. Bridges, and R. S. Harwick. This adaptation differs from earlier revisions in that credit for items passed was given in points instead of months of mental age.

YERKES-DODSON LAW. Strong motivation interferes with learning a difficult discrimination problem but helps to learn a simple one.

YERKES REGIONAL PRIMATE CENTER. A regional primate center at Emory University, Atlanta, Georgia. It is a central colony kept for the benefit of researchers from regional universities because it reduces the high cost of acquisition and care of primates. After Yerkes' retirement in 1942, the center was first named the Yerkes Laboratory of Primate Biology. Yerkes had established the first primate laboratory at Yale University, the Yale Laboratories of Primate Biology. He was its director from 1929 to 1941. It was later moved to Orange Park, Florida, and then to Emory.

YERKES-WATSON DISCRIMINATION APPARATUS. An apparatus for testing abstraction in animals. A row of up to nine boxes, open and closed, is set before the animal. The animal determines which of the open boxes has food in it. It is then required to remember the box in subsequent testing.

YERKISH. Computer-mediated language, devised by Duane Rumbaugh, for communication with chimpanzees. It consists of arbitrary symbols and some grammatical rules for connecting the symbols. The name derives from the Yerkes Regional Primate Center at Emory University where the language was developed (D. Rumbaugh et al., *Behav. Res. Meth. Instr.*, 1973, *5*, 385–391).

Yerkes, Robert Mearns. American psychologist (b. Breadysville, Pennsylvania, May 26, 1876, d. New Haven, Connecticut, February 3, 1956). Yerkes received a Ph.D. in psychology from Harvard University in 1902. He was at Harvard from 1908 to 1917, at the University of Minnesota from 1917 to 1924, and at Yale University from 1924 to 1944. Yerkes was one of the pioneers in the experimental study of animal behavior. He produced many comparative psychological studies on a variety of species, but especially the primates, and is remembered for having written such books as *The Great Apes* (1929, with Ada Yerkes) and *Chimpanzees: A Laboratory Colony* (1943). During World War I, Yerkes headed a group of psychologists who developed the first group intelligence tests for screening recruits, the Army Alpha and the Army Beta tests. The Point Scale was first published in 1915. The first paper on the Yerkes-Dodson law was published by the two authors in 1908 (*J. Comp. Neurol. 18*, 459–82). It was supplemented by Dodson in two additional papers (*J. Anim. Behav.*, 1915, *5*, 330–36, and *Psychobiol.*, 1917, *1*, 231–76). The Yerkes-Watson discrimination apparatus was described by the two authors in 1911 (*Behav. Monogr., 1*, No. 2).
   Biographies: Biog. Mem. NAS, 38; L. Carmichael, *Psychol. Rev.*, 1957, *64*, 1–7; *DSB*, 14; *EB*, 23; R. M. Elliott, *Amer. J. Psychol.*, 1956, *69*, 487–94; W. R. Miles, *Amer. Psychologist*, 1946, *1*, 175–78; *NCAB*, 43; *WhAm*, 3; *Yearb. Amer. Philos. Soc.*, 1956.

Bridges, James Winfred. Canadian psychologist (b. Cascumpec, Prince Edward Island, September 14, 1885, d. August 3, 1979). Bridges received his Ph.D. from Harvard University (1915). After two years at Harvard, Bridges taught at Ohio State University (1917–1921), the University of Toronto (1921–1924), McGill University (1924–1938), and Sir George Williams College (1940–1963). He specialized in personality development, personality dynamics, attitudes, and, later, history and systems.
Biographies: AMS, 1968S; *APA Dir.,* 1975; *PR,* 3.

Dodson, John Dillingham (b. n.a., d. n.a.). Dodson obtained his Ph.D. from the University of Minnesota in 1918. He was at Central College, Pella, Iowa, in 1915 when he wrote the first of his own papers on the Yerkes-Dodson law. The second paper (1917) was the result of his dissertation work.
Biographies: Unavailable.

YOUDEN SQUARE. An incomplete Latin square for designing blocks of experimental treatments, such that every treatment and every pair of treatments occur equally often. For instance, in this Youden square,

a b c d e f g

b c d e f g a

d e f g a b c

the design is read downward, resulting in seven blocks of three treatments each.

Youden, William John. American mathematical statistician (b. Townsville, Queensland, Australia, April 12, 1900, d. Washington, D.C., March 31, 1971).

Having obtained a Ph.D. in chemistry (Columbia University, 1924), Youden started as physical chemist but gradually turned to statistics. He worked for Boyce Thompson Institute for Plant Research from 1924 to 1948 and then, from 1948 to 1965 when he retired, for the National Bureau of Standards. Youden presented the square in 1937 (*Contributions from Boyce Thompson Institute, 9,* No. 1 [Nov.], 41–48). It was named after Youden by R. A. Fisher and F. Yates in the introduction to their *Statistical Tables* (1938, p. 18).
Biographies: Amer. Statistician, 1971, *25*(3), 51; *AMS,* 1960P; *DSB,* 16; *NCAB,* 56.

YOUNG-HELMHOLTZ THEORY OF COLOR VISION. Thomas Young had hypothesized that all colors could be produced if only three principal ones—red, green, and blue—were mixed in the right proportion and that the retina would therefore need only three kinds of color receptors to reproduce all visible colors. Helmholtz, referring to Young's formulation, presented a full-fledged theory, the essence of which was that there are three kinds of retinal receptors for color, three kinds of chemical substances, and three kinds of nerve fibers. When stimulated by radiant energy of the appropriate wavelength, this apparatus gives rise to the sensations of not only red, green, and indigo but, through their combinations in different amount, all other colors as well, including black and white.

Young, Thomas. English physicist and physician (b. Melverton, Somersetshire, June 13, 1773, d. London, May 10, 1829). Young became a doctor of physics at the University of Göttingen in 1796 and doctor of medicine at Cambridge University in 1808. From 1799 to 1801 he was a physician in London, held a position at the Royal Institution from 1801 to 1803, and served as foreign secretary of the Royal Society from 1802 to 1829. In addition to his many contributions in physics, such as the demonstration of the wave nature of light, Young was the founder of physiological optics. In 1793, he explained the phenomenon of accommodation, and in 1801 he described and explained astigmatism. In the same year he determined the extent of the visual field and described how acuity decreases toward the periphery. His most notable contribution was the formulation of a color vision theory. Young first mentioned it in a paper read on November 12, 1801 (*Philos. Trans.*, 1802, *92*, 20ff.). Helmholtz considered Young's color vision theory in two papers, published in 1852 and 1854, but he makes the definitive presentation of the arguments in the second volume of his *Handbuch der physiologischen Optik* (1860).

Biographies: F. Arago, *Biographies of Distinguished Scientific Men*, Ser. 2, 1972, pp. 280–350; *Asimov; DNB,* 21; *DSB,* 14; *EB,* 23; H. B. Williams, *J. Opt. Soc. Amer.*, 1930, *20*, 35–50; A. Wood & F. Oldham, *Thomas Young: Natural Philosopher*, 1954; *Talbot.*

Helmholtz, Hermann von. See under eponyms beginning with HELMHOLTZ.

Z

ZEIGARNIK EFFECT. The empirical observation that incomplete tasks are remembered better than completed tasks. The phenomenon was noted by both Max Wertheimer and Kurt Lewin, but it was Lewin's student, Blyuma Zeigarnik, who performed the experiments that linked her name to the effect.

Zeigarnik, Blyuma Vul'fovna. Russian psychologist (b. Prienai, Lithuania, November 9, 1900). Upon obtaining her Ph.D. in psychology from the University of Berlin in 1927, Zeigarnik returned to the USSR to work with L. S. Vygotskiǐ at the Institute of Experimental Medicine on behavioral disturbances resulting from brain damage (1931–1942). During World War II, Zeigarnik did research at the Neurosurgical Hospital in Kisegache and worked on the rehabilitation of wounded soilders. In 1949, she became associated with the Moscow Research Institute of Psychiatry and with Moscow State University, where she pioneered in experimental psychopathology and trained cadres of psychopathologists (clincal psychologists). She received the post-Ph.D. doctoral degree in 1959 for her work. Zeigarnik described the experiments showing the incomplete task effect in 1927 (*Psychol. Forsch., 9, 1–85*).
   Biographies: Vopr. Psikhol., 1975, 20(6), 159–60.

ZENER CARDS. A deck of twenty-five cards containing five repetitions each of the symbols circle, square, triangle, star, and wavy lines, used in experiments on extrasensory perception.

Zener, Karl Edward. American psychologist (b. Indianapolis, Indiana, April 22, 1903, d. Durham, North Carolina, September 27, 1964). After graduating from Harvard University in psychology (Ph.D., 1926), Zener, after a year's stay at Princeton, went to Duke University, where he remained from 1928 to 1964.

Most of Zener's scientific papers, of which he did not write many, are on problems in conditioning. The work for which he is best known is the phenomenological analysis of perceptual experience, a subject that occupied him for the last fifteen years of his life. Zener designed the ESP cards in about 1930 when he and J. B. Rhine of parapsychology fame were in the Psychology Department at Duke.

Biographies: AMS, 1960P; E. E. Jones, J. Pers., 1964, 32, 511–13; S. Koch, J. Pers., 1969, 37, 179–89; NYT, Sept. 8, 1964, 29; PR, 3.

ZIPF'S LAW. In its graphic form, the Zipf curve, Zipf's law shows the relationship between the frequency with which an event occurs and the number of events occurring with that frequency. For instance, concerning language, the relationship between the length of words and their number and frequency with which they occur within a given work or type of work follows Zipf's law: there are many very short words that occur with high frequency and progressively fewer words of greater length that occur with progressively lower frequency. In a general form, the law states that there is an equilibrium between uniformity and diversity. Zipf called it the principle of least effort.

Zipf, George Kingsley. American scientist (b. Freeport, Illinois, 1903, d. Newton, Massachusetts, September 25, 1950). Zipf received the Ph.D. degree in comparative philology from Harvard University in 1930 and remained at Harvard for the rest of his life. The last ten years Zipf occupied himself with sociology and wrote three books in that area. With respect to language, the principle of least effort was stated in *The Psycho-Biology of Language* (1935) and subsequent papers on language. The more general form of the principle was presented in *Human Behavior and the Principle of Least Effort* (1949).

Biographies: G. A. Lundberg & S. C. Dodd, Amer. Sociol. Rev., 1950, 15, 804; NYT, Sept. 27, 1950, 31; School & Society, 1950, 72, 236.

ZOLLNER ILLUSION. When short bars cross long vertical and parallel bars at forty-five degrees, with the direction of slant alternating from one vertical bar to the next, the latter are perceived as no longer vertical but slanted in the direction opposite to the slant of the cross-bars. Because the overall pattern of the illusion is that of a herringbone-patterned fabric, the illusion is also known as the herringbone illusion.

Zöllner, Friedrich. German astrophysicist (b. Berlin, November 8, 1834, d. Leipzig, April 26, 1882). Zöllner became professor of physics and astronomy at the University of Leipzig in 1872. He was one of the founders of astrophotometry. He was also a believer in spirits and gained notoriety when he investigated the fraudulent American medium Henry Slade and expressed belief that Slade's slate writing was accomplished in the fourth dimension. He described the Slade experiments (in which both Gustav Fechner* and E. H. Weber participated) in his

1880 book, *Transcendental Physics*. Zöllner described the illusion in 1860 (*Ann. Phys. Chem., 186*, 500–20).
   Biographies: Shepard, 3.

ZOTH'S ACOUMETER. An older form of the audiometer, a device for measuring sound intensity thresholds in which the intensity of the sound was varied by varying the height from which a pellet dropped unto a sound-producing surface.

Zoth, Oscar. Austrian physiologist (b. Padua, Italy, August 28, 1864, d. 1933). Zoth received an M.D. from the University of Graz (1888). From 1885 to 1902 he worked with Alexander Rollet at the Physiological Institute of the University of Graz and was at the University of Innsbruck from 1902 to 1904. He succeeded Rollet at Graz in 1904, retiring in 1926. Zoth studied circulatory physiology, physiological optics, and motion and was a methodological innovator and constructor of instruments.
   Biographies: Fischer, Biog. Lex.; Rothschuh.

ZURICH SCHOOL. The adherents of the psychoanalyst Carl Gustav Jung* and of his system of analytical psychology. Analytical psychology differs from Freudianism* mainly in its deemphasis on the sexual factor in both personality development and psychopathology and the addition of and emphasis on the collective aspect of the unconscious. Also central is the recognition that every psychological phenomenon implies the opposite of itself. Extroversion implies introversion, and thinking and feeling are the opposites of sensation and intuition. The principle of opposites also implies that both manifest and latent tendencies need to be recognized and dealt with if one is to live in harmony with oneself. In the human personality, it is the components of the ego, persona, shadow, animus or anima, the personal and the collective unconscious that the individual must become aware of and bring into balance. The process of attaining a healthy, creative personality, the process of individuation, involves the differentiation of as well as the compensatory balancing of opposite facets of personality in relation to its core, the self.

Zurich. The school is named after Zurich, Switzerland, where Jung taught and practiced psychiatry from 1900 to 1961. It is also the site of the first Jungian training center, established in 1948.

ZWAARDEMAKER OLFACTOMETER. A device for delivering measured amounts of volatile substances to the nose. It consists of a glass tube, one end of which fits into a hard rubber cylinder saturated with the odorous material, the other entering the nostril. By varying the position of the rubber cylinder, different amounts of the material are allowed to enter the nose.

ZWAARDEMAKER SMELL SYSTEM. A classificatory system for smells consisting of nine fundamental odors, with several subclasses of each. This classification prevailed until Hans Henning introduced his smell prism.

Zwaardemaker, Hendrick. Dutch otolaryngologist (b. Haarlem, May 10, 1857, d. Utrecht, September 19, 1930). Zwaardemaker received his medical degree from the University of Amsterdam in 1883. From 1897 to 1927 he was at the University of Utrecht. Zwaardemaker spent much of his professional life looking for the physical key that makes substances odorous. He measured olfactory thresholds, designed the odor-proof room, and introduced the unit of olfactory intensity, the olfactie. His book, *Die Physiologie des Geruchs* (1895), was a classic and the first scientific treatise on smell. He also did important work on hearing. Zwaardemaker got the idea for the olfactometer in September 1887, and he published it in 1888 (*Berliner klin. Wochenschr., 25*, 950ff.). He described the smell system in his *Physiologie des Geruchs* (pp. 207–238).

Biographies: HPA, 1; A. K. M. Noyons, *Amer. J. Psychol.,* 1931, *43*, 525–26; *PR,* 3.

Index

Note: *Italic* page numbers indicate the location of biographies.

About the Author

LEONARD ZUSNE, Professor of Psychology, University of Tulsa, is the compiler of *Names in the History of Psychology* and *Biographical Dictionary of Psychology* (Greenwood Press, 1984), as well as the author of scholarly works on perception and anomalistic psychology and nearly sixty journal articles.